IRELAND

HISTORY • CULTURE • PEOPLE

IRELAND

HISTORY • CULTURE • PEOPLE

EDITED BY PAUL BREWER

COURAGE BOOKS

AN IMPRINT OF RUNNING PRESS
PHILADELPHIA · LONDON

© 2001 Salamander Books Ltd
8 Blenheim Court
Brewery Road
London N7 9NY
England

A member of the Chrysalis Group plc

This edition published in the United States by Courage Books, an imprint of
Running Press Book Publishers,
125 South Twenty-second Street
Philadelphia, Pennsylvania 19103-4399

9 8 7 6 5 4 3 2 1

Library of Congress Cataloging-in-Publication Number 2001094407

ISBN 0-7624-1269-0

Credits
Cover Design by Justina Leitão
Interior Design by Heather Moore
Index compiled by Nigel D`Auvergne

Production Phillip Chamberlain
Editorial Director Charlotte Davies
Color reproduction Media Print (UK) Ltd

This book may be ordered by mail from the publisher.
But try your bookstore first!

Visit us on the Web!
www.runningpress.com

Contents

Introduction

by Terence J. Sheehy

Physically and literally part of the continent of Europe, the island of Ireland is the most northwesterly part of the continental shelf. The Irish Sea separates Ireland from its closest neighbours, ranging between 60 and 120 miles of water, the channel separating Scotland from Ireland narrowing in the north-west to rather less than twenty miles.

The earliest people to set foot on the Emerald Isle found a small island to explore, not more than three hundred miles at its greatest length from north to south, and about 170 miles in its greatest width from east to west, and no point inland much more than eighty miles from the sea. The battered and indented coast-line of several thousand miles outlines a total area of 32,500 square miles.

In modern times, viewed from the air, by a weather satellite, or from an incoming passenger plane, this tiny Atlantic outpost appears to be shaped roughly like a saucer of mountains and highlands on the rim, and, in the middle, a central limestone plain. Today, this central plain is largely covered by bogland, thousands upon thousands of acres of peat, once mighty forests of oak and other majestic trees. The lordly Shannon, over 160 miles in length, one of the largest rivers in Europe, and the largest in Great Britain and Ireland, drains this central area, which accounts for one-fifth of the land of Ireland. The Shannon rises in the "Shannon Pot," high up in the Cuilcagh Mountain, in the county of Cavan, over 2188 ft (666 m) high. On the southern flank of the mountain, in barren country, on the borders of the counties of Fermanagh, Leitrim and Cavan, the "pot" is a small brown pool of water, surrounded by low trees and shrubs and, at this very source, a good young athlete could almost leap across this bubbling pool from which the mighty river springs.

Add to this mixture of mountains and plain the steady westerly winds of Ireland, blowing in from the Atlantic Ocean, and you have an ever-tumultuous sky of clouds like an army in full retreat with tattered and billowing banners all over the country from west to east. The light over Ireland is quite out of this world for sheer luminosity. The tree lines and scrub lines and gorse bushes and blackthorns and

BELOW: The ruins of Dunluce Castle, in County Antrim, stand on the site of an earlier Irish fort.

hedges of Ireland seem bent to the west winds, and yet such is the warming influence of the Gulf Stream, as it turns south along the coast of Ireland, that much of the vegetation is surprisingly Mediterranean, as can be seen in the fuschia-hedged lanes of Kerry and the abundance of arbutus and rhododendron and gorse and hawthorn bushes. The climate is moist and mild.

To such a mixture of mountains, lakes, rivers, and weather came the first human inhabitants of Ireland. Whence they came, nobody really knows, because so much is lost in the mists of time, and nothing was written down until many centuries after Christ. About three hundred years before Christ, we can begin thinking of Celtic Ireland with its own Gaelic culture. The really vast chasm of difference between the culture of Ireland and the rest of Europe, was that the Four Green Fields of this island were never occupied or raided or touched by the Roman Empire. The result was Ireland remained Celtic. No dead straight and boring highways but a multiplicity of tracks and winding paths, and fords across rivers.

The Celts themselves brought Christianity upon themselves, when Irish pirates swept up a young oby named Patrick in one of their many hit-and-run raids on Britain. He eventually escaped, but returned as a bishop sent by Rome, determined to convert his pagan captors. After the death of Patrick, the Celtic civilization of Ireland took to Christianity like the proverbial duck to water.

Norse raiders appeared as raisders of the coast of Dublin Bay towards the end of the seventh century. They made settlements in Dublin and in other coastal places now bearing their Norse names, such as Waterford and Limerick.

The story of England's involvement with Ireland begins with Henry II getting a Papal Bull from Pope Adrian, the only English pope, to put the Irish house in order. A horde of Welsh and Norman knights moved in, and very shortly the Norman conquest of Ireland was over, with Strongbow seated in power in Dublin. Came the Tudors and Henry VIII took

over. The Irish Ireland was confronted by an English-speaking, entirely difrrerent sytem of values – imposed on them by force. The conflict between them has continued at many levels even up to the present day. The Thirty-Two Counties of Ireland today are still the prisoners of history, and their relationship with Britain remains to be resolved by men of goodwill. But even history cannot prevent fifteen men in green jerseys from all the counties of Ireland taking on the Scots, the Welsh, the English, the French, and the Italians in the friendliest of competitions for the Six Nations' Rugby Championship.

GAELIC GAMES AND IRELAND AT SPORTS

Sport in Ireland expresses both unity and its division. The games unique to the country are hurling and Gaelic football. They are to the nation as a whole what soccer is to Britain, baseball and American football to the United States of America, and cricket to Australia.

Like the Football Association annual cup final at Wembley, in England, the All-Ireland Finals in hurling and in Gaelic football, attract enormous audiences. Up to ninety thousand spectators will roar their support for their respec-

BELOW: The 1972 Gaelic Football Championship replay between Kerry and Offaly. Offaly won.

tive county teams at the finals in Croke Park in Dublin, and hundreds of thousands more will gather around their television sets and their radios on these nationally important annual sporting fixtures.

Hurling has its origin in the mists of time, in the days of folk-lore, and all the great warrior legendary heroes such as Cuchullain and Finn MacCool were expert hurlers. That is to say they wielded the four foot stick of ash, the "camán", with total skill in striking the leather ball, which is about the same size as a cricket ball. Throughout the centuries the game was played at parish level, with almost whole parishes taking part, but in due course it became refined to a team of fifteen men. Women, too, not to be outdone, play the game under the title of "camogie", in a slightly modified form. The south-east, the county of Kilkenny, and the south, the counties of Tipperary and of Cork, and in the west the county of Galway, were the traditional fortresses of the game. Originally more blood and guts and physical, it is now reckoned to be the fastest and most scientific game in the world after ice-hockey. The speed of play is incredible and the wrist-work has cricket beaten into a very poor second place. It has to be seen to be believed for its dexterity and skills.

Gaelic football – Australian Rules football is very similar – is less like soccer and rugby, and has no "offside" rules to slow it down. Players can leap for the ball and catch it, hop

BELOW: The road between Ennis and Ennistymon in County Clare, a part of the country that has eluded thte modern world to some extent.

it or knock it, and the whole game is fast and open. Many a good rugby player is all the more skilful for having been a good Gaelic footballer. The counties of Dublin, Cork, Kerry and Tipperary have been to the fore in the championships but Northern county teams, such as Armagh, Derry, Tyrone and Fermanagh, have all shown their paces in recent years.

Both games, and camogie, are, of course, strictly amateur. Allied to these Gaelic games is the sport of handball, and handball alleys are found throughout the country. This game, too, has travelled with the Irish abroad, to America and to Australia.

Road "Bowling" in Ireland is quite a unique attraction which is played in well defined areas in the county of Cork and in the counties of Armagh, Limerick and Waterford. As old a game as hurling, it consists in flinging a weighty iron ball in the shortest number of "flings" over a set course of a public road (sealed off for the occasion, one might add), or over a good minor road. Throws can vary from sixty to two hundred yards, according to the conditions of the road, and the greatest skill is shown in cutting the corners by "lofting" the ball over the bends from one spot on the road to another.

Trinity College, Dublin, introduced Rugby Union Football to Ireland in the 1850's and from there it spread to Cork and to Belfast, and, by 1879 a thirty-two counties of Ireland Union was established and all-Ireland matches began against England, Scotland and Wales.

Associated Football, soccer, arrived in Ireland in the 1880's, the two big clubs being Bohemians and Shelbourne in Dublin. The scene is divided into two soccer bodies, one for players from the Twenty-Six Counties, and one for players born in the Six Counties. The Republic of Ireland team enjoyed the glory of qualifying for two successive World Cup finals – 1990 in Italy and 1994 in the United States – and if the Irish soccer eleven were chosen on a Thirty-Two County basis, like the rugby team, they would make a very formidableteam indeed.

Hockey, cricket and lawn tennis are played in Ireland, but the one game which is universally played, and at which Ireland had achieved international repute, is golf. With over two hundred golf-courses throughout the land, the game has become famous for its Irish Amateur Championship. The four provinces of Ireland hold their own championships, and school-boy golf championships have been well developed over recent years.

IRISH LITERATURE

With a dual heritage of Gaelic literature, and Anglo-Irish literature, Ireland has a very rich heritage indeed for such a tiny island, and so small a population. Literature embodies what it is that makes up the very soul of a nation, and probably the earliest written records we have are the writings of Saint Patrick himself, who was a powerful, but simple orator, in Latin, and who had this oratory written down for him. The Druids, who were converted to Christianity by Patrick, were the holders of all poetry and learning and law in an oral tradition, which they passed on to their successors, the Christian monks. The first folk tales, by word of mouth, were the *Tain*, the Irish *Iliad*, which tells of the Cattle-Raid of Cooley, of Queen Maeve of Connaught, and Cúchulain, the Hound of Ulster, and the Kings of Ulster. These stories were generally known as the stories of The Red Branch Knights.

All the time the language of the ordinary people, and their poetry and stories, was Irish, and English, under the Norman ascendancy, was spoken in a limited area extending outside Dublin known as the "Pale." Gradually, the bards and the poets gave way to the seventeenth century Anglo-Irish conquerors. In the eighteenth century the ordinary people were virtually dispossessed of their own Irish language and literature.

However, the chief paradox in Irish literature then came about – namely that the Anglo-Irish writers began to take their place in the literary world. Came Jonathan Swift, the mad genius dean of Saint Patrick's, and his satirical *Gulliver's Travels*. A contemporary of Swift's was the bishop of Cloyne, George Berkeley, a product of Kilkenny College, and the College of the Holy and Undivided Trinity, in Dublin. He gave Ireland, and the world, his *Principles of Human Knowledge* and *The Querist*. About this time also were Sir Richard Steele, born in Dublin, who, with Addison, founded the *Spectator* and the *Tatler*, and established the art of the essay, and Oliver Goldsmith. The latter, in addition to his work as a playwright, proved himself a first-class essayist, and won popular appeal with his poem, *The Deserted Village* and his novel *The Vicar of Wakefield*.

Thus began the pageant of Irish literature in English, which encompasses the politician Edmund Burke, the nov-

ABOVE: James Joyce's three major novels changed the way people think about literature.

elist Maria Edgeworth, whose writings such as *Castle Rackrent* were said to have influenced the Russian writer, Turgenev, and Sir Walter Scott, and a writer who was racy of the soil, and writing in English, and who captured the hearts and minds of his people then, and ever since, was Charles Kickham, of County Tipperary. He lived from 1826 until 1882, and his best loved and remembered novel is *Knocknagow*.

While these writers were among the best of their time, Irish literature really made its mark on history in the twentieth century. James Joyce was one of the founding fathers of Modernist literature, and gave the world *Ulysses, Dubliners, A Portrait of the Artist as a Young Man* and his *Finnegans Wake*. Any one of them alone would have been a landmark.

After him comes Samuel Beckett, with at least three significant novels to his credit, in addition to his plays. More recently, the literary successes of Edna O'Brien, Brian Moore, and Roddy Doyle, among others, have continued the rich Irish literary tradition down to the end of the century.

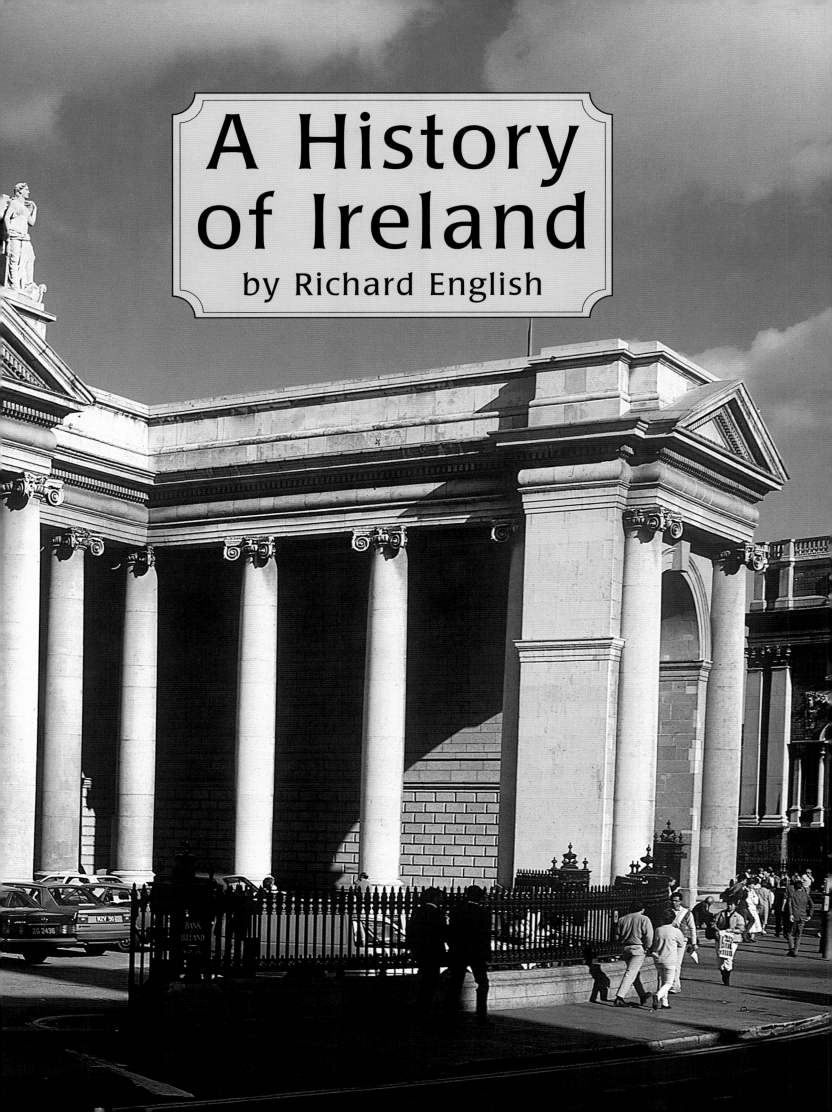

A History of Ireland

by Richard English

1
Ireland's Early History

Writing in the first century A.D., the Roman historian, Tacitus, claimed that Ireland lay "between Britain and Spain." No such confusion persists today. Yet much does remain unclear about Ireland's history, and the awkward task facing the Irish historian is that of clarifying while avoiding simplification.

The first traces of human settlement in Ireland date from 7000 B.C. These people appear to have lived by hunting and fishing. By 4000 B.C., the inhabitants of New Stone Age Ireland had developed a more advanced approach to subsistence with their ability to cultivate land. These Neolithic farmers also built a variety of megalithic (large stone) tombs – further evidence of a certain sophistication. Around the year A.D. 200 Ireland's Bronze Age metalworkers were making use of domestic deposits as well as engaging in trade beyond the island. Irish daggers and axes found their way to Europe, while some of the tin used in Ireland appears to have originated in Spain. The fact that Ireland lay on the periphery of Europe did not mean it was aloof in terms of culture or economy. As one authority, Michael Richter, has observed:

> Ireland was remote only in the geographical sense. Both in antiquity and in the Middle Ages, the sea proved more of a link with the outside world than a barrier.

Evidence from such periods is sketchy, but the Late Bronze Age in Ireland produced many artifacts which tempted and taunted historians. Its distinctive bronze swords and shields suggest a pride in truly martial arts, and Dublin's National Museum possesses a fine collection of such pieces.

OPPOSITE: The entrance to the passage grave at Newgrange is an extraordinary example of Neolithic architecture. The bones of many chieftains were interred here.

Early Ireland is associated in many people's minds with the Celts. Yet on their arrival during the latter part of the first millennium B.C. their character was that of immigrant bullies. They came as a powerful minority, influenced by the indigenous population which they encountered and dominated. Iron-using farmers, the Celts shifted east, south and west from central Europe and arrived in Ireland by a variety of routes. They came to dominate the island, and while traces of pre-Celtic languages can be found it was Irish-Gaelic which came to prevail. The Irish-Gaelic language represented a distinctive, locally influenced version of Celtic. Early Irish literature contains evidence of certain continental traits – including head-hunting – but this should not lead one into the assumption that all in Ireland was continentally Celtic. Tara (County Meath) held a symbolically crucial place in the kingship world of the Celts in Ireland. But it was a cultural focal point long before the Celts arrived on the island. Continuity as well as change helped mold the life of the Irish Celts.

It has often been commented upon that Ireland did not experience Roman invasion. In his life of Agricola (a Roman governor of Britain during the first century A.D.), Tacitus tells us that, "The whole side of Britain that faces Ireland was lined with Agricola's forces." The historian further asserts that he

> often heard Agricola say that Ireland could be reduced and held by a single legion and a few auxiliaries, and that the conquest would also pay from the point of view of Britain, if Roman arms were in evidence on every side and liberty vanished off the map.

But while no attempt was made by the Romans to conquer Ireland, there was a Roman influence. Archaeological evidence points to contact with

Roman culture prior to the departure from Britain (in A.D. 409) of the last Roman legions. There appears, for example, to have been a notable trade in wine, and some Roman objects date from as early as the first century A.D. Remains in Ireland demonstrate that during the fifth century A.D. there was considerable contact with Roman culture.

Indeed, the inhabitants of Ireland on occasions harassed those of the neighboring island. From the third century A.D. onwards Roman Britain experienced significant attacks from a variety of marauders, among them the Saxons and the Irish. In A.D. 367 a threefold threat materialized from the north (Picts), the east (Saxons) and the west (Irish). With the effective demise of Roman authority early in the fifth century A.D. raids appear to have resulted in settlements and more lasting conquests. The Irish established themselves most significantly in what are now Scotland and Wales. In Scotland the language of the Picts was soon replaced by that of the incoming Irish, so effective was the incursion. Indeed, the name of the region derives from the title of the Irish (or *Scoti*) who established themselves there. It was from the northeast of Ireland – the kingdom of the Dal Riada – that the Irish who settled in Argyll originated. Exactly when and why they did set out for the neighboring land is not clear. Whatever their motivation, the Argyll base facilitated further settlements; though naturally the development of Irish influence in the new land was one of gradual progress. There is at least one literary reference to a Pictish king still ruling over Argyll during the latter part of the sixth century A.D. But the Irish conquest in Scotland was certainly impressive – if invasion and settlement can ever be deemed so. This was the most successful process of Irish colonization in Britain, and the Dal Riada dynasty came eventually to take control the land of the Picts with Cinaed macAilpin (Kenneth mac Alpin) ruling a united kingdom of Dal Riada and the Picts between 843 and 858.

LEFT: World-famous Neolithic tombs, built in the fourth millennium B.C. at Newgrange, County Meath. The earthen mound is 250 feet (75 meters) in diameter, and the ceiling of the central chamber is 20 feet (6 meters) high. An aperture allows the sun to illuminate the whole of the central passage at sunrise on the winter solstice.

There was also important Irish settlement in Wales. To the north (Angelsey, Carnarvonshire and Denbighshire) colonists from Leinster ruled for a time. They left their mark on Gwynedd in the name of the Lleyn peninsula, derived from Leinster's Laigin dynasty. During the fifth century A.D. these Irish rulers were driven out by Cunedda (a British king) but there was more significant – and permanent – Irish settlement in South Wales (Cardiganshire, Carmarthenshire, and Pembrokeshire). Coming from what is now Cork, Kerry, and Waterford, the Irish rulers belonged to the Deisi dynasty and brought with them their Irish language.

The famous *Ogham* inscriptions provide valuable evidence of such settlement patterns. *Ogham* script was a simple style of lettering which used lines and notches carved along the vertical edge of a stone. The alphabet employed is based on the Latin, and these stones therefore reflect the meeting of Irish and Roman cultures. Employed on the memorials of lead-

ABOVE: Tomb interior at Newgrange, County Meath.
BELOW: The Petrie Crown, an example of early Irish Celtic metalworking.

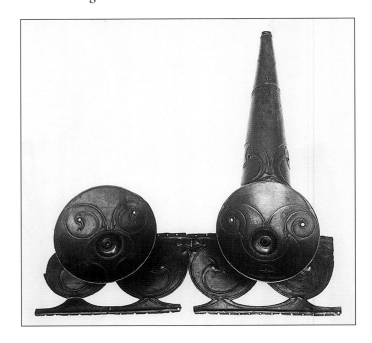

ing figures, *Ogham* is the earliest written Irish, and although the inscriptions are mostly very simple they none the less provide valuable evidence of early Irish culture. *Ogham* stone memorials have been found in

BELOW: Stone fort known as Dun Aengus, on Inishmore, probably built during the last centuries B.C.

Wales and throughout Ireland (particularly to the south). They date from a lengthy period (fifth to seventh centuries A.D.) and provide tangible proof of the extent of Irish settlement in Britain. Not only did Irish culture persist in parts of the larger island, but at least some of the Irish plainly maintained their language while in Britain. Inscriptions written in

Irish indicate that this language was familiar to those of the more elevated classes whose status merited *Ogham* memorial stones.

The interaction of cultures was having its effect in Ireland too. It appears that Romano-British culture reached the smaller island, and it is also possible that the process of Irish raiding in Britain affected power relations back in Ireland. The Laigin, as we have seen, made significant inroads into Wales and evidence exists within Laigin literary culture of words borrowed from the Latin. Invasion appears to have led to a process of cultural exchange. This, again, was to

ABOVE: Dun Eoghanachta, Inishmore – a ring fort built during the last centuries B.C.
OPPOSITE, TOP: Early settlement near Bray Head.
OPPOSITE, BOTTOM: A cross-slab, Kerry, dating possibly from the seventh or eighth century A.D.

prove a resilient – though complicated – feature of Irish experience in relation to Britain.

Indeed, Irish Christianity itself owed much to British influence, and the most celebrated figure in Ireland's Christian history – Patrick – was himself born in Britain. The case of Ireland's patron saint in

some ways reflects much that has been important in Irish experience. Patrick is, perhaps, an appropriate figure for Ireland to celebrate. The dates of his birth and death are not known, though it is generally accepted that he was active as a missionary in Ireland during the fifth century A.D. Much is still vague, but he was the son of a Roman official and was born in the west of Britain. During his teens he was captured by Irish raiders and taken to Ireland, where he worked as a shepherd and where he stayed for approximately six years. During this period he became a devoted Christian, though it was by means of a pagan crew that he managed to effect his escape from Ireland, having first travelled two hundred miles (320 km) to reach the coast. The ship was bound for the European mainland, but Patrick eventually returned to Britain. There, thoughts of Ireland lived with him and he returned to the island of his captivity – this time with the intention of preaching the Christian gospel.

Patrick is often given credit for the conversion of the pagan Irish and the establishment of the church in Ireland. But the shift to Christianity was much more complicated than this and deserves some attention, particularly in the light of the religion's subsequent importance through centuries of Irish life. The chronicler, Prosper of Aquitaine, records for the year 431 that Pope Celestine sent Palladius "as the first bishop to the Irish who believe in Christ." The traditional date given for Patrick's missionary landing in Ireland is 432. In fact the 432 tradition is unreliable, but there is other evidence which suggests the borrowing of Latin Christian terms into the Irish language during the first half of the fourth century A.D. Thus it may be assumed that a sturdy Christian community existed in Patrick's chosen island during the century *preceding* his missionary activity there. The cult of Patrick had become widely popular in Ireland by the late seventh century, and indeed it continues to enjoy widespread adherence (at least once a year)

RIGHT: The ancient Drombeg stone circle, near Glandore, in County Cork, the shape of which dates from about 2000 B.C. Also known as the Druid's Altar, it is one of the best-known stone circles in Ireland. The turf was stripped and the site levelled to create the structure, which aligns roughly with the midwinter sunset.

ABOVE: Statue of St Patrick near the foot of Croagh Patrick, a cone-shaped mountain in County Mayo.

ABOVE: Shrine of St Patrick's Hand in possession of the Lord Bishop of Down and Connor.

even in modern times. But it would be simplistic to attribute to Patrick the winning of the Irish to the faith. It is simply not known when the first Christian missionaries started to proselytize in Ireland. It is possible that the solidly structured church of Gaul provided the godly troops for the religious invasion during the fourth century.

Some scholars have suggested that our understanding of Patrick in fact represents the bringing together of accounts relating to two separate figures, the confusion arising because Patricius was the second name of the aforementioned bishop, Palladius. Certainly it could be argued that there has been an over-concentration by historians on the words and actions of Patrick, to the detriment of a

wider and fuller grasp of events surrounding fourth and fifth century Christianity in Ireland; other missionaries have perhaps been short-changed in accounts of this period. Yet, whatever the merits of figures such as Auxilius or Iserninus, it is to Patrick that we are forced repeatedly to turn. Muirchu's *Vita Patricii (Life of Patrick)* – written towards the end of the seventh century – asserts that Iserninus and Auxilius were made bishops in Gaul along with Patrick, but mentions them no further. Patrick, however, is portrayed as the medium controlling the elements and even bringing the dead back to life. Even if healthy scepticism is applied to such accounts, Patrick remains an important figure for the study of this period in Ireland's past. The two surviving texts attributed to him (the *Confession* and the *Letter to the soldiers of Coroticus*) are different in purpose. The first includes a justification of his work in Ireland and a personal confession of faith by the author. The *Letter,* on the other hand, was written with a view to securing the liberation of some of Patrick's recent Irish converts to Christianity, who had been sold to the Picts as slaves. These two works are important items but they leave many questions unanswered. The *Confession,* for example, contains no specific dates, and neither of the works was meant by its author to offer a detailed, historical account of Ireland's conversion to Christianity. It does appear that Patrick boldly went where no Christian missionary had gone before, but he is unfortunately rather vague about these newly penetrated areas.

What is certain is that Ireland did in time become a Christian island. While pre-Christian, Irish Celtic tradition was preserved (at least in literary form) in the twelfth century *Book of Invasions,* it was Christianity which was to define much of the developing Irish culture. Patrick seems to have encouraged people towards monasticism, and with the spread of Christianity in Ireland monasteries provided valuable centres for the corporate expression of the new religion. Great monasteries such as those of Clonard, Cork or Kildare were powerful ecclesiastical communities. They enjoyed enviable wealth and influence, and were well connected with the powerful in society. Early in the ninth century, for example, the king of Leinster lived at Kildare as did his brother (who was abbot) and his sister (who was abbess).

BELOW: Gallarus Oratory, south of Smerwick Harbour at the end of the Dingle Peninsula. The date of its construction is uncertain. The earliest suggested is the eighth century A.D., the latest the twelfth century. An oratory associated with St. Brendan stands nearby.

As with many other areas of Irish life, significant individuals appear to have become important cult figures and to have left tangible monuments to their particular vision. St Finnian, for instance, founded the monastery at Clonard (County Meath) in the sixth century. He was also reputed to have been the inspiration for other monastic founders such as St Ciaran, who established a monastery at Clonmacnois (County Offaly). In addition, Ciaran appears to have been influenced by St Enda of Aran who was – in turn – reputedly taught by the fifth century British saint, Ninian. Thus a web of monastic cult and foundation influenced the Irish church. For even if the supposed mentor-pupil relationships mentioned above did not

ABOVE: Beehive huts, such as these excavated at Sleahead, County Kerry, have been built in western Ireland since prehistoric times.
LEFT: Kilnasaggart inscribed cross-pillar, County Louth.
OPPOSITE, TOP: Ruins of the monastery of Clonmacnoise, County Offaly, founded by St Ciaran.
OPPOSITE, BOTTOM: Monastery ruins, Ballynacallagh Dursey Island, County Cork.

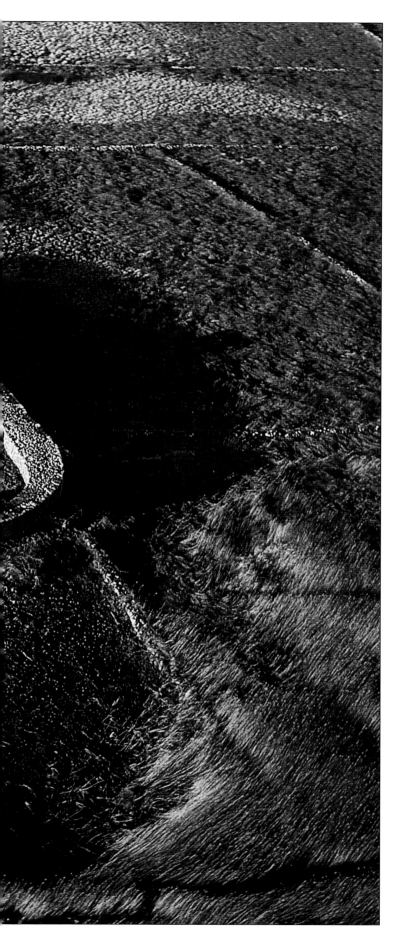

in reality exist, it would still be instructive that such traditions were *created* surrounding these major monastic figures. St Colum Cille – for whom, again, Finnian was reputedly a source of inspiration – is important not only because of his contemporary influence, but also because of Adomnan's Life; this account of Colum Cille – written c.700 by an abbot of Iona – offers us helpful insights into the life of the period. Colum Cille (or Columba the Elder) was born in 521-522. Having established the monastic communities at Derry and Durrow he moved (in 563) to Iona, an island off the west Scottish coast. It was here that he came to base his work and it was here that he died, in 597. The membership of the initial community at Iona included monks of Irish, British and Germanic extraction. The monastic existence on Iona was rather isolated and austere. Geography and climate saw to that! But there is considerable divergence of opinion regarding the severity of discipline called for by Colum Cille.

Accounts such as that by Adomnan must be treated cautiously. After all, it was written about a century after Colum Cille's death and is far too reverential. But it does touch on important themes regarding the society and culture of the contemporary Ireland. Adomnan records, for example, that Colum Cille ordained a king of the Ui Neill dynasty (Aedan) on Iona. Too much should not be read into such accounts. But the relation of the church to the wider society is indeed vital. During the seventh and eighth centuries there emerged legal writings which have greatly enhanced our perception of the ecclesiastical and of the wider culture at this time in Ireland. Scholars in Ireland had maintained and cultivated Irish; to this Latin was added. It seems that rigorous study of this additional language began in Ireland in the latter part of the sixth century. During the following two centuries law tracts started to be written down. *Senchas Mar* (a collection of tracts apparently compiled in the early eighth century) and the *Collectio Canonum Hibernensis* (originating from the same period) provide much legally focused information about Irish society and in particular about

LEFT: An early monastic settlement found at Irishmurray, County Sligo. The Celtic saint Murtagh, associated with the sixth century St. Colum Cille is believed to have lived here.

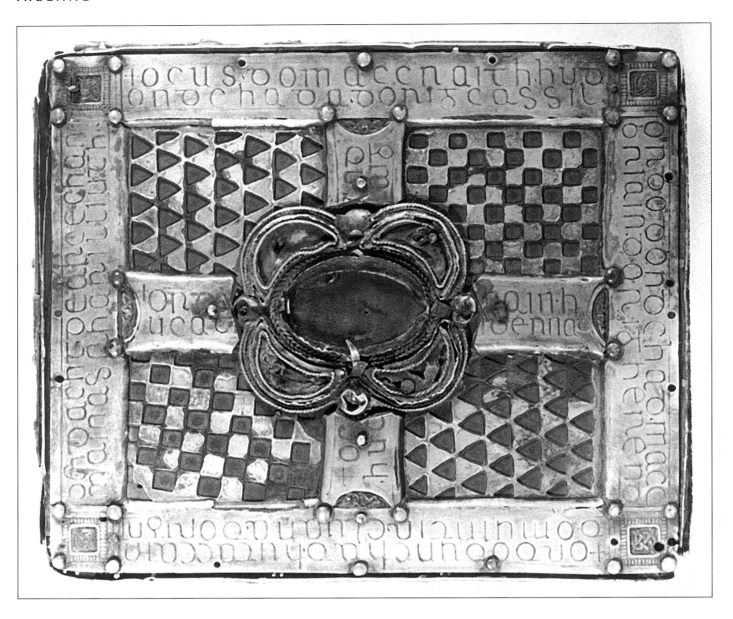

church culture. For it was within the church's orbit that scholarly sophistication developed. In Latin and in Irish, for secular as for religious society, ecclesiastical scholarship provided the foundation for seventh and eighth century law.

The Old Testament was important in this process: In the *Collectio Canonum Hibernensis* considerable time is taken up with quotations from this source as well as from significant church fathers. The *Collectio* in fact also deals with widespread social issues, including those of theft and inheritance. Sanctuary, too, was dealt with in this text. The area around a sacred site was held to ensure protection for laity as it did for clerics. At the end of the seventh century "Adomnan's Law" (the Law of the Innocent) had

ABOVE: Back of the Shrine of the Stowe Missal, which is dated to A.D. 800. It is also known as the Lorrha Missal, and the liturgy it contains is of the Celtic Church.
OPPOSITE: Pre-Christian bronze belt buckle found at Lagore in County Meath, with the characteristic swirling motifs of Celtic art.

placed not only the clergy but also women and children under protection for the duration of war. Thus ecclesiastical law-makers greatly influenced the world beyond as well as that within the church.

The writings of clerics at this time also reflect the development of the idea of the divinely ordained monarch. So in medieval Ireland the Almighty came to play a significant role in the theory of monarchy.

This was a naturally complementary relationship. Competing kings could only gain through religious sanction – who better to have on your side than God? For their part, clerics belonged to a religious culture which enjoyed much wealth and status; solid, favourable royal authority offered a welcome basis for stability. A passage drawn from a treatise written in the seventh century reflects this emphasis upon the blessings of good kingship:

> The justness of the king is the peace of the peoples, the protection of the land, the invulnerability and protection of the people, caire for the weak, the joy of the people, mildness of the air and calmness of the sea, fertility of the soil, consolation for the poor, the heritage of the sons, the hope for future salvation, the abundance of corn and the fruitfulness of the trees.

An impressive catalogue indeed!

Despite their ideological reliance upon ecclesiastics, medieval Irish kings were a truly powerful force. In fact, ideas of royal rule seem not to have drawn solely from the Christian well. The *Audacht Morainn (Bequest of Morann)* displays very few debts to Christian thinking. Written around the year 700 and emerging from southern Ireland, the *Bequest* presents the ruler as the embodiment of his people, with appropriate responsibility: His good behavior results in great benefit for those over whom he presides. The problem with such priceless sources is that persistent attempts to inculcate good behavior suggest, if anything, a gap between noble ideal and contemporary action. Strong oral tradition can be traced in the *Bequest,* for exam-

ple; more than one generation plainly felt it necessary that the advice which this treatise contained regarding healthy kingship should be expressed.

Much remains unclear about Irish kingship in the middle ages. There seem to have been layers of monarchy, from the person presiding over a local kingdom (the *ri tuaithe),* through the ruler who was Lord over a number of local kings (the *ruiri),* to the provincial king (the *ri ruirech)* who actually exercised considerable influence, certainly by the eighth century. The annals (chronicles, the first of which appears to have been begun on Iona in the latter part of the sixth century) reflect the dominance of this provincial class of monarch and, again, the intermingling of church authority and secular rule can be detected. In the south of Ireland Artri mac Cathail was ordained at the end of the eighth century as king of Munster; he in turn permitted the church which had ordained him to demand tax from the province over which his rule had been religiously sanctioned.

The notion of a high king (or *ard-ri)* is an important one and has generated much debate and speculation. It has been suggested that Niall of the Nine Hostages (Niall Noigiallach, from whom the Ui Neill dynasty took its name, and who died around the middle of the fifth century) might have been the first Irish ruler to adopt the title of high king. If this is true, then it was a royal claim lacking substance. *Effective* rule over the whole island eluded even later Irish kings, though it was closest to being brought to life at the very point at which twelfth century invasion rendered it impossible. Despite the power of cer-

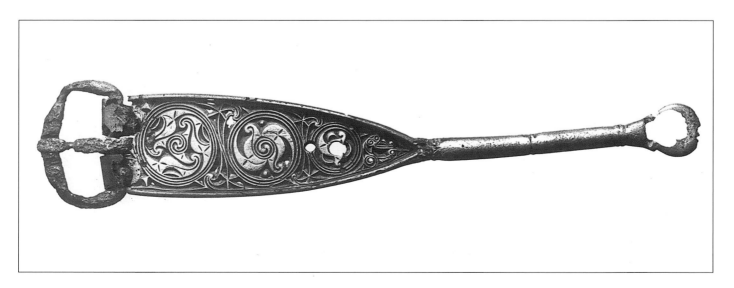

tain rulers – particularly those of the Ui Neill – it is too convenient (and unhistorical) to assume a high king model for Ireland in this period. Claims of authority over the whole island contrast with a fierce reality of local dynastic power and competition.

Less lofty heights existed than those inhabited by kings. The ruler presided over his people (or *tuath)*. The royal *derbfine* (the close family clan) enjoyed the right of succession. The early eighth century law tract *Crith Gablach* uses the word *tanaise* to denote the individual due to succeed the existing ruler. The identity of this person appears to have been agreed upon during the lifetime of the king from whom they were due to inherit. Below kings lay lords (or *flaithi)*. Members of this class had clients – the more the better, in terms of one's social status! Those bound to a nobleman in this way consisted of freemen, and the relationship was a contractual one. The lord offered protection and the loan of cattle for grazing his client's land; in return the freeman provided rent. The freeman class contained gradations of status, but they were all of higher standing than the serfs (or *senchleithe)*. Legal writers divided this class into different categories and its members were bound to their noble's estate. The complicated picture was compounded by the prevalence in the period of polygamy, divorce and remarriage.

Just as in pre-Christian Ireland druids had fulfilled the role of a learned as well as a priestly class, so after the coming of Christianity scholarly, intellectual functions were performed by ecclesiastical figures. Although most clerical scholars in the early Christian period had noble backgrounds, they are perhaps better seen as a distinct class; certainly their contribution was a distinctive one. Irish illuminated manuscripts are justly famous. The most celebrated are the *Book of Durrow* (seventh century) and the *Book of Kells* (eighth century) – both held now by Trinity College, Dublin. Sculpture and metalwork also survive and, again, the role of the church was vital here. Indeed, there are discernible similarities between these various art forms. The motifs on certain sculpted crosses resemble those in illuminated

texts such as the *Book of Durrow.* Metalwork had had a long pedigree in Ireland even by the seventh century. Pre-Christian workers had been familiar with the processes involved in enamelling for many centuries, and we are fortunate in the survival of medieval Irish pieces such as bells and brooches. The famous Tara Brooch and Ardagh Chalice are classic examples of Irish metalworking expertise.

Large numbers of Irish artifacts were taken to Scandinavia by a group of actors whose role in medieval Irish history was both important at the time and famous well after it – the Vikings. Attitudes towards the Viking impact on Ireland (as elsewhere in Europe) have varied greatly. The image of the rampaging hooligan has come to be complemented by that of the more constructive contributor to Irish society and culture. Neither stereotype will do; the important thing is that both must be examined.

OPPOSITE: From St Luke's Gospel, Book of Kells.
LEFT: From St Matthew's Gospel, Book of Kells.
The Book of Kells is one of the finest illuminated manuscripts extant, and contains the Four Gospels.
FOLLOWING PAGE: Ardmore church and round tower, County Waterford. The monastery founded here was one of the first in Ireland, dating to the early sixth century, although most of the remains of the

the Scandinavian intruders were greeted with understandable horror on the part of the clerical community and this response is (not surprisingly) evident in monastic chronicles of the period.

By 823 the whole of the Irish coast had been negotiated by the unwelcome tourists, and although Irish retaliation was not unknown the trend was with the Vikings (most of whom came to Ireland from Norway). During the early decades the attacks had a random quality, but Viking involvement was to change in character after the first third of the ninth century. Attacks intensified and in the 830s there occurred the first known inland raid of any significance. As with the first wave, Irish experience reflected a broader pattern. In 793 – just two years before Lambay and Iona were hit – Lindisfarne monastery, off the northeast coast of England, had been attacked. So in the 830s raids in England as in Ireland became more concentrated. In 837 major Viking fleets cruised the rivers Boyne and Liffey. Three years later Scandinavians wintered in Ireland, a telling indication of the settlement which was to follow.

Monks wrote about many horrific experiences at the hands of the Vikings. But the historical record for a long time underplayed those aspects of the Norsemen's contribution which were positive. Many important Irish towns (among them Dublin, Cork, Limerick, Waterford and Wexford) have their origins in Scandinavian settlement. Naturally enough, once the Vikings took root they "went native" and became involved in the locally based dynastic conflicts which Ireland had known prior to their arrival. As early as the 840s, indeed, there is evidence of collusion

Violence had been known in pre-Viking Ireland, but the late-eighth-century attacks by Scandinavians represented the beginning of an important phase in the island's historical development. In 795 the east coast island of Lambay was raided. Colum Cille had founded a monastery on this island, and another site of his monastic work – Iona – was also attacked in 795. Iona, indeed, was to suffer again at Viking hands, and after the killing of monks there in 806 the surviving members of the community moved to mainland Ireland, setting up a monastery in Kells, County Meath, which they completed in 814. Although the Viking raids were geographically concentrated, they nonetheless represented a significant tide of onslaught. Monasteries were ill-equipped to fend off marauders, and Viking mobility gave them a fearsome advantage in these early raiding years. Oblivious to rules regarding sacred Christian sites,

between Norse and Irish, and this was soon to become a frequent phenomenon. Dublin was the first Viking settlement and was destined to become the most significant one. Its foundation dates to 841.

Ten years later tussles began between different

OPPOSITE: Monastic complex, Holy Island, County Clare.
BELOW: The Grianan of Aileach, County Donegal, was built by Eoghan, one of the sons of the high king Niall of the Nine Hostages, and was destroyed in 1101 during raiding between the kings of Aileach and the O'Briens of Kincora. It was restored in 1870.

groups of Scandinavians. The arrival of Danes in 851 appears to have irritated Norwegian Dublin, though the newcomers eventually established a place for themselves there. In considering such developments the links with England should not be forgotten. It was via their raids and settlements in England that the Danes had come to Ireland, and they seem subsequently to have kept up contact with Scandinavian settlers there. The interests of the Viking newcomers to Ireland altered as their approach shifted from one of raiding to that of establishing a more lasting base on the island. They began to direct their energies

towards longer term economic strategies. Irish ports grew in relative importance, and Dublin witnessed its first minting of a silver coinage. Killers and traders, destroyers and builders, bullies and innovators – their role was a complicated one. Violence did not, of course, disappear with settlement. While the Ui Neill swept the northern coast free of Scandinavian strongholds during the latter ninth century, it should also be noted that sporadic Viking attacks on northern Irish sites continued, Armagh suffering on more than one occasion during this period.

The newcomers certainly altered the details of Irish kingship as a result of particular campaigns and conflicts. Following the start of the second Viking wave early in the tenth century, there occurred in 919 a battle in Dublin which resulted in victory for the Scandinavians over Niall Glundub (king of the Ui Neill) who was himself killed. But is it possible, from such instances, to discern some wider pattern of Viking influence over the important structure of the Irish kingdom? Comparison with English experience provides a useful perspective. There the Vikings took control of entire kingdoms; in the eleventh century, indeed, the Danes gained influence over the national

kingship. This was not the case in Ireland, where Scandinavian kingdoms were comparatively small and where innovation lay in the fact that the new towns often provided useful focal points for the development of trade. Any general impact which the Viking immigrants did have on kingship would probably have occurred anyway. The existing small kingdoms began to disappear in this period, with the *ri tuaithe* gradually diminishing in importance. But this shift appears to have begun prior to the arrival of the Vikings.

During the ninth century three dynasties had come to dominant prominence: The Ui Neill, the Eoganachta and the Dal Cais. Cashel (where the

OPPOSITE: Full-length view of the Cross of the Scriptures, Clonmacnoise, County Offaly. Clonmacnoise was a major religious center founded in 545 by St Ciaran. There are eight churches, two round towers, two holy wells, and an extensive collection of memorial slabs. It was burned by the Vikings in 844, but a monastery continued to serve God and Irish literature here, creating beautiful illuminated manuscripts, until it was burned by the English in 1552.
BELOW: Ruin of Staigue Fort, County Kerry.

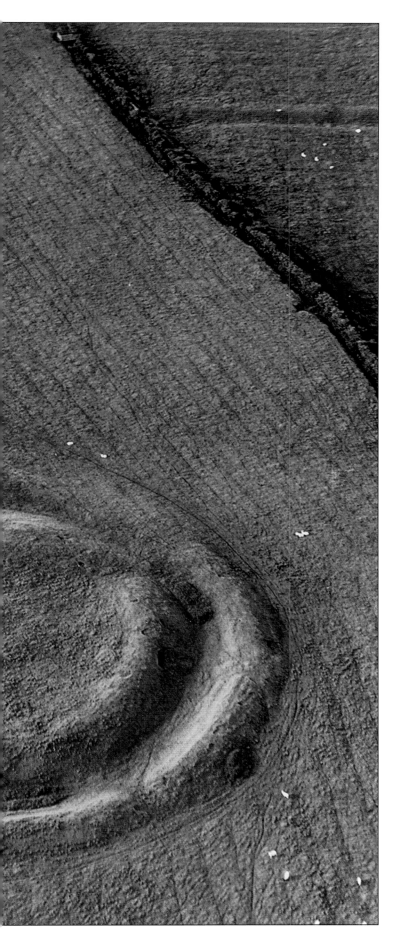

Eoganachta were based) fell in 964 to the Dal Cais, and with the succession to the Dal Cais monarchy of Brian Boru in 976 there arrived on the dynastic scene one of Ireland's most famed heroic figures. Born around the year 940, Brian came to achieve notable success against allied Norse and Irish, and by the 980s controlled the southern part of Ireland. His aim was to become effective high king of the island, and by 1002 Mael Sechnaill II (king of the rival Ui Neill) had yielded to him. Between then and 1014 Brian enjoyed wide authority. In 1006 he even travelled unchallenged around the north of Ireland – far from his Munster base. During these comparatively peaceful years he contributed, among other things, to the restoration of churches and libraries in Ireland. But in 1014 he was killed at the battle of Clontarf (situated now on the north side of Dublin).

While this contest has become encrusted with legendary status as one of the milestones on the journey to make an Irish nation, in its own time it looked a different sort of affair. Brian did not have as his objective the freeing of Ireland from Viking authority; he had in fact shown himself perfectly prepared to ally with Waterford Vikings. While Clontarf was indeed fought against an alliance of Vikings and Leinstermen, it should be understood for what it actually was: Part of the familiar pattern of dynastic conflict within Ireland. Its most significant consequence, and perhaps the reason why it has become a national milestone, was to ensure that Ireland would not, as England was in 1016 under the Dane Canute, be united by rulers with Scandinavian roots.

Although the battle was won by Brian's army, his death in the fighting halted him precisely when he seemed to be on the point of giving some real substance to the idea of a kingship of Ireland. Battles between chieftains for overall control were also evident in the following century. The tussles between twelfth century kings were complex and protracted, and it was as a result of such a conflict that one of Ireland's most famous events emerged: The invasion of 1169.

LEFT: The hill of Tara, County Meath, was an important symbolic site in the history of Irish kingship. It has been a sacred place since Neolithic times, and it became a ritual center of kingship in Celtic Ireland.

2
The English Invasion

The year 1169 was indeed an important point in Ireland's history. It introduced the island to a new and more lasting phase of incomplete conquest. The reasons behind the Anglo-Norman invasion are at once complex and simple. The Norman assault on England had taken place in 1066. During the twelfth century significant economic links existed between Ireland and Britain; trade involving Dublin and parts of the west of Britain appears to have flourished in the early twelfth century during the reign of Henry I in England. But if Ireland was part of a wider economic unit, the prize of effective Irish kingship remained a cherished (though elusive) one. Efforts towards cohesion were, as ever, complemented by the tensions. This should not lead one into any casual dismissal of the idea of an Irish nation in this period. Nationhood was rather undeveloped at this time. Nor, however, can one happily swallow the idea of a united nation, harmonious and undivided.

Into this picture of ambiguous nationhood were drawn external forces, from England. In the early twelfth century Turloch O'Connor of Connacht pressed a claim to the kingship of Ireland, and his son (Rory O'Connor) continued the trend later in the century. Rory's ally, Tiernan O'Rourke (king of Breifne), celebrated O'Connor's assumption of the

Gilbert and Richard de Clare (strongbow)

high kingship in 1166 by attempting to gain revenge over Dermot MacMurrough (king of Leinster). MacMurrough had abducted O'Rourke's wife (Dervorgilla) in 1152 and, although she had in fact returned to O'Rourke, the latter appears to have retained considerable feelings of hostility towards the Leinster ruler. The rivalry between the two men did not derive solely from the conflict over Dervorgilla, but their mutual antipathy was given extra bite by this episode. With his ally as high king, O'Rourke was in a position to punish his rival and MacMurrough was driven out of Leinster. The dethroned Dermot turned to Henry II (king of England, 1154-89), to whom he gave his allegiance. In return Henry granted MacMurrough permission to seek aid from among his subjects. The idea of invading Ireland was not entirely alien to Henry's thinking; it had, in fact, been considered shortly after his accession. Indeed, Pope Adrian IV had blessed Henry and his heirs with the right to rule Ireland – an irony, given the religious contours which Anglo-Irish relations were later to follow.

It was not, however, Henry II who invaded Ireland in the first instance; his own inheritance in England had been shaky enough at the start of his reign and he decided against personal intervention in Ireland at first. Certain of his nobles did, however, take up the challenge. The Anglo-Norman, Strongbow (Richard FitzGilbert de Clare, earl of Pembroke), accepted an exchange which was to have huge historical side effects. Strongbow was to receive in marriage Aoife,

OPPOSITE: Cashel, County Tipperary, once the seat of a medieval archbishop.
ABOVE: The seal of Strongbow, displaying typical Anglo-Norman pride in their military prowess.

ABOVE: The tomb of Strongbow, who died in 1176.
OPPOSITE: The ruin of Cashel Cathedral, County Tipperary.

MacMurrough's daughter, and was also promised the Leinster succession upon Dermot's demise. In return Strongbow pledged to help put MacMurrough back on the Leinster throne. It was actually in 1167 that Dermot travelled back to Ireland (accompanied by a small, mixed force of Welsh, Normans and Flemings) but the more famous date of 1169 marked the arrival of the first significant Norman contingent in Ireland. Landing in County Wexford, they were met by a force of local Vikings but these quickly gave way to the invaders. In 1170 Strongbow himself arrived, captured Waterford and married Aoife. Dublin soon fell to the incoming soldiers, and when Dermot MacMurrough died in 1171 Strongbow became king of Leinster. Predictably, Rory O'Connor fought on, laying siege to the Normans in Dublin. But Strongbow's military superiority made possible their successful defence of Dublin in 1171. The newcomers were not going to be dislodged.

This point was not lost on Henry II, who decided to set himself up as overlord of Ireland and who consequently landed at Waterford in October 1171, backed by a formidable army. It is possible that the thinking behind this move was not quite as simple as it might initially seem. Certainly Henry did not want

to allow the emergence of an independent Irish kingdom under rival rule, and was therefore keen to emphasize his own authority over Strongbow. This he quickly achieved, with Richard offering his submission to Henry's supremacy and being allowed to hold Leinster as a fief. The English ruler retained Dublin, and his power was further underlined by the submission of the kings in southeast Ireland. Large tracts, to the west and to the north, were still beyond his grasp, but his intrusion into Ireland had none the less proved effective. Even the Irish clergy pledged him their allegiance.

But the tugging of Strongbow's lead was not necessarily the only thought in Henry's mind when he directed his attentions toward Ireland. Ireland provided a possible lordship which Henry could bestow on his young son, John. Furthermore, he might have wished to capitalize on the papal endorsement which he had received regarding Ireland. The famous Bull, *Laudabiliter,* by which Adrian lV had given Henry permission to rule Ireland, might have been interpreted as lending a certain legitimacy to the king's own desires. Such a claim must undoubtedly be judged to have been spurious. But its usefulness would not have been lost on the English king, particularly in the light of the recent killing of archbishop Thomas à Becket in December 1170. The murder had caused strained relations between the king and the church, but Henry's keenness to portray himself as a church reformer demonstrates his awareness of the value of a favorable relationship with the ecclesiastical community. In 1172 he made his peace with the church and was actually endorsed in his authority by Pope Alexander III.

In fact, the Irish church had been significantly reformed without help or influence from England. St Malachy was the most influential of the reformers of this period, apparently born at the end of the eleventh century and becoming archbishop of Armagh in 1132. Five years later he retired to Bangor. But he was later sent to Rome to procure proof of papal endorsement for the archbishops of Cashel and of Armagh. This trip was to emerge as an important one. For on his way to Rome Malachy encountered and was impressed by St Bernard, leading French ecclesiastic and founder of the abbey at Clairvaux.

Malachy later sent people to be trained at Clairvaux (where Bernard was the head of the Cistercian order) and in 1142 Ireland's first Cistercian foundation was established at Mellifont (County Louth). Further foundations followed and the Cistercians subsequently became an influential order within Ireland.

The synod of Kells in 1152 (four years after Malachy's death) restructured the Irish church, with Armagh, Cashel, Dublin and Tuam all being recognized as archbishoprics and thirty-six dioceses being established throughout the island. The archbishop of Armagh was declared to be the Primate of All Ireland, and so the northward shift in influence which Malachy had helped bring about thus became institutionalized in Irish ecclesiastical structure. Lasting, too, were the architectural results of twelfth-century church reform. New dioceses received new cathedrals, many of which survive in ruined form to this day. So prior to Henry II's intervention the Irish church had been shuffling itself into a different order, reorganizing and restructuring and reforming on a significant scale.

What of the wider society and culture of twelfth-century Ireland? One of the most important sources for this period is the record of Gerald of Wales.

Giraldus de Barri – referred to as Giraldius Cambrensis owing to his having originated in Cambria (Wales) – was born in Pembrokeshire c.1146 and died c.1223. He made four visits to Ireland, in 1183, 1185, 1199 and 1204. Related to a number of the Norman lords who were involved in the invasion of Ireland, Gerald was a cleric and a writer of some significance. He wrote seventeen works, all in Latin, including *Topographia Hibernica (Topography of Ireland)*, the first significant written portrayal of Ireland by a foreign person who had visited the place. He also brought with him a certain breadth of European learning, having spent many years in Paris by the time he first set foot in Ireland. Having studied in France for over a decade, he became archdeacon of Brecon in 1175 and would have become bishop of St David's had not the king (Henry II) refused to appoint a Welshman to a see in Wales.

In 1184, however, Gerald became a member of Henry II's entourage, and it was with John (the king's son, to whom Gerald was tutor) that he visited Ireland a second time in 1185. Thus the *Topography* was drawn from Gerald's vision of Ireland in the mid-1180s, and it is an extremely valuable period piece for Irish historians. It is divided into three parts. In Gerald's own words:

> The first part treats of the Position of Ireland....
> The second part treats of the Wonders and
> Miracles of Ireland....The third part treats of
> the Inhabitants of the Country.

Gerald's work addresses itself respectively, therefore, to the *geographical,* the *remarkable,* and the *human/historical* – this third section looking at the history of Ireland from the "first arrival" up to the twelfth-century inhabitants. It is a text which has been the object of severe attacks. As historians, we must ask certain crucial questions regarding Gerald. Where did he go in Ireland during the visits upon which the *Topography* was based? What do his background and connections suggest regarding the views, the presuppositions which he would have brought to

LEFT: The Rock of Cashel, Tipperary, was traditionally the royal seat of the kings of Munster. It became an important religious center in the ninth century, and the ruins include a Cathedral, Cormac's Chapel, a round tower and the Archbishop's Palace.

his writing? Above all, for whom and in what context was the work written?

On his first visit it is evident that he became familiar, to some degree, with the regions of Cork and Waterford – beyond that we do not know how far Gerald's experience reached. His second visit was more extensive. He certainly saw Waterford, Meath, Kildare and Dublin, and was quite possibly also in Wicklow and the Athlone region. Much of the rest of the island was unknown to the Normans anyway. So his sight of Ireland was partial, though (particularly on his second trip) not insubstantial. As to his background and connections, it is important to recognize that Gerald was woven into a web of people instrumental in the twelfth-century invasion of Ireland. His uncle, Maurice FitzGerald, was one of the leaders of that invasion. Thus Gerald – if he is to be understood in an appropriate historical setting – must be seen as one surfing to Ireland on a wave of Norman incursion. As we have observed, his second visit to the island was in the company of Henry II's son, John, and Gerald actually dedicated the *Topography* to the king whose entourage he had joined in 1184. Indeed Gerald at times was thoroughly sycophantic:

The victories of Henry the Second, king of the English

Your victories vie with the whole round of the world. Our western Alexander, you have stretched your arm from the Pyrenean mountains even to these far western bounds of the northern ocean. As many as are the lands provided by nature in these parts, so many are your victories. If the limits of your expeditions are sought – there will be no more of the world left for you before there will be an end to your activities. A courageous heart may find no lands to conquer. Your victories can never cease. Your triumphs cannot cease, but only that over which you may triumph.

So Gerald's account has to be examined in its partisan context. What does he say of the late-twelfth-century Ireland which he encountered? Much of it is unflattering. "It is only in the case of musical instruments" – he wrote – "that I find any commendable diligence in the people. They seem to me to be incomparably more skilled in these than any other people that I have seen." Rare praise, for he also claimed that Ireland's saints "seem to be of a vindictive cast of mind" and that her inhabitants

are a wild and inhospitable people. They live on beasts only, and live like beasts. They have not progressed at all from the primitive habits of pastoral living.

Indeed, Gerald's condemnation of the Irish was as

merciless as it was generalized; "above all other peoples" – he wrote – "they always practice treachery. When they give their word to anyone, they do not keep it."

Beyond such generalized abuse – and in addition to tales of bestiality in Connacht and Paris – Gerald does offer certain nuggets which must be judged of greater value to the historian. The third section of the work, in particular, presents useful insights regarding late-twelfth-century Irish people, since Gerald's account here must have relied heavily on the perceptions of people in Ireland. There emerges from his account a "stages" view of Irish history, with different arrivals successively contributing to the population of the island. It is also intriguing that Gerald lays

OPPOSITE : The ruined Augustinian abbey at Cong, County Mayo. It was founded in the twelfth century, and the beautiful Cross of Cong, now in the National Museum of Ireland, was kept there for centuries.
BELOW: Another Romanesque doorway built at Clonfert Cathedral, County Galway.

stress on there having been in Ireland a tradition of united kingship ("Slanius became the sole king of the whole of Ireland") though it should also be noted that he argued "that Ireland can with some right be claimed by the kings of Britain."

Kingship continued to be a crucial aspect of Irish society after the twelfth-century invasion. This was true not only in Ireland. As the historian, J.R. Lander, put it, "In the medieval and the early modern world there was no substitute for a mature and vigorous king, for a king had to rule as well as reign." If skepticism had to be applied regarding the claims of pre-invasion rulers in Ireland, what of the situation after 1169? In April 1172 Henry II concluded his Irish visit – the only one he was to make. Henry's performance in Ireland had been an impressive – albeit an intruding – one. What was the situation which he left behind him? On departing from Ireland Henry appointed Hugh de Lacy as justiciar (or administrator). De Lacy was now the representative of Henry's power in Ireland, and he was also granted Meath and appointed to specific authority over Dublin. Royal garrisons provided symbolic and practical evidence

An Irish native

CHAPTER XX
OF THE BADGER AND ITS NATURE

There is also here the badger or melot, an unclean animal which bites sharply, frequenting the mountains and rocks. It makes holes under the ground for its refuge and protection, scratching and digging them out with its feet. Some of them, whose natural instinct it is to serve the rest, have been seen, to the great admiration of the observers, lying on their backs with the earth dug out heaped on their bellies and held together by their four claws, while others dragged them backward by a stick held in their mouth, fastening their teeth in which, they drew them out of the hole with their burthens.

FROM GIRALDUS CAMBRENSIS (GERALD OF WALES) TOPOGRAPHY OF IRELAND (1188)

of Henry's rule, and soon after his departure Hugh de Lacy had emphasized his own strength by killing Tiernan O'Rourke, king of Breifne. But the English royal hold on Ireland was in fact far from total. This was tacitly stated by Henry in 1175 with the Treaty of Windsor between himself and Rory O'Connor. This agreement involved O'Connor yielding to Henry's authority in return for lordship over those regions which Henry had not been in a position to take over. Thus a formal division was recognized between Irish and English spheres of influence, and the pattern of incomplete conquest once again became evident.

In 1177 Henry bestowed on his son (John) the title "Lord of Ireland". But the struggle for control of Ireland was a continuing and contested one. Henry in fact reneged on the Treaty of Windsor, granting new lands to certain of his barons – behavior reminiscent of that which Gerald of Wales had chauvinistically attributed to the Irish. Norman castles continued to sprout, and by the middle of the thirteenth century the Normans had come to control most of the island. Tir Conaill and Tir Eoghain in the north stood outside the conquest and Connacht was less densely affected than the east, but the Norman settlement

was, nevertheless, a significantly successful one. The personnel soon changed: Strongbow died in 1176, Maurice FitzGerald (Gerald of Wales' uncle) in the same year, and Hugh de Lacy was killed ten years later. But the seat of Norman occupation remained. Indeed, the commitment to control over Ireland became, if anything, more resolute owing to the potential economic advantage to be derived from access to Irish agricultural land. Grants were followed by cultivation, as well as by defence, and the

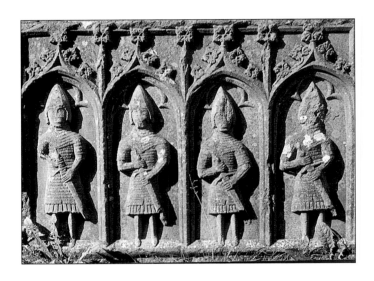

OPPOSITE, TOP: *Detail of tomb, Roscommon Abbey.*
OPPOSITE, BOTTOM: *Jerpoint Abbey, County Kilkenny.*
BELOW: *Incised effigy, tomb slab, Jerpoint Abbey.*

Normans introduced to the island a feudal system of landholding common not only in England but also throughout much of mainland Europe. In this instance, therefore, English rule in Ireland actually resulted in greater Irish conformity to European practice – a theme which was to recur, though more direct links between Ireland and Europe also continued. The feudal system, in essence, involved the king owning all the land but granting it out in return for allegiance and the provision of services or payments. At lower levels, too, there was a feudal relation, with major nobles dividing their land between less major nobles who themselves had tenants. Thus a pyramid of economically based allegiance took hold and, in a sense, this was reflected by the political change which Norman intrusion brought to Ireland. The justiciar headed the military, civil, and judicial structures, and was assisted by an influential council of officials. By the end of the thirteenth century local representatives were in fact being called to a parliament. This was primarily concerned with taxation, and although its influence was limited it is a further indication of the moves made under Norman rule towards a form of effective government. This should not be overplayed. The Normans' role in Ireland was a less all-embracing one than the one which they had played in England. It is as another layer in Ireland's past – admittedly an influential one – that the incoming Normans should be viewed. The twelfth-century invasion was actually less of a straightforward fault line than has often been assumed. Precisely because there was no solid, central, governmental edifice of which they could assume possession, the Normans found their power in Ireland less universal than might otherwise have been the case. For the same reason, their moves towards the creation of governmental machinery should not casually be dismissed.

Another notable contribution was in the language spoken by the people. The creation of new towns was a significant and lasting aspect of invader culture – with Athlone, Galway and Kilkenny among those whose roots lie in Norman innovation – and it was in the towns of the eastern side of the island that linguistic change was most concentrated. Towns tended to be in a state of direct subjection to the crown, and so English became the spoken language. Other cultural changes also grew. Early Norman defenses were

ABOVE: An elaborate Irish Romanesque doorway, Killeshin Church, County. Laois, built in the twelfth century by Diarmid Mac Murchada, king of Leinster.
OPPOSITE: Mellifont Abbey, County Louth.

towers, constructed of wood and situated on artificial mounds. But there quickly developed among the newcomers an understandable preference for sturdier fortifications, and between the late twelfth century and the earlier part of the fourteenth century stone castles were built. A common design involved a central keep, often built into its surrounding walls. Such structures that have survived remain impressive even today, Carrickfergus Castle (to the north of Belfast) being a good example.

While such traces of Norman influence proved resilient, English rulers were distracted by other concerns from a more extensive conquest. It is also worth noting the toughness of will of the old chieftains. Irish rulers continued to enjoy control in Connacht during much of the thirteenth century in the form of the O'Connors. In 1270 Aedh O'Connor scored a victory over an army led by Ralph d'Ufford (royal justi-

ciar) and Walter de Burgo (who had become earl of Ulster in 1263). Walter's son, Richard, later became an influential figure in northern Ireland between 1286 and 1320. Under his influence English authority was to spread into Donegal. The picture of power in Ireland at this time was a complex one (involving a mixture of cooperation and coercion), with a variety of claimants to royal rule.

To complicate matters further, Edward Bruce invaded Ireland from Scotland in 1315, landing at Larne in the northeast of the country. The events preceding this invasion involve, in part, the conflict between England and Scotland. King Edward I, who ruled England at the end of the thirteenth and beginning of the fourteenth century, had enjoyed significant success in his efforts to conquer Welsh territory in the early 1280s. But his overtures in a Scottish direction met with less fruitful results. Inroads were made, but the conquest of Scotland remained elusive. By the time that Edward II became English king in 1307, Robert Bruce had emerged as a powerful leader of Scottish resistance to English advances. In 1314 the famous battle of Bannockburn saw Robert inflict a defeat on English forces, and it led to the Larne landing of 1315. Edward II had utilized human and other resources drawn from Ireland, and Robert Bruce held that an attack on Ireland might not only provide a kingdom for his brother, Edward, but might also help to dent English power in the process. Edward Bruce's expedition eventually failed, but not without first having achieved notable success. Edward – who had built alliances with a number of Irish leaders – defeated Richard de Burgo (earl of Ulster) at the battle of Connor in 1315 and was finally crowned king of Ireland in May 1316 at Faughart (County Louth).

English rule in Ireland was thus exposed as vulnerable – at least in the short term. The Scottish incursion also prompted at least one effort to undermine England's attempt to rule Ireland. When he arrived in Ireland in 1315 Edward Bruce had allied himself with the king of Tir Eoghain, Donal O'Neill. In 1317 O'Neill communicated with the pope, John XXII, asking he should back Edward's claims to Irish kingship. The arguments which O'Neill employed are interesting. For although it could not be claimed that he represented a united Irish people, his assertions embodied ideas of Irish freedom and of the illegitimacy of English claims on the island of Ireland. Prior to English intrusion, claimed O'Neill, the people in Ireland had been characterized by religious devotion and also by liberty; the Norman invasion which ended this situation had been wrongly sanctioned by Pope Adrian IV (who happened to be English). Not only was Adrian's Bull unacceptable in itself – O'Neill continued – but the subsequent actions of the English in Ireland would anyway have undermined the legitimacy of the conquest. For if the English were supposed to master Ireland in order to reform its church, then their role was a Christian one. Yet in reality, O'Neill's Irish Remonstrance maintained, the English had acted in a deeply unchristian spirit – rather than displaying a zeal to draw the Irish back to truly holy ways they had instead oppressed them. Thus English rule was not legitimate in Ireland, and the authority of a Scottish king had been supported in its place.

But although this document is a fascinating one it lacked both historical substance and practical effect. To suggest that the Irish people had been free, that their freedom had been impinged upon by twelfth-century invasion, and that they had responded by seeking a Scottish alternative to English authority – this would be to simplify the complex reality of Irish political life. To claim instead that the Irish peoples had been free, to recognize that the Norman invasion had in fact been greeted by a telling variety of responses from an equally telling variety of Irish rulers, and to admit that attitudes to the Bruce invasion had also been mixed – these responses would be more historically reliable.

Whatever one makes of it Donal O'Neill's plea to the pope had little effect. The issue of Bruce's kingship was decided by force. In 1318 Edward Bruce was

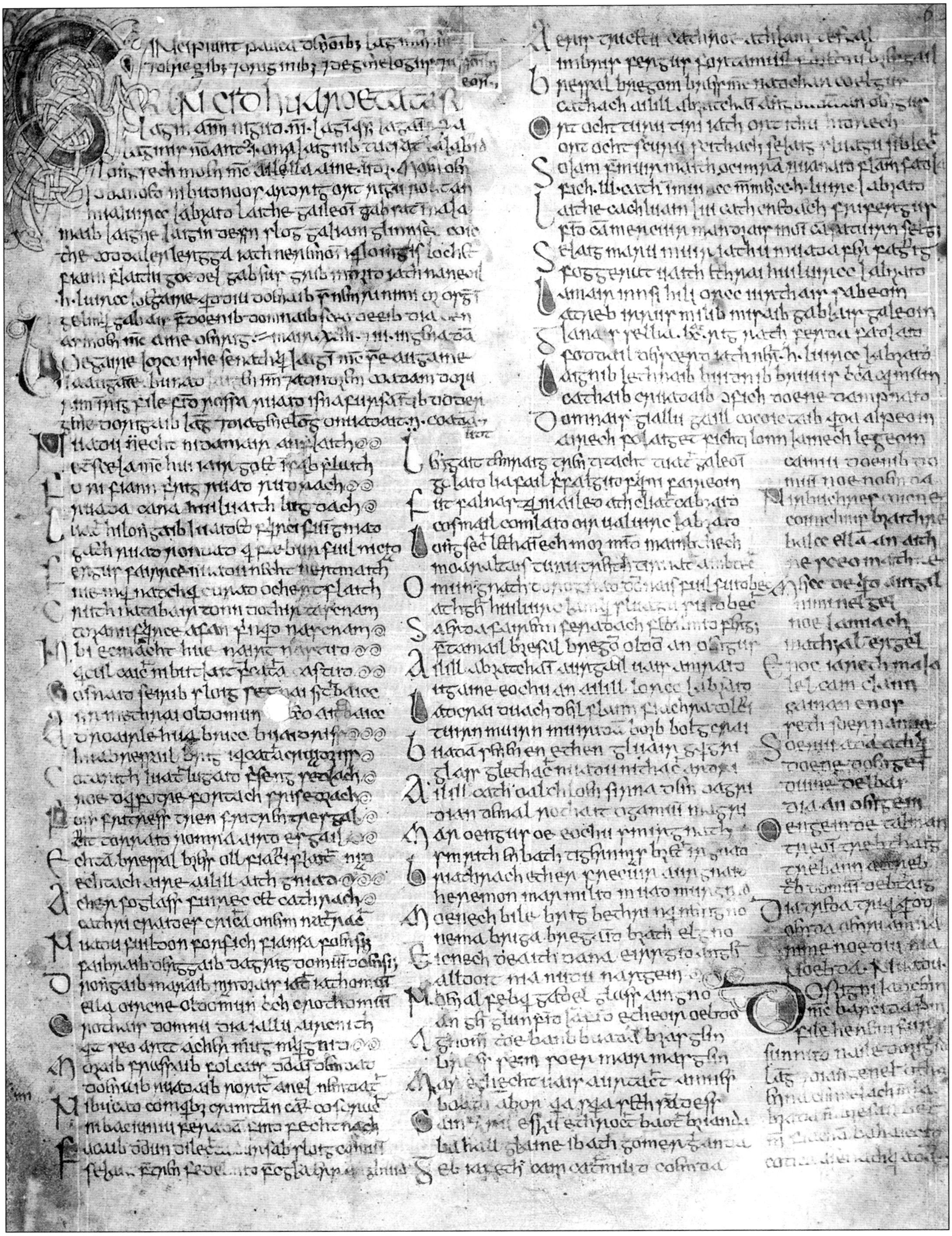

defeated and killed in battle at Faughart (not far from Dundalk) by a colonial force led by John de Bermingham.

The following year de Bermingham became earl of Louth, an example of the prevalent process of the granting of privileges to Anglo-Irish nobles. Indeed, the attempted securing of England's Irish rule was an ongoing effort within which patronage played a crucial part. Edward III – king of England between 1327 and 1377 – stated early in the 1330s that he intended personally to visit Ireland. But this proposed trip never materialized, and in fact English royal rule of Ireland continued to be pursued by envoys sent by the king. Anthony Lucy (the justiciar) and William de Burgo (earl of Ulster) pushed royal interests; but we should be cautious regarding the notion of effective Anglo-Irish authority in Ireland. In this period power was exercised in the context of a patchwork of claims to authority. And within this pattern there were clashes, such as that between the de Burgo and the FitzGerald factions.

There was a certain anxiety on the part of the royal authorities in the early fourteenth century regarding the way in which certain Norman nobles showed themselves prepared to team up with Gaelic leaders. Such alliances – it was held – threatened to undermine the power of the English king in Ireland. Edward III in 1361 gave his son, Lionel of Clarence, the role of king's lieutenant in Ireland, and this appointment led to the famous Statutes of Kilkenny, which emerged from a parliament held by Lionel in 1366. These statutes were addressed to the king's subjects and sought to ensure that, although the conquest of Ireland might be incomplete, there would nevertheless be a maintenance of a loyal, royally ruled, English-style part of the island of Ireland. Under the laws of 1366 it was enacted that English colonists should have no trade with the Irish, nor any marital or concubinary relations with them. They were not even allowed to have contact with Irish poets or musicians lest the artists should act as spies. It was further stated that colonists (and indeed the

OPPOSITE: *The Rawlinson B 502 manuscript, now in the Bodleian Library, Oxford, England, is the earliest Irish manuscript to contain genealogical material, in this case about the kings of Leinster.*

loyal Irish) should use only the English language, and that neither Marcher Law nor Irish (Brehon) Law should be observed. Irish people were to be given no religious rights. Wars between the English in Ireland were proscribed, as were privately pursued wars against the Irish. The Statutes of Kilkenny represented a development of earlier attempts to preserve the distinctively English quality of English Ireland. During the two decades which had preceded the Kilkenny parliament there had, for example, been efforts to control marriage between English and Irish partners and also to consolidate the use of English rather than of Irish law. Such moves testify to the degree to which Ireland's mid-fourteenth-century English population had immersed itself in Irishness. The Kilkenny laws of 1366 can be seen as a kind of legislative breathalyzer, with those Anglo-Irish who did not conform being judged to have stepped over the acceptable limit and to have absorbed a dangerous quantity of Irishness.

If the Statutes of Kilkenny point to certain concerns of the English authorities regarding Ireland, what of Gaelic political culture at this time? There was something of a reassertion both of hope and of influence by the native rulers, with lands and castles being taken from the colonizers by the Irish. The area controlled by the English colony shrunk during the fifteenth century. At the end of the previous century the English king, Richard II, had attempted to halt the sinking of the colonial ship in Ireland and had made two expeditions there. The first (in 1394) saw the king bring a large army and achieve some success in winning submission from Irish leaders. In 1399 Richard returned, but on this occasion a power struggle in England decided the issue. Henry of Derby claimed the English crown and, with Richard being compelled to abdicate, Henry became King Henry IV. Thus Richard's efforts in Ireland were scuppered. The eastern portion of the island was the part in which royal rule was maintained, but this was a territorially small foothold. In the latter part of the century a defensive fortification was constructed to protect the Dublin-centered Pale, which was still subject to English royal authority. This area took in territory from counties Louth, Meath, Dublin and Kildare. But beyond this region lay most of the island, ruled over by a variety of native and Anglo-Irish lords. Neither group achieved anything like dominance over Ireland during this period. Indeed, the Anglo-Irish nobles held a pivotal position in terms of fifteenth-century influence, and English government in Ireland relied on harmonious relations with these powerful figures. The earls of Desmond and of Kildare (both earldoms being held by branches of the FitzGerald family) enjoyed considerable strength, the Kildare House coming to prominence with successive earls filling the position of chief governor of Ireland during the late-fifteenth and early-sixteenth centuries.

This kind of political stability was to be jolted during the crucial sixteenth century. Again it is possible to trace the tensions in the era preceding it. The reign of King Henry VIII (1509-47) was to witness the powerful reassertion of English royal rule in Ireland. But the tussle involving Henry's father (Henry VII, king of England between 1485 and 1509) and Garret More FitzGerald had already hinted at the direction which Anglo-Irish relations would later

take. Born in the mid fifteenth century, Garret More FitzGerald had become earl of Kildare in the 1470s. He became the most famous and the most powerful of the fifteenth century Anglo-Irish earls, and in 1487 he even supported the claims of Lambert Simnel (whose pretensions to the English throne represented a challenge to the authority of Henry VII). Having resisted English efforts to remove him as justiciar, Garret was eventually arrested in 1495 and taken to London. Yet he was subsequently restored as justiciar by Henry VII, whose intelligent pragmatism led him to recognize the authority which Garret possessed in Ireland. In fact, up until his death in 1513 the 'Great Earl' cut an impressively authoritative figure.

But there was another element within this period – Edward Poynings. Sent to Ireland by Henry VII, Poynings called a parliament which met at Drogheda in 1494. This not only accused Garret More FitzGerald of treason, but also produced the measure with which Poynings' name has become lastingly and

OPPOSITE: Three manuscript illustrations from the thirteenth and fourteenth centuries showing monks at prayer (far left), rowing a curragh boat (top right), and attacking a tower (bottom right).
ABOVE: Bunrathy Castle, County Clare, was built by John of England during his lordship of Ireland.

famously associated. 'Poynings' Law' decreed that future parliaments would only be able to meet in Ireland if they had royal license to do so. It also stated that prior royal approval of all intended parliamentary legislation would in future be required. Thus, well before the death of the Great Earl in 1513 there were signs of a Tudor intention to take more control of Ireland. Too much should not be made of this, of course. There were huge differences – in personality as in policy and historical context – between Henry VII and Henry VIII. But the Drogheda parliament of 1494 should certainly not be overlooked in our wide-angle appreciation of the history and politics of early modern Ireland.

Following Garret More FitzGerald's demise his son, Garret Og, became the ninth earl of Kildare and also the lord deputy of Ireland. During the 1530s Garret Og FitzGerald was called to London, and during his absence there occurred a rebellion which was directed at English authority and which was led by his son – Thomas FitzGerald, Lord Offaly. Better known to history as 'Silken Thomas', Lord Offaly's 1534 resistance to English authority in Ireland represented a restatement of Kildare strength, the message to Henry VIII being that English rule in Ireland depended on the House of Kildare. But in Henry VIII Thomas faced one to whom swaggering pride was far from alien, and in October 1534 William Skeffington's arrival in Ireland signalled the start of a process of suppression. Henry's appointment of Skeffington as deputy in Ireland was underlined militarily by the large force with which the new appointee was equipped. By 1535 Silken Thomas' Maynooth base had been taken, and the severity of the royal attitude was reflected in the killing of those who surrendered to the king's forces. Thomas himself was executed in London in 1537 and, as his father was also dead, the Kildare faction was left considerably weakened. The resistance of 1534 had resulted in the forceful

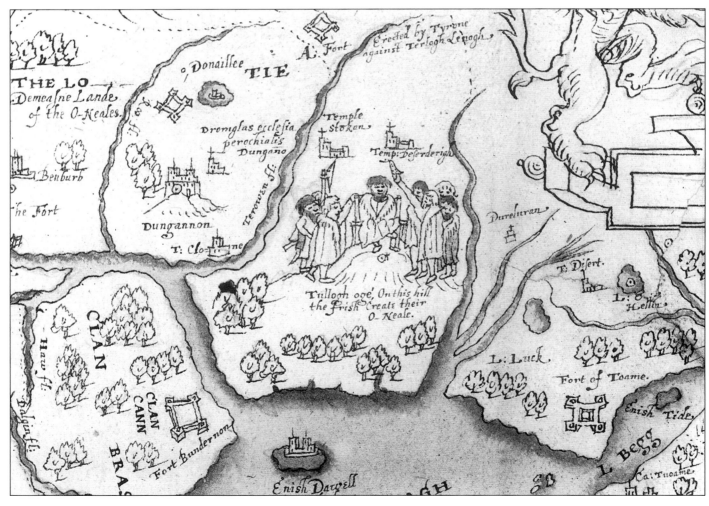

reassertion of English authority in Ireland.

The reign of Henry VIII in England also brought religious reformation, resulting in a distinctively English form of Protestantism. The relationship between religion and political life rendered it vital that Henry's authority be recognized in the religious as in the temporal sphere. An Irish parliament met in 1536 under the new deputy, Lord Grey, and confirmed Henry as supreme head of the church. The English parliament had taken a similar step in the course of the king's messy break with Rome, and this Irish law reinforced through statute the power of the Tudor dynasty in Ireland. In the same year as this parlia-

OPPOSITE, TOP: Dungary Castle, County Clare.
OPPOSITE, BOTTOM: A map with a detail showing the area of County Tyrone where The O'Neill would be inaugurated.
ABOVE: Henry VIII (1509–47), whose rule saw the reassertion of English rule in Ireland.

ment had come together, George Browne was appointed archbishop of Dublin. During the following reign (that of Edward VI, 1547-53) Browne attempted to continue the process of pushing the cause of religious reform in Ireland. As in parts of England, however, there was some strong opposition to alterations regarding the Mass. As is so often the case, religious habit conflicted stubbornly with attempts at theological change. But the Reformation, once planted in Ireland, proved to have sturdy roots. In part this was due to extremely worldly considerations – not even the passionately Catholic Mary Tudor (queen of England between 1553 and 1558) embarked, for example, on the restoration of monastic land and property which had been dissolved as part of the reformation process.

What of other areas of Irish administration? The undermining of the Kildare interest led to certain problems for English rule. Certain Gaelic nobles challenged the people of the Pale by means of raids. The government replied in kind via military missions and also by garrisoning the edges of the Pale. In the end, however, Silken Thomas was perhaps proved right, with the FitzGerald family heir having his title and some of his lands returned to him. In contrast, Gaelic rulers of the Irish midlands – over whom the earls of Kildare had enjoyed a certain dominance in the past – again lost out, being dispossessed and shunted west. There was an option available, but it was a humiliating one: Gaelic rulers could obtain the recognition and support of the English monarch if they acknowledged that monarch to be their legitimate ruler. But the process went beyond this. The Gaelic leaders were also to abandon military practices – an important concession from the English point of view – and to further the process of extending English administration within the Gaelic-controlled areas.

In 1541 an Irish parliament had confirmed England's King Henry VIII as king also of Ireland. In the decade after Henry VIII's death there were further steps taken to entrench the English influence in Ireland, with lands seized in the counties of Laois and Offaly being provided for settlement by people from England or from the English Pale in Ireland. But no all-Ireland effective government emerged at this point, and the story remained one of partial control and of varying political cultures.

3
Building the Ascendancy

The last in the sequence of Tudor monarchs, Elizabeth I, came to power in 1558. Elizabeth sought to continue the development of an English form of Protestantism. In 1560 an Irish parliament confirmed her position as head of the Irish church – again, the importance of religion in affairs of state should be stressed. A further piece of legislation pressed upon clergy the Elizabethan *Book of Common Prayer* (which revised the 1552 book) and although there was comparatively little practical religious persecution under Elizabeth I, it should nevertheless be noted that objection to Tudor rule and objection to Protestantism undoubtedly became intermingled.

There was certainly resistance to Elizabethan rule in Ireland. Ulster proved resilient, with the successive military efforts advocated by Thomas Radcliffe (earl of Sussex) failing to have their desired effect. In 1569 there was further trouble for the English rulers when James FitzMaurice FitzGerald was among the leaders of a rebellion which had arisen in response to claims made on land in the possession of the FitzGeralds and the Butlers. Peter Carew had been the claimant. But he was only one of a number of English adventurers who had participated in a scheme sponsored by Henry Sidney, who became governor of Ireland during the 1560s. Sidney proposed taking lands from Gaelic owners who had militarily opposed the English monarch, or from those whose land was held not to be their own but rather to be the legitimate property of the English crown. The hostility of people such as James FitzMaurice FitzGerald can hardly

OPPOSITE: The English conquest of Ireland was effectively completed during the reign of Elizabeth I (1558–1603).
FOLLOWING PAGE: Cattle raid, a 1581 woodcut by John Derrick, showing Irish pillaging of the English Pale.

be judged to have been one of Irish history's most surprising phenomena. In the event James's rebellion was not successful and he fled to the European mainland. A decade later he returned with an avowed aim of fighting on behalf of the Catholic faith. Equipped with a papal ambassador and a small military body composed of Italians and Spaniards, FitzGerald was again unsuccessful. But prior to defeat there had been notable backing for this venture – particularly in the south – and Elizabeth had responded to this challenge with a sizable force and considerable brutality.

Following the suppression of this rebellion there emerged an extensive English settlement on confiscated land. Important trends can be detected in this episode. Religious undertones are evident in the rebellion and also in the subsequent plantation, for with settlement came a strengthening of Protestant Ireland (in Munster, at least). Also traceable in the 1569 and 1579 revolts is the cycle of rebellion following provocation. Implicit here is the attempted furtherance of the English hold on Ireland; and yet even after the settlements English control of Ireland was far from complete.

One further feature of this rebellious sequence of events was the European connection. Not for the last time mainland European players were to be involved in conflict between Irish challengers and the English government. A European dimension of a different kind entered Irish history during the 1580s, with Anglo-Spanish hostilities resulting in the famous but unsuccessful Armada. Certain of those Spanish ships which had not been destroyed in this celebrated defeat looked to the Irish west coast to provide refuge. The fate of those crew members who made it safely to land reflected the political variations in Ireland. Little mercy awaited Spaniards except in the

province of Ulster, most of which had managed to evade Tudor advances. Yet English governmental ambitions in the Elizabethan period included the aim of bringing Ulster into the English political orbit. The consensus among the English administrators appears to have been to pursue the aim of breaking up the territory, even if considerable influence were to be left with the O'Neill dynasty.

O'Neill authority represented the major problem for English government in this region of Ireland, and the toughest incarnation of this authority was Hugh O'Neill, who had become earl of Tyrone in 1585. O'Neill's career illuminates some of the complications of early modern Irish history. Born in 1550, he was the heir to the baron of Dungannon, Matthew O'Neill, whose inheritance of the earldom of Tyrone was contested and who never realized his claim. Indeed, Hugh O'Neill's accession to the earldom grew out of his immersion in English culture and politics. After his grandfather (Conn O'Neill, first earl of Tyrone) had died, Hugh had been taken to England and put through the process of an English lord's education. Returning to Ireland in the 1560s, it was as a result of his loyal service to Elizabeth that he was given the Tyrone earldom. Having acted in shrewd collusion with English allies in opposition to his

dynastic competitors in Ulster, O'Neill then set himself more ambitious aims than English administrators were prepared to accept. He sought to regain the whole lordship of Tyrone, and during the last decade of the sixteenth century tension brewed between this talented soldier and the English authorities. In 1595 Hugh embarked on rebellion and, with his ally Red Hugh O'Donnell (from Tyrconnell), he made overtures seeking Spanish assistance. Another ingredient of the continental dimension can again be tasted here. O'Neill's military success in 1598 at the battle of the Yellow Ford demonstrated his potential. Indeed, the Spanish king, Philip III, provided Hugh with an army which landed at Kinsale in 1601. O'Neill, O'Donnell and their continental comrades were, however, severely beaten by the forces of the government. The battle of Kinsale was followed by further resistance on O'Neill's part, but in 1603 – just days after the death of Elizabeth I – Hugh surrendered. Sturdy Gaelic opposition had eventually been overcome by English power.

Hugh O'Neill's challenge had been a major one. His defeat was correspondingly significant, and important changes were indeed to occur in the wake of this turbulent episode. In 1607 – four years after his surrender – Hugh and many other Ulster lords opted for

Irish Bards

Iren: There is amongst the Irishe a Certaine kynde of people called the bardes, which are to them in steade of Poetes, whose profession is to sett forth the prayses and disprayses of men, in theire Poems or rymes the which are had in so high regard and estymacion amongst them, that none dare displease them, for feare to rvn into reproch, through theire offence and to bee made infamous in the mouthes of all men, for theire vearses are taken vpp with a generall applause, and vsuallie sounge at all feastes and metinges, by certaine other persons whose proper function that is, which also receyve for the same greate rewardes, and reputacion besides.

FROM EDMUND SPENSER A VIEW OF THE PRESENT STATE OF IRELAND (CIRCA 1596)

OPPOSITE: A 1581 woodcut showing an Irish chieftain entertained by a harpist during a feast.
ABOVE: An Irish chief and attendants from the same year.

voluntary exile in Europe, O'Neill himself dying in Rome nine years later. To the administrators of English rule in Ireland the lesson was that Gaelic, Catholic lords were a dangerous breed as far as crown rule was concerned. Things were not quite this simple, however, for there appears also to have been a measure of concern regarding the reliability of the Old English nobles – those whose ancestors had pioneered the Anglo-Norman conquest of Ireland. The insecurity of the English hold which is highlighted by these attitudes galvanized the authorities into measures aimed at securing English rule. Another pivotal point in Irish history had therefore been reached.

Following the "flight of the earls" to Europe in 1607 the English government was given a chance to consolidate its strength in Ireland. James I had followed Elizabeth on the English throne in 1603 and, like her, he included Ireland among his monarchical possessions. The lord deputy in Ireland – Arthur Chichester – took six of Ulster's nine counties after the fleeing earls' territory had been declared forfeit to the English monarchy. In 1609 the Articles of

Plantation emerged, facilitating a process of settlement which brought Scottish and English people to the island. Some land was also allotted to Irish people, though these landlords were obliged to farm according to English practice. The bullying nature of the plantation process and the dispossession of the Irish cannot be morally condoned simply because it appeared to be tactically sensible. But the variation of settlement patterns should be noted, particularly as the shapes of later Irish political life were beginning here to be molded. It was in eastern Ulster that the process of colonization took firmest root. Counties Antrim and Down witnessed the fiercest example, with Scottish Protestant immigration resulting in the forcible uprooting of Irish Catholic natives. Already one can trace the emerging characteristics of northern Irish political history. It was not merely a case of dispossessor and dispossessed, nor solely one of Protestant and Catholic, or of Scottish versus Irish; the politics of this region derived from the fact that all three distinctions were relevant. Religion, ethnicity and the process of plantation combined to produce a most significant and resilient cultural fault line.

The situation in county Londonderry was different, however, from that in south Antrim or north

LEFT: A sixteenth-century English soldier.
ABOVE: An Irish Gallowglass of the same era.
OPPOSITE: Irish soldiery displaying the haphazard armament typical of their armies of this time.

Down. Insufficient numbers of Scottish or English people could be drawn to Londonderry, and so Irish tenants formed an important part of the new picture there. More broadly, plantation also affected many other parts of seventeenth-century Ireland, including Carlow, Leitrim, Longford and Wexford. In every Irish county, indeed, there came to be at least some landowners who originated from the neighboring island. Englishness, in fact, was seriously in vogue, to the extent of some native landowners stepping down the road of emulating things Anglo. English power brought with it a coercive logic tending in the direction of assimilation. Linguistic, sartorial, architectural and legal developments reflected as much.

During the 1630s a significant development in Anglo-Irish politics was heralded by the appointment of Thomas Wentworth as lord deputy. Later to become the earl of Strafford, Wentworth embarked on a rigorous policy of attempting to increase royal revenue and also royal power in Ireland. Once again the tensions of English political life had an important bearing on Irish affairs. Charles I (king of England between 1625 and 1649) experienced increasing problems during the 1630s, and this decade in English politics exported some of its turbulence to Ireland. Wentworth's espousal of Laudianism represents an important example here. William Laud – archbishop of Canterbury from 1633 – was zealous for the enforcement of uniformity within the Church of England. But Wentworth's assumption of religious authority in Ireland alienated many in Ireland's English community. Similarly, his failure to grant promised concessions to Catholics generated irritation, while his harsh line on Ulster – with people being punished for their non-adherence to the 1609 Articles of Plantation – caused further resentment still. Hostility to Wentworth, therefore, was widespread in Ireland, and the next stage in the English crisis also influenced Irish experience significantly.

The year 1642 witnessed the start of the English Civil War. The preceding year has achieved a high place in Irish history. In Ulster certain people within the Catholic landowning class sought advancement of their interests through the medium of force. A number of local risings resulted in a combination of humiliation, expulsion and killing directed at recent settlers in the region. But Ulster was not the only scene of revolt in 1641. Rory O'More – whose family had suffered as a consequence of plantation in county Laois – colluded with Phelim O'Neill in his plan to subvert the government in Dublin. An attempt to take control of Dublin Castle failed, but the rebellion was not to be snuffed out so easily.

The rebels declared that they had the support of King Charles I and an alliance was forged between the Old English in Ireland and the native Irish. Cracks began to show quickly enough between the partners in this intriguing relationship. But the strength of religious identification is unmistakable none the less. Catholics, though massively different in other ways, united as Catholics in the face of Protestant adversaries. Religious vision clearly meant much to these adversaries as well. When the English response to events in 1640s Ireland finally came, it turned out to be a cruel one. In a history peopled with simplistically portrayed good guys and bad guys, Oliver Cromwell has tended to be placed among the latter group. Charles I had been executed in January 1649, and seven months later Cromwell arrived in Ireland, enjoying both civil and military authority. The English Civil War had gone very badly for the Irish. In 1642 leading representatives of Catholic Ireland had gathered in Kilkenny, and tied their colors to the king's mast. There were stresses within this Catholic

grouping, reflected by respective attitudes to Owen Roe O'Neill. Nephew of Hugh O'Neill, Owen Roe had spent considerable time in the Spanish army in a Europe which was experiencing the Thirty Years' War. In 1642 O'Neill agreed to lead Ulster's rebels. But the fragility of the alliance can be gauged by the fact that Old English Catholics were reluctant to give O'Neill the backing he needed in the Ulster theater of war. For O'Neill's approach involved the belief that Irish chiefs should try to rid Ireland of English power. The Old English, however, were less enthusiastic about severing links with the crown.

Whether they were thoroughly hostile to English rule or keen on royal reconciliation, the rebels were perceived by Cromwell in a fully negative light. Parliament had won the day in the civil war and Irish Catholic affection for crown authority was hardly likely to win friends in post-monarchical England. Cromwell was determined to avenge the slaughter of Protestants which had taken place in the early part of the decade. He also wished to restore English order to

unruly Ireland, and to stamp on the head of any Irish remnants of royalism. In September 1649 the violence began, carried out by a tough military machine. Drogheda was attacked and, following its refusal to surrender, the garrison was killed by Cromwell's forces. A similarly atrocious procedure occurred in October at Wexford. Military suppression succeeded in bringing about the defeat of the Irish. Cromwell himself departed from the island in 1650. Henry Ireton then acted as the enforcer, followed after his death by Charles Fleetwood. Between these two, English military command was effectively exercised by Edmund Ludlow, and this succession of figures – Cromwell, Ireton, Ludlow, Fleetwood – oversaw the defeat of Irish resistance.

BELOW: Detail from the O'Connor Sligo wall memorial (1624) at Sligo Abbey, in honor of Sir Donogh O'Conor Sligo.
OPPOSITE: Thomas Wentworth, 1st earl of Strafford (c. 1633), attempted to use Ireland to buttress the authority of England's Charles I in a struggle with Parliament.

But the mission went beyond the eradication of Irish military potential. Protestant conversion might not have been foremost in the mind during the carnage at Drogheda or Wexford. But conversion was none the less part of the overall vision for Ireland. It was also part of the less than grand design that Catholic lands should be confiscated. The English parliament in 1652 passed an Act of Settlement which facilitated the taking of land from owners who had not demonstrated their loyalty during the years of the rebellion. Many soldiers were rewarded with such forfeited lands. Catholics were forced to take land in Connacht. Thus the 1640s and 1650s present a painful and all too familiar pattern – rebellion mingled with a search for revenge; severe reaction by those in authority; massacres; economic and religious marginalization; the creation of myths portraying the viciousness and treachery of one's opponents – these features overlay one another and represent a complicated catalogue of bloody and ugly conflict.

Cromwell's reputation in Ireland continued well after his death; non-monarchical rule in England did not. He died in 1658, and within two years Charles II was king of England, Scotland, and Ireland. But the Irish parliament which met in 1661 was heavily Cromwellian in complexion. In 1662 an Act of Settlement facilitated claims from those who had not been guilty of rebellion, regarding lands of which they had been dispossessed. But in practice widespread re-transfer did not occur. The 1665 Act of Explanation attempted to compensate Protestants who had lost land returned to Catholics. Although some Catholics did regain land, Catholic land grievance remained. At the start of the 1640s Catholics had held over half of the land in Ireland. But in the 1660s the picture was very different. In the period after the Act of Explanation, Catholics held less than a quarter of Irish land. Thus religious difference was carved into patterns of land ownership.

Late-seventeenth-century Catholicism made ground in terms of organization and control. The Church of Ireland also made progress, enjoying land restoration and a strengthening of its hierarchy. Variety rather than uniformity persisted, a trend

OPPOSITE: Tomb erected in 1632 in St Patrick's Cathedral, Dublin, by Richard Boyle, earl of Cork, for his wife Katherine.

emphasized by the continued vitality of northern Presbyterianism. The Church of Ireland was the officially established church. If numbers provided an index of potential, then it was the Catholic tradition which had most to anticipate. In a sense this proved to be the case. This process took time to develop, but there were hopes of great things among sections of the Catholic population when, in 1685, the Catholic James II came to the throne. It was assumed by many that land and influence would surely follow. Certain changes did take place. An eminent Irish Catholic, Richard Talbot, was given the title earl of Tyrconnell in 1685. He took charge of the army and reorganized it with an infusion of Catholic blood. Catholics became judges and came to sit on the Privy Council, and when Talbot became lord deputy in 1687 Protestant anxiety increased still further. Such fear could only be rendered even more acute by consideration of Talbot's determination that the Cromwellian confiscations of land be undone.

In fact the reign of James II was a short one. Although he lived until 1701 he was driven from power in 1688, to be succeeded the following year by William III and Mary II as king and queen of England. In 1689, James II landed in Ireland from France. His Scottish followers having been beaten in battle, Ireland appeared to offer James a last chance to regain power. He had the backing of Louis XIV of France, who found the exiled James his sole ally in a war against German, Dutch, Spanish, and Italian enemies. But events unfolded unhappily for the ousted ruler. Londonderry had stood against James' supporters and a famous siege failed to break the resilient town. William III landed in Ireland in June 1690. At the battle of the Boyne in the following month, July 1, 1690, Protestant William gained the day over Catholic James. The religious labels are all too tragically relevant here. While the conflict between William and James was in one sense a contest between multinational armies about who should control England, it reflected very Irish realities. James had called a predominantly Catholic parliament in 1689. The Act of Settlement was repealed – further evidence of the vital significance of land in Irish political consciousness. Those who had held land in 1641 were now able to seek restitution of losses incurred in the Cromwellian period.

This Dublin "patriot" parliament was prevented from producing effective legislation by military reality. Because religion overlapped with questions such as land ownership it was a forceful phenomenon. The situation by 1689-90 was one in which the religious boundary reigned supreme. Religion, politics and economics were woven together in this period. The interrelation of these crucial factors underlines the integral importance of late-seventeenth-century Irish religious identification: it was present in all spheres of contemporary life.

Following the clash at the river Boyne James left for France. But the conflict continued after his departure. William also left Ireland in 1690, Patrick Sarsfield's Limerick Jacobites having repulsed the king's forces. But the absence of the figureheads did not remove the violence. In 1691 the Williamites took Athlone and inflicted defeat on their enemies at Aughrim. Eventually Sarsfield agreed to a treaty. Like the battles of Aughrim and the Boyne, the Treaty of Limerick has become lodged in Ireland's complex historical memory. Signed on 3 October 1691, it gave Irish soldiers a variety of choices, including the most popular one of going to France. It also provided for a measure of toleration where Ireland's Catholics were concerned. But it would be naive to attribute too great a role in 1690s political culture to the practice of religious toleration. The year 1695 saw the emergence of parliamentary acts which restricted Catholic rights regarding education and the bearing of arms. Parliament also legislated – in 1697 – for the banishment of Catholic clergy. So the flavor of the 1690s was a religiously sour one. The Penal Laws characterized the attitude of the victorious powerful. This attitude should not be condoned. But it was wholly predictable none the less. The 1640s and the 1680s had each, in their respective ways, instilled a measure of fear into the Protestant culture which thrived after the Williamite triumph.

In 1704 – two years after the accession to the English throne of Queen Anne (1702-14) – the penal legislation was extended with the introduction of restrictions on Catholic land-holding rights and on Catholic participation in public office. Prior to Anne's arrival on the throne legislation had gone some way toward directing Irish economic development in accordance with English designs. In 1696 Irish linen manufacture was encouraged, while in 1699 Irish woollen exports were restricted. Thus the English exertion of influence over Irish affairs represented self-defensive muscle-flexing on the part of the powerful. To non-Catholics in Ireland the bitter history of the post-1640 period told its own tale – Catholics were a threat to your property, position, and even to your life. Members of the Dublin parliament represented a centre of enthusiasm for penal legislation directed against Catholics. But to the English authorities, too, there was a recognition of the special position of the Roman Catholic religion in Ireland. Even James II – hero of the Catholic cause – appreciated the politically different implications of Irish as opposed to English Catholicism.

And here we come to the really distinctive aspect of the appalling penal measures in Ireland. For religiously punitive legislation was not an unknown phenomenon in contemporary Europe. The distinguishing feature of the Irish case was that here it was a religious majority rather than a minority which was experiencing suppression. The penal process could not realistically be hoped to convert the Catholic population of Ireland to the Protestant faith. At the root of the process was the intention that Catholics should be kept out of positions of influence. Excluded from parliament, the legal profession, the armed or governmental services, Catholics were the victims more of a structure of repression than one of attempted conversion. It should, however, be noted that many Catholics of higher social status did make the required shift into Protestant respectability. This was important, for instance, if a wealthy Catholic wanted his land to be passed on intact to one son. Only a Protestant could inherit in such a way. If conversion did not take place then the land would be divided up among the various male heirs, rather than going in one piece to the eldest. The application of this mechanism would ensure the subdivision of Catholic holdings, and would plainly bring about a decline in Catholic landed influence.

The Penal Laws will not be forgotten, but in order

OPPOSITE: A portrait of Oliver Cromwell, from the painting by Robert Walker. His black reputation in Ireland has sound foundations in a systematic anti-Catholicism that obliterated any remaining sizable Catholic landholdings.

fully to understand their operation two further points should be made. First, a distinction should be drawn between the passing of legislation and the effective implementation of the laws so enacted. There was, in fact, considerable variation in the application of penal legislation in Ireland. The ban on Catholic arms-bearing, for example, soon lapsed into disuse, and the laws which impinged on practices of religious worship came increasingly to have little impact. There was greater alertness regarding those elements of the code which were seen as truly vital to the maintenance of Protestant ascendancy. Exclusion from parliament was to remain an important grievance until the early nineteenth century. And land, as always, focused the fears of the powerful and the resentment of the marginalized. In the early eighteenth century Irish Catholics represented approximately three-quarters of the island's population. Yet they owned only a tiny fraction of the land.

The second point worth adding to this discussion of penal pressure concerns Dissenters. Northern Irish Presbyterianism was a vibrant force in this period, but was officially penalized in certain ways. For religious discrimination was really a pro-Church of Ireland mechanism. The Dissenter tradition had less to complain about than did the Catholic one with which it was eventually to lock vicious horns. A parliamentary act of 1704 made it obligatory that those holding public office should take the sacrament according to Church of Ireland practice. Thus Presbyterians, too, were on the receiving end of discrimination. Even when the 1719 Toleration Act liberated Protestant Dissenters from the requirement of attending the services of the established church, their obligation to pay tithes still remained. Thus distinctions within Irish Protestantism – which have often been underestimated by observers – can clearly be detected within this era.

Argyle a muckle Scotch Knaue in gude faith Sir.

OPPOSITE: Captain Thomas Lee, executed for treason in 1601, was one of the English Protestant officers who helped to build the ascendancy. This portrait was painted by Marcus Gheeraedts, the younger (1561–1635).
ABOVE, RIGHT: Satirical portrayal of Scottish Presbyterians, whose settlement in northern Ireland during the seventeenth century created another group that would benefit, if not as fully as Irish Anglicans, from the Ascendancy.

What of the eighteenth century economy? The parliament in London helped direct the development of Irish trade. (Though it should be noted, for example, that in 1699 legislation aimed at limiting Irish export of woollens was passed in the Irish as well as the English parliament). Irish brewing underwent expansion; this trend was hampered by the parliamentary decision that hops could only be imported into Ireland from Britain. The linen industry was to flourish (especially in Ulster) following the encouragement it received. Thus Irish economic developments generally followed a pattern friendly to England.

Good pasture land facilitated the emergence of a prospering body of farmers in parts of Munster and Leinster – a development less common in the west of Ireland. In rural regions the role of the infamous absentee landlords, whose estates were leased and

subdivided in their absence, has been the focus of much debate. But to attribute too much blame to non-resident aristocrats exempts from blame many rural actors lower down the social league table who were themselves happy to thrive at the expense of Ireland's poor. The pasture-farming class is one example. Domestic graziers became the focus of rural resentment later in Ireland's history, when the landlord class had been effectively bought out.

The relation between politics and economy was an intimate one. England's political hold on Ireland was reflected in the 1720 Declaratory Act, which recognized the right of the parliament at Westminster to legislate for Ireland. Two decades before to the passing of this act, a sophisticated case on behalf of a kind of Irish nationalism had been presented. William Molyneux (1656-98) was educated at Trinity

LEFT: *James, 1st duke of Ormond, served the Stuart kings well in Ireland during the 1640s, and in 1660-1668.*
BELOW: *Charles Fort, Kinsale, Cork.*
OPPOSITE: *William III (1650–1702), a Dutch prince, married into the Stuart family.*

College, Dublin, and in addition to his contributions to the world of Irish philosophy he also had political experience as member of parliament for Dublin University during the 1690s. His pamphlet, *The Case of Ireland's being Bound by Acts of Parliament in England Stated* (1698), grew out of his consideration of the consequences of English laws for Irish industrial life. Molyneux's argument is important in representing a particular kind of "national" sentiment. His argument effectively pointed in a nationalistic direction. But it is crucial to stress, given the modern-day identification of Irish nationalism with the Catholic tradition, that to the Anglo-Irish, seventeenth-century mind of William Molyneux the Irish nation was the Protestant Irish nation. The Protestant Ascendancy was precisely that, an ascendancy based on an exclusive definition of who constituted the nation.

ABOVE: Tailor's Guild Hall, Dublin, is the only medieval guild hall that still exists in the Irish capital.
RIGHT: The Mansion House, built in 1705, and bought in 1715 to serve as the residence of Dublin's Lord Mayor.

4

The United Kingdom

Questions of English power and Irish life in the years following the Declaratory Act of 1720 drew the attention of the first great Irish writer in English, Jonathan Swift (1667-1745). Born in Dublin, Swift was educated at Kilkenny Grammar School and then (like William Molyneux, another Anglo-Irishman who helped develop an Irish national consciousness) at Trinity College, Dublin. In the 1690s Swift was ordained and in 1713 he became the Dean of Dublin's St Patrick's Cathedral (a position he held right up until 1745). Both Swift and Molyneux espoused a form of constitutional Irish independence. Swift's anonymous pamphlet from 1720 advocated the use of Irish manufactures, as did his *Drapier's Letters,* published in 1724. In these he opposed the license issued to an Englishman, William Wood, to mint brass coins for use in Ireland. The patent in question had been granted by the government to the duchess of Kendal and in turn had been bought by Wood, who had hoped to make a significant profit from the project. In 1723, however, the Irish parliament protested against the scheme and in the end, with Swift's prod-

LEFT: *Portrait of Jonathan Swift. Born in Ireland of English parents, he came to identify with the land of his birth.*
ABOVE: *Statue of Henry Grattan, City Hall, Dublin.*

A Loyal critic

You state, what has long been but too obvious, that it seems the unfortunate policy of the Hour, to put to the far largest portion of the Kings Subjects in Ireland, the desperate alternative, between a thankless acquiescence under grievous Oppression, or a refuge in Jacobinism with all its horrors and all its crimes. You prefer the former dismal part of the choice. There is no doubt but that you would have reasons if the election of one of these Evils was at all a security against the other. But they are things very alliable and as closely connected as cause and effect. That Jacobinism, which is Speculative in its Origin, and which arises from Wantonness and fullness of bread, may possibly be kept under by firmness and prudence. The very levity of character which produces it may extinguish it; but the Jacobinism which arises from Penury and irritation, from scorned loyalty, and rejected Allegiance, has much deeper roots. They take their nourishment from the bottom of human Nature and the unalterable constitution of things, and not from humour and caprice or the opinions of the Day about privileges and Liberties.

**FROM A LETTER FROM EDMUND BURKE
TO THE REVEREND THOMAS HUSSEY
(LATER CATHOLIC BISHOP OF WATERFORD), 1796.**

The Irish gentry

...Then he fell to singing the favourite song he learned from his father - for the last time, poor gentleman - he sung it that night as loud and as hearty as ever with a chorus...

"He that goes to bed, and goes to bed sober,
Falls as the leaves do, falls as the leaves do, and
dies in October;
But he that goes to bed, and goes to bed mellow,
Lives as he ought to do, lives as he ought to do,
and dies and honest fellow."

Sir Patrick died that night: Just as the company rose to drink his health with three cheers, he fell down in a sort of fit, and was carried off; they sat it out, and were surprised, on inquiry, in the morning, to find that it was all over with poor Sir Patrick. Never did any gentleman live and die with more beloved in the country by rich and poor. His funeral was such a one as was never known before or since in the county!

FROM CASTLE RACKRENT, A NOVEL BY MARIA EDGEWORTH, 1800

OPPOSITE, TOP: Irish peasants stacking turf.
OPPOSITE, BOTTOM: The speaker enters parliament.
ABOVE: The Irish parliament in 1790.

ding, the plan was abandoned.

Swift's witty brilliance excels within this Ascendancy tradition of Irish patriotism. But the Ascendancy intelligentsia had other heroes to offer to posterity, among them the orator Edmund Burke (1729-97), and the philosopher George Berkeley (1685-1753). Berkeley's assertion that truth was "the game of the few" might perhaps be applied also to Irish politics in the latter part of the eighteenth century. For these were highly elitist times. Two charismatic figures were influential in differing ways during the late eighteenth century: Henry Grattan and Theobald Wolfe Tone. Born in 1746, Grattan was educated at Trinity College, Dublin, and during the 1770s was called to the Irish Bar and entered the Irish parliament. His oratorical gifts brought him quickly to prominence, and he emerged as leader of the "patriot" party, an opposition group in the Dublin parliament that had developed during the 1760s. The patriots sought and gained greater Irish independence

from England. But the nature of this independence was limited. Patriots were the backbone of the Irish Volunteers, a militia force established at the time of the American Revolution for defense against possible foreign invasion. Grattan campaigned for the removal of the remaining restrictions on Irish commerce and for Irish legislative independence. The achievement of these two goals represented an important development in Irish political history. "Grattan's parliament," as the 1782-1800 Dublin body came to be known, had legislative independence under the crown. It was not absolute independence from England that Grattan and his colleagues sought; it was autonomy within an English orbit. The Volunteer movement helped the patriots to these legislative victories, and some members became interested in a more radical agenda.

The achievements of 1782 should not be sneered at. In June the Declaratory Act (which had recognized the right of the London parliament to legislate for Ireland) was repealed. In July Poynings' Law was amended. As we saw earlier, this law had stated that Irish parliaments could only meet if they had royal license to do so, and stipulated the necessity of prior royal approval for Irish parliamentary legislation. Now, however, the situation was to be different. After 1782 a royal right of veto remained, but not a right to alter Irish legislation.

Henry Grattan's parliamentary instincts were not only evident in his pursuit of Irish parliamentary independence, but were further reflected in his career after 1800. Having opposed the parliamentary union with Britain that emerged in that year, he none the less sat in the union parliament in London between 1805 and 1820. Parliament was his natural medium. A leading member of the Protestant Ascendancy himself, Grattan nevertheless argued – with typical rhetorical flourish – that "the Irish Protestant could never be free till the Irish Catholic had ceased to be a slave." In the early nineteenth century he espoused the cause of Catholic emancipation.

This issue of religious toleration brings us on to our second late-eighteenth-century focal figure. Theobald Wolfe Tone was born in 1763 and, like Grattan, he attended Trinity College, Dublin. Like Grattan, too, he pursued legal studies, but the two men were in fact highly different. Tone's *Argument on Behalf of the Catholics of Ireland* (1791) reflected his political enthusiasm, and later in the year he was involved in the foundation of the United Irishmen in Belfast. The radical spirit that had tentatively emerged among the Volunteers now found a new outlet. This movement began as a debating society with reform on its mind. But Tone and the United Irishmen are inescapably linked in historical memory with the rebellion – or rebellions – of 1798. Tone's ideology developed into a dreamy blend of republican separatism and religious tolerance, his thinking classically epitomized in seductive rhetoric:

(1796:) To subvert the tyranny of our execrable government, to break the connection with England, the never failing source of all our political evils, and to assert the independence of my country – these were my objects. To unite the whole people of Ireland, to abolish the memory of all past dissensions, and to substitute the common name of Irishman, in the place of the denominations of Protestant, Catholic and Dissenter – these were my means.

(1798:) The great object of my life has been the independence of my country ... looking upon the connexion with England to have been her bane I have endeavored by every means in my power to break that connexion ....

But the events that actually materialized in 1798 deviated in many ways from the envisaged pattern. For one thing the rebellion failed; Tone's arrival with French forces could not alter the outcome and he himself was captured and sentenced to death before in fact committing suicide. In addition to this, the violence of 1798 took on a sectarian aspect in various places – precisely the division which Tone had sought to eradicate from Irish life. As so often in Irish experience, rhetoric and enthusiasm had an undeniable impact without bringing about the changes at which

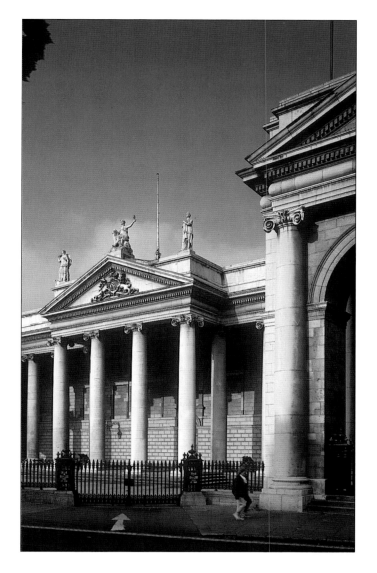

OPPOSITE: The memorial to Wolfe Tone at Collins' Barracks.
ABOVE, RIGHT: A 1798 memorial to one of the ordinary soldiers, the "Croppy Boys" of the 1798 rebellion in Tralee, County Kerry.
ABOVE, LEFT: Today's Bank of Ireland building was once home to the Irish parliament.

they were in fact directed.

The cult of Theobald Wolfe Tone was to become a resilient one, with his being celebrated (or condemned) as the founding father of modern Irish republicanism. This description is a dangerous one. Yet in a way Tone has indeed been a figure for apostles of the Irish republic to celebrate. For later republican thought and practice were to reflect themes associated with Wolfe Tone. Separatist zeal; romantic conceptions of nationhood; aspirations to cross-sectarian unity; effective rhetoric; the rather less effec-

tive use of violence; striking commitment, even unto death; indulgence in political simplification; a good measure of Anglophobia – each of these elements was to recur in subsequent Irish republican experience and in this sense Tone's celebrated status is fitting.

More immediately, the rebellion with which he is associated helped convince the prime minister, William Pitt, of the need for a union between Ireland and Great Britain. Thus "Grattan's parliament" was brought to an end. The Act of Union which passed through the Irish parliament in 1800 came into effect at the start of January 1801. The century which began in this way witnessed the development in Ireland of mutually hostile political and cultural traditions. Indeed, the persistence of conflict in modern Ireland owes much to this phenomenon – the simultaneous validity of apparently contradictory stances.

The United Kingdom of Great Britain and Ireland

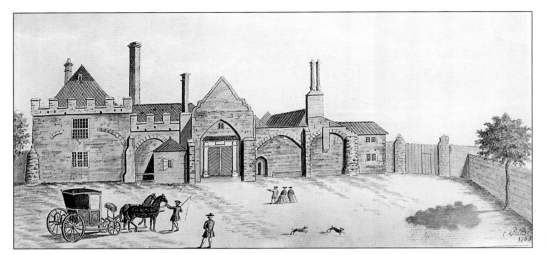

TOP: *The Archiepiscopal Palace in Dublin in 1765. At the time the Archbishop had two palaces, one at the village of Tallaght, and the other in Kevin Street.*
MIDDLE: *Ships in the Foyle Estuary, Londonderry 1793.*
BOTTOM: *This view of Dublin Castle, the headquarters of English administration, was published in 1728.*

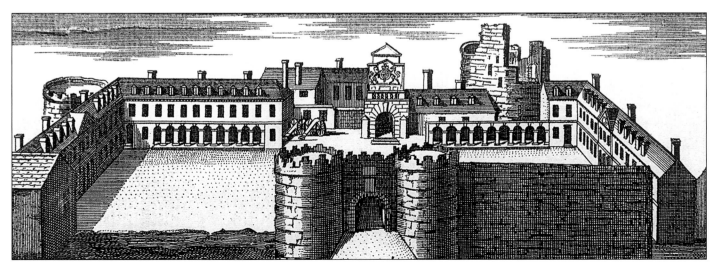

ABOVE: *Belfast High Street in 1786. The city was then a center of the thriving linen industry in Ulster.*

BELOW: *The Viceregal Lodge in 1783. It was originally built in Phoenix Park in 1751 as a residence for the park ranger.*

was reflected, in parliamentary terms, in Irish representation to a Westminster body. Certain distinctive elements remained in the realm of Irish government after 1800; Ireland was not simply absorbed indiscriminately into the British political world. Financially there was Irish difference, and the vice-regal and Castle structures – so important before the Union – remained. The Union was certainly important. But in a sense it reflected rather than created Irish reality. Ironically, the degree of post-1800 continuity is evident even among those looking for drastic change. Robert Emmet (1778-1803), brother of an eminent United Irishman, led an unsuccessful rebellion in 1803 and was subsequently hanged. Thus the United Irish connection lived on, and physical force earned a place in the history of the early nineteenth century, just as it had at the end of the eighteenth. The significance of violence was to be elevated to sophisticated heights. But in the early nineteenth century it was the emergence of a very different tradition which dominated the agenda.

Daniel O'Connell (1775-1847) came to be known as "The Liberator," but "the mobilizer" might be a

more appropriate nickname. It was under O'Connell that Catholic Ireland acquired political maturity, and he deserves to be recognized as one of Irish history's truly inspiring figures. Born in County Kerry, he was educated abroad and became a barrister on his return to Ireland. Talented and Catholic, he was in a perfect position to experience, respond to and do something about the injustices which Catholics suffered in the early nineteenth century. Debarred from sitting in parliament or holding high office, Catholics none the less had the potential within Ireland for the

OPPOSITE, TOP AND BOTTOM: Monuments to Daniel O'Connell, who helped overturn some of the anti-Catholic discriminatory legislation can be found across Ireland. These examples are from Ennis Town (top) and Dublin (bottom). ABOVE: The museum of Trinty College, Dublin, during the early nineteenth century.

achievement of dominance. Focusing on the issue of Catholic emancipation, O'Connell helped Catholic Ireland to begin to realize this potential. In May 1823 he founded the Catholic Association, which sought the attainment of full political rights for Catholics. Charisma, oratory, and organizational skills combined to make the man a formidable figure. And it was in the last of these spheres – that of organization – that the crucial development occurred. The "Catholic Rent" was a small subscription paid by thousands, and it offered both financial foundations and widespread political involvement. Thus mass politics arrived in Ireland and, significantly, the focus was a Catholic one. In 1828 O'Connell was elected MP for County Clare – as a Catholic he was unable to take his seat – and the following year saw the Catholic Emancipation Act, enabling Catholics to enter parliament and also to hold most public offices.

5
Emigration and Revolution

The victory of 1829 facilitated a shift in the focus of political activity: parliament was now open to Catholic politics. During the 1830s O'Connell worked diligently in this different sphere, and through it he achieved notable changes for Ireland. Supporters of the tradition of physical force in Ireland have tended to be scathing about what can be achieved through compromise. Yet O'Connell's achievements – partial though they often tended to be – must surely be compared against the practical results which his physical force critics could offer. Hard-line Irish republican movements have never been in particularly short supply of ambition. In terms of practical delivery of goods, their cupboard is slightly more bare. The exception to this is the phenomenon of physical force activism representing a strong hand in the background, a hand which can enable constitutional forces to exert greater pressure where it matters. Arguments could be made out along these lines with regard to Charles Parnell, or even to events concerning Northern Ireland in the 1980s. But such suggestions in no way damage the argument that constitutional methods of Irish political expression have enabled certain tangible results to be achieved.

Unfortunately for O'Connell, the latter years of his political career formed an anti-climactic end to his story. He sensed by 1840 that the Whig administration of Lord Melbourne would shortly be replaced by a less appealing Tory regime led by Robert Peel. O'Connell had publicly protested against the Union as early as 1800; now, in 1840, he founded the Repeal Association. This was to set the tone for important developments in the 1840s, and O'Connell returned to mass movement tactics in pursuit of repeal. The famous Clontarf episode of 1843 has become a lasting litmus test of attitudes to O'Connell; a repeal meeting planned for 8 October of that year was proscribed by the government and, rather than risk confrontation, O'Connell cancelled the gathering.

This raises the important question of O'Connell's hostile attitude toward political violence. O'Connell was firmly in the constitutionalist rather than the physical force camp. Right up until the present day there has been an ambiguity about the precise relationship between the violent and non-violent agendas in Irish nationalism. The former has largely been the preserve of an enthusiastic minority. Yet at certain crucial times the physical force approach has

OPPOSITE: Kilmainham jail, now a museum, housed plenty of Irish patriots over its history, and was the scene of the execution of those charged with treason after the Easter Rising of 1916.
ABOVE: The Irish Nationalist leader William Smith O'Brien in Kilmainham jail, 1848, after being sentenced to transportation to Australia.

ABOVE: The opening of the Dublin & Kingstown Railway, the first in Ireland, in 1834.
OPPOSITE: An Ulster linen mill, around 1840.

19th-century Limerick

Passing by it, and walking down other streets,- black, ruinous, swarming, dark, hideous,-you come upon the barracks and the walks of the old castle, and from it on to an old bridge, from which the view is a fine one. On one side are the grey bastions of the castle; beyond them, in the midst of the broad stream, stands a huge mill that looks like another castle; further yet is the handsome new Wellesley Bridge, with some little craft upon the river, and the red warehouses of the New Town looking prosperous enough. The Irish Town stretches away to the right; there are pretty villas beyond it; and on the bridge are walking twenty-four young girls, in parties of four and five, with their arms round each other's waists, swaying to and fro, and singing or chattering, as happy as if they had shoes to their feet. Yonder you see a dozen pair of red legs glittering in the water, their owners being employed in washing their own or other people's rags.

**FROM AN IRISH SKETCH BOOK,
WILLIAM MAKEPEACE THACKERAY, 1843**

gained a wider measure of support (or at least of favorable acquiescence). To suggest that political violence in Ireland has always been the work of a few people with no connection to the wider public is to simplify a complex and important relationship. This extreme end of the political spectrum has tended to represent a concentrated and more narrowly conceived form of the wider nationalist rainbow.

During the 1840s something of this ambiguity came to life in the midst of the repeal agitation. In October 1842 the *Nation* was first published, a newspaper around which the Young Ireland movement developed. Young Ireland emerged within the context of O'Connell's repeal movement, but it was eventually to give birth to the next in the sequence of failed nationalist rebellions, that of 1848. The figures involved in Young Ireland included Thomas Davis (1814-45), Charles Gavan Duffy (1816-1903), John Blake Dillon (1816-66), John Mitchel (1815-75) and

James Fintan Lalor (1807-49). Thus some of Irish nationalism's most famous names were associated with the Young Ireland movement. Of them all, Thomas Davis is perhaps the most attractive. A Protestant born in county Cork, he was educated at Dublin's Trinity College, became a lawyer, and between 1842 and 1845 effectively led the Young Ireland grouping. Like Wolfe Tone, Davis is an appealing and useful figure to cite if your creed is that of nationalism. As Protestants and anti-sectarians, these two men seem to some to provide a means of squaring an awkward circle. For nationalists face the problem in Ireland that the nationalist tradition early on became firmly fixed in the Catholic constituency. And it has been its Catholic identity which has done much to give it cohesion and meaning. In an attempt, however, to create a genuinely united Irish nation some separatists have maintained that true Irish nationalism involves non-denominational assumptions. The problem is clear. To maintain a Catholic ethos was to give nationalism an important identity; but this approach would result in the exclusion of a sizable minority of the people from your nationalist world. To reject a

Catholic ethos was to offer the hand of friendship to non-Catholics; but this approach would risk the loss of Catholic-generated momentum.

Thus Tone and Davis serve as useful icons. As Protestants they seem to deny the accusation that Irish nationalism is Catholic nationalism. They appear to present a model of nationalist Irishness which welcomes all creeds. The clash between unity and identity seems resolved. But this argument is deceptive, as events repeatedly proved. It is one thing to declare yourself opposed to sectarian division; it is quite another to achieve in practice the cross-sectarian unity that you desire. It was one thing to invite Ireland's Protestants to participate in the nationalist game; it was quite another – as Tone and Davis themselves found out – to establish a nationalist crusade in which significant numbers of Irish Protestants did in fact participate. Tone and Davis must be seen less as examples of any natural Protestant affinity with Irish separatism than as unrepresentative dissidents. That some (albeit charismatic) Protestants have joined the nationalist movement in less telling than the fact that the vast majority of Protestants have not done so.

Whatever the gulf between ideology and practice, Young Ireland left a major mark on Irish nationalist

consciousness. Many people associated with the movement – such as the fiery Mitchel, or the agrarian radical Lalor – have become central figures within nationalist Irish history. And indeed the 1840s illuminate much about the development of Irish nationalism. There was, for example, considerable ambiguity about the precise nature of the objective which nationalists were pursuing. Roy Foster's assertion that, "By 'Repeal' O'Connell probably meant, first, a recognition of the illegitmacy of the Union; and then negotiation of an alternative mechanism of government" nicely reflects the blend which existed within the emerging nationalist tradition. This combination was to persist. Mitchel came to embody republicanism, while in comparison Davis showed signs of flexibility regarding federal arrangements. The historian Richard Davis has observed that, "If there was considerable doubt amongst Young Irelanders as to the ultimate ends of their movement, there was corresponding inconsistency on strategy." As evidence of this he points to "warlike exhilaration," "passive constitutionalism" and "insurrectionary aspirations."

Yet such distinctions should not be overplayed. The fact that there was a variety of nationalist opinion should not lead us to dismiss the nationalist cause. The nineteenth century in Ireland witnessed the maturing of a political culture of autonomy. It should also be remembered that "repeal" did offer a center of gravity. As an aim it might have masked differences of outlook, but despite this it still represented a bonding ambition. The ambition was not achieved, however – it was to be the next century before the Union was fractured. Daniel O'Connell died in 1847, his career having fizzled rather unspectacularly in its latter stages. Thus the era of the mobilizer came to an end.

O'Connell's demise occurred in Italy at a time when Ireland was experiencing famine. Famine was in fact no newcomer to Ireland, but the horrors of the late 1840s were exceptional. Understandably tattooed on the memory of the island, the trauma emerged as a result of a fungal disease which struck the potato in Ireland. The potato having become a staple food by the 1840s, its infection wrought atrocious results. Despite the speedy relief inaugurated by the prime minister, Robert Peel, massive tragedy hit the island.

ABOVE: The Port of Dublin as it looked in the 1880s.
OPPOSITE: Eviction scenes during the last quarter of the nineteenth century. Cloncorey.

Before the Famine

I visited Anne's home, and found her with many little comforts not common to her class. "Why do you not wear a bonnet?" I inquired. "I came back," she replied, "from New York to live in a cabin, and I must not put myself above others who associate with me." John was industrious and thrifty, and proud of a visit from the mistress of the girl who had come from the other side of the waters. Twice while in the parish a cleanly-dressed woman called to see me, but did not invite me to her cabin, because, she said, she would be ashamed to do so, though she really wished me to go.

FROM WRITINGS ABOUT IRELAND BY AMERICAN-BORN ASENATH NICHOLSON (1792-1855).

Disease, starvation, exposure, and emigration between them decimated the Irish population. Between 1845 and 1851, it has been estimated, over two million inhabitants died or emigrated. This remains a staggering haemorrhage.

The authorities' behavior contributed to the extent of the suffering. Lord John Russell (prime minister between 1846 and 1852) adhered to *laissez-faire* economic thinking, with the result that state intervention was limited. The idea was that local rather than central initiative should primarily be relied on to deal with the situation. Though fashionable, this notion was deeply unrealistic.

Accusations that the British engaged in the partial genocide of the Irish are historically daft. But it remains the case that the government was hopelessly inept at dealing with conditions in famine Ireland. The impact of the tragedy, of course, was far from evenly distributed. Regional and class-based differences of experience were enormous. The east of Leinster and the northeast of Ulster escaped compar-

ABOVE: Statue of the Apostle of Temperance, Father Matthew, in Cork
OPPOSITE: Wellington Memorial, Phoenix Park.

The Famine's impact

And the strange thing was that it was the big farmers who were the first to fall. The man who owned only a small farm, with the grass of six or seven cows, kept his grip; the man who owned a big farm was soon ruined when the circumstances changed. The man who owned little lost but little. He had not a big rent to pay, nor were there any great calls on him. He was accustomed to meagre living. He did not find it too hard to retrench a little more, and to meet small claims without too much hardship. But the owner of a big farm was accustomed to expensive living. He was independent while the farm paid. When the change came, the yield form the farm stopped at once. The loss was too great, the expenditure was too great, the claims were too great. They could not be met, and they swept him off is feet. I well recall how I would hear the news being told and wondered at: "Oh! Did you hear? So-and-so is broke! His land is up. He's gone, He stole off. His land is up."

**FROM AN tATHAIR PEADAR Ó LAOGHAIRE
MO SCÉAL FÉIN [MY OWN STORY] (1915)**

atively unscathed, for example. In terms of class it was laborers and smaller farmers who suffered most heavily. Yet distinctions such as these have often been obscured in more generalized reactions to the period.

One important nineteenth-century trend to which the famine significantly contributed was that of emigration. The scale of this was such that "Irishness" became less reliant upon the island itself. The growth of Irish communities in Britain, Canada, Australia and – above all – the United States added a new layer to the complexity of Irish experience. The problem for Irish nationalism in Ireland was that significant numbers of people there rejected the emerging nationalist tradition. Yet outside Ireland there existed many people with a sturdy commitment to this same tradition. The mobilization of this non-resident sentiment was one aspiration of the Fenian movement. This secret society was launched on St Patrick's Day, 1858, in Dublin by James Stephens (1825-1901). Mystery was to be an important element within the Fenian tradition and even the organization's name was initially hard to locate. The Irish Republican Brotherhood (IRB); the Irish Revolutionary Brotherhood; the Fenian Brotherhood; the Fenians; more menacingly, perhaps, the "organization" – each of these terms has been used in connection with the same grouping. Its concentration on the objective of Irish independence tended to eclipse all other concerns. And while not every leading Fenian was a traditional republican, there was a distinctly republican flavor to this conspiratorial tradition. Indeed, it seems that the initial Fenian oath – which originated with Thomas Clarke Luby – included a commitment to create an Irish republic.

The Fenians aimed to achieve independence by force. Dallying with constitutionalism was held to be a fruitless pastime. They argued that English conversion to the idea of Irish independence could only come as a result of the use of violence. Now there emerged an approach firmly committed to physical force; where the rebellions of the 1790s or 1840s had occurred after constitutional methods had failed, the Fenians embarked from the start on the road to bloodshed. Yet there were similarities between Fenian

OPPOSITE, TOP: The Irish Parliamentary Party, 1886.
OPPOSITE, BOTTOM: Old Belfast City Hall.

Belfast at play

We penetrated into Smithfield-court, which is not unworthy of its patronymic. This is, as we learned on the spot, the battle-ground of the whole neighbourhood; and wrathful pugilists resort thither, even from the most distant parts of the town, to settle their disputes after their own fashion, undisturbed by impertinent policemen. How far these explosions of brutality are connected with the drinking habits of the people, may be gathered from the fact that Saturday night and Sunday are the times when these fierce, and often bloody, struggles take place. The court is somewhat spacious, but very filthy, and the house filled with as many human beings as can huddle together within their walls.

FROM WALKS AMONG THE POOR OF BELFAST, 1853.

violence and that of earlier rebellions. The nineteenth-century Fenians failed in practical terms, just as the attempted insurrections of 1798, 1803 or 1848 had, and the Fenian rising of 1867 was comfortably crushed by the authorities.

A further similarity which the Fenians shared with earlier Irish revolutionaries was that their military gestures subsequently came to achieve celebrity status in the republican tradition of the twentieth century. Thus 1867 joined the other magic numbers – 1798, 1803 and so on – in an ever-expanding collection of historic dates. One other point about the Fenians which is worth consideration is their social composition. Writing to Engels in November 1867, Karl Marx claimed that, "Fenianism is characterized by a socialistic tendency (in a negative sense, directed against the appropriation of the soil) and by being a lower orders movement." There were better grounds for the latter than for the former of these claims. It is interesting also to note Marx's comments on the Fenian attempt on 13 December 1867 to rescue one of their number from London's Clerkenwell prison; the explosion which formed part of the rescue bid caused numerous deaths and injuries. In a letter written the following day to Engels, Marx commented that:

Rural Ireland, c.1900

DANNY

One night a score of Erris men,
A score I'm told and nine,
Said, "We'll get shut of Danny's noise
Of girls and widows dyin'".

"There's not his like from Binghamstown
To Boyle and Ballycroy,
At playing hell on decent girls,
At beating man and boy.

"He's left two pairs of female twins
Beyond in Killacreest,
And twice in Crossmolina fair
He's struck the parish priest.

"But we'll come round him in the night
A mile beyond the Mullet;
Ten will quench his bloody eyes,
And ten will choke his gullet."

It wasn't long till Danny came,
From Bangor making way,
And he was damning moon and stars
And whistling grand and gay.

Till in a gap of hazel glen –
And not a hare in sight –
Out lepped the nine-and-twenty lads
Along his left and right.

Then Danny smashed the nose on Byrne,
He split the lips on three,
And bit across the right hand thumb
Of one Red Shawn Mageee.

But seven tripped him up behind,
And seven kicked before,
And seven squeezed around his throat
Till Danny kicked no more.

Then some destroyed him with their heels,
Some trapped him in the mud,
Some stole his purse and timber pipe,
And some washed off his blood.

And when you're walking out the way
From Bangor to Belmullet,
You'll see a flat cross on a stone
Where men choked Danny's gullet.

A POEM (1907) BY JOHN MILLINGTON SYNGE

The last exploit of the Fenians in Clerkenwell was a very stupid thing. The London masses, who have shown great sympathy for Ireland, will be made wild by it and driven into the arms of the government party. One cannot expect the London proletarians to allow themselves to be blown up in honor of the Fenian emissaries.

Sound sense indeed. And yet prisoners have played a vital part within the Irish republican tradition. More successful propaganda than the Clerkenwell explosion could and did emerge from the phenomenon of republican incarceration.

At this stage we should perhaps move on to look at one of Irish history's most influential figures: Charles Stewart Parnell (1846-91). Parnell's career was to be influenced by his relations with the physical force tradition. Born in County Wicklow, Parnell had an Anglo-Irish, landowning father and an American mother with Ulster Presbyterian roots. He went to Cambridge University and was in 1875 elected to parliament as a Home Rule MP. In 1870 the Home Government Association had been founded by Isaac Butt (1813-79), with a view to the achievement of an Irish parliament. In 1873 the association matured into the Home Rule League. The election of 1874 saw the emergence in the London parliament of a Home Rule party led by Butt, and Parnell entered the political arena in this parliamentary context.

To Isaac Butt, home government meant the establishment (or re-establishment) of a domestic Irish parliament which would exist within an imperial framework. Thus it was not total separation from Britain that was being espoused; rather the call was for a form of legislative autonomy for Ireland. The Home Rule movement which grew from Butt's beginnings was to become very much Parnell's crusade. In 1877 Parnell became president of the Home Rule Confederation of Great Britain. In 1880 he became chairman of the Irish Parliamentary Party. But Parnell's political importance was associated with the breadth of his vision and practice. Not only did he lead the charge towards Home Rule, but he also

OPPOSITE, TOP: Workers leaving the Harland & Wolff Shipyard, Belfast.
OPPOSITE, BOTTOM: Dublin University cricketers in 1905.

issues and the national question. In 1879 the Irish National Land League had been founded, with Parnell becoming its president. The League's stated aims were:

First, to bring about a reduction of rack-rents; second, to facilitate the obtaining of the owner-ship of the soil by the occupiers.

The 1870s and 1880s in Ireland were heavily colored by the questions of Home Rule and land politics. And Parnell was now crucial in both realms. The precise relation between land and national politics in this period is a complex one. Michael Davitt's influential role in the politics of the land is interesting here, given his Fenian credentials. And Parnell's own rhetoric could hint at a practical relationship between the land and national movements in this period. At Galway in October 1880 he argued that, while wishing to see Irish tenant farmers prosper, he would not have dived into the land agitation "if I had not known that we were laying the foundations by this movement for the recovery of our legislative independence."

Thus Parnell wove a web of political alliances which – for a time, at least – held diverse forces in a seemingly implausible pattern. A parliamentarian, he won admiration from devotees of violence. Successful in the attainment of Catholic Church support for Home Rule, he also threw out lines towards the phys-ical force tradition against which the church had firmly set its face. Parliamentary party, tenant farm-ers, Catholic church, physical force people – and even for a time the London government – each of these powerful ingredients was involved in the politics of Parnell. Thus in 1886 William Ewart Gladstone (1809-98) introduced the first Home Rule Bill, which would have established an Irish parliament within an imperial context. In the mid 1880s Parnell found himself holding the balance of power at Westminster. Gladstone could only take office should Parnell give him his backing. This Parnell did; Gladstone became prime minister and the relationship between the two men and their respective parties was cemented.

ABOVE, LEFT: Irish are encouraged to enlist during World War I.
OPPOSITE: Countess Markiewicz runs guns for Irish Nationalists in 1916.

threw out seductive hints in the direction of those who might seek a fuller degree of independence for Ireland. Thus, in January 1885 Parnell declared:

We cannot ask for less than the restitution of Grattan's parliament .... We cannot under the British constitution ask for more than the resti-tution of Grattan's parliament, but no man has the right to fix the boundary to the march of a nation. No man has a right to say to his coun-try, "Thus far shalt thou go and no further," and we have never attempted to fix the ne plus ultra to the progress of Ireland's nationhood, and we never shall.

Grattan's parliament represented Irish legislative independence within a British framework. Yet here Parnell was being deliberately unclear about Irish national ambitions. Was Grattan's parliament the goal? Were things meant to go on beyond the attain-ment of legislative independence under the crown?

Ambiguity of a different kind can be detected in the late-nineteenth-century relation between land

ABOVE: The Irish citizen army drawn up in ranks outside outside Liberty Hall.

The first Home Rule Bill was in fact defeated in the House of Commons by 343 votes to 313. The later Home Rule Bills (of 1893 and 1912) also met unpleasant ends – though the Home Rule idea was eventually to triumph. Gladstone's 1893 measure was defeated in the House of Lords. The Bill which emerged in 1912 reached the statute book in 1914; but it was decided that its operation should be suspended until after the end of the First World War. By the time that the war did in fact end, in 1918, circumstances had greatly changed. Parnell's political and then actual demise only partially, therefore, marked a break in Irish history. One of Ireland's most sophisticated and influential political leaders was gone, and it was natural that a kind of vacuum should ensue. But much continued after 1891 of the world which Parnell had helped to mold. As noted, the concept of Home Rule persisted. Above all, perhaps, the land revolution was fundamental to the development of the modern Ireland. In 1870 Gladstone's first Land Act had recognized certain principles of tenant protection and,

although in practice little change was effected, this measure proved to be a sign of the direction of the coming tides. In 1881 a further Land Act provided for a land court which would fix rents fairly, decreed that those who paid such rents should be guaranteed against eviction, and made a further gesture regarding a tenant's right of free sale. In 1885 the Ashbourne Act made moves in the direction of land purchase. In 1891 a further step was taken along this path, while in 1903 the Wyndham Act located land purchase as the answer to Ireland's land question.

So it was that peasant proprietorship set the tone for modern Irish rural society. And the other two subversive forces of significance, unionism and nationalism, undoubtedly involve much complexity. Thus the logic of past interests crystallized in the form of Catholic, Gaelic nationalism and Protestant, non-Gaelic unionism. Plainly, not everybody fell neatly into this scheme. But the lines of division were clear enough. Unionist opposition to Home Rule was fierce and massive, as was reflected in the signing of the Solemn League and Covenant in 1912:

Being convinced in our consciences that Home
Rule would be disastrous to the material well-

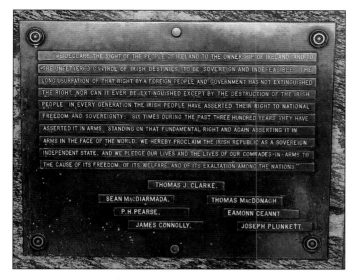

ABOVE: Part of the 1916 Proclamation of Independence.

The spirit of resistance

When that story is written by a man or woman with an honest heart, and with a sympathetic insight in tot he travail of the poor, it will be a record of which Ireland may well be proud. It will tell of how the old women and young girls, long crushed and enslaved, dared to risk all, even life itself, in the struggle to make life more tolerable, more free of the grinding tyranny of the soulless Dublin employers. It will tell of how, like an inspiration, there came to those Irish women and girls the thought that no free nation could be reared which tolerated the enslavement of its daughters to the worst forms of wage-slavery, and how in the glow of that inspiration they arose from their seats in the workshop or factory, and went out to suffer and struggle along with their men.

FROM AN ARTICLE ABOUT THE 1913 DUBLIN "LOCK OUT" BY JAMES CONNOLLY

being of Ulster as well as the whole of Ireland, subversive of our civil and religious freedom, destructive of our citizenship, and perilous to the unity of the Empire [we] do hereby pledge ourselves ... to stand by one another in defending for ourselves and our children our cherished position of equal citizenship in the United Kingdom and in using all means which may be found necessary to defeat the present conspiracy to set up a Home Rule Parliament.

The perception of threat is illuminated here by the words, "disastrous", "subversive," "destructive," "perilous," and "conspiracy." The following year the Ulster Volunteer Force (UVF) was established. Plans were drawn up for a provisional government, and by the time firearms and ammunition were landed in 1914, the basis for a sturdy bout of resistance had unquestionably been laid. The UVF could also rely on sympathy from some British officials and army officers.

Cultural and paramilitary resistance was also emerging from another quarter. The Irish Volunteers were established in November 1913 to provide a nationalist counter-gesture. It was fitting that the genesis of the Irish Volunteers should owe so much to Eoin MacNeill, since he reflected the trend towards cultural Irish nationalism which was so important at the turn of the century. In 1884 the Gaelic Athletic Association had been set up. And in 1893 the Gaelic League had been established, with Douglas Hyde as its first president and with MacNeill as its first vice-president. The emphasis on Gaelic culture was to have

vast influence in twentieth-century Irish nationalism. The most significant icon in modern Irish republicanism was Patrick Pearse (1879-1916). Born in Dublin, Pearse was called to the Bar, but chose instead a kind of alternative professionalism expressed through cultural, educational, and in the end revolutionary, enthusiasm.

In a sense Pearse's career followed the logic of the nationalist condition. The Gaelic Athletic Association would aim to guard and develop native Irish sports; the Gaelic League would seek to promote the Irish language. These were cultural attempts to fight against the Anglicization of Ireland. But these were mirrored by a political struggle, to free Ireland from English control in that realm also. Pearse was a feverishly dedicated Gaelic Leaguer, and in 1913 he was a founder member of the Irish Volunteers. He also joined the Irish Republican Brotherhood (IRB) and indeed it was as a revolutionary that he was to attain later celebrity status. Pearse's fame rests primarily on the 1916 rebellion – though over-concentration on this part of his career has tended to obscure the importance of his earlier enthusiasms. The Easter 1916 insurrection ostensibly aimed to establish an independent Irish republic. In reality its significance

ABOVE: Easter Week, 1916, showing the scene in the General Post Office just before its evacuation.

lies in its quality of military gesture. By the time that the rebellion actually began (on 24 April 1916), it had little realistic chance of success. But the proclamation which Pearse read out in Dublin on that opening day of the revolt became one of the sacred texts of the Irish republican tradition:

We declare the right of the people of Ireland to the ownership of Ireland, and to the unfettered control of Irish destinies, to be sovereign and indefeasible. The long usurpation of that right by a foreign people and government has not extinguished the right, nor can it ever be extinguished except by the destruction of the Irish people .... The Irish republic is entitled to, and hereby claims, the allegiance of every Irishman and Irishwoman. The republic guarantees religious and civil liberty, equal rights and equal opportunities to all its citizens, and declares its resolve to pursue the happiness and prosperity of the whole nation and of all its parts, cherishing all the children of the nation equally, and oblivious of the differences carefully fostered by an alien government, which have divided a minority from the majority in the past .... In this supreme hour the Irish nation must, by its valor and discipline, and by the readiness of its children to sacrifice themselves for the common good, prove itself worthy of the august destiny to which it is called.

Signed on behalf of the provisional government, Thomas J. Clarke, Sean MacDiarmada, Thomas MacDonagh, P.H. Pearse, Eamonn Ceannt, James Connolly, Joseph Plunkett.

The reference to sacrifice is important. The rebels were defeated in 1916, surrendering on 29 April. Pearse was executed on 3 May, and thereby won the right to the status of nationalist martyr. As we have seen, the cult of the dying hero had roots in earlier Irish history; Pearse himself, incidentally, made much of Theobald Wolfe Tone. As one of the most charismatic of twentieth-century republicans – Ernie O'Malley (1897-1957) – put it: "As a Republican one was evidently never sufficiently tested until one had died in the Republican faith." The republican faith was propelled forward, ironically, by Britain's involvement in the First World War. Not only did the war seem to some to offer an opportunity of striking at a distracted England, but the threatened imposition of conscription on Ireland served powerfully to alienate many people from the authorities.

A combination of factors therefore united to stimulate nationalist Ireland into a new stage of activity – the suppression of the 1916 rising, the reorganization of the Sinn Féin movement in 1917, the tactless handling by the British of the conscription issue. But even at the point of Sinn Féin's apparent triumph – when it thrashed the Irish Parliamentary Party in the 1918 general election – the picture was far less neat than might initially have been assumed. For one thing the election also demonstrated the strength of unionist opposition to nationalist aspirations. The twenty-six unionists elected in 1918 were greatly outnumbered, it is true, by the seventy-three Sinn Féiners. But the geographical concentration of unionist commitment in Ireland was destined to present problems for Irish nationalists. If nationalist Ireland

BELOW: Members of Michael Collins' squad of assassins and spies played a crucial role in the IRA's campaign against the British during the war for independence in 1919-1921.

derived strength and cohesion from its Gaelic, Catholic identity, then what did this imply about the 'Irishness' of non-Gaelic non-Catholics who lived on the island? And what use was it anyway to invite unionists into your proposed all-Ireland nation if they firmly rejected your offer; would you – could you – force them to accept your invitation?

Such problems were to cause lasting and painful headaches for Irish nationalists. The tradition which produced nationalist leaders such as Arthur Griffith (1871-1922) and Eamon de Valera (1882-1975) was matched in commitment, though not in numbers, by that which produced unionist figures such as Edward Carson (1854-1935) and James Craig (1871-1940). But in the immediate post-war period the tide seemed to flow with the nationalist cause. The Anglo-Irish war began in 1919 and was to continue until 1921. An ambush in County Tipperary can be interpreted as inaugurating the military conflict – though it took some time for momentum to develop. On the same day, 21 January 1919, in Dublin took place the first meeting of an alternative Irish parliament – *Dail Eireann*. The membership of the Dail was composed of 73 people who had been elected to the Westminster

House of Commons in the general election of December 1918. Thus it was out of the womb of the United Kingdom's electoral process that the independently-minded Irish nationalist child emerged.

Ambiguity surrounds the Anglo-Irish war. The exact relationship between the military and non-military forces for independence; the precise interpretation which nationalists gave to their objective; the question of whether what eventually emerged from the conflict would have emerged anyway without it – these and other areas remain open to a lot of debate. What can safely be said is that a multi-pronged independence movement succeeded by 1921 in prodding the British government into the granting of partial independence. The Anglo-Irish war was ended with a truce in July 1921. Negotiations between British and Irish representatives resulted in the fiercely disputed 'treaty' of December 1921. This arrangement offered substantial rather than total independence for twenty-six of Ireland's thirty-two counties.

The six northeastern counties excluded from the new state were Antrim, Londonderry, Tyrone, Fermanagh, Armagh and Down. But partition had effectively existed prior to the signing of the 1921 treaty. The Government of Ireland Act of 1920 provided for the setting up of a northern and of a southern parliament – each enjoying powers of local self-government – and the former was in fact opened by King George V in June 1921. The Government of Ireland Act southern parliament had not become a reality, but when *Dail Eireann* approved the treaty in January 1922 the process of partition became more firmly established. For the setting up of the Irish Free State under the terms of the 1921 treaty carved a territorial division in Ireland which has ever since persisted. In part this merely recognized realities. A sizable concentration of people in the northeast of the island wanted nothing to do with Irish independence, and so remained attached to Britain. Yet the split between north and south was anything but neat. The historic province of Ulster contained nine counties, not six, and many Protestant people were cut adrift by partition and left in counties Donegal, Monaghan and Cavan. There was also in Northern Ireland a large minority of Catholic people who now faced life on the "wrong" side of the border. In truth, the six-county

OPPOSITE: Members of the Black and Tans, the British reprisal squad of unemployed ex-soldiers .
BELOW: The wreckage of a County Cork farm after a visit from the Black and Tans.

state was chosen since it provided the largest area over which a unionist regime could securely preside.

Partition also served to increase the likelihood of self-deceptions regarding an Irish identity. One vital theme in Ireland's history has been the persistence of the desire for dominance and the failure to secure it completely. In a partitioned Ireland. Rival concepts of Irishness – the conviction that "Ulster was British" versus the spirit of Gaelic Revivalism – colluded in discriminating politically, socially, and intellectually against their respective minority communites.

6
A Disunited Ireland

Partition was not, however, the main topic of debate during the Dail's discussion of the proposed treaty. While the 1921 Anglo-Irish agreement had offered substantial autonomy to the intended southern state, it was none the less objectionable to many within the independence movement. The narrowness of the vote in the Dail in January 7, 1922 – sixty-four in favour of the treaty, fifty-seven against – pointed to some of the difficulties which lay ahead. But it also suggested a willingness to give the treaty a chance. In a sense the nationalist achievement of the Anglo-Irish war had been one of propaganda and of personality. Violence was impressively portrayed in terms of victories and of atrocities. The Irish Republican Army (IRA) which grew out of the Irish Volunteers was celebrated in heroic terms. To quote again from the eminent IRA man, Ernie O'Malley: "I was told stories of myself, what I had said or done in different places. I could not recognize myself for the legend" In contrast, the actions of the forces of the crown – some of which were indeed atrocious – became celebrated in a negative sense. The establishment of the Dail – an alternative Irish government – symbolised the maturity of nationalist Ireland. Was not here a governmental culture in waiting? Was it not obvious that legitimacy rested with this body elected by Irish people?

But the civil war which occurred in 1922-3 shone a spotlight on the tensions which had existed within the independence movement. Personality might have

LEFT: Four Courts building, the scene of fighting in 1922.
ABOVE: The anti-treaty leader, Eamon de Valera .

seemed to pioneer the way to freedom up to 1921. But in the post-treaty split the gods were shown warring amongst themselves. Michael Collins (1890-1922) – who, perhaps, did more than anyone else to achieve the successful draw of 1921 – was important in pushing through the treaty. Arthur Griffith – with Collins, a co-signatory of the 1921 agreement – was another influential pro-treatyite. Yet to their anti-treaty opponents these figures had betrayed the republic, had settled for less than was Ireland's right and had cooperated in a disgraceful compromise. The fact that the treaty offered complete independence in domestic matters did not count for anything – so the argument ran – for the Irish Free State was not the Irish republic. Michael Collins argued that

After a national struggle sustained through many centuries, we have to-day in Ireland a native Government deriving its authority solely from the Irish people, and acknowledged by England and the other nations of the world.

But neither this, nor the assertion that the "substance of freedom" had been attained, could convince anti-treaty opponents. The anti-treaty republicans opposed the idea of the oath with passionate hostility. Under the terms of the 1921 treaty, members of the Free State parliament were obliged to take an oath of allegiance to the British monarch. The ferocity of response which this provoked indicated the quality of opposition to the agreement. Just as a republic had been fought for, so the British crown was what had been fought against. The republic embodied all that was desired; the crown represented all that was detested. To fight for the former and end up owing

ABOVE: Eamonn de Valera and the Archbishop of Dublin review Irish soldiers in 1936. De Valera's government built a close relationship with the Catholic Church.

allegiance to the latter was unthinkable to many in 1922.

In April 1922 anti-treaty republicans took over Dublin's Four Courts building and set up headquarters there. On 28 June the Four Courts was attacked by the forces of the pro-treaty government. Two days later the republican garrison surrendered. This battle of the Four Courts marked the beginning of the Irish civil war. The war lasted until the following year. In 1923 Eamon de Valera – the anti-treaty leader – issued a proclamation addressed to the republican army:

> Further sacrifice on your part would now be vain and continuance of the struggle in arms unwise in the national interest. Military victory must be allowed to rest for the moment with those who have destroyed the Republic.

The IRA chief of staff, Frank Aiken, issued an order for republican forces to cease fire and dump their weapons. The civil war was officially over. The Free State – which had come into formal existence in December 1922 – had won the day. But the election of August 1923 reflected the fact that deep divisions remained within the infant state. In March 1923 the pro-treaty party, Cumann na nGaedheal (Party of the Gaels), had been launched, and in the August election this grouping won 63 seats in a Dáil of 153. The republicans won 44 Dail seats, and though their policy of parliamentary abstention rendered this less dramatic, it was none the less an indication of resilient support. The republic may have been betrayed in the treaty and defeated in the battlefield of the civil war, but the republican tradition still breathed.

William Cosgrave (1880-1965) led the Cumann na nGaedheal government which ruled the Free State between 1922 and 1932. Far less charismatic than many contemporary figures in political Ireland, he presided over a swiftly maturing state. At first glance the emergence of a stable Free State out of the dislocation of two wars seems striking. Having experienced a conflict with a powerful external enemy between 1919 and 1921, Ireland then witnessed a vicious contest between internal political groupings

Approach

The tightening eyes, tendrilled of sympathy,
The accepted secret before a third;
The unrequired gesture, imperfect denial of
contact.

The flaunt, the posture, display of the self,
Under appraisal relenting to seriousness,
And sudden tenderness lightening in simple
actions;

The gaze, responded to, steadying in brave
request;
Prolonged at acceptance; the attitude
Breaking in mutual and offered laughter.

A POEM BY CHARLIE DONNELLY (1932)

BELOW: Leinster House, Dublin, where the parliament sits.

between 1922 and 1923. The civil war as much reflected as created the tensions of the territory. Its legacy of bitterness has often been noted. That this legacy developed is hardly surprising. Incarceration, assassination, execution and hunger strike encouraged acrimonious memory. On 7 December 1922, pro-treaty Dail member Sean Hales was killed by republicans. The government speedily responded; on 8 December 1922 four republican prisoners were executed in Dublin's Mountjoy Jail.

The republican hunger strike for unconditional release, occurring in October/November 1923, reflected the strength of commitment of the post-civil war republicans while pointing to their weakness. The strike was called off in November 1923 without any promise of release having been wrested from the Free State authorities. Defeated in the Dáil over the treaty, defeated militarily in the civil war, the republic was now beaten in the post-war prisons.

And this should not surprise us. For all its seductive rhetoric and commitment, the Irish republican-

ism of the revolutionary period was destined for defeat. Its aspirations for the total independence of the thirty-two counties implied the inevitability of disappointment. British and Ulster resistance to the idea of an Irish republic was too high a fence for revolutionary separatists to clear. They could generate the conditions within which important concessions would be granted. But they had not the power with which to force their ambitions to completion. Part of the 1919-21 nationalist experience was the adoption of strong poses regarding the aims that were sought. But commitment to the poses greatly varied. So, for some a thirty-two county "republic" was the least they would accept. Yet others, plainly, were ready quite swiftly to climb down from the high ground of republican hope to the less lofty level of the Irish Free State. Compromise, indeed, was implicit in any serious approach to negotiation; thus the 1921 Anglo-Irish negotiations might seem to have implied some willingness to compromise. And compromise was, in practice, inevitable given the respective strengths and commitments involved. But to intransigent republicans there could be no backing down. In arguing that the 1921 treaty represented "the betrayal of the Republic," Liam Mellows embodied this tradition; "I stand now where I always stood, for the Irish Republic ... I hold you cannot deny the existence of the Irish Republic and remain a Republican. This Treaty is a denial of the Republic."

Mellows was a mystical soldier of the republic, a crusader on behalf of Irish independence. But the crusade lacked the power to overcome the obstacles in the way of its full success. Offered a substantial measure of freedom in 1921, a majority chose compromise. The diehard republicans could only succeed when their concerns were shared by large numbers of the people. This was the case in 1920; it was no longer so in 1923. Ironically, perhaps, the person who did most to marginalize the hard-line republican tradition in the southern state was Eamon de Valera. De Valera came to recognize the necessity for compromise. In 1926 he formed a new political party, Fianna Fail (Soldiers of Destiny), which was to come to dominate southern political life. In 1927 for the first time Fianna Fail entered the twenty-six county Dail. They thus balanced the previously lop-sided, Cumann na nGaedheal-dominated institution. In 1932 Fianna Fail came to power, having mobilized much support among the old anti-treaty constituency. During the 1930s de Valera's party set about the removal of numerous elements of the treaty arrangement. The land annuities payments to Britain, the oath of allegiance to the British crown, the office of governor-general, the senate – each of these features of the treaty state was abolished.

In 1937 de Valera's new constitution set the philosophy of his Ireland. It named the state, 'Eire, or in the English language, Ireland'. It also recognised realities in its attitude to Northern Ireland. The national territory was defined as including all thirty-two counties. Thus the heritage and identity of Irish nationalist aspiration were respectfully enshrined in the sacred text of de Valera's Ireland. But the inability of nationalist Ireland to achieve the united independence of the island was also recognized. For the constitution declared that, pending the restoration of the six counties, the jurisdiction of the Dublin government would extend only over the twenty-six county area. This approach epitomized the contradictions of Irish nationalism. The constitution asserted an all-Ireland case; yet it simultaneously embodied certain attitudes guaranteed to provoke hostility among Ulster unionists. The "special position" of the Catholic church (acknowledged in this 1937 document) was hardly likely to win many Protestant friends in counties Down or Antrim!

But two other points should perhaps be given greater stress. First, the nationalist tradition had for years derived strength from its Catholic, Gaelic emphases. The fact that these had tended to exclude non-Gaelic non-Catholics had not in fact eroded their importance in giving momentum to the nationalist march. Indeed, it was extremely convenient that the northeastern counties were partitioned. Second, it should also be noted that Ulster unionist hostility to Irish unity was sturdy enough regardless of the 1937 constitution. There was little sign that unionists were willing to move toward unity in any circumstances anyway.

OPPOSITE, TOP: Priests at Maynooth Seminary, the vital heart of the Irish Catholic Church.
OPPOSITE, BOTTOM: Outside Trinity College, Dublin, a Protestant institution in the Republic..

If his *constitution* was a crucial document, de Valera's *party* held a dominant position in the life of the southern state. This was reflected in the fact that Fianna Fail were in office for two impressive sixteen-year stretches (1932-48 and 1957-73) and it was during the first of these periods that Ireland underwent her distinctive Second World War experiences. In September 1939 the southern state adopted a neutral stance. This was a position it maintained throughout the conflict, though not without certain tensions developing at times with belligerent nations.

Three years after the end of the war Fianna Fail fell from power. Between 1948 and 1951 the state was governed by a coalition led by John A. Costello as Taoiseach (or prime minister). Costello's party – Fine Gael – had emerged from the Cumann na nGaedheal pro-treaty tradition. There was therefore an apparent irony in the fact that it was Costello's government which enacted legislation declaring an Irish republic. The 1948 Republic of Ireland Act led to the formal inauguration of a republic in April 1949. Thirty-three years after the Easter Rebellion, therefore, a republic was established in Ireland. But it was established by a government whose largest participant – Fine Gael –

had grown from the side that had *beaten* the republicans in the 1922-23 civil war. In fact the irony was more apparent than substantial. Certainly the 1948 act brought Irish unity no nearer to realization. This was underlined by the passing at Westminster of the 1949 Ireland Act which stated that no part of Northern Ireland would leave the United Kingdom without the consent of the Northern Ireland parliament. The south might be called a republic, but the all-Ireland republican dream was still well beyond reach.

In 1959 the man who had for many been a symbol of the republic – Eamon de Valera – was elected to the presidency and Sean Lemass took over as Taoiseach. Lemass had lengthy political experience, having been influentially involved in Fianna Fail since its inception. Having promoted protection of domestic industry as a Fianna Fail minister in the 1930s, Lemass shifted ground, now pushing for foreign investment in Ireland and for freer trade. One manifestation of the latter was the signing in 1965 of the Anglo-Irish Free Trade Agreement (which provided Irish industry with immediate tariff-free access to the British market). In the same year Lemass met the Northern Ireland prime minister, Terence O'Neill, in Belfast and in Dublin. But prime ministerial cross-border gestures proved not to be prophetic and the painful contradiction of the northeast of Ireland were soon to explode into tragedy.

Within Northern Ireland a majority-leaning state had been maintained. Whatever discrimination occurred was directed against the Catholic minority. Sectarian tension and sectarian violence are not recent developments in the northeast of Ireland, though their more recent forms have taken distinctive and particular forms. The political dominance of the unionist tradition was firmly rooted in the Northern Irish parliament at Stormont (on the outskirts of Belfast). The vibrant local cultures did coexist. But tension was a persistent motif.

James Craig (who had been involved in pre-partition unionist politics) had become Northern Ireland's first prime minister in 1921. He remained in this position until his death in 1940. He was succeeded by J.M. Andrews. Then in 1943 Basil Brooke assumed office and retained the premiership until 1963. In that year Terence O'Neill became Northern Ireland's prime minister, and it was his period in office which witnessed the ugly eruption of the continuing violence within the northern state. In 1967 the Northern Ireland Civil Rights Association was set up to redress grievance. Demands were met with mixed responses, including that of violence. The late-1960s saw the reappearance of bloody, tribal fighting with the British army called in during 1969 to part the waves of sectarian hostility. In 1972 the Stormont parliament and government were suspended, with direct rule from Westminster being imposed.

OPPOSITE: Shipbuilding at Harland & Wolff's, Belfast, was a vital element in the economy of Northern Ireland.
BELOW: The first turf-fired generating station built in Ireland at Portarlington, County Laois.

Claiming All Ireland

Article 3. Pending the re-integration of the national territory, and without prejeudice o the right of Parliament and the Government established by the Constitution to exercise jurisdiction of the whole of that territory, the laws enacted by that Parliament shall have the like area and extent of application as the laws of Saorstat Éireann and the like extra-territorial effect.

FROM THE CONSTITUTION OF IRELAND (1937); THIS ARTICLE WAS MODIFIED BY REFERENDUM FOLLOWING THE GOOD FRIDAY AGREEMENT OF 1997.

7

The Troubles and the Tiger

by Antony Shaw

Ireland's 20th-century transition from a poor, rural nation at the fringe of Europe into a state led by the wealthy new economy based around Dublin and vigorously participating in the European Union has been undertaken at a dramatic pace since 1973. Gemma Hussey, the former minister of education, has commented that "Irish society has changed more in the two decades leading up to the 1990s than in the previous hundred years."

In 1973, when the Irish Republic and Northern Ireland both joined the European Community (EC), Fianna Fáil had held power for 16 consecutive years. However, a pre-election deal between Fine Gael (FG) and the Labor Party, and an electorate concerned about prices, housing, and social welfare issues threw out Jack Lynch's Fianna Fáil administration which was far more interested in security issues as the crisis in Northern Ireland entered its fourth year. There followed one of the Irish Republic's most politically unstable periods, with the exception of Fianna Fáil's surprise landslide victory in 1977. There were no fewer than seven general elections between 1973 and 1989, a period of time that

should have seen three or four. A series of coalitions and short-term minority administrations ensued.

Economic affairs were a major cause of this turbulence. The oil crises in 1973 and 1979 and the global recession of the early 1980s led to soaring unemployment and increased emigration.

The inability of any party to solve the crisis led to votes dispersing among smaller political groups offering an alternative to the traditional Fianna Fáil/Fine Gael divide. In 1985 a new party, the Progressive Democrats (PDs), was created out of a split in Fianna Fáil, with a program of free-market economics and liberal social policy. The Labor Party's support surged under the skillful leadership of Dick Spring, and it became a key element in building governing coalitions. The Green Party, with its environmental concerns, caught the public mood in the late 1980s. During the 1970s and 1980s the conservative values of the main parties seemed increasingly out of touch as the Women's Movement and the "anything goes" social mood of the time brought them into question.

These changes in Irish politics were reflected by the election of President Mary Robinson (1991-97). She became the first female president and the first not to be nominated by the dominant FF party. The president's gender, her background as a human rights lawyer and a representative of causes outside those of

OPPOSITE: Dublin's pubs are enjoyed by both visitors from abroad and natives.
ABOVE: Charles Haughey's political career ended in scandals of bribery and tax evasion.

ABOVE: Garrett FitzGerald (center left) and Margaret Thatcher (center right) negotiated the breakthrough of the Anglo-Irish agreement of 1985.
BELOW RIGHT: Mary Robinson, Ireland's first female president, was by profession a barrister.

the traditional parties gave new life to Irish politics. The attention she attracted outside the state helped modernize the international view of Ireland. During a period of political scandals many hoped she heralded a new era of integrity in public life.

The scandals revolved around Fianna Fáil and the controversial Charles Haughey, its leader for twelve years. Haughey has always been dogged by allegations involving his personal, political, and business life. In 1992, claims that he had knowledge that journalists hostile to Fianna Fáil had their telephones tapped in 1982 caused his resignation. In May 2000 the Tanaiste (the deputy prime minister), Mary Harney, alleged that Haughey had received Ir£8.6 million between 1979 and 1996 from various sources. Haughey himself, before a judicial inquiry in July 1997, admitted receiving Ir£1.3 million from a supermarket owner.

Haughey's successor as leader of Fianna Fáil, Albert Reynolds, himself became embroiled in controversy during the inquiry into fraud and political favouritism in the beef industry, and a scandal surrounding delays in extraditing a priest charged with pedophile offenses in Northern Ireland. Reynolds resigned, and the so-called "Rainbow Coalition" of Fine Gael, Labour and Democratic Left took over.

During the 1997 general election, Fianna Fáil's new leader Bertie Ahern ran on a common platform with the PDs. Though they fell short of a majority,

LEFT: *The Republic of Ireland qualified for soccer's World Cup in the United States in 1994, boosting national pride.* ABOVE: *The death of Bobby Sands in a British prison in 1981 created a new martyr for Irish republicans.*

they held enough seats to form a minority coalition government. That same year the Catholic nationalist Mary McAleese became president, with the support of Fianna Fáil. She was the first president from Northern Ireland and continued the peacemaking efforts of her predecessor.

The relative political stability since 1992 followed an economic upturn that began in the late 1980s after tax rates on company profits were lowered and foreign investment courted. European Union membership offered multinationals barrier-free access to continental markets via Irish subsidiaries.

Northern Ireland, however, did not enjoy this boom. Since 1974 it experienced decline due to a general U.K. downturn, "deindustrialization" in sectors such as shipbuilding, the slow pace of commercial modernization and lack of foreign investment because of security fears.

In the years after Northern Ireland returned to direct rule, both sides of the border were left in despair as bitterness and brutality imposed tremendous human and economic suffering on the province. The 1973 Sunningdale Agreement to form a power-sharing executive in Northern Ireland provided hope to governments in the United Kingdom and the Republic. But Unionists opposed to power-sharing won a landslide victory in the 1974 U.K. general election with the slogan "Dublin is only a Sunningdale away." A Unionist-led general strike then crippled Northern Ireland and direct rule was restored.

For the next 20 years militant republicans continued an armed struggle, convinced their campaign would make it too politically costly for the British to retain the province. Sectarian killings claimed many innocent lives.

An attempt to break this cycle of violence was made by the Women's Peace Movement during the 1970s. Mairead Corrigan and Betty Williams, its founders, received the 1977 Nobel Peace Prize for organizing mass demonstrations and raising questions about the conflict.

In 1976 Britain withdrew the Special Category for prisoners charged with offenses related to the Troubles. This denied them the status of political prisoners. Nationalist inmates in Belfast's Maze Prison launched a "blanket protest" by refusing to wear uniforms in accordance with their new status. This escalated into the "dirty protest" with inmates smearing walls with excrement rather than slopping out. From 1980-82 a hunger strike then claimed ten lives. One hunger striker, Bobby Sands, was elected an MP before his death. This attracted massive international and domestic political attention.

One of the most substantial steps towards a peace process was the 1985 Anglo-Irish Agreement. It provided for Dublin's regular participation in Northern Ireland's political, legal, security and cross-border affairs. An underlying motive behind the agreement was a desire to push Sinn Féin to the political margins but its electoral strength rose. In 1996 the

Assembly created by the agreement was dissolved following constant Unionist attack.

In subsequent years contact between the Irish and British governments was maintained through an intergovernmental conference framework. In 1993 the Downing Street Declaration issued by Ireland and Britain set out basic principles to underpin a peace process for relationships in Ireland and Anglo-Irish entente. It was based upon self-determination and consent. IRA and Loyalist paramilitaries then declared a cessation of violence (1994). Senior republican figures believed all-party talks could now yield results. In April 1998 the Good Friday Agreement created an historic breakthrough. It proposed an elected assembly, a North-South Ministerial Council, a British-Irish Council and commissions for decommissioning arms and police. Ireland would also give up its constitutional claim to the North. Prisoner releases would take place. Referendums in the South and North supported the agreement. Ulster Unionist leader David Trimble and SDLP leader John Hume received the Nobel Peace Prize.

Almost every aspect of the agreement has caused controversy. Prisoner releases spark disagreement as recently freed paramilitaries on both sides have been implicated in exacerbating sectarian divisions and launching terrorist actions. A resumption of terrorist violence has posed a grave threat to the peace process. In August 1998 the Real IRA, an anti-agreement republican faction, killed 29 people in a bomb attack on Omagh, County Tyrone. It was the worst atrocity in the history of the Troubles. Dissident republicans and unionists groups continue to launch sporadic attacks.

The European Union has sought to play a more active role in resolving the conflict over Northern Ireland since the European Parliament released the Haagerup Report in 1984. This advocated power-sharing and increased cooperation between governments, both of which have been, to some extent achieved. The European Commission has also been generous in its financial aid.

The European Union (EU) has provided a new focus for the Irish nation. A 1987 referendum in the Republic supported the Single European Act on economic and political integration. Voters in the Republic then approved the far-reaching 1991 Maastricht Treaty although it had to agree that future EU legislation would not affect its abortion laws. EU coins and notes have been the sole legal tender since February 28, 2002. Since 1999 monetary policy has been controlled by the European Central Bank. It has also enjoyed regional development funding from the EU for infrastructure, culture, and education.

The badger as metaphor

SIGNS

It is all too previous.
In the poet's house years gone

Sleeping over on my way
To interview by appointment

I heard a living world on the BBC.
Badger's funeral with digging and dirges –

More dignity than pipes and snuff,
Natural religion not for them,

A brock circle of backs turned,
A grave pissed on for solidarity

Under little red tearcups upsidedown,
Ovidian imported fuchsia.

So, too am I watched
By the disappeared, from a tree.

**FROM A POEM "MARIE WILSON"
BY HUGH MAXTON (2000)**

The final decades of the 20th Century saw the Irish people increasingly questioning the Catholic Church's dominance over society. The Women's Movement, European legislation on equality, and the greater influence of secular and liberal thinking led to challenges to established social, moral and political conventions. In 1995 the constitutional ban on divorce was removed by referendum, and the prohibition on abortion was hotly debated.

The ability of the Catholic Church to resist these challenges was hampered as its moral authority was greatly undermined by a series of clerical scandals that shook public confidence in its religious leaders. Despite this turbulence the Church still plays a powerful role in Ireland. It is adapting to the "New Ireland" and, under the influence of the Church in Europe, is widening its moral debates to encompass pressing issues such as poverty. Increasing numbers of Catholics still believe in the broad message of the Church without feeling compelled to follow specific

OPPOSITE, TOP: Gerry Adams of Sinn Féin has shown great political still during the peace negotiations in Northern Ireland. BELOW: U2 are perhaps the world's best-known Irishmen. Their successful career in rock music has also given their lead singer, Bono, a platform for his political views.

aspects of Church teaching. Mass attendance, remains uniquely high for a European state.

The decline of traditional morality has led to wider recreational use of illegal drugs and the resulting boost that this gives to organized crime. Public concern heightened after the 1996 murder of Veronica Guerin, a journalist investigating underworld figures. Two men have since been found guilty of her murder and sentenced to life imprisonment.

In spite of these problems, Ireland entered the 21st Century with optimism. Cultural life since 1973 has thrived. There has been an explosion of activity on both sides of the border. During the 1980s and 1990s Ireland's international profile was enhanced by its musical talent. Traditional music, as played by the Chieftains, and modern pop, represented by U2, both gained worldwide recognition. Novelists (Christy Brown, Roddy Doyle, Iris Murdoch, J. P. Donleavy), playwrights (Brian Friel, Tom Macintyre) and poets (Nobel Prize-winner Seamus Heaney, Tom Paulin, Eavan Boland, and Derek Mahon) created a vibrant literary scene. Ireland has always produced great actors but it also now cultivates film directors (Neil Jordan, Jim Sheridan). Past and present have fused in the revival of traditional culture and interest has increased in the ancient language of Gaeltacht.

Ireland's Provinces

The Province of Connacht

by Cormac MacConnell

For about 25 years after the War of Independence between Britain and Ireland, which resulted in the Anglo-Irish Treaty, approved in Dáil Eireann on 7th January 1922, what is now the Republic of Ireland was officially called the Irish Free State – a fine name indeed.

While the title has long since been replaced, I would argue gently that, in its most literal sense, the Irish Free State still exists, in a very real way, inside those allegedly merely geographic boundaries of the province of Connacht. Certainly, visitors from Northern Ireland, when summer comes, pour into Connacht in their tens of thousands and always refer to it, in their sharpened accents, as the "free state."

Connacht is in many ways indeed the "Irish free state." It is "Ballyescape." It is for holidays; for feasting the eyes, and the spirit. It is for what we call "the Craic." It is the place where the clocks seem to run without the urgencies of elsewhere. It is the region where some mysterious alchemy has subtly married the best of Ireland's yesterworlds to the better elements of a nation's social and economic progress. Although by far the poorest of the provinces economically, it is, by common consent, infinitely the richest in what it has to offer those who come to see, to hear, to smell, to touch; to taste the core of a culture.

Gaelic is still the musical mother tongue in parts of Connemara, as it is on many of the offshore islands where the tough, yet delicate, currachs nimbly dance their darkened shadows from wavetip to spumed trough, durable as the culture itself. There are more musicians per acre, of flute and fiddle and accordion,

than anywhere else, except maybe in County Clare. In the quietest corners of the great mountains of the west there are still hardy bands of moonshiners servicing a ritual which, though illegal, is almost as old as the hills themselves. Hay is still cut and saved the old slow way on many of the small farms; more turf is burned aromatically through old and venerable chimneys; salmon are still poached from the rivers as they have always been poached, and the huntsmen and women of The Galway Blazers still ride as recklessly pell-mell as they ever did. Yet, there is a modern factory just around the corner, its spaces full of new cars; a new hotel tucked cunningly, almost unseen, against the side of that mountain; supertrawlers costing £10 million sharing the seas with the currachs and bright new bungalows facing setting suns with golden windows.

This rugged unofficial "Irish free state" now attracts more tourists annually than even fabled

Opposite: Kinvarra, County Galway.
Right: Ashford Castle, County Mayo.

125

Killarney. A few are so captivated that they never leave again. The coastline areas of Galway and Mayo, from which, ironically, many natives still emigrate, are now liberally dotted with colonies of mainly European young people. They, like the Norman invaders of centuries past, are well on their way to becoming more Irish than the Irish themselves.

Galway and Mayo, Sligo and Roscommon and lovely little languid Leitrim, these are the stops along the twisting road which runs west into the heart of Connacht. Along the edge of that road, where the tourists' maps turn brown and airy, in a small place called Rosmuc in Connemara, one can still visit Patrick Pearse's cottage, the summer holiday home of the schoolteacher-poet who championed the clandestine Irish Republican Brotherhood and was later executed for his part in the Easter Rising of 1916. One imagines he must have often sat inside the small windows dreaming his revolutionary dreams, and writing poetry which was perhaps sometimes a little on the maudlin side, an Irish trait.

From that place you can still see the unfettered sweep of the great, granite mountains, awesomely empty and clean, being casually stroked by suns that turn furze bushes into whorls of gold, and lakes into pools of molten silver; a scene that inspired Pearse to write these evocative lines:

> The little fields where mountainy
> men have sown,
> And soon will reap,
> Close to the gates of Heaven.
> FROM: "THE BEAUTY OF THIS WORLD"
> BY PATRICK PEARSE (1879–1916)

In 1649, when Oliver Cromwell came to Ireland, determined to bring the entire population to the Protestant faith, he once ordered the Irish natives to go "to Hell or to Connacht...," to make room for his planters. Maybe he, too, got it right through happenstance. Many millions of visitors would, today, join with the natives in claiming that Connacht is so far away from Hell that it is, in the words of Pearse, as close as you can get on this earth to the gates of Heaven.

RIGHT: County Down farmland, seen from Scrabo Hill.

Galway

Cradle of the "hidden Ireland"

Galway is a county, is a city, is a state of mind. Galway is a republic within a republic; a principality of all the Irish pleasures; a dominion of dreams; a myth that is a rock-tipped reality; a myth upon which real purple heather grows; against whose shoreline the long Atlantic waves murmur mysteries.

Galway City and its great sweeping county hinterland is not just the capital of Connacht. It is also, in a spiritual way, the unchallenged capital of what people are now commonly terming the "hidden Ireland." Here, one of Europe's fastest growing cities has somehow contrived to marry the very best of

modernity and economic development to all the worthwhile elements of a colorful history.

There are many areas of Ireland, especially towards the east coast, where one could argue that Europeanization has impacted heavily upon both the places and their people. Mainstream cultural and lifestyle changes are clearly evident at every level. The national media, largely headquartered in Dublin,

BELOW: Approaching the shore at Cana, County Galway. OPPOSITE: The Galway races are held on the Tuesday, Wednesday, and Thursday before the first Monday in August.

today generally portrays the Irish as differing less and less from our European brethren. International lifestyle trends, for whatever commercial reason, are powerfully hyped, frequently adopted. And yet, against this background, the "hidden Ireland" of which Galway is the capital continues to flourish.

In this world the old values still hold sway. Gaelic football and hurling are still far more popular than soccer, for example. Irish musicians and balladeers draw larger audiences than any others. In County Galway, in the Gaeltacht (Irish-speaking) region of south Connemara, not only is Irish the mother tongue for at least 40,000 people, it is also a live and vibrant element in the social intercourse of the city itself. In this world, people still go to church on Sundays; eat more potatoes than pasta; know their family trees, and folklore, and how to dance the old set dances. In all of Galway, both city and county, the "hidden Ireland" is not hidden at all and this is probably the reason why the region so powerfully plays the heartstrings.

From each corner of Eyre Square, in the heart of Galway City, run four roads which all lead to some understanding of the Galway mystique. The road which runs north from Eyre Square, before swinging somewhat to the west, ends up hugging the shores of the lordly Corrib the great lake which meets the Atlantic near the ancient fishing village of the Claddagh. Further to the west is the town of Oughterard, which goes mad each May when the mayfly begin to rise and excite both the trout and the anglers. The Corrib hereabouts is at its most majestic. On its shores, quiet places like Conbur and Corrhanmona look over to horizons of drifting boats of anglers, blue skies, and peace.

The road that runs west from Eyre Square penetrates a totally different Galway. It runs again for about 60 miles (96 km) through some of Ireland's most strikingly rugged scenery, right through the heart of Connemara to Clifden.

Connemara, under its sculpted weight of great

RIGHT: The still waters of Killary Harbor, near Leenane, a place that attracts hiking enthusiasts. According to local legend, an escarpment near here was caused by the Devil, who attempted to drag St Roc away using a chain that scraped the ground up into the slope.

mountains called The Twelve Pins, is as different from north and east Galway as chalk from cheese. Here, Gaelic is spoken to a man, and the people seem somehow smaller and quicker that their brethren towards the River Shannon. It is probably the difference between the fisherman and the farmer. Most Connemara men fish. To see their traditional boats, currachs, which they use the way farmers use tractors, dancing on the sea, is to observe artistry. Their ancestors needed to be quick and hardy to eke out a living between seas and rocks and harder places. Times are easier now with the explosion of new industries, such as aquaculture, but Connemara remains a law unto itself. Despite heavy penalties, they still make poitín by the gallon here, especially at Christmas. The colorless, fiery moonshine, distilled in quiet glens or on remote offshore islands, tastes of bog and heather, a little of Heaven and a little of Hell.

The three Aran Islands, Inishmore, Inishmaan and Inisheer, which groan under the weight of tourists all year round, are like fragments of Connemara flung offshore. Dun Aenghus, mysterious clifftop fort on Inishmore, the largest of the three, is awe-inspiring. Inisheer, closer to the Clare coast, is the most serene.

The road south from Eyre Square runs through another world again. Past the village of Oranmore, heading towards Clare and Limerick, it runs through oyster country; through hunting country; through green fields and tall trees. Villages like Oranmore, Clarinbridge and Kilcolgan all lie inshore from the world-famous oyster beds of Galway Bay. Each autumn, when the oysters are in season, a jetsetters' Oyster Festival in Galway City attracts scores of revellers.

The infectious passion with which Galwegians play is reflected in another way in many areas along the road which runs east. En route to the shore of the River Shannon, it passes between the towns of Tuam and sprawling Loughrea where, Sunday after Sunday, great games of Gaelic football and hurling are played with rare fire, skill and competitiveness. Once, in the 1960s, the Tuam football team won the All-Ireland Championship three years in a row, a most difficult feat. The players who accomplished this triple

OPPOSITE: A slice of daily life – drawing water in Galway Town, County Galway.

triumph, now in their sixties, are still regarded almost as demigods by the young boys and men who can be seen practising and honing their skills in the playing fields along the roadside.

The strong market town of Ballinasloe, in the heart of the west's horse country, reveals another element of the real Galway. Here, at the beginning of each October, is staged what is now Europe's largest traditional horse fair. On the first Monday of the month, Ballinasloe's great amphitheatre, Fair Green, is swamped by thousands of horses. Many of them are the horses of Ireland's travelling people who, from dawn until dusk, can be seen riding furiously bareback up and down through the thick of the action. Deals involving dozens of horses are going on everywhere. There is back-slapping, hand-slapping; all the tricks of buying and selling. There are trick-o-the-loop men slipping through the crowds like ghosts, fortune-tellers, three-card-trick men. Usually, on the fringes of the fair, the strong men among the travellers engage in bareknuckle fisticuffs in prearranged bouts to determine, in effect, who is the "king of the tinkers." Two centuries ago, so great was the reputation of the Ballinasloe Fair that the purchasing officers for the armies of the czar of Russia used to come here to buy their cavalry mounts.

For one of the finest examples of the Galway spirit, one should follow the road east to Ballybrit, just off the edge of the city, where, at the end of July, the Galway Races are held for an entire week. The Galway Races are different from any other race meeting in Ireland. It is significant that many tens of thousands of visitors who come to Galway for Race Week never go to the track at all; never bet on a horse. They come for the almost feverish merrymaking which is the climax of the region's summer tourist season. More champagne is drunk in Galway during that week than anywhere else in Ireland. There are more high jinks, more card games for incredibly high stakes, more street fun for the masses. The skies are full of private helicopters heading to and from the track in a spending spree worth at least £20 million to all the local tills. Each year the total betting take is higher than ever before. This happens even during periods of economic downturn! Galway Races, fabled in song and story, are an experience for all the senses. Only Galway could stage them.

133

Leitrim

The Cinderella county

Clichés are often very apt. They call Leitrim "the Cinderella county" and you would not find a better description. She is a waifish scrap of a thing, tiny, with a smudged nose and a crystal slipper that glitters at the waterfall of Glencar. She has even got her very own Garden of Eden!

It is outside Rossinver. Here, there has always been a townland called Eden. A gentle Englishman called Rod Alston visited Eden 20 years ago. He saw a cottage there, empty, as were many by emigration. It even had

an apple tree, although it lay on its side beside the cottage, its roots drying and dying inside a thin uprooted sod. Alston bought the cottage and almost the first thing he did was to right the tree, stake it and then feed its famished roots. Today it brings forth good fruit and surrounding it is one of the west of Ireland's best organic gardens. The story of this garden of Eden is in many respects the story of Leitrim.

The west, economically, is the poorest region in Ireland. Leitrim is the poorest county in the west. Her drumlin soil is acidic and thin. Her winters can be harsh, wet, windy. In the 1950s and 1960s her population was so ravaged by emigration that it was reduced to below 30,000. At one time there were even doubts about whether the county could survive as a viable unit.

Just as in the Cinderella story, help came from outside – one hesitates to say from "a fairy godfather" – but in the shape of a man with imagination. His name was John McGivern, otherwise known as Johnny Macaroni. He came back from America in the darkest days of the early 1950s, and in the small village of Glenfarne he built the "Ballroom of Romance," a dance hall to which he brought the biggest dance bands in all of Ireland. Thereafter, every Sunday night, without fail, the dapper, tuxedoed, Italian-shod McGivern went onstage, turned the lights low, and sang, *Have You Ever Been Lonely?*. Then, as the band played softly, he encouraged Leitrim boy and Leitrim girl, dancing shyly together, perhaps for the first time, to exchange names and perhaps peck each other on the cheek if they felt bold enough. McGivern called it the "Romantic Interlude," and it was a major attraction, especially for tongue-tied young men. Years later, before William Trevor wrote his classic short story, "The Ballroom of Romance", John McGivern had statistics to show that his ballroom, a blazing bright light on a darkly drumlin horizon, had indeed created hundreds of marriages.

Today, there are many bright nightspots and clubs to visit in prospering towns like Carrick-on-Shannon and Mohill and Manorhamilton and Ballinamore. Maybe the best index to the new vitality of a county once threatened with extinction is the fact that its Gaelic footballers recently won the Connacht Championships and made a gallant attempt to win the All-Ireland title. Nothing so sharply defines the county's identity and pride. Yet there is something poignant, too, in all the subcurrents of modern Leitrim. So much hurting by the past generations; so much poverty then; so many tens of thousands of enforced emigrants, all mean that, even in the midst of summertime gaiety, the strong folk memory of loss and regret is never too far away. It is neither intrusive

OPPOSITE: A cascading waterfall in the area known as Glencar Lakes, County Leitrim.

nor depressing – rather the opposite nowadays – but it is there. The setting sun that X-rays the breathtaking valleys clearly exposes the shadows of the potato ridges and furrows of the past. Crops grew here to feed thousands whose crumbling gables testify to eventual defeat. When the potato crop failed during the Great Famine of 150 years ago (1845–49), few areas suffered more. In a Leitrim pub there comes a special silence when someone sings any of the many emigration songs that recall the era:

> I am bidding them all farewell,
> With an aching heart I will bid them adieu,
> For tomorrow I sail far away,
> All across the wild foam, for to seek a new home
> On the Shores of Amerikay.

However, in Leitrim that mood will not last long. No sooner will the echoes of the song have died away than some fluter or fiddler will strike up a lively tune and, before the night is over, the visitor is likely to be told in detail of how the abused tenantry of this region at last ended the allegedly cruel career of the county's most hated landlord of the last century.

When Lord Leitrim of Mohill was murdered in 1878 in nearby County Donegal, where he also owned huge estates, the police thought they had a clear clue to the identity of one of his murderers because, in the dead lord's fist, they found a "clump" of red hair which he had torn from the head of one of his assailants. However, when they went to investigate, they found that every redheaded male within 70 miles (112 km) had willingly undergone a similar semi-scalping experience. Today the great Lough Rynn House near Mohill, from which the autocratic lord once ruled over 90,000 acres (36,423 ha) in four counties, is one of the area's premier tourist attractions.

Survival was always the name of the game in Leitrim. Even in modern times the people are ultra-sensitive about the integrity of their identity. They react sharply, usually en masse, to any media criticism of their own place. They strongly dislike the political reality that, for voting purposes, their beloved county is annexed to neighboring Sligo. There is also continuing opposition to forestry developments in the county which springs largely from a fierce wish not to surrender farmland to trees.

Mayo

A sacred "queendom"

The third largest county is not pronounced "mayo" at all in the local dialect. It is infinitely more of a "mmayOO" sound, softly and proudly articulated. That final vowel rides as high and airy above the rest as the holy mountain of Croagh Patrick soars above the animated picture postcard that is the town of Westport on the surf line of Clew Bay.

Hunched slightly forward over the town, the summit almost always cloud-wreathed, the holy mountain has the profile of a shawled matriarch kneeling in prayer before a smoking turf fire. It looks formidable, somehow indomitable, yet calm, like a seashore grandmother scanning the bay for the first sight of the family fishing boat beating for home, an appropriate metaphor, as it happens, for a county where formidable females have left an indelible imprint on both the past and present.

There is a great national pilgrimage to Croagh Patrick on the final Sunday of July, known as Reek Sunday. Up to 100,000 pilgrims climb to the summit – an awesome sight – to hear Mass and receive Holy Communion in a grey little oratory up in the mists. The climbs used to take place at night, the pilgrims' torches creating a writhing golden-skinned 235 foot (72 m) serpent; the only one St Patrick never banished from Ireland. In those years the local people employed a herd of donkeys to ferry supplies of tea and soft drinks to canvas-roofed bothies along the way and on the summit itself. I once paid five old shillings (now 25 pence), then a huge price, for a single cup of tea, to a feisty local woman who justified the price by saying she had climbed the mountain four times in the previous two days to bring up supplies. Outside, as I drank the best tea I've ever tasted, stalwarts like her, many in bleeding bare feet, toiled towards the clouds. Faith, it seems, can move mountains; the centuries-old pilgrims' path is constantly being eroded and broken down by the tens of thousands of feet.

In the nearby village of Knock an event took place in 1879 which would have a profound effect on the county of Mayo. Here, on a warm August evening, 15 local people claimed to have seen an apparition of the Blessed Virgin Mary on the outside gable wall of the local chapel. Today, in consequence, Knock is Ireland's leading pilgrimage center – 1.5 million pilgrims visit the village annually – and numerous miracles are claimed to have occurred there. The village also now has the country's largest church – Our Lady's Basilica – which can accommodate 20,000 people and often needs to. Even cynics are impressed by a very special serene atmosphere surrounding this gentle place.

On all the roads that lead to Knock, everywhere in the county, the scores of Marian shrines and roadside grottos are the best maintained in Ireland. Around almost every bend, in robes of blue and white, the Lady of Mayo is to be seen surrounded by flowers and homage. Her molded features, rendered hereabouts as Celtic and serene, but with a powerful directness about them, never fail to remind me of drawings of the other great lady who once ruled this mountain matriarchy, the warrior queen Grace O'Malley, commonly known as Granuaile.

Beautiful, wild, wily, passionate Grace O'Malley, the queen of all the seas around Clew Bay; a pirate queen; a female free-booter in a totally male-dominated era. The Mayo historian, Anne Chambers, has written a splendid history of her lifetime achievements and daring exploits in the years from about 1550 to 1600. I love the image of Granuaile, at the prime of her powers, sailing proudly up the mouth of the River Thames to London in her own fierce warship to meet with Queen Elizabeth in the Elizabethan court on equal terms. The "virgin" queen is said to have been fascinated and hugely impressed

OPPOSITE: Dramatic ribbed, layered cliffs and pounding seas around Achill Island, off the coast of County Mayo. The island has at times been a popular tourist destination for writers and artists, such as Heinrich Böll, Peadar O'Donnell, and Graham Greene.

by her, as well she might. Today, on striking Clare Island, off the Mayo coast, the remains of one of her castles, cliff-perched still, after all these centuries, seem to echo with her powerful presence.

Perhaps because of the early power of Granuaile, County Mayo, even more than the other western counties, has the heft of a matriarchy about it even now. In most agricultural societies with a Catholic tradition and large families, mothers played a vital role, and the women of Mayo, who have always been noted for their thrift, energy, and enterprise, are no exception. There is a common saying often used to illustrate the shrewdness and vitality of Mayo's mothers: "She would mind mice at a crossroads!"

The first woman president of Ireland, Mary Robinson (who was elevated from the presidency to become United Nations' Commissioner for Human Rights in 1997), is in many ways the Granuaile of her era. Already an internationally-famed constitutional lawyer and feminist before she was proposed for the state's highest office, the Ballina woman was not expected to win. But she sailed forth against all the odds and won over the people of Ireland in a decisive election victory. Since then, with intellect, with elegance, and with a forceful kind of compassion for all humanity which has seen her catapulted onto the international scene, President Robinson has enhanced both the office which she holds, and, in the wider context, the entire proud reputation of Mayo matriarchs. A welcoming light burns always in the window of the presidential palace in Dublin; a token of the welcoming lights that have always been burning in Mayo's windows for the homecomings of generations of both seasonal and long-term emigrants.

It is said that although 400 people died in a dreadful famine march along the shoreline of Doo Lough (Louisburgh) in 1847 – they were seeking food from workhouse authorities – many more would have died had it not been for the womenfolk among them. It was they who drove the survivors on.

LEFT: A timeless agricultural scene in County Mayo, against a backdrop of still water and bare hills. Mayo is a very rural county. Its most important towns are Castlebar, Westport, and Ballina. Ballina has a cathedral, and Westport is the closest town to the pilgrimage site of Croagh Patrick.

Roscommon

Evoking the ancient

On a midsummer evening a dying sun illuminates Rathcroghan, in the green heart of County Roscommon. This ancient stone, which seems to grow much taller than its six feet (2 m) in the lowering light, is said to mark the tomb of the fierce King Dathi, the last pagan ruler of Ireland. Beyond it are Relig na Ri, Rath na Tarbh and Rathbeg, just some of the seemingly endless megalithic tombs of those rulers who preceded Dathi, including Maeve, the legendary Queen of Connacht who also ruled and loved in this place in the days before St Patrick.

There is a general view that Roscommon's colorful present tends to be over-shadowed by her exotic past. Certainly, the county's past and present are fused in a

compelling way not matched anywhere else even in the west of Ireland. Barely a month passes when the scuba divers, fishermen and boatmen who ply the ever-busier Shannon, bordering the county to the east, do not find artifacts that evoke the centuries: stone axes, bone buttons, coins, the heavy pikes of the wars and rebellions.

In Lough Gara, off the road between Boyle and Ballaghaderreen, the lowering of the water level 30 years ago recently revealed 400 drowned crannogs (lake dwellings), hitherto unknown. Nearby were the well-preserved remains of 40 dug-out canoes.

Likewise the county's green acres are fairly littered with historic memorabilia. Ogulla Well is here, in the shade both of a bloodstained O'Conor Castle and a broken Dominican priory, veined now with ivy and the clawings of centuries. It was in this place that St Patrick is said to have baptized the daughters of the high king of Ireland, Eithne and Fidelma, thereby ensuring the success of his Christianizing of the paganlands. He did it under the raised eyebrows of another of those pagan hills, Carnfree, where the kings of Connacht are thought to have been crowned.

Clonalis House, outside Castlerea in the west of the county, typifies the sheer height and width of Roscommon's history. It is the ancestral home of the Clan O'Conor, a family which produced no less than 11 high kings of Ireland and 24 kings of Connacht. Today it houses a rich display of artifacts, including the harp of Blind O'Carolan, the greatest of the Irish harpists whose compositions reputedly include the music for "The Star Spangled Banner." There, too, one can learn the well-documented story of "Lady Betty," a convicted murderer, who had her sentence commuted on condition that she carried out the hangman's grisly duties without any fee. The jail, in which it is said she enjoyed her work, still stands, a mighty stone building in the center of the town. In Fuerty graveyard lies another of Connacht's anti-heros, Robert Ormsby, known as Riobard na nGligearnacht, "Robert of the Jingling Harness" who is remembered darkly in the local folklore for his many cruelties towards his tenants in the Cromwellian era.

All of this co-exists with a vivacious modern way

OPPOSITE: A thirteenth-century castle still stands at Roscommon, County Roscommon.

of living. The pubs in the main Roscommon towns are second only to some of the country pubs for their nightlife and the quality of the music. More often than not the visitor is likely to hear at least one of the famous bitter-sweet songs of the satirical troubadour, Percy French:

> You remember young Peter O'Loughlin, of course,
> Well, here he is here at the head of the Force.
> I met him to-day, I was crossing the Strand,
> And he stopped the whole street wid wan wave of
> > his hand;
> And there we stood talking of days that are gone,
> While the whole population of London looked on,
> But for all these great powers he's wishful, like
> > me,
> To be back where dark Mourne sweeps down to
> > the sea.

FROM: "THE MOUNTAINS O'MOURNE"
BY PERCY FRENCH (1854–1919)

He had a fine way with words, the Strokestown man. So, too, have his fellow countymen and women. I gave one a seat in my car recently near a somnolently serene Lough Gara. I asked what the fishing was like. The answer was immediate: "The best fishing is to be found around those signs that say 'No fishing'!"

There is a castle outside Roscommon town called Donamon Castle. Curving like a sickle around the River Suck, this site has been fortified since 1154. It was then the powerhouse of the ferocious O'Finaghty family who owned all the lands they could see from their highest windows in all directions.

Today it is a seminary for a gentle order of priests called the Divine Word Missionaries. I heard them singing a Mass here, the shadows of their chapel almost visibly tenanted with the gentled spirits of old warriors, princes, kings. The silent river seemed to take the music away with it on its eddies and currents, as it flowed past other old ruined monasteries and castles, passage graves, and burial mounds; flowed over the hidden bronze daggers and rusted spears and pikes, past the holy wells and unholy hanging places. At some point on its journey it passed the extended shadow of that still-living tombstone of the last of the pagan kings of this county and of all the kings there ever were.

Sligo
County of poets and painters

I met a merry, unpublished poet in the city of Sligo. He was 60 years old and there was the froth of a pint of Guinness on his upper lip when he uttered a few of his lines:

> The working men of Sligo,
> Don't care a damn for Yeats,
> All we want are pints of porter,
> Spuds and bacon on our plates!

This happy poet's name was Melody, an appropriate surname for a bright spark of Sligo's soul. He was one of the many thousands of ex-soldiers that the garrison town of Sligo has given to the armies of the world down the centuries. In his case the army was the US Army and his war was the Korean War.

I contrast those eyes that were still so bright and lively with the gloomy and foreboding epitaph etched on the gravestone of the more famous poet, W. B. Yeats, a few miles out on the road in Drumcliff cemetery.

> Cast a cold Eye
> On Life on Death
> Horseman pass by!

The real ethos of County Sligo, as I have known and experienced it for more than 30 years, was infinitely better captured by the "unknown soldier" who laughed at life than by the poet laureate whose dark and essentially tormented presence still hangs over Sligo as distinctively as the silvered forelock hung

over his own forehead; as lonely Benbulben Mountain looms over Sligo town.

Sligo is often known as "Yeats Country," an accolade which at one level his powerful literary genius deserves. Also it is good for tourism. But at a deeper level it is a flawed attribution in many ways. The real and very earthy Sligo never belonged to William Butler Yeats any more than he belonged to it. He was actually born in Dublin and spent the greater part of his childhood in London. His was the Sligo of the visitor, and a relatively privileged one at that.

Indeed I would claim that his brother, Jack Yeats, the painter, whose work is increasingly in vogue nowadays, could properly lay more claim to the

OPPOSITE: Traditional transport is still seen in County Sligo.
ABOVE: Drumcliff Church seen looking toward Glencar Lough.

tribute. Jack Yeats' paintings of popular Sligo events, like fair days and horse races, do catch the soul of this county. His faces, animated and at ease with themselves, are the kind of faces one still sees on the streets of Ballymote and Tobercurry; in the fields around Gurteen; walking the golden sands of Strandhill. They are real. You can shake their hands and they will smile at you. William's strange people seem tenanted more to the superstitious county of his genius that to the county of which he was so fond.

Once, while visiting Drumcliff cemetery, I watched a fiery farmyard rooster, the picture of a primitive kind of vitality, fly up onto one of the tombstones, sadly not that of Yeats, where he cock-a-doodle-dooed for the whole wide world. That's my Sligo.

For those that seek tombland and ancient castles, archaeology, history, echoes of centuries, they are all here. There are books galore that will tell you all about the misted and essentially heartbreaking Celtic legends attached to the empurpled mountains and caverns of Sligo. Go south to the Strand of Streedagh and you can still almost hear the grinding noise of the waterlogged Spanish Armada foundering here.

But Sligo people, though well-versed in the richness of their own history, and proud of it too, are more likely to get a bright light in their eyes at the mention of Michael Coleman than at the mention of either the poet or the slaughtered Spaniards. Coleman, an accomplished and truly lively fiddler, evocative of the local spirit, emigrated to the United States and began a brilliant recording career there 60 years ago. His records, in that era and beyond, were as popular as those of the Athlone tenor, Count John McCormack. Coleman is still one of the father figures of Irish traditional music and thanks to his influence, Sligo continues to have a spirited corps of musicians who manage very sucessfully to "make the timber talk."

When I think of Sligo I think of good nights in good company; of exciting modern theater by companies like the Hawk's Well group in the city; of children singing and dancing and playing at the Sligo Feis (competitive festival); of the awesome beauty of Easkey, south of Sligo, whose very name is an amalgam of the words "sea" and "sky." I think of Gurteen and the prized racing greyhounds, and of Enniscrone, where the salty baths, they say, would bring a dead man to life, if you could get him immersed in them quickly enough. And I think of the fabled Coney Island, after which it is claimed the New York counterpart is named. It is off the road between Sligo and the resort of Strandhill. At low tide, with care and local advice, you can drive across golden strands out to an island of gentle wonder and serenity.

There is another special place along the Sligo coastline. It is near the now empty little town of Aughris, ruined by emigration. It is called Coragh Dtonn. The Gaelic name springs from the fact that the cliff hereabouts is concave. The sea, in its green, heaves against it, especially on summer nights, producing an eerie sound which is unforgettable, but, somehow, not sad. It sounds a bit like a tumult of ancient warriors celebrating a battle long ago; a battle won rather than lost. It is elemental, exciting, enchanting. It is the growl of life in Sligo's throat.

RIGHT: An inviting sweep of sandy shoreline near Moneygold, County Sligo.

The Province of Leinster

by Seamus Martin

The Atlantic Ocean, that vast machine which daily churns out the weather for western Europe, dashes against the shores of three of Ireland's four provinces. Leinster is the exception. Apart from a tiny strip of coastline on the southern slopes of County Wexford, the province is bathed by the milder waters of the Irish Sea, a stretch of water which in comparison is little more than a large lake.

While the Atlantic has carved out massive gashes and has flooded river valleys in the coastlines of Ulster, Connacht, and Munster, the Irish Sea coast of Leinster runs in more or less a straight line from north to south.

There is little of the savage grandeur of mountains tumbling into the sea that characterizes the rest of the Irish coastline. In Wicklow there are mountains indeed, but they slope gently towards sandy shores, while elsewhere the sea is bordered by lush, flat pasture.

Leinster looks east. It is less remote from the rest of Europe and its coastline in earlier times lay open to invaders and immigrants from Britain and the mainland. The Vikings founded many of the coastal towns, the indigenous population being rural rather than urban dwellers. The Normans began their conquest in Leinster, and so, too, did the English who followed them.

Large settlements grew, and for centuries – until the industrial revolution – Dublin, the province's and the country's capital, was the only place on the entire island which could justifiably call itself a city by international standards.

OPPOSITE: Kilkenny Castle was bought by James Butler, the third earl of Ormonde, in 1391. It remained the seat of the Butler family 1936.

Dublin remains the largest urban agglomeration, and one person in five in the island of Ireland – one in three in the Republic – lives there. It dominates the country and dominates the province even more.

The extent of this dominance can be shown by some comparisons: if the same population ratio of capital city to country existed, as does that between Dublin and the Republic of Ireland, London would have almost 20 million inhabitants; in the United States, Washington would be a city of 100 million; in Germany, Berlin would house 27 million souls; Moscow would harbor 50 million Russians and Beijing would be home to 400 million Chinese.

But the Republic is a very small country, and Dublin, by European standards, is no more than a medium-sized city; only Helsinki and Luxembourg, of the 15 capital cities of the European Union, are smaller in size.

The dominance, however, remains. In Leinster the next largest town, Dundalk, in County Louth, is just one-thirtieth of Dublin's size. There are, of course, historical reasons for this. Ireland's population is now little over half what it was before the Great Famine began in 1845, while the Dublin urban area has grown four-fold in the same period.

Dublin's pre-eminence has not only been in the area of population. In architecture, despite the ravages of time, it outshines all other urban areas; in music, the arts, medicine and science it has produced the leading Irish exponents. In industry, Belfast left Dublin far behind, but the advent of computer technology has given Dublin a boost.

It is, however, in the field of literature that Dublin has made its greatest contribution, not only to Ireland but also to the world. What other city of its size has produced writers of the stature of Jonathan Swift, Sir

Richard Steele, Richard Brinsley Sheridan, Oscar Wilde, Bernard Shaw, W. B. Yeats, James Joyce, Samuel Beckett, Sean O'Casey, Brendan Behan and, in the field of political letters, Edmund Burke?

Dublin, despite this, is not Ireland, and neither is it totally representative of Leinster. The great plains of Meath and Westmeath; the vast boglands of Offaly; the mountain fastnesses of Wicklow; the long stretch of the River Shannon to the west; the unique county of Wexford; the ancient town of Kilkenny, all have attractions of an entirely different nature from the Georgian streets and squares of Dublin.

Leinster has what could be described as two coastlines, that of the Irish Sea to the east and of the Shannon to the west. The sea coast has long stretches of sandy shore from Clogherhead in County Louth all the way to the popular beaches of Wexford and Wicklow. The Shannon is by far the longest river in Ireland. Described by Edmund Spenser as "the spacious Shenan spreadeing like a sea," it flows from north to south along the shores of Longford, Westmeath and Offaly, bursting forth at one point into the expanse of Lough Ree, where it takes little imagination to consider oneself out of touch with land.

The remains of the ancient monastic settlement of Clonmacnois, founded by St. Kieran, borders the river in County Offaly, rivalled only by St. Kevin's foundation at Glendalough in County Wicklow.

There are other rivers of importance. The Barrow and the Nore flow in a southeasterly direction and are navigable in parts. The Boyne runs from east to west reaching the Irish Sea at the ancient town of Drogheda, and few rivers in Ireland run by more historic sites.

The Battle of the Boyne at Oldbridge, near Drogheda, where William III defeated James II, with the British monarchy at stake, changed the whole order of Ireland for centuries. Much earlier the banks of the Boyne were home to prehistoric people, as the burial grounds of Newgrange – older than the pyramids of Egypt – Knowth, and Dowth bear witness.

Leinster offers, uniquely in Ireland, the amenities of a capital city coupled with the quiet pleasures of the countryside, the one accessible to the other in minutes rather than in hours.

RIGHT: One of Ireland's many splendid golf courses, the Tranmore golf course in County Waterford.

Carlow

County of the nearly famous

Carlow is a small county, the second smallest in Ireland. Its claims are modest, but its land is productive. It is here that the coastal mountain ranges of the east meet the rich, if featureless, central plain. It was in Carlow, too, that the Normans, following their 12th century arrival in neighboring Wexford, began to consolidate their conquest; it was here that they built their first castles, thus leaving their mark permanently on the landscape.

The rugged beauty of the Blackstairs Mountains quickly slope to a rich pasture, watered by the broad and navigable River Barrow which was envied and taken by a succession of invaders who themselves blended with the Celtic inhabitants to produce a population, unpretentious in the main, but with more than its average share of eccentrics.

Like many parts of Ireland, Carlow supplied migrants to the rest of the English-speaking world. But in many cases they were well-to-do, Protestant rather than Roman Catholic, and far from the archetype of the famine-stricken who crowded the cities of Britain and the United States in the 19th century.

Those fortunate enough to own large holdings were prosperous and such people find time to devote their mental energies to matters other than managing their estates. Many, in any event, were wealthy enough to employ professional managers while they got on with their pet, often unconventional, projects.

BELOW: The Blackstairs Mountains mark the boundary between County Carlow and County Wexford.

Others, from the merchant class, in what was, and to a great extent still is, a prosperous corner of Ireland, made enough money to involve themselves in similar activities.

Samuel Haughton was one of the eccentrics who abounded in the Ireland of the Victorian era. Born in Carlow, he was a scientist and mathematician and graduated in mathematics from Trinity College Dublin before turning his attention to medicine. He is best remembered for a discovery which combined all three disciplines at which he was adept. It took some time to work out, mind you, but in the end his formula was of benefit to a tiny percentage of the population, although it stopped dramatically short of saving their lives.

Haughton worked out a mathematical, scientific and medical computation known as "Haughton's Drop." The "drop" was not one of medicinal liquid but an instruction to the hangman when dealing with prisoners sentenced to death. Until this time, the unfortunate wretches sentenced to be "hanged by the neck until dead" usually suffered from a slow and agonizing process of strangulation, something which the mob that gathered for executions thoroughly enjoyed.

"Haughton's Drop" took the "fun" out of execution day. It determined the precise length of rope; the exact depth of fall which a condemned man of a certain weight required in order to die instantly rather than linger half-alive in front of his viewers.

Carlow appears to have had the knack for producing "once famous sons and daughters," those talented men and women who made well-known contributions to society in their time, but who are now half, or totally, forgotten.

While everyone has heard of Henry Ford, whose ancestors came from County Cork, the name Frederick York Wolseley may not immediately ring a bell or blow a horn. The Wolseleys came from Mount Wolseley in the county and Fred was an ambitious chap who headed off to New South Wales in 1867 where he invented an ingenious device to shear sheep mechanically.

From there he came back to the "home countries" settling in England where he and Herbert Austin produced the first British automobile, the Wolseley Three-Wheeler. The Wolseley dominated the British auto market for some time and the name was only withdrawn from the market in 1975. Frederick died in London in 1899 and his grave was unmarked until 1988 when the Australians celebrated their country's bicentenary.

So it is that many Carlow people have made names for themselves both at home and abroad. Patrick Francis Moran, from the quaint village of Leighlinbridge, became cardinal archbishop of Sydney where his statue adorns St. Mary's Cathedral. John Tyndall, from the same village, was the 19th century scientist who discovered why the sky was blue and then spent most of his life getting as close to it as was possible. He was the first person to climb the Weisshorn in the Swiss Alps and one of the first to climb the Matterhorn.

Tyndall was also a pioneer in the field of fibre optics which play a major part in the communications industry of today. This achievement is commemorated by a monument erected at Alp Lusgen by his distraught and remorseful widow in 1911. Mrs Tyndall had every reason to be unhappy, her unwitting application of an overdose of chloral to her unfortunate 73-year-old husband in 1873 having been the cause of his sad demise.

Others to escape, and I use the word advisedly, from Carlow were Peter Fenelon Collier of Myshall who founded the US publishers of *Collier's Magazine* and William Dargan, Ireland's great railway entrepreneur who worked with Thomas Telford as a surveyor, made a vast fortune, donated some to found the National Gallery of Ireland and died in Dublin in 1867 almost penniless after a fall from a horse incapacitated him.

The greatest Carlow escape artist of all was Patrick Robert "Paddy" Reid, who was the British escape officer at the German prisoner-of-war camp in Colditz. As well as engineering many daring escapes from the notorious castle in eastern Germany, Reid managed to make an unscheduled exit himself.

Those sons and daughters of Carlow who stayed at home may have failed to make a name for themselves, but they live in a pleasant place bordered by the Blackstairs Mountains to the east and watered by the great River Barrow. It is one of the few counties in Leinster which does not form a section of Ireland's large but often featureless Central Plain.

Dublin

A splendid city

At the beginning of the 17th century the Great Duke Ormonde proclaimed that "it was of vital importance to keep up the splendor of the government;" that the populace of Dublin, and therefore of Ireland as a whole, should know who was in power and the importance of that power should be impressed upon them. The political motivation behind this statement may have been open to question, but it was from this pragmatic principle that the glories of Dublin's architecture stemmed.

The Phoenix Park with its 1,750 acres (708 ha), the sum of all the public parks in central London put together, was the first project. Next came the Royal Hospital in Kilmainham in 1680. Ormonde vetoed plans which would have seen the great houses of Dublin, like those in many cities and towns in Great Britain and Ireland, turn their backs on the central

river and thus be hidden from view. He insisted on the Parisian model: houses should face the water; quays should be built and the "splendor of the government" displayed.

Ormonde's principle dominated the development of Dublin for more than a century. However, by 1690 the balance of power had swung dramatically towards the "Protestant Party" with the defeat of the Catholic King James II by King William III at the Boyne, just 30 miles (48 km) north of Dublin. Catholics were debarred from office, high and low, their churches closed and their places of worship confined to small rooms in back alleys.

Unprincipled and undemocratic as the new regime was, it led to a period during which the city's Protestants – and Dublin was largely a Protestant city – became secure enough in themselves to settle more comfortably into Irish life.

In Dublin, a period of stability and self-confidence, not to mention considerable wealth, ensued which soon found its expression in an unprecedented expansion of the city. This growth, unlike elsewhere in Europe, took place to the east of the old town rather than to the west.

Development came thick and fast. Great town-houses were built for titled landowners, first north of the River Liffey and later to the south. In 1713 the city decided that there should be a "Mansion House...for the honor and advantage of this city, and a convienency (sic) to the Lord Mayor," so a large house, built by Joshua Dawson in 1705, was purchased and extended. It stands today on Dawson Street.

As well as encouraging architectural development, the period of stability began to engender among the Irish Protestant ascendancy a feeling of separateness, even of independence, from their cousins in Britain. It

LEFT: A statue of Thomas Parke, traveller and doctor, stands outside the Natural History Museum in Dublin.
OPPOSITE: The spiral staircase inside the National Gallery of Ireland.

was a phenomenon not dissimilar to the quest for independence from London on the part of the colonists in North America.

By 1729 the first stone of a new Irish Parliament House was laid on College Green. The building was to be an essay in classical elegance, and on a far more monumental scale than the buildings that then housed the Parliament in London which had supremacy over its Irish counterpart. Its colonnades inspired Robert Smirke's design for the British Museum a hundred years later.

The Irish Parliament, scene of many dramatic incidents in later years, voted subventions for the rebuilding of Trinity College across the road and soon the two buildings formed the northern and eastern sides of a stylish plaza.

In 1741 the "Musick Hall" was opened in Fishamble Street, site of the medieval "Fish Shambles," and a

year later the fame of the burgeoning city in the far west of Europe had spread to the extent that when George Frederick Handel, out of favor with London society, wished to take himself and his music to another capital, it was to Dublin he turned. He had hoped, as his biographer, Mainwaring, wrote in 1760, to "find that favor and encouragement in a distant capital, which London seemed to refuse him."

This is precisely what happened, and on 13th April 1742 he gave the first performance of his new oratorio, *Messiah*, at the "Musick Hall" to an audience of 700 people who were fitted in tightly. Ladies were advised that they should not wear hoops in their

BELOW: Government Buildings, Merrion Street.
OPPOSITE: Dublin has become a more Europeanized city with a thriving boutique-and-café culture.
FOLLOWING PAGES: The reading room, National Library.

skirts, and gentlemen that they should leave their swords at home.

Performed with the help of the choirs of the two Anglican cathedrals, Handel's great work received an ecstatic response with the Revd. Dr Patrick Delany so overcome by the performance of "He was Despised" by Susanna Cibber, that he rose from his seat and exclaimed: "Woman, for this, be all thy sins forgiven."

The architectural bonanza continued. Lord Powerscourt built his own town mansion in 1771; Fitzwilliam and Mountjoy squares were laid out in 1791 and Aldborough House, another city mansion for another lord and his family, was opened in 1796. The two most majestic buildings of all, the Custom House and the Four Courts, though north of the Liffey, were constructed right up on the quays to be viewed from the south bank. Confidence abounded, further expansion was expected, but at the height of its growth, events changed Dublin from one of Europe's capitals into a provincial town.

The insurrection of 1798 in counties Antrim, Down, Wexford and Mayo, put an end to stability. Plans were laid for the Union of Great Britain and Ireland. The Irish parliament voted for its own dissolution in a welter of bribery and corruption. Dublin society, for all the grandeur of the architecture, the literature and the music, had become thoroughly debauched. "Men of quality" surrounded themselves with rogues and thugs; claret was consumed in such vast quantities as to astound visitors from abroad; great estates were gambled away; favors were bought and sold, and eventually, the parliament itself was sold to London for money, land and titles.

The chief architect of Union in Ireland was Lord Clare, known to Dubliners as "Black Jack FitzGibbon." He was given a final accolade by the populace when they pelted his coffin with dead cats as his funeral procession passed through the city.

Dublin's decline was almost instantaneous. The aristocracy, who had built their town-houses to attend the House of Lords, and the landed gentry who had constructed similar mansions to attend the Commons, had no reason to maintain premises in Dublin. The Georgian buildings with their magnificent fan-lit doors fell, first, into the hands of

professional men, the lawyers and doctors, then to unscrupulous slum landlords, and then to decay.

By the start of the 20th century, living conditions in Dublin were among the worst in Europe. The child mortality rate was reportedly higher than in Calcutta. Large families crowded into single rooms of tenements which had once been mansions. Magnificent plasterwork and stucco Cupids, Venuses, and Apollos gazed down on scenes of indescribable squalor.

Dublin had once again reached an abysmally low point in its long history of ups and downs. It had thrived as a Viking trading center. In the early Middle Ages it already had two cathedrals, one within and another outside the city walls. It had been fought over continuously and by the time of Ormonde's arrival, its fortunes had hit the bottom of a trough following half a century of conflict throughout Ireland. But it always had the resilience to rise from the depths.

The impoverishment of the city following the Union in 1800 left the great public buildings intact, but the private mansions suffered. Later, in the struggle for independence and the civil war which followed in the 1920s, the Four Courts and the Custom House were badly damaged in the fighting, but decently restored by the government of the new Irish Free State, perhaps due to a subconscious memory of Ormonde's dictum.

But things got worse before they began to get better. In the second half of the 20th century, many great houses fell to a misguided prosperity rather than to poverty as previously had been the case. Property developers knocked down elegant buildings to replace them with glass-and-concrete structures. The people protested, at first without being listened to. There was a residue of bitterness in the hearts of some people, including those in government, who saw the splendid houses as reminders of former British occupation. However, gradually this has been overcome, but only gradually.

Now, at the close of the century, a construction boom, the likes of which has not been seen since Georgian times is under way. The city is looking to the future with as much confidence as it did more than 200 years ago, but this time with a cautious eye on its heritage as well.

LEFT: O'Connnell Bridge and O'Connell St., Dublin.

159

Kildare

County of the horse

After Newbridge, on the main road from Dublin to the south, pasture and parkland suddenly disappear to be replaced by a high treeless plain dotted with gorse bushes. This is The Curragh, and if you are early enough on the road, you are likely to see strings of thoroughbred racehorses undergoing their daily exercise.

At any time of day, mist and rain permitting, the starting gates and the large grandstand of Ireland's leading racecourse can be seen. This is the center of the country's great bloodstock industry with its training establishments – meticulously-kept stud farms owned by some of the richest families on earth – and in the village of Kill, the auction ring of Goff's Bloodstock Sales.

I have sat by that ring and watched spindly-legged yearlings, colts and fillies, make their way shakily round as the auctioneer spies a raised finger and in modulated English public school tones announces the process of the bidding in guineas, not pounds.

The guinea represented one pound and one shilling in earlier times; now it means one pound and five pence. It remained the fictitious unit of currency at Goff's long after decimalization.

Traditions die hard in the bloodstock world. After all, its very basis is in lines of breeding which stretch back to three imported stallions from the east: the Brierley Turk, the Godolphin Arabian and the Darley Arabian. From this trio all thoroughbreds are descended, so every little yearling to stagger its way round Goff's ring is likely to be related at some stage in its ancestry.

In the not so distant past, the stud farms and the bidding at Goff's came from the old Anglo-Irish ascendancy: the county magnates; the great landowners; and the more astute judges of horses from the lower ranks of the "nobility and gentry of Ireland." This has now changed. The big bidders' blood lines nowadays can be as eastern as those of the horses put up for sale. Sheikh Mohammed al Maktoum of Dubai has raised his finger at Goff's to bid in millions of guineas. A line of Their Serene Highnesses, The Aga Khan, have also had strong connections with Irish bloodstock over the years.

The old horsey families of Kentucky and the racing men and women of Britain, France and Italy are represented too, and for those who do not arrive by private helicopter from Dublin airport, there is a large car park to house the Rolls Royces, Bentleys, Mercedes and Porsches of the lesser fry. The bloodstock business is centered on very serious money.

It was always a bit like that, even in Irish legend when The Curragh was reputedly a place for chariot racing and the ancient Brehon Laws listed a complicated set of rules and regulations for the practice of the sport by young men of noble birth.

But racing as we know it today began in Kildare in more modern times, and by 1727, when Cheney's Racing Calendar was published for the first time, The Curragh had already become the headquarters of the "Sport of Kings" in Ireland.

Early on, the great contests were in the form of "match races' in which one great champion was pitted directly against another. In a contest of this type in September 1751, a steed called Black and All Black took on a rival named Bajazet for a prize of 1,000 guineas. The side bets came to a total of 10,000 guineas, a vast fortune in those times.

By 1812 a new phenomenon arrived on the scene in the form of Patrick Connolly who set up as a "public trainer" of racehorses at Waterford Lodge. Up to then the landed proprietors trained their own champions, but Connolly and his successors have taken over and the famous training establishments of Kildare and other counties further afield, now dominate the racing industry.

Then came the railways, which made The Curragh

OPPOSITE: Conolly's Folly was built in 1740 in the grounds of Castletown House, Maynooth, County Kildare, in honor of William Connolly, the speaker of the Irish House of Commons from 1715-29.

easily accessible to the metropolis in Dublin less than 30 miles (48 km) away. When the first Irish Derby was run in 1866, a "racing special," 30 carriages long, set out from the then Kingsbridge (now Heuston) Station in Dublin bearing the well-to-do, and perhaps some of the ill-intentioned of the capital, to their day's outing of sport.

On that first Derby Day the band of the Third Buffs Regiment was on hand to play martial airs for the ladies and gentlemen, but there was an audible sigh of disappointment when only three runners turned up for a sweepstake of five sovereigns each. The first Irish Derby winner was an Englishman, James Cockin of Staffordshire, whose horse, Selim, ridden by a

jockey with the propitious title of "Lucky" Maidment, won by eight lengths.

Cockin won again the following year with Golden Plover, again with Maidment as jockey, and this led to unsuccessful attempts of a less than sporting nature to limit the race to horses owned and trained in Ireland.

Even the dark days of civil war in Ireland failed to dim the glory of Derby Day on The Curragh. In 1922, when the country was riven by a conflict between those who supported the treaty which established the new Irish Free State and those who were intransigent in their republicanism, the Derby was held in calm and quiet. The race, with its prize of £4,715, was won

by Spike Island, owned by Major Giles Loder, who, it was noted, represented a class which at that time preferred neither the Free State nor the Republic, but a maintenance of the Union with Great Britain.

The Derby was later sponsored by the old Irish Sweeps Trust and by the Anheuser-Busch brewing company of St. Louis in the United States, raising the prize money to astronomical levels and attracting further private helicopters to The Curragh in June every year to augment the ordinary racegoers who flock there from all parts of Ireland and abroad.

County Kildare was also the scene of a unique

*ABOVE: The Tully Japanese Gardens were part of an Edwardian-era trend for the exotic world of the Orient.
OPPOSITE: The library of Carton House, an impressive aristocratic manor that has been repeatedly remodelled according to prevailing fashion during its 300-year history.*

kidnapping in 1983 when the former Derby winner, Shergar, was abducted from the stud of his owner, The Aga Khan, and has never been recovered, despite offers of vast rewards by His Serene Highness.

But horseracing in Ireland and in Kildare is not confined to the super rich. The classics on the flat may be the domain of the wealthy, but racing over jumps, or National Hunt Racing, as it is formally known, is a far more egalitarian sport, with small farmers testing their horses, often successfully, against wealthier opponents.

Not surprisingly in a county where the horse is king, there are a number of large country houses of the old Anglo-Irish ascendancy who spent a great deal of time hunting and racing. One anonymous lady was described by the satirical writer Brian O'Nolan (alias Flann O'Brien and Myles na Gopaleen) as being "not in the least bit self-conscious when off a horse."

163

Kilkenny

City of medieval charms

Inland towns in Ireland are, in the main, 18th-century creations, the work of "improving landlords," their houses being of Georgian vintage with their backs turned to the river on which they were founded. Kilkenny is different. True, like other Irish urban foundations, Dublin excepted, it shuns its great river, the Nore, but here the similarity ends.

Kilkenny is in essence a medieval town, with a great castle, a magnificent cathedral, some well-preserved merchant, houses and a sprinkling of abbeys, churches, and inns from the Norman period. By size it is a market town, by ancient charter, and from its cathedral status, it is a city.

Its location made it a convenient place for the holding of parliaments, and one of these, in 1366, introduced the "Statutes of Kilkenny," an early form of "apartheid" which aimed to separate the Irish from the Normans. Intermarriage was forbidden, so too was the use of Irish surnames and dress. Clerics and monks of Irish origin were refused admittance to churches and monasteries under Norman control. The ancient Irish game of hurling was expressly prohibited.

These Draconian measures were taken because of fears that the Norman colonists were becoming overly Hibernicized in dress and tongue and recreational habits. However, by the time the statutes were introduced the process of assimilation had advanced to such a stage that most of the Norman inhabitants had Irish blood and many of the Irish were part-Norman. In short, it had become almost impossible to distinguish between one race and the other.

The futility of this attempt at racial separation is most apparent today when one sees young men and boys walking through the city's medieval streets with their hurleys tucked under their arms. In Kilkenny, a county which has won the All-Ireland Hurling Championship more than 20 times, the game has

acquired an almost religious fervor among its players and supporters.

The failure of the statutes has produced in Kilkenny a unique cross-fertilization between old Irish and Norman which is epitomized in the city itself, a place in which more medieval architecture and lore is compressed into such a small area than in any other town in Ireland.

Kilkenny's heyday came in the six-year span in which it proclaimed itself the capital of Ireland under the "Confederation of Kilkenny" from 1642 to 1648, when the Roman Catholics, of Irish and Anglo-Irish origin, united briefly and held court with the Papal-Nuncio, Cardinal Rinuccini. But the experiment, bedevilled by rivalries between the two ethnic groups, came to an end with the triumph of the Cromwellians in England and the execution of Charles I. Two years later Cromwell himself arrived and took control after four major assaults over five days.

Built in 1172, Kilkenny Castle has been altered significantly since its original construction by Strongbow, the first Norman conqueror of Ireland. On his death, his nephew, William the Marshal, replaced the original structure with a stone fortress. The Butlers, one of whom had been made Chief Butler of Ireland, took over the castle in 1391, from which time Kilkenny became an Anglo-Irish town with its original inhabitants clustered around St. Canice's Cathedral in a small area which is still known today as Irishtown. For the next six centuries, the Butlers, who later became the earls of Ormonde, kept their eye on their lands by establishing Catholic and Protestant branches. If the regime in London favored Protestant ownership, there were Protestant Butlers to fit the bill; if, as it did on occasions, Catholic ownership found favor, there were Catholic Butlers on hand to take over. The castle and some of the grounds were finally handed over to the Irish state by the 6th marquess of Ormonde in 1967.

At the bottom of the gently sloping hill from the castle, the old city begins at Shee's Almshouse, which

OPPOSITE: Cattle graze peacefully outside the ruins of Kells Priory, County Kilkenny. This fortified Augustinian priory was founded by Geoffrey de Monte Marisco, Strongbow's representative in Leinster.

was built in the quaintly named Rose Inn Street in 1588 by Sir Richard Shee and his wife as an institution for the relief of the poor in the town. Nearby in St. Mary's Lane is the 13th century church of St. Mary and, close at hand, St. Kieran's Lane which is famous for its inns and hostelries. The "Slips," a collection of narrow alleyways which run up from St. Kieran's to High Street, were the principal thoroughfares of the medieval town. Today, their modern storefronts mask many much older façades.

Close to "The Ring," once a center of medieval bull baiting, stand the remains of the Franciscan Friary, built in 1232, where Friar John Clyn was an annalist in 1348 and 1349 when the Black Death devastated the city and disease hung in the air like an avenging angel. Friar Clyn's annals end as follows: "I leave parchment to carry out the work if perchance any man survives…" After that entry, the annals continue in a different hand. The Friary now stands in the grounds of Smithwick's Brewery, a Guinness subsidiary, whose Kilkenny Beer sells in "Irish" pubs from Moscow to Milan.

Towering over the town, is the magnificent St. Canice's Cathedral which was built by Bishop de Mappleton in 1251–56. The second largest medieval church in Ireland – after St. Patrick's Cathedral in Dublin – St. Canice's stands on the site of an ancient monastic settlement founded by St. Cainneach (anglicized as Canice or Kenny) the only remnant of which is its 100 foot (30.5 m) round tower. During Cromwell's brief stay in Kilkenny, in 1650, he left his iconoclastic mark on the cathedral, destroying the "idols" and using the nave as a stable for his horses.

Just to the south is Kilkenny College or "the Grammar School," built by the 1st duke of Ormonde in 1666. Among its early alumni are several famous men. One was Jonathan Swift, the great satirist and later dean of St. Patrick's in Dublin; another was the poet and playwright William Congreve. George Berkeley, the philosopher and bishop of Cloyne, who gave his name to the university city of Berkeley in California, was a third. One cannot help feeling that the unique city in which they received their secondary education, before moving to Trinity College, Dublin and onwards, must have played a part in developing their imaginations and preparing them for the careers which brought them international renown.

Laois

A French refuge

The town of Portarlington, which lies on a bend in the River Barrow not far from the border with the county of Offaly, is now a quiet backwater of County Laois. Once it was the scene of a remarkable demographic experiment which made it a place unique in Ireland; a place in which a language was spoken, a religion practiced, and a culture installed, which was totally distinct from the surrounding region.

Following the revocation in 1685 of the Edict of Nantes, which had ensured religious tolerance, French Protestant refugees flocked to what was then the United Kingdom of Great Britain and Ireland in search of places in which they could live in peace. One of the many places they settled was Portarlington, and nowhere did their culture, religion and language survive more tenaciously.

Why did the separate identity remain intact for so long? There are many theories put forward. First, Portarlington was surrounded by bogs and forest and therefore sufficiently isolated from the rest of the countryside to maintain a separate identity. Second, the settlement was large enough to be self-sufficient and third, the place had a distinctive character in that an astonishingly high proportion of its families were of noble origin.

The establishment of the French communities took place at a time when, in another Irish paradox, Roman Catholic Irish soldiers were fleeing to France after the Jacobite defeat at the hands of King William III, and it was one of William's senior lieutenants, the Huguenot Henri Massue, Marquis de Ruvigny, later styled earl of Galway, who got the Portarlington project under way.

Portarlington had been laid out for English settlers with a market square and four streets leading from it. But the little town had suffered severe damage during the war, and de Ruvigny personally financed the construction of over 100 houses of unique design. The entrances and gardens were to the rear and blank walls faced the streets.

The first wave of immigrants arrived in 1692, many of whom were pensioned-off soldiers and their families. Most came from the officer class, which, at that time, was made up of sons of noble families. There were six ensigns, one cornet, 16 lieutenants, 12 captains and one lieutenant-colonel. The most elegant and magnificent of all, with his scarlet cloak and silver-buckled breeches, was Robert d'Ully, Vicomte de Laval, a man of the royal blood line of King Henri de Navarre.

However, the nobles of that era could hardly have been expected to fend for themselves, and a second group of laboureurs, 13 families in all, arrived from the Swiss cantons where they had taken refuge, and gave the colony a more balanced character.

So by the start of the 18th century the foundations of a lasting settlement were laid. There were stories from visitors from neighboring areas of noblemen sipping a strange drink called tea from tiny china cups under trees in the village square; of the wine of Bordeaux being favored over the whiskey of the surrounding countryside.

Very soon, however, a number of forces combined to change the situation. The French Calvinists had initially been given freedom from interference by the episcopacy of the established Anglican Church of Ireland. But the arrival of a high-church bishop, William Moreton, from England changed all that. Exceptionally tolerant (for a man of his time) of the Roman Catholic majority in his diocese, he had an abhorrence of Protestant dissenters and was determined to enforce Anglican conformity on the French enclave.

The minister at the Eglise Française de St. Paul, Revd. Benjamin de Daillon, practiced a very strict Calvinistic form of worship which was by no means to the bishop's liking. Daillon was replaced in 1702 by a former army chaplain, Antoine Ligenier de Bonneval, who had already embraced Anglicanism and thus began a schism, a major split in the community, which lasted for 26 years.

The turning point came when 37 families left for Dublin to worship at the French Calvinist churches in

ABOVE: Looking north from Slieve Bloom Mountains

the capital, where their distinct language and customs were overwhelmed in a city which was quickly growing to become one of the most populous in Europe. Meanwhile, Portarlington was becoming increasingly Anglican and, therefore, more of an Anglo-Irish town.

Today, there are still Irish and Catholic families in the county who bear names such as Blanc and Champ, and families in other parts of Leinster, both Catholic and Protestant, whose Huguenot forebears gave them names such as Dubois, Perrin, Du Moulin, and De Mange.

All that remains of the Portarlington French connection now are its meticulous records, a few of the old noble houses and an annual French Festival at which the wine of Bordeaux is imbided in great quantities and snails and frogs legs are eaten in abundance, some by the English-speaking descendants of the original French settlers, but more by those of Gaelic and English origin.

Huguenots made a remarkable, if not fully recognized, contribution to Irish history. The less noble branches of the immigration, notably the

weavers who established the Irish poplin industry, now vanished like the immigrants themselves, contributed greatly to the economy of a country which had been ravaged by more than half a century of warfare prior to their arrival. Their memory survives in a county of moorland and bog, pasture and parkland, in the heart of Ireland's Central Plain; a county of level land, except in the northwest where the Slieve Bloom mountains once housed rebel Gaelic chieftains.

Portarlington is now a backwater marked by cooling towers of a peat-powered electricity plant. The county town, Portlaois (formerly Maryborough) houses a giant prison, but the best place in which to lock yourself away with the memories of the French and their descendants is the town of Abbeyleix, planned in the 17th century by the local landlord, Viscount de Vesci, a nobleman of Norman descent. Here, on the main street, and not mentioned in the guidebooks, is Morrissey's pub, a halting place for the discerning imbiber, in a land where imbibers are discerning in the extreme. One of the most convivial and best-preserved bars in Ireland, it might just be the place to raise a glass of Bordeaux to the French who have passed on.

Longford
Loveliest county of the plain

Longford figures little in the epic sagas of the Ossianic or Ulster Cycles, and it was never a strategic center in the long history of battles, victories, and defeats which other places have endured or exulted.

It is a quiet place, a place where water as often as land appears to make up the topography. Low hills, an abundance of lakes, streams and rivers flowing into the great River Shannon – which on its Longford shore takes on the appearance of a broad lake – and an artificial extra, in the form of the Royal Canal, give the county a watery aspect which is remarkable even in Ireland.

What remains of Oliver Goldsmith's body lies in the Poets' Corner in Westminster Abbey in London, where his epitaph, composed by Samuel Johnson reads: "He touched nothing which he did not adorn." His most prominent statue stands alongside that of Edmund Burke outside Trinity College, Dublin, where he was educated. However, Goldsmith first saw the light of day in Pallas in the county of Longford, one of the least spectacular places in Ireland, but a region every bit as gentle and attractive as this quotation from his poem, "Deserted Village," suggests.

Sweet Auburn, loveliest village of the plain,
Where health and plenty cheered the laboring
swain,
Where smiling spring its earliest visit paid,
And parting summer's blooms delayed,
Dear lovely bowers of innocence and ease,
Seats of my youth, when every sport could please,
How often have I loitered o'er thy green,
Where humble happiness endeared each scene.
FROM: 'DESERTED VILLAGE "BY OLIVER GOLDSMITH

The countryside abounds with places connected with the poet and author. At Pallas, his birthplace, there is a replica of Foley's Trinity College statue, and at Forgney Church, where his father, Revd Charles Goldsmith, was rector, there is a beautiful stained glass window depicting "Sweet Auburn."

As a young man, Goldsmith spent three years under the tutelage of Revd Patrick Hughes in Edgeworthstown, a place with another literary connection. The town was the seat of the Edgeworth family since 1583 and, in the 18th century, the scion was a Richard Lovell Edgeworth, an eccentric inventor and surveyor. One of his 24 children from his many marriages was Maria Edgeworth, the novelist, who wrote the much admired *Castle Rackrent*. Sir Walter Scott wrote in a preface to the Waverley Novels: "I feel that something might be attempted for my own country of the same kind as that which Miss Edgeworth so fortunately achieved for Ireland."

Another member of the extended family was the Abbé Edgeworth, a Roman Catholic priest, son of a Protestant clergyman, and a devotee of royalist France, who attended to the final religious needs of Louis XVI before he was executed, and later escaped to Russia.

Edgeworth House is now a nursing home, run by the religious Sisters of Mercy, who have maintained it in good condition, and the Edgeworth family vault is situated in the local St John's churchyard. Richard Lovell and Maria Edgeworth are buried there.

Longford figures strongly, too, in the Irish struggle for independence, and near Edgeworthstown one encounters a type of paradox which is not uncommon in Ireland.

Ballinalee was the home of General Sean McEoin, a guerrilla leader in the 1920s, known as the "Blacksmith of Ballinalee," who was captured and sentenced to death on 14th June 1921. However, he

OPPOSITE: Peat-burning power station in the countryside of County Longford. Electricity from burning peat is a relatively modern technology, having been experimentally tested in Scotland in 1959. The Irish government has made a significant investment in generating power through the burning of peat, a resource of which it has plenty. Peat emits more "greenhouse" gas than natural gas, but less than coal, and it is cheaper than the latter.

was later released and eventually became minister for justice and minister for defence before unsuccessfully contesting two elections for the presidency of Ireland.

Just south of Ballinalee is Currygrane, the birthplace of an Irishman of a very different political and religious hue. He was Field Marshal Sir Henry Wilson, Chief of the Imperial General Staff, who favored repressive measures to crush militant Irish nationalism. Wilson was assassinated in London by Irish republicans in 1922.

Longford's newest attraction is in fact its oldest. In 1984, in a bog in the townland of Corlea, near the small town of Kenagh, "trackway", made from large oak planks and dating from the early Iron Age, was discovered. Following excavation work four more "trackways" were found. This was followed by the discovery of a further 16. Now 57 of these prehistoric roads have been uncovered in the area, and a major exhibition center has been built at the site to inform visitors of the importance of these ancient remains.

The county town of Longford offers little in the way of architectural interest save for St. Mel's Cathedral which has been described as one of the "better post-emancipation churches" in Ireland. The architect, Augustus Welby Pugin, was less kind. It was, to his taste, "A bad copy of that wretched compound of pagan and Protestant architecture, St. Pancras New Church in London."

Like most of Ireland's counties, Longford has been depopulated by emigration over the years, but the Longford emigration, like that of its neighboring county of Westmeath, differs somewhat in that, as well as the traditional movements to Britain, North America and Australia, there was a considerable migration to Argentina from 1842 to 1860, during and after the Great Famine.

The Longford familes settled mainly in the province of Buenos Aires, where large tracts of land were being offered to European settlers. Edelmiro O'Farrell became President of the Republic of Argentina in 1914 and a kinsman of an even earlier emigrant, Romulo O'Farrill, is Mexico's leading media magnate.

RIGHT: Ireland's loughs and the favorable winds make windsurfing a popular leisure and competitive activity among the younger Irish.

Louth

A tale of brown bulls and battles

A spur of mountainous granite juts out like a thumb into the sea from the flat limestone plain of Louth, the smallest county in Ireland, to form the Cooley Peninsula. In ancient times, Louth was a borderland between the province of Ulster and, today, lies on the border of the Republic and Northern Ireland. Here, more than anywhere else in the province of Leinster, the landscape bears a resemblance to the jagged Atlantic coast. The pattern of settlement, too, is similar, and its barrier of mountains made it less open to the process of anglicization which quickly took hold elsewhere to the east of the River Shannon. The area around the picturesque village of Omeath was Gaelic-speaking into the beginning of this century, the last indigenous outpost of the ancient tongue in eastern Ireland.

The Cooley Peninsula, with its hills tumbling to the Irish Sea on the southern shore, and to Carlingford Lough on the north, is the site of one of the great epics of Irish mythology, the Táin Bó Cuailgne, "the Cattle Raid of Cooley", which tells how Queen Maeve of Connacht set her forces, under the

BELOW: Mellifont Abbey, County Louth, was the first Cistercian abbey in Ireland. It was founded in 1140 at the urging of St Malachy Ó Morgair.
OPPOSITE: Ruins of the sixth-century Monasterboice monastery, supposedly founded by St Buithe.

IRELAND

command of Ferdia, against those of his friend, Cuchullain of Louth, for the capture of a highly coveted bull owned by a Cooley farmer.

The exploits of all concerned were superhuman and the battles raged over vast stretches of territory; tops of mountains were sliced off by the swords of the combatants. Cuchullain, the epitome of epic heroes, slew hundreds of enemies single-handedly each day before the battle culminated in a four-day duel between him and his friend, Ferdia, at a place still known today as Ardee Ath Fhirdia, "Ferdia's Ford." Each night, regardless of the hostilities, Ferdia sent food and medicine across the ford to Cuchullain, until the third night when no messages were passed between the two men. On the fourth day Ferdia ran Cuchullain through with his sword and gravely wounded him, but Cuchullain finally produced the coup-de-grâce with his magic spear, the Gae Bulgach, and Ferdia was no more.

As all this went on, the wily Queen Maeve had smuggled the Brown Bull of Cooley back across the Shannon to Connacht, so the two friends had fought, and Ferdia had died, in vain. True to a tradition in which words were as potent as weapons, the conflict ended with Cuchullain reciting an encomium over the body of his friend in which he praised his opponent's courage and lamented the death of a great hero.

Over in Connacht, Maeve had a surprise waiting for her, the Brown Bull of Cooley having entered into his own personal battle with the white-horned bull belonging to her husband, Ailell, which he killed before heading back eastwards to his beloved hills of Cooley. For all its heroism the Táin also carries a subtext on the futility of war.

The southern part of Louth has its seaside resorts and its historic connotations, centered mainly on the town of Drogheda where the River Boyne completes its journey to the sea. Down river on the north bank from the town is Baltray, home of one of the finest golf links in Ireland. The East of Ireland Amateur Championship, one of the four major provincial golf competitions in the country, takes place here

OPPOSITE: Baled straw awaits collection on the Cooley peninsula, County Louth. The Cooley peninsula separates Carlingford Loch, the border with Northern Ireland, and Dundalk Bay on the east coast of Ireland.

annually.

Drogheda itself is remembered historically for the lack of quarter given to its residents by its most unpopular tourist, Oliver Cromwell, in 1649. At that time Sir Arthur Aston held Drogheda for King Charles I against the Roundheads, and on 10th September the town fell to Cromwell's third assault. Cromwell, a symbol of democracy in most parts of the world, was a man of his time, an era when the line between progress and barbarity was thinly drawn. He ordered the execution of some 2000 of the town's defenders, including Aston, and many of the survivors were transported to the West Indies.

In the 12th century, Drogheda's strategic position near the mouth of the Boyne was not wasted on the Anglo-Norman colonists who set up a castle and a bridge here, and by the Middle Ages, Drogheda, along with Dublin, was one of the most important English towns in Ireland. There was even a parliament which passed an Act, in 1465, for the setting up of a Drogheda University.

Although Drogheda's significance would diminish over the centuries, there are still some magnificent architectural examples extant of the town's former splendor. The most impressive of these is St Lawrence's Gate, a magnificent barbican complex at the junction of St Lawrence Street and Palace Street, with its pair of great circular towers linked by double arches and topped by a battlement.

In more recent times, parts of Louth have formed the borderlands with Northern Ireland in the course of the "Troubles." Moments of carnage, such as the deaths, in 1979, of eight British paratroopers near the narrow stretch of water in Warrenpoint – a place clearly seen from Cooley – and, in true Irish fashion, moments of comedy too, as when a detachment of Britain's most feared professional troops, the Special Air Service (SAS), was arrested by a village policeman in Omeath after they strayed across the border claiming they did not know how to read their maps.

For the moment all is peaceful in this borderland. The most sought after shells in the beautiful fishing port of Carlingford, where the 1935 foot (590 m) Slieve Foye Mountain tumbles into the sea, are those of the local oysters and prawns which are washed down with Guinness or Harp lager from a brewery in the county town of Dundalk.

Meath

A seat of kings

The Fenian cycle, Ireland's equivalent of the mythology of the Greeks and the sagas of the Norsemen, tells tales of great heroism, of Tír na n'Og, "the land of the young," an island to the west whose inhabitants never grow old, and of the great tragic love story of Diarmuid and Grainne.

The place at the center of these great tales was Tara, a name indelible in the minds and hearts of the Irish. It was not in any way accidental that the great house in which the heroine of *Gone with the Wind*, Scarlett O'Hara, was raised was given this name by her Irish father. No name could have been more synonymous with his Irishness.

All that remains of Tara today is a green meadow on a low hilltop, rutted with earthworks which provide the few discernible traces of the presence of a distant glory. All that is now gone, as the romantic poet Thomas Moore wrote:

No more to chiefs and ladies bright,
The harp of Tara swells,
The cord alone that breaks at night
Its tale of ruin tells,
Thus Freedom now so seldom wakes,
The only throb she gives,
Is when some heart indignant breaks,
To show that she still lives.
FROM: "THE HARP THAT ONCE THROUGH TARA'S HALLS"
BY THOMAS MOORE

The visitor to Tara now must come equipped with imagination; the ability to picture the great banqueting hall of King Cormac Mac Airt, close to half a mile (0.9 km) in length, where the kings became gods through a symbolic ritual mating with the Earth Goddess while their warriors feasted.

The hall, the Teach Midhchuarta, was believed to have been divided into five aisles, according to the medieval chroniclers. In the central aisle stood the great cauldrons, the fires for roasting and the flaming torches. On either side were aisles with booths in which the host's guests sat, in places allocated according to the nobility of their birth and their current social status.

Other pagan ceremonies included the games and fair, Aonach Tailte, which were held on the Hill of Tailte about half-way between the market towns of Navan and Kells. The foot races and the throwing of weights continued at this site for centuries into the Christian era and were held formally for the last time under the patronage of Roderick O'Connor, the high king of Ireland, in 1168, one year before the arrival of the Norman knights from Britain. In the early years of Irish independence, romantics in the new Irish Free State attempted to revive the games, but their efforts at mock-Celticism quickly petered out.

Another great festival of the ancient Celts was Samhain, which was held every three years on the Hill of Ward, overlooking the County Meath town of Athboy, on the eve of a pagan feast, the night known to us now as Hallowe'en. This was a wild and savage occasion with human sacrifices offered and victims burned as offerings by the druids to the gods; this was the true "Hallowe'en 1," far more frightening than the most horrific of horror movies.

These old Celtic traditions and the places intimately associated with them are, for all their mysticism, for all their embellishment over the millennia, younger than other more mysterious traditional places in this county. Along the banks of the Boyne, and particularly in the area surrounding

OPPOSITE: Slane Castle, with the River Boyne in the background. William of Orange's forces crossed near here during the battle of the Boyne in 1690. The original castle was built for a Norman family named Fleming, but in the late 17th century it passed to the Conyngham family, who had a new building put up in 1785. Rock concerts have been held here regularly, and the gatehouse appears on the U2 album "The Unforgettable Fire". Curiously in 1991, after this photograph was taken and the album was released, the castle was badly damaged by fire.

one large loop of its journey to the Irish Sea, an unknown people settled; their great burial grounds, some nearly 5000 years old, remain.

Who these people were, no one knows, but they knew of the cycles of the sun and they buried their chieftains in splendor. The complex at Newgrange has been dated scientifically to be from 3100 B.C. Each year, on the days around 21st December – the winter solstice – a shaft of light penetrates the dark, 30 yard (27 m) passageway and focuses on the very center of the tomb chamber. The precision of the event and the design of the "roof box" through which the sun's rays are admitted, rule out suggestions of a fluke, an accident, a mere coincidence. The great chamber, it seems, was designed 5000 years ago as a solar observatory.

The arrival of the sun's light at the very doors of the dead on the shortest days of the year must have symbolized rebirth and renewal; new light and new hope to the not-so-primitive people who lived in the bend of the Boyne.

From where did those people come? Legend is virtually unanimous that the earliest inhabitants of Ireland arrived directly from Spain, the land of the sun. More likely, however, is the far less romantic but more scientific notion that they made their way from continental Europe by the shortest sea routes: across the English Channel and the narrow sea between the southernmost tips of Scotland and the northeast coast of Ireland. Wherever they came from, they found their way to Meath; to the center of the mystical in Ireland; to the valley of the River Boyne which saw the birth of Celtic myth, legend and civilization in Ireland, but also witnessed its death.

At the town of Oldbridge, not far from Newgrange, on the first day of July in the year of 1690, two great armies faced one another across the river. On the northern bank stood 36,000 Dutch, English, Danish and German troops loyal to King William III and the reformed Protestant religion; to the south the ground

OPPOSITE: Remains of the church and college on the Hill of Slane, County Meath. According to legend, the first Paschal fire in Ireland was kindled here by St. Patrick, and a church was founded here by St Earc. The existing ruins consist of a church and the ruins of a college founded in 1612 and occupied at one time by Capuchin monks.

was held by 26,000 mainly Irish and French soldiers loyal to William's father-in-law, the Stuart king, James II, and the Catholic faith.

Among the first to run when the battle swung in William's favor was James himself, although, his army remained intact to fight again at Aughrim in County Galway a year later – and this time to lose more disastrously. The old Gaelic civilization, debilitated 89 years earlier by defeat at Kinsale, in County Cork (where, incidentally, James had landed to begin his campaign) was now on its last legs. The landed Catholic families fled to the continent just as the losers at Kinsale, the Ulster princes of the O'Neill and O'Donnell lines, had done following that earlier defeat.

O'Neill and O'Donnell, the earls of Tyrone and Tyrconnell, left for Spain; those defeated at the Boyne went initially to France and spread from there throughout Europe. Some of them, and their descendants, did well for themselves. Richard Hennessy and his successors prospered in the region of Cognac; the Taaffe family provided a first minister to the Habsburgs.

Those left behind were less fortunate. Lands and estates were lost; the peasantry – not that their lot was prosperous under their indigenous landlords – fell into despair and a destitution unparalleled in western Europe. Old traditions petered out. The stories of former glory lived on but were told in the English language and thus diminished from great saga to tales spoken in impoverished cabins.

Ironically, Meath today is the only county in the province of Leinster where the Gaelic tongue is still spoken as the vernacular. The Gaeltacht region in the parish of Rath Chairn near Athboy is not, however, the result of the tenacity of a small group of the indigenous population, but stems from a social experiment of the 1930s in which families from the beautiful region of Connemara left their infertile, rocky and tiny parcels of land in the west to take up small-holdings on an estate which was divided amongst them.

Unlike the rest of Gaelic-speaking Ireland, where the ancient language is in peril, the number of Irish speakers in Rath Chairn is growing as time goes on. Thus the language still lives, albeit artificially, in the cradle of Gaelic civilization.

Offaly
Reaching for the stars

The county of Offaly is best known for its stretches of bogland and for its wild Slieve Blooms, which, rare for Irish mountains, are not close to the sea. It is also the site of "St Kieran's City" at Clonmacnois, on the banks of the Shannon, where the impressive remains of a large and significant monastic settlement, dating from 545 A.D., describe a time when it was a center of Celtic learning, literature and art, an era when most of the rest of Europe was being engulfed by the barbarian invasions.

Another of Offaly's sources of repute rests in the demesne of Birr Castle, home of the Parsons family, earls of Rosse for 14 generations. Here in its Gothic-style housing lies the tube of what was, from the 1840s until 1917, the greatest telescope in the world, the "Leviathan of Birr" which was constructed by Lord Oxmantown (later the 3rd earl of Rosse) in 1845.

In the first half of the 19th century when work began there had been a tradition of secrecy among the experts in glass and mirror-making, so Oxmantown,

deciding to make his mirror from metal rather than glass, built a forge and enlisted the services of a blacksmith, a carpenter, and laborers from his own estate. He then invented a steam-driven apparatus to polish the metal, and the final result, known as the "Three Foot Telescope," was installed in 1839.

However, within a year, plans were already underway to build an even greater telescope. In 1840, Dr Thomas Romney Robinson, director of the Armagh Observatory, reported that, "Lord Oxmantown is about to construct a telescope of unequalled dimensions. He intends it to be six feet aperture and fifty feet focus...his character is an assurance that it will be devoted, in the most unreserved manner, to the service of astronomy, while the energy that could accomplish such a triumph and the liberality that has placed his discoveries in this difficult art within reach

BELOW: Hough's pub, Banagher, County Offaly.
OPPOSITE: A landscape transformed by peat cutting.

of all, may justly be reckoned among the highest distinctions of Ireland."

Work on the mirror presented, according to Robinson, a spectacle of "sublime beauty" in which "furnaces poured out huge columns of nearly monochromatic yellow flame, and the ignited crucibles during their passage through the air were fountains of red light, producing on the towers of the castle and the foliage of the trees, such accidents of color and shade as might almost transport fancy to the planets of a constrasted double star."

On 13th April 1842 the vast mirror had been cast. By February 1845 the great tube was in place and had been officially opened by Dean Peacock of the Church of Ireland who, to demonstrate its great size, paraded through it wearing his top hat and carrying his umbrella above his head.

The occasion was a great one, but its timing was inauspicious. In that year the potato crop was blighted and Ireland's Great Famine was underway. The earl, who sat as a representative Irish peer in the House of Lords in Westminster, ceased his astronomic activites and devoted his time to relief work. The "Leviathan" was left virtually unused until 1848 when the worst of the famine was over and the population of the country had collapsed through hunger, disease and emigration.

From the 1850s onwards, the fame of the telescope began to spread. The opening of the railways made Birr more accessible and the visitors' book at Birr Castle, intact today, recorded those who came to gaze further into space than was possible anywhere else on earth. A special feature in The Illustrated London News extended the fame of the 'Leviathan'.

The first entry is devoted to the visit of Charles Babbage, the scientist and inventor of the mechanical calculator, who came to see the stars on 9th September 1850 and was followed quickly by a Mr John Morrison of New York, Professor E.J. Santamour of Geneva and, with a flourish, Le Chevalier Sigismund Neukomm of Geneva who arrived at this place set among the peat bogs of central Ireland in August 1852. Many others followed from places as far afield as St Petersburg and Budapest. The voyages

OPPOSITE: Mount St. Joseph Abbey in Roscrea, County Offaly, was founded in 1878 by some Cistercian monks.

made by Dr Browne from Van Diemens Land (now Tasmania) in 1854 and that by the first New Zealander recorded in the visitors' book, a certain Mr Studholme, in 1892, beggar description.

When these intrepid astromers arrived at Birr their problems were by no means over. There was often cloud and consequently long waits for the night skies to clear. Mirrors became tarnished and had to be removed for polishing. All in all, it was a business that required not only painstaking study and endurance, but also a great deal of patience.

So it continued into the early years of the 20th century until, in 1916, Birr's full time astronomer, Otto Boeddicker, from Germany, was forced to leave Ireland as an "enemy alien" in the course of the First World War. A year later a larger telescope than the Leviathan was built at Mount Wilson in the United States with a 100 inch (254 cm) reflector and the great days of Birr had ended.

But in the three-quarters of a century of its operation the great telescope made remarkable contributions to the science of astronomy. The 3rd earl of Rosse had died in 1866 having left behind fine drawings of the planets and having discovered the spiral nature of nebulae.

The small market town took its important visitors in its stride. It had been laid out by the earlier members of the Parsons family in the 18th century with a neat square and the fine Georgian Oxmantown Mall which leads to the entrance of the castle and its demesne.

A statue of the duke of Cumberland, scourge of the Jacobites, had been commissioned to be placed on a Doric column in the center of the square but was never erected. The column stands bare to this day. The buildings of the town's center exude the classical elegance of their period and perhaps the finest is "John's Hall," an Ionic temple, built in 1828 to the memory of John Clere Parsons, the 3rd earl's brother, a brilliant mathmatician, who died of typhoid in his twenties.

Close by, on John's Mall, stands the fine statue, by John Henry Foley, of William Parsons, the 3rd earl of Rosse, who made his front lawn the center of world astronomy, and who shared his discoveries and his great telescope with all who expressed a serious interest in the science.

Westmeath

With its 'golden voice'

Westmeath was hived off from the ancient province of Meath by a decree of Henry VIII which declared: "For as much as the shire of Meath is great and large and the west part thereof is beset with divers of the King's enemies and his writs have not been obeyed, in consideration thereof it is thought meet that the said shire should be divided."

In short, the Gaelic way of life had persisted longer here than in most of the province of Leinster. The chieftains with their poets, bards and musicians lingered on in this region, which borders on the still-Gaelic province of Connacht.

Two market towns today dominate this intensely rural county which is famous mainly for its beef herds, but also for one man who took the musical world by storm in the early part of this century.

It is certain that somewhere, silently, in an attic near you, there is a "golden voice," first heard in County Westmeath in 1884. Our grandfathers and, more particularly, our grandmothers – for the voice

belonged to a "fine figure of a man" – whether in Ireland, Britain, the United States or further afield in Australia and New Zealand, might have collected the records of the tenor, John McCormack. Some of them may still be in your own attic to this day.

It is a long artistic way from the narrow streets of Athlone, Ireland's most central town, to the auditoriums of the Teatro alla Scala in Milan and the Metropolitan and Carnegie Hall in New York, but that is the journey McCormack made.

His parents, Scottish-born of Irish origin, had returned to the "old country" where his father obtained work at the Athlone woollen mills. Their son was a bright lad who gained a scholarship to a boarding school in Sligo, won several singing competitions but was astute enough to realize that his tenor voice needed training, and that Italy was the place where the job should be done.

He set about raising the funds to achieve this and, after some months tuition with Maestro Vincenzo Sabbatini, made his debut as a 22-year-old in the title role of Mascagni's L'Amico Fritz in the Teatro Chiabrero in Savona.

After that bright start things went badly, but McCormack was a tough working-class boy from Athlone at a time when Ireland was one of the poorest countries in Europe and Athlone was by no means to be counted among its more prosperous centers. He was full of determination to make a name for himself and, according to those who knew him, was possessed of "language so earthy a docker might blush to hear him." Odd, is it not, that the tongue which held a voice which rivalled that of Caruso, which lilted the muscial phrases of Mozart's *Il Mio Tesoro*, could be capable of strong language that could put a stevedore to shame?

It is odd too that the rivalry between McCormack and Caruso was of the friendliest of natures. No hard feelings were entertained. Each tenor deferred to the other as the greatest of the day. Both became millionaires, of course, and both became mainstays of the RCA Victor recording company. The rivals were also personal friends.

But there was more to it than that. Caruso was an

OPPOSITE: An aerial image of Athlone. The city's strategic position on the main road between Galway and Dublin has given it a turbulent history.

actor and an artist, as shown by his affectionate caricatures of McCormack in pen and ink. Caruso excelled in the flamboyant settings of Grand Opera. McCormack was a bad actor, but was the master of the individual concert appearance.

McCormack's success was phenonemal. He was the first mega-star of music and this success led to a mansion in Hollywood and a grand estate in Ireland which was once the seat of the earls of Drogheda. He, too, was ennobled by being made a Count of the Papal Court, and for a great part of his life was known as "John, Count McCormack," or simply as "the Count," to his thousands of admirers.

He was lionized in America, being the guest of honor at President Wilson's Fourth of July concert in 1918, having a year previously renounced "all previous allegiances" to the United Kingdom – which included Ireland – to become an American citizen. This act was virtually ignored in Ireland, but, officially, England took offence, as his change of nationality had taken place a few months before America had entered the "Great War." There was an irony here, too, for it was in England, after his voice and his fortune had failed, that his most loyal audiences remained.

Failure of voice was a natural phenomenon, but the failure of fortune was self-inflicted, with the help of a weakness for slow racehorses. The story persists of a meeting on The Curragh in County Kildare between the trainer of "the Count's" expensive charges and a stable boy.

"I thought you would be in Dublin today, sir," the boy suggested. "Why, son?" asked the trainer. "The Count is singing in the Theater Royal, sir," the boy replied. This elicted the immortal response: "My dear boy, when we are finished with him, your Count shall be singing outside the Theater Royal."

It didn't quite end up like that, but the young man who set out from Westmeath to conquer the world was, to a large extent, successful in his quest before the world conquered him. Having achieved world-wide fame in the sphere in which he was talented, he, in his insecurity, sought fame in a sphere, that of the turf, in which his talents were limited in the extreme. Still, his memory remains in the minds of the operatic cognoscenti and his voice, in brittle Bakelite, lies in the attics of Westmeath and the world.

Wexford

Crucible of the 1798 rebellion

Wexford is truly a place apart. It is separated by natural barriers from the rest of Ireland but with close connections by sea to Britain and to mainland Europe. For this reason the county has provided access to immigrants from abroad from the earliest times; to invading armies later. Now, at Rosslare, it provides ferry connections to South Wales and to Le Havre and Cherbourg in France.

It was in Wexford, in 1169, that the Anglo-Norman conquest of Ireland began. This was followed by settlers from England and Wales. Here, as well as the Gaelic surnames of Kinsella, Murphy, O'Connor and Kehoe, can be found families called Dake, Fleming, Devereux, Furlong, and Harvey.

For centuries Wexford has been mainly an English-speaking county. Even in the 1798 rebellion, when the county rose up against British rule, the rebels tended to be English speakers, while their loyalist opponents included Gaelic-speaking militia from the province of Munster.

Today, the English language is delivered in Wexford with a unique accent. In earlier time, in certain parts of the county, people conversed in a dialect known as "Yola," which bore strong resemblance to that of Somerset in England, especially regarding the

BELOW: Fishing boats, Kilmore Quay, County Wexford.
OPPOSITE: J.F. Kennedy Memorial Park, Slieve Caoilte.

tendency to pronounce the letter "S" as "Z." Remnants of the old way of speaking persist in the southern baronies of Forth and Bargy, a flat sea-bound area entwined with little roads.

The English of Ireland is full of dialect words, but in the vast majority of cases these are survivors from the Gaelic which was once the dominant language. What makes Wexford, and Forth and Bargy in particular, different in its speech from most of the rest of the country, is that the dialect words are essentially English in origin, with some Flemish undertones to complicate matters further.

To keek is to peep, to prime a water pump is to hench it, if there is a cold easterly wind it is a "hash day." Wexford is famous, too, for its "mummers" – bands of singers who move from house to house at certain times of year. It is also home to the country's only indigenous Christmas Carol, "The Wexford Carol." All those traditions have been imported from abroad, as have the blood-lines of many of the people, yet Wexford is essentially Irish, as Irish as anywhere in Ireland and more Irish than most places.

In the summer of 1798, inspired by the ideals of the United Irishmen (a nationalist group imbued with the spirit of the French and American revolutions), the Catholic peasantry of Wexford united against loyalist forces in a war of short duration but intense bloodiness. The rebels had some spectacular successes early on and fought bravely in the hope of a landing by sympathetic French forces. However, it was all over in six weeks. The Wexford rebels, armed with pikes, were defeated by the might of loyalist forces in the form of regular soldiers, mercenaries from Hesse and a tough regiment of the north Cork militia, and treated brutally in that defeat. Towards the end, the idealism of the rebels had degenerated into sectarianism, the major outrage being the burning alive of Protestant loyalist families in a barn in the townland of Scullabogue. The French landed at Killala in County Mayo six weeks after the rising in Wexford had been put down. Their intervention was too small and too far away to make any difference.

Bitterness and repression haunted the county for

OPPOSITE: The gothic, nineteenth-century Johnstown Castle, County Wexford, is now an agricultural college and a museum of the history of farming in Ireland.

many years after that fateful summer and, even today, the year of 1798 is still engraved on the hearts of the people of Wexford. It was the greatest calamity in the history of a county which was spared the worst of the Great Famine in the 19th century. Almost every Wexford town and village has its commemorative statue of a 1798 rebel, pike in hand.

> What's the news, what's the news
> Oh my bold Shelmalier,
> With your long-barrelled gun of the sea.
> Goodly news, goodly news,
> Do I bring youth of Forth,
> Goodly news do I bring Bargy man,
> For the boys march at dawn,
> From the South to the North,
> Led by Kelly the boy from Killane.
> BALLAD OF THE WEXFORD REBELS OF 1798

The county town of Wexford is one of delightful, narrow streets in which some famous people and some interesting people were born. Jane Francis Elgee, mother of Oscar Wilde, was born in Wexford town and her epigrams were almost as famous as her son's. On "respectability," for example, she is reputed to have said: "Respectability is for tradesmen. We [the Wildes] are above respectability."

But the true character of Wexford is shaped by the sea. There is a seafaring tradition here which is stronger than anywhere else in Ireland, with the possible exception of the town of Arklow in the neighboring county of Wicklow, and this latter is truly an extension of the Wexford tradition.

The Irish Sea coast along the east of the county and the small Atlantic coastline to the south, which are dotted with beaches and quaint villages with their local pubs, has become the prime holiday haunt of Dubliners. It is close enough for a day trip, yet far enough to be completely uncontaminated by the city.

Almost the entire coast of Wexford is important in the ornithological sphere. The North Slob, hardly an enticing name, is situated across the bridge from Wexford town and contains the Wexford Wildfowl Reserve, where 30 percent of the world's Greenland white-fronted geese spend their winters. Perhaps this is no wonder since Wexford has more hours of sunshine annually than anywhere else in Ireland.

189

Wicklow

The "Garden of Ireland"

At Powerscourt in Enniskerry in County Wicklow, a mere 12 miles (19 km) from the bustling center of Dublin, the pointed Sugarloaf Mountain provides a perfect backdrop for the artificial lake with its fountain, its terraces and its statues of Pegasus, with the effect that the gardens appear to lead naturally and seamlessly to the true countryside. No line of division can be perceived.

Nowhere else in Ireland could this have been possible; certainly not in the ruggedness of the Atlantic coast where the contrast between the gentility of the 18th-century Anglo-Irish landscapers and the savage grandeur of the terrain would have been impossible to reconcile.

But Wicklow is the "Garden of Ireland." Its scenery is naturally graduated; the great massif slopes gently to the sea on the east and to the Central Plain on the west. Here, there are no great cliffs battered by the ocean's rage, no deep inlets, no craggy shores, but instead sloping pastures filled with black-faced sheep ushered from pasture to pasture by the slender-faced Wicklow collie. Where Wicklow reaches the sea there

BELOW: Gorse bushes in Glendalough Forest Park.
OPPOSITE: A cemetery, part of the extensive remains of a monastic site at Glendalough. St Kevin founded a hermitage here which became an important destination for pilgrims during the Middle Ages.

are long beaches, some of them, such as the three-mile (5 km) strand at Brittas Bay, crowded at weekends because of their proximity to Dublin, but others, known to a few, virtually empty whatever the weather and whatever the day of the week.

Wicklow, the county town, is also a Viking foundation and takes its name from that of the 9th century settlement, Vikingalo. Now, long after the northern warriors have departed into history, Wicklow is a small port and a seaside town set in gentle countryside.

Rugged beauty does exist, but mainly in the deserted center, on the crests of Ireland's largest mountain chain, where Dubliners, at weekends in summer, hew peat, and picnic, and fill their lungs and, on the occasional clear day, view the mountain tops of Snowdonia in Wales.

The rest of the county slopes gently to the sea, its great houses and gardens nestling in valleys and glens which were gouged from the land in the harsh Ice Age, but which now provide generous micro-climates in which palms and yuccas are able to flourish, albeit at the northernmost limits of their existence.

From the time of the Norman conquest 800 years ago – a mere millisecond in the Irish historical mind – the families which ousted the O'Byrnes and O'Tooles from their traditional lands, settled, discarded their rough colonial ways and, in succeeding generations, opened their hearts and minds to the land and culture which surrounded them.

Before all that there had been houses and gardens in Wicklow, notably in the great 6th century monastic settlement established by St Coemgen, "Kevin," in Glendalough, "the valley of two lakes." After Kevin's death in 619 ad the monastery continued to flourish through the centuries. It began to decline following an attack by the English of Dublin in 1389, but was not finally put down until the conquest of Wicklow by the English in the 15th and 16th centuries.

The unused buildings, and there are so many of them that the place has been described as a "monastic city," then fell into decay. The more enlightened hands

OPPOSITE: The Great Sugar Loaf Mountain, near Enniskerry reaches a height of 1660 feet (506 meters). At its foot are the beautiful gardens of Powerscourt.

of the restorers of the Office of Public Works have been in action since 1873 and have saved the settlement with its chapels, cathedral and hermitages from total ruin.

Kevin was, of course, a holy man and celibate, according to legend, to the point of violence. The stories say that he once flung an aspiring temptress to her death from the heights above the lakes.

Much later, another man of Wicklow, in times of greater sophistication, was to take a woman to his heart instead of dashing her to the rocks with consequences which led to one of the great personal and political tragedies of the 19th century.

Charles Stewart Parnell was born at Avondale, near Rathdrum, in 1846, the year that saw Ireland broken by the Great Famine. In 1875, he took his place in the House of Commons, in Westminster, where he devoted his life to returning the seat of power in Ireland to College Green whence it had been wrested in a welter of bribery in the final days of the 18th century.

Many of the "honorable" members had accepted hard cash to relieve their encumbered estates, while others were tempted by "ennoblement" and accepted "Union Peerages" in return for their votes which dissolved the Irish parliament and created the United Kingdom of Great Britain and Ireland.

Intent on undoing their work, Parnell succeeded in casting a spell on his country. He was "our poor dead king" to Joyce; the "uncrowned king of Ireland" to the dispossessed peasantry; and finally the tormented leader, politically broken by his love for Kitty O'Shea, the wife of a fellow member of the nationalist Irish Party at Westminster.

The "Parnell Affair" carved the heart of the nationalist cause in two, with provincial Ireland, a geographical pocket or two apart, and its Roman Catholic clergy, denouncing him as an adulterer, and Dublin's open-hearted artisans, strongly supporting the "poor king" until his untimely death.

Avondale is an elegant "Big House" of its time, set in 500 acres (202 ha) of tranquil and pleasant woods and gardens. Its true significance, however, and overwhelming attraction, stems from the great man who was born and lived there; the poignant redolence of a great political and personal tragedy is its strongest feature. A place of beauty mixed with sadness and tragedy, it captures the soul of Ireland.

The Province of Munster

by Damien Enright

Munster is the largest province in Ireland. It is a rich and confident province, having three of the Republic's six cities, four of her great rivers, and the great flow and estuary of the Shannon, longest river in Britain and Ireland. It has a massive diversity of landscape, from the most fertile, the Golden Vale, to the least fertile, the naked limestone plains of north Clare. There, in the Burren, it has the greatest polarity of botany, where indigenous flowers found elsewhere only in the Alps and Mediterranean lowlands grow side by side. It is at the northernmost range of Lusitanian vegetation, and Kerry and Cork have fuchsia hedges, rhododendron forests, and plants found nowhere else north of Spain.

Of all the provinces, it has the longest Gulf Stream coast and the mildest climate. It may rain, deep in the west, but there are a greater number of frost-free days here than anywhere north of the Channel Isles. Migrant birds flock in their hundred thousands to Munster estuaries in winter, and Cape Clear is the oldest bird observatory in the Republic.

The Munster coast is the native vacationers' favorite, and who would know better than the Irish themselves? Of Ireland's 66 Blue Flag beaches (those meeting European Union standards relating to water quality and general cleanliness), 26 are in Munster. For the saltwater fisherman, it is lapped by the most fertile sea – three-quarters of all specimen sea fish are caught in southwestern waters. Here, the first sharks of summer are hooked, tagged and released, drifting north on the Gulf Stream. Whales pass by, and giant leather-back turtles circumnavigating the Atlantic from their nesting beaches in the Caribbean. For the

inland angler, Munster rivers hold the most bountiful stocks of brown trout, and almost every river has a respectable salmon run. Waterville is one of the best sea-trout lakes in Europe.

Kerry also has a very large colony of natterjack toads which live in the dunes backing the five-mile (8 km) long strand at Inch. The elegant snow white egret, a new visitor, favors the southwest and if it nests in Ireland, as is the birders' hope, it is likely to be in Munster. Munster has, also, a richer variety of warm-blooded wild creatures than any other province, being the main redoubt of the pine marten, bank vole and red squirrel. The Munster people are warm blooded themselves, and famous for sport and song.

Munster was the nursery of many a journeyman saint who set out from stone cells by lake and sea to carry the Christian light to Dark Age Europe. The oldest surviving Christian church in Ireland is Gallarus Oratory, near Slea Head, and the first Protestant church built in Ireland is in Bandon, County Cork. Everywhere the landscape is dotted with relics of an earlier worship: stone circles and dolmens, their capstones like altars under the vault of the sky.

Munster has always produced Irish patriots and liberators. It was Brian Boru, from Clare, High King of Ireland, who defeated the Vikings. The ancient abbey that tops the Rock of Cashel-of-the-Kings rises dramatic and lovely out of the Tipperary plain. Daniel O'Connell, "the Liberator," was born in Kerry; Michael Collins, who led the fight for Irish independence in 1919–1921, was born and died in west Cork. The cottage in which De Valera, our first Taoiseach, was reared was at Bruree in the Golden Vale.

Cashel is only one of thousands of ruins of old Ireland still extant in Munster. Cork has 2000 prehistoric sites, and Limerick's Lough Gur offers fine

OPPOSITE: A waterfall in the Comeragh Mountains.
FOLLOWING PAGE: Adrigole Harbour on Bantry Bay.

examples of early lake dwellings. County Limerick, alone, has 400 castles. Everywhere in Munster one comes upon elegant, roofless abbeys; squat oratories; ivy-bound churches; gutted stately houses.

It is also quite likely that Munster was home to the first potatoes, imported from America and welcomed at Youghal by Sir Walter Raleigh, also an import to Ireland, but not so welcome himself. At Youghal, also, was possibly smoked the first pipe of the insidious tobacco – but we can blame Raleigh for that.

Munster has some of the finest progenitors and practitioners of Irish music among the people of Clare. Ireland's composer, Wallace, of Waterford, was Munster born, as was the modern composer, Sean O'Riada, and the great poet in Gaelic, Aodhagán O'Rathaille. In science, Munstermen also made their mark – Boyle, of Boyle's Law, was born at Lismore Castle in 1627.

For sporting, the Munster people are famous. Jack Doyles, the boxer, was born at Cobh on the Shannon Estuary. Cork also has more All Ireland Hurling medals than any other county, and was home to the legendary hurler, Christy Ring. Its road bowlers sling a bowl with greater flair and accuracy than any others, lobbing hedges and curving corners, champions of Ireland again and again.

Munster vies with Leinster for fame in horseflesh. The first steeplechase ever was galloped between the steeples of Buttevant and Doneraile, in County Cork. The fine stud farms of Tipperary and north Cork are famous everywhere. Sons of Shergar, prince of stallions, can be seen grazing the parklands on long, slim legs. Vincent O'Brien, doyen of trainers, has his stables, still in business, at Ballydoyle.

Master MacGrath, the world-beating greyhound, was pupped in Waterford. Munster offers the finest, most scenic golf in Europe, with four world-class links courses close together in Kerry and Clare. The oldest yacht club in the world is on Cork harbor.

Being the most beautiful, Munster is the most filmed province. Moby Dick was made off the Cork coast; Ryan's Daughter, on the coast of Kerry. Craftsmen abound, and the finest crystal glass in the world, often imitated but never equalled, is made in Waterford.

In Munster, the softest Irish and the most melodious English is spoken. When Cork men or Kerry women speak, you might think they were singing to you. This is, perhaps, one reason why visitors fall in love with Munster.

The old Irish Tourist Board slogan claimed, 'The most interesting people come to Ireland..." Many come to Munster, and they stay. There is hardly a village along the southwest seaboard that isn't host to a well-known expatriate writer, painter or film-maker and stars of stage, screen and pop choose Munster to bring "quality" and privacy into their lives. These glitterati are welcomed, but in no way do they eclipse the light of local talent. Humor is the breath of life and the tradition of talk, song, dance and banter is treasured. Native vernacular brilliance blossoms behind every bush.

Clare

County of stone and song

The awesome Cliffs of Moher in north Clare rise 700 feet (213 m) out of the sea like black ramparts. Great slabs of paving stone, etched with the fossil tracks of creatures of a million years ago, wall off the more dangerous corners along the cliff path. The bare cliffs wear a toupee of green fields, across which the wind blows. It blows towards the Burren where there are no fields at all.

Someone once told Cromwell that the Burren was a "savage land, yielding neither water enough to drown a man, nor a tree to hang him, nor soil enough to bury him…" Cromwell, being interested in doing all these things to the Irish, didn't bother to go there.

However, the description is hardly accurate. There are no trees, but scoops in the limestone plains support dense thickets of hazel and scrub. In spring, the 116 sq miles (300 sq km) of Burren stone is a wild rock garden, colonized by a disparate and wonderful botany. Blue Spring Gentians, Cinquefoil and plants rare or absent elsewhere in Ireland grow in profusion. Mountain Avens, found in the high Alps, bloom side-by-side with orchids normally confined to the Mediterranean.

It is a surprise, almost a shock, to come upon the Burren landscape. It is hard to believe one is still in Ireland, indeed hard to believe one is on earth, for the miles of flat, naked rock, stretching as far as the eye can see, are more reminiscent of our image of the moon. The low, bleached hills, also of limestone, might be outcrops in the Sahara, more so when seen through the staggering air of a hot summer's day.

These grey plains, or pavements – and pavements they are, with deep fissures between – were made from the compressed skeletons of plants and animals which, 340 million years ago, died on the floor of a warm, carboniferous sea. Limestone easily erodes, and the cracks are the result of water running over the pavement and finding their way underground.

On green oases, small farms dot the landscape. A red barn may appear in one's carefully framed photo of a dolmen, with washing in the yard on a line. Sheep graze the fields, eating, perhaps, rare Alpine flora. One imagines that at least a few of these weird plants have taken the opportunity to escape to richer pasture.

Here, stone forts, wedge graves and dolmens are much more common than farms. Man settled on the Burren 10,000 years ago and from his visible remains one might think that in Neolithic times the place was a veritable metropolis. In fact this was not the case. It is simply that the stones have been left undisturbed, there being no land to plough around them, and no need to use them for building. Loose stones are plentiful on the Burren.

Poulnabrone is one of the more accessible, and famous, of the table stones. It has featured on Irish postage stamps. One can stand beneath the canopy stone and, should the rain clouds pass over, it would make an adequate shelter from the weather. It is set on a slight mound, stark and dramatic against the sky.

Deep within Ailwee Cave, which is on the edge of the Burren, it is so dark that one's eyes could never become accustomed, however long one stayed. Long gone are the Irish bears that once slept there in winter. Cave bones have also included those of African wildcats, reindeer and Arctic foxes, animals as disparate in habitat as today's plants. We, ourselves, probably made homes in these caves not so very long ago in the scale of time. Stalagmites, no thicker or longer than a pencil, rise from the cave floor. Many commenced growing before the birth of Christ.

Holy wells are everywhere in the Burren, each patronized for its particular cure. Thus, the waters of St Senan's Well in Kilshanny were held to cure blindness, while sufferers from backache went to the well at Killnaboy. St Brigid's Well, a cure for all ills, is still a place of pilgrimage on Garland Sunday, at the end of July.

At Corcomroe are the ruins of a great abbey, open to the sky. At Kilfenora, a sleepy town on the

OPPOSITE: Bunratty Castle, County Clare

pavement's edge, are found three High Crosses and the remains of a fourth, their Burren stone carved with intricate detail.

Perhaps it was the wind over the limestone pavements of the Burren, or the waves breaking on the treeless coast that inspired the airs of Clare, but whatever the cause, the county has nurtured the very soul of Irish traditional music, from the piping of Willie Clancy to the lilting ballads of Christy Moore. Each year at Lisdoonvarna, the capital of the Burren, a summer musical festival draws folk singers and musicians from all over the world.

As well as being a musical center, Lisdoonvarna is also a mecca for lonely bachelors. Each September, following an old tradition, unmarried farmers from all over Munster leave their cows, and spinsters their spinning wheels, to come to the town in search of life partners. For a whole month, match-makers ply their ancient trade while their clients dance, drink and make eyes at one another. By the time they leave, some will have sealed a bond. Others, not having found their fancy, will wait for another crop, another year.

Cork

"On the banks of my own lovely Lee"

Cork is Ireland's biggest county. It stretches from the rich lands of the Golden Vale in the north, to the flat lands of the east, to the Poor Law peninsulas and mountains of the west. To the south is the sea.

Long ago, it was the hub of Neolithic settlement and worship. The county boasts more stone circles per acre than anywhere in these islands, more than 2000 prehistoric sites, littered, as casually as furze bushes, over the landscape. Look behind a bush and you may find an undiscovered dolmen. The more notable sites, like Drombeg, are advertised; it would require a forest of finger-posts to announce them all.

Cork, the county capital, is a sleepy city. Compared with Galway, Limerick or Kilkenny, it is still in the Edwardian era. But with the Shandon bells ringing out over it, the Lee flowing through it, and high hills rising from its riverside streets, it is a romantic place.

It is famous for "de paper," the Cork Examiner, now gone national and dropped the "Cork." "Cork" is a name of mixed blessings, translated from Corcaigh, "a marsh," on which the city was built. When the notorious Black and Tans and British Auxiliaries burned Cork city in 1920 during the War of Independence, they went west looking for trouble with burnt corks in their hats.

East County Cork is noted for Ballycotton, a small fishing port, which, along with Ballymacoda, is a great estuary for wintering birds. Youghal, where tradition has it that Sir Walter Raleigh planted the first "spud" and smoked the first cigarette, is an old walled sea port. It is a popular summer resort for the Irish, with a hurdy-gurdy amusement park and fair still there 40 years after my childhood visits – Perks Amusements, it is called.

LEFT: The ruins of Charles Fort, Kinsale, County Cork.
OPPOSITE: Historic churchyards abound in Cork.

WARNING
BEFORE KISSING THE
STONE REMOVE ALL
LOOSE VALUABLES

ABOVE: Fish for sale at "The English Market", Cork.
OPPOSITE: Kissing the Blarney Stone, Blarney Castle.

Cork north of the River Blackwater is the Golden Vale of rich grasslands, cheese, butter and fat farmers. Here, Edmund Spenser, of *Faerie Queen* fame, had vast lands at Kilcolman, whence the gentle poet preached repression of the Irish so bloody that even Elizabeth I's colonizing government would not entertain it.

If Dubliners think of Cork city as the "sticks," they consider west Cork as an arcane island on the southern seaboard. With the exception of Galway's Connemara, no other county has a region so distinct and a people so distinctive that it is given its own name. "North Cork" refers to geography; "west Cork" stands for a culture. It is a culture much sought after by "blow-ins." Coast and hinterland are speckled with the renovated cottages and mansions of famous writers, film-makers and artists. However, the "native" culture remains thick on the ground.

Much of west Cork is a hilly land of small, colorful fields, with lichen-grown rocks that look like they have had orange paint splashed on them. Washed by the warm Gulf Stream, it is, in popular perception, the exotic land of rhododendron, fuchsia hedges, and picture postcard islands upon which peacocks roam. As one goes west from the city, the coastal strip of rocky land, with breaks of gorse and heather, becomes wider. Forty miles (64 km) from Cork, it stretches on both sides of the road, south to the sea and west to the Kerry mountains.

The west Cork people are no less colorful and individual than their landscape. It was here, during the war for Irish independence, that Flying Columns practiced their daring guerrilla tactics. The ill-fated Michael Collins was born in west Cork and shot there by other Irishmen, at Beal na mBlath, "the mouth of the flowers." Today, west Cork people are still proud and independent, a nation unto themselves, crowing at one another in sing-song voices, imaginative, rebellious and out of date.

The agricultural citizenry of Cork are fierce followers of sport, none more so than the west Cork farmers. Sulky racing and road bowling are favorites. "Sulkies" are game little horses that pull a light cart and driver around a track which may be a stretch of country road, or a beach with the tide out. It is unforgettable to watch horses and drivers raise spray from the near pools or race far off in a string against the sun-bright Atlantic. It is intoxicating to hear the cries of the bettors, the galloping commentary on the p.a. system. Here is racing in the vernacular: sulky and saddle racing; county men and women riding flat out across the sun-blessed Irish sands.

As a state of mind, west Cork may well be retreating west. Twenty miles (32 km) from the city, the up-market, yachting town of Kinsale – 'gourmet capital of Ireland' – bears little resemblance to, say, wild west Dunmanway or Skibbereen. In Dunmanway, on market day, one sees battered cars and tractors, men in caps with rolled down Wellington boots, and sheep in the back of Toyotas. This kind of exotica has long since disappeared from Kinsale.

The division is also economic. The farmer of the rugged hills and coast is a grizzled, hard-working heir to Poor Law land, a turf cutter, fisherman and all-round dealer, keeping his family on 50 acres (20 ha), 20 of them arable, the rest rock and bog. But, they say: "When God made time, he made plenty of it." So, he finds leisure time for beagling – pronounced "bageling" – with hounds that rarely catch a fox, sulky racing, road bowling and hurling. He does not shave on weekdays, and has a drink at weekends, driving the tractor to the pub.

West, in the Irish-speaking area of Ballyvourney, on the rocky farms of Hungry Hill or Roaring Water Bay, we are a long way from the huge, rich fields of the Bandon Valley and Barryroe where the milk quotas are high, the new bungalows have central heating, and the farmers sport four-wheel-drive jeeps. Yet, there is an affinity among the people. The landscape may be drained and tamed, but let no stranger say that the people are any less "west Cork."

LEFT: The waterfront of the River Lee, in the city of Cork. The city has always had something of a "foreign" quality, being settled in the Middle Ages by Norse and English, as well as Irish.

Kerry

Little climate, but much weather

The Kerry people are held, by the rest of the Irish, to be "cute," not in the American sense of being pretty – although, of course they are that – but in the sense of being able to outsmart their fellow countrymen at every turn.

They are also, out of jealousy, the butt of jokes, such as, "Did you hear the one about the Kerrymen who decided to climb the mountain? The scaffolding collapsed at 500 feet…" Kerry people are also known for their ability to answer a question with a question – this is part of their "cuteness." Asked if there is any chance of catching a few fish in his local wide stretch of the Atlantic Ocean, the dyed-in-the-bog Kerry person will eye one cutely and respond, "Is it the way you're fond of fish?"

Everything in Kerry is superlative. In Sneem, there is "the best selection of woollens in Ireland." Near Waterville, a bar claims "the most famous view in Ireland." Caherdaniel boasts "the only beach bar in Ireland." On a lonely bog road to the Skelligs, a guest house *cum* wine bar suddenly appears offering "the best Chinese and Indian food in Ireland." In self-confidence, the kingdom is next door to Texas.

Whatever the hyperbole, the physical beauty of Kerry is world class. It can indeed claim elements of greatness. If a Greek friend told me about Ephesus or an American friend about Big Sur, I would take them to the Ring of Kerry.

In summertime, the landscape of the Iveragh Peninsula is splashed with color. There is scarcely a square foot of grass that is not speckled with wild flowers; each small field a jewel in "the Ring." Heather purples the road side; fuchsia reddens the paths; montbretia edges the verges; loosestrife brightens the bogs. The rock faces are painted with contrasting grey and yellow lichens. Above, the clouds, moving across the sun, pattern the hills.

Kerry is a county with little climate, but much weather. The warm waters of the Gulf Stream wash between the open fingers of land. Temperatures are rarely less than 41°F (5°C) in winter, or more than 68°F (20°C) in summer. But, for all that, the main constant for much of the year is change. Mists or rain clouds drift in like veils off the western ocean. The sun, bright a few moments before, shines between them like a spotlight sweeping over the hills. "Softness" is the theme, and water, a pellucid, magical light.

The misty lakes and grandiose mountains were the epitome of the scenery celebrated by the romantic movement led by Sir Walter Scott. When Queen Victoria visited them, she was smitten instantly. Although familiar with the loveliness of the Scottish Highlands, she pronounced the Kerry panoramas the finest in her empire.

Turf cutting is big in Kerry. The drying black shocks of turf stand in the summer bogs among the yellow flag irises, the white bog cotton, and the deep and bronze pools. To strip the bogs is a pity. They sit like brown, hump-backed animals in the mix of landscape. It takes a million years to make a bog and its unique flora, once gone, is irreplaceable.

Kerry is known for the romance of its islands, the Blaskets and the Skellig Rocks. The Blaskets, hard berths for man or beast, are thrown out into the Atlantic, off Dingle, the last land in Europe. Until the 1930s they were home to a mere 30 souls, including one Tomás Ó Crohan, whose book, *The Islandman*, is a testament to the faith and stoicism of a simple man and his island neighbors. When measles and whooping cough came to the island, he wrote, "Three months I spent sitting up with those of my children who took them worst, and I got nothing for the time I spent, only the two best of them were carried off. That was another discouragement for us, God help us. I fancy the sorrow of it never left the mother, and from that time she began to fail, for she was not to live long, and never lasted to be old."

But, if there was tragedy on the island, there was also great joy and humor, and a great spirit in the

OPPOSITE: The Ring of Kerry.

people. He speaks of selling lobsters to a passing vessel in a rare time of plenty, "It was a good life in those days. Shillings came on shillings' heels…." He tells of the bonanza of cut timber swept off the deck of a ship; of his childhood; his first visit to the mainland. He writes of match-making and wedding feasts; of gathering seaweed; of seal hunting. He brings to life the love and faith of these unique folk. "We are poor, simple people, living from hand to mouth. We were apt and willing to live, without repining, the life the Blessed Master made for us, often ploughing the sea with only our hope in God to bring us through. We had characters of our own, each different from the other, and all different from the landsmen. I have done my best to set down the character of the people about me so that some record of us might live after us, for the likes of us will never be again."

Limerick

A deceptive county

Limerick people will tell you that Limerick women are the prettiest in Ireland. They point to the pages of the Irish Tatler, and photos of pretty girls at race meetings. Almost invariably, they are Limerick girls they say. However, to insist that they are beautiful above all other women in Ireland is extravagant. Women in every county are pretty, although this was not always the case. In the 1950s, farmers daughters tended, more than they do today, to plaster over their natural beauty with make-up and black mascara.

The natural outdoor looks of Irish women have since become fashionable, and the soft Irish climate is good for the skin. Irish women are extremely confident and "well able" for the men. They are not short of words, or wit, or character. In ancient Ireland, they were total equals, and Brehon Law absolutely upheld their right to divorce a husband on the important grounds that he was weak in bed.

Limerick women, much prized, are like their county, neatly manicured. In Limerick, one does not find the wild disarray of Kerry, Clare or west Cork. Fields by the road side are flat and lush, with the finest growth of grass in Ireland along the Golden Vale. Here, happily, in early summer, old meadows

BELOW: Limerick and the Shannon.
OPPOSITE: A quiet stretch of the River Shannon, County Limerick.

still sway with the heads of tall and diverse seed grasses, dock, dandelion, clover and plantain.

The roads through the back country are mainly straight. As we drove, the world about was entirely pastoral and gentle, the villages few and far between, the cottages by the roadside small and built before the age of shoe-box bungalows. On a mound heaved out of the plain, a square keep, with the ruin of a tall gable, once a Norman fortress, broke the skyline.

At Bruff and indeed at crossroad pubs all that Saturday afternoon, we saw cars parked, small boys in suits and little girls playing in their First Communion white dresses, pretty veils and bouquets askew. A few carried little white purses, no doubt crammed with their communion gifts of £5 and £10 notes.

Everywhere is lovely in May in Ireland, but for those who enjoy wilderness, as embodied in the wildness of migrant birds, the Limerick shore of the Shannon Estuary is most spectacular in the winter. The Shannon, the longest river in Britain and Ireland,

daily deposits a rich icing of silt in which billions of humble invertebrates breed, providing fat fare for the many birds that fly extraordinary distances to winter there. Knots breed 2000 miles (3218 km) away, in the thin tundra of the high Canadian Arctic; tiny dunlin, after breeding, fly south from Iceland. From Greenland, white-fronted geese wing in to Shannon. The great river obligingly recedes twice daily, exposing thousands of acres of invertebrate rich-mud.

The survival of the estuary is vital to the survival of its indigents which Ireland has an international obligation to conserve. No less than six species of birds are present in internationally important numbers. They are as much natives of Ireland as anywhere and spend half the year here. They may be born north of the Arctic Circle, but which comes first, the goose or the egg?

Out on the marshes of the Shannon, one realizes that Limerick is a deceptive county. The great estates and sylvan softness of the grasslands might be a thousand miles away. Limerick has been well-settled for millennia; Stone Age forts, castles, keeps, churches and modern towns abound. But the shores of the vast Shannon confluence are as wild as anywhere in Ireland. They are especially magnificent on a winter evening when the mudflats are gilded by the dying sun.

On the low islands, a thousand lapwing stand facing into the wind, their topknots dancing. Between them, dunlin skitter like clockwork mice. On the creeks, rafts of teal and widgeon drift in the evening silence, heads under wings.

Every now and then, as if by some unknown telepathy, all the waders rise together. Lapwing lift and wheel, black and white wings checkered against the sky. Above them, great flocks of golden plover soar and circle. Curlew beat into the wind. Then they all descend, light as feathers.

My favorite moment is when dunlin come. At breathtaking speed, they flash and bank in formation over the roosting flocks. You can see this wildness any winter evening on the Shannon marshes. Just a short distance from Limerick city, but it is timeless. It is glorious. It is free.

LEFT: Rural workers, County Limerick.

Tipperary

Hunters and hurlers

Tipperary is a rich inland county with a town called Golden and mountains called the Silvermines. Approaching from the south, mountains edge the Tipperary plain on both sides of the main Cork to Dublin road, made more dramatic by snow in winter and blazing gorse in summer.

The great plain of Tipperary has many impressive raised bogs, one of the best known being the Littleton Bog. Here, pollens from the peats and mosses that have grown and decayed in the bog over the last 12,000 years provide geologists with an very accurate record of the vegetation, climate and agriculture of a geological period which has since become known as the "Littletonian" era.

The history and ruins of time abound in Tipperary. One of the most magnificent of ancient Irish relics is the Rock of Cashel-of-the-Kings which emerges out of the Tipperary plain like something out of a medieval fairy tale, an Irish Avalon. Seen from afar, it epitomizes the legendary grandeur of early Christian Ireland and the power of the Irish Kings. It is even more impressive close to.

Tipperary is the only county in Ireland with a North Riding and a South Riding. The term "riding" was first used in Domesday Book to define an administrative district. Ireland did not have William the Conqueror's census-takers, but all the same

BELOW: Cahir Castle was built by the Butler family in the 15th century, then badly restored in 1840.
OPPOSITE: The Glen of Aherlow is an important pass between Tipperary and Limerick.

"riding" is a division very appropriate to a county associated with horse flesh and horsemanship. Hunting is the sport of Tipperary's landowners. Hurling is the vernacular sport, and is followed with a passion. Tipperary horses and hurlers are some of the greatest that have ever graced a field.

The county is full of Norman names: Delaney, Delahunty, D'Arcy – the one-time hunters – now mixed with the old Irish names: the Ryans, Mahers, Dwyers, and so on. So many Ryans are there that they often enjoy local distinction in an agnomen. I remember, as a child in Thurles, being told that my friends, whose surnames were Ryan-Bishop and Ryan-Bucket, came from two different branches of the family and therefore "lived on different sides of the tracks." Whether this was literally true, I'm not sure, but certainly the main Cork to Dublin railway line, which crosses Tipperary and neighboring Kilkenny, still runs through Thurles.

Both counties are hurling mad. When the "Tipp" team was in competition, flags would be hung out of windows and the towns bedecked in the county colors. The same applies today. When driving along the Cork to Dublin road, the visitor will notice that on crossing the border into County Kilkenny, trees, lampposts, overhead wires and suspended teddy bears, hitherto dressed in the blue and gold of Tipperary, abruptly convert to the black and amber of Kilkenny.

Hurling is one of the fastest, fiercest games ever devised. It is played on an oversized football pitch, and the small leather ball, seamed with ridges, is almost constantly in the air as it is pucked or run from one end of the field to the other. The hurley sticks – or camáns – are hip high blades of ash, slimmer than hockey sticks, with broad bosses often bound with metal hoops.

Unlike a hockey stick, a hurley stick may be swung

at any height, and the famous "clash of the ash" occurs when two or more hurlers leap for the descending ball, their camáns colliding against the sky. It is a miracle – and a testament to the skill of the hurlers – that no player is decapitated, or suffers the full force swing of the instrument across the face. Nowadays, some hurlers wear helmets, but it is a recent innovation and not favored by many experienced players who would rather trust the opposition not to harm them than suffer the discomfort of a helmet during the 70-minute long, sweaty game.

Hurling is – with the possible exception of steeplechasing – the most exciting sport in Ireland. The score tallies are high and smacking the ball over the high posts from 70 yards (64 m) out is a favorite scoring ploy. This is not easy while running full pelt, hopping the ball on the boss – it is against the rules to "hand" the ball for long – and dodging the gauntlet of swinging sticks wielded by the opposition. It requires a cool head and deadly accuracy to score – look up for a second, toss the ball high, aim, swing and let fly.

Southern Tipperary is hunting country. While some hunters may hurl, and some hurlers hunt, average citizens can more easily afford a hurley than a horse. If they follow the hunt, it is likely they will use the traditional transport of Shanks's mare.

At the other end of the scale, the "sons" of the legendary stallion, Shergar, still walk tall across the south Tipperary grasslands. The Derby winner, spirited away in 1983 in a failed ransom bid, is still mourned and his bones are sought like relics. His bloodline is perpetuated in Tipperary stud farms and his progeny remain much prized by horse breeders all over the world.

Coolmore Stud is one of the most important bloodstock breeding stations in the world, with associate farms in the USA and Australia. Flat race and National Hunt mares are brought here, where 40 to 50 stallions provide service. Open to the public, the best time to visit is undoubtedly in the early morning when the horses tend to be standing knee high in mist, their nostrils issuing fine smoke into the Tipperary dawn.

RIGHT: The dairy farming town of Tipperary, immortalized in the song "It's a Long Way to Tipperary," on the River Ara can trace its roots back to the twelfth century.

Waterford

Ireland's best kept secret

Waterford defies gravity. While other Irish counties boast of statues that move and windowpanes that reflect the Virgin Mary, in only one will a car run uphill when one releases the emergency brake. The phenomenon can be relished at Waterford's Mahon Falls.

The people of Ireland rightly believe there are more things in heaven and on earth than our philosophers have ever dreamed of. Leprechauns are an endangered species, but the paranormal is still extant. Happily, pishoges, or supernatural valedictions, remain potent forces, protecting duns, raths and standing stones from the incursions of drainers, developers and European Union grants. It was intelligent of their

builders to attach such warnings, and the curses pertaining to their removal, unwritten but passed down locally over thousands of years, are as old and durable as the artifacts themselves.

Waterford is a "sleeper" among Irish counties, as beautiful in its way as any, but largely ignored and unknown. The Waterford people are private and laid back, and haven't pursued tourists with the same vigor as commercial Kerrymen or "quaint-ifying" Galway city burghers. Used to employment on the great estates, with which the county is replete, they were satiated or stultified beyond bothering. It is extraordinary, for instance, that in the lovely town of Lismore there was hardly a rooming house available

until five years ago, and one still can't buy a meal after six o'clock.

Waterford is a "corridor" county. Folk disembark from the U.K. ferry at Rosslare, in Wexford, and rush through Waterford en route to Killarney, as if the latter were Mecca and there was nothing but desert in between. This, apparently, bothers the Waterford people not a whit. They don't mind keeping their beautiful inland mountains and stunning seaside strands a secret. Far be it from them to tout for custom. Let the visitors shoot through to Killarney, only alighting for the briefest of moments.

It is a source of amazement to many native Irish that tourists bother to go anywhere at all. It is almost certain, anywhere in our fair country, that unimagined beauty is only a short walk away and, in any case, to understand Ireland and feel that much-sought lack of stress and hurry, one is better staying put.

With a little patience, inner peace is reached: a herd of cows strolls at evening through the village; in the

morning the children can be heard singing their tables in the National School; the church bells ring for the Angelus in a street where there isn't a cricket stirring, and at night the village pubs are filled with a buzz transcending worldly cares. Yet, nightly in rooming houses, visitors survey their maps: Kinsale tomorrow; Killarney and the Ring next day; Connemara the day after and "we'll do" the lakes of Leitrim before a mad dash cross-country to catch the boat home. Such insanity defeats the object of the exercise, and nowhere is this more evident than in the tourist's gallop across Waterford, one of the loveliest, most tranquil counties in Ireland's crown.

The city of Waterford, famous for its crystal glass, was a Viking port, the name honoring Odin's father. Captured by Strongbow, the Norman invader, in 1170, it uniquely proved too strong for Cromwell in 1649. His "by Hook or by Crooke" threat referred to siege routes via Hook Head or Crooke village on the estuary. In the event, he had to eat his words. The city's medieval walls are better preserved than any in Ireland, except Derry, and the townscape and wharves are a wonderful sight from the Kilkenny side of the River Suir.

Dungarvan is the county town, with a large square, without a statue, little changed from what it might have been in the 1940s or 1950s – one can imagine asses and carts tied to the lampposts as farmers did their business on market day. Down a short street behind it lie the docks, where is evidenced that symbol of recent Irish "quaint-ifying," a large building with exposed and re-pointed stone. As usual, the sandstone blocks of which it is built are colored from deep red to umber, and it emulates a mini-Canary Wharf in London, only it is old and real. Here, too, are a few colorful pubs, outside which one can sit in clement weather and watch the yachts in the basin.

On a positively continental sweep of the Cork road above Dungarvan town, the motorist will be arrested by a magnificent view in his rear mirror; he should pull into a lay-by and get out. Below him, or her, will be seen the vast panorama of Dungarvan Bay, with bird-friendly wetlands and mudflats reflecting the sky. The itinerants camped nearby enjoy one of the finest views

OPPOSITE: Ardmore Round Tower, part of a site dating to the fifth century, although the tower was built in the twelfth.

in Ireland, and their piebald ponies a fine diet as they graze the "long acre' – the county name for lush, roadside verges – rich with a diversity of flowering weeds and grass.

Ardmore, on the coast, is distinguished by a ruined cathedral, not very large, but with a fine, pencil-slim round tower rising above it. This tower is one of the best examples in Ireland. The door is 12 feet (3.7 m) up the wall, the better to pre-empt Viking brigands and house-breakers, although the assailants were, as often, Christian Irish chieftains who saw no reason why monks should be richer than themselves.

The tower is still almost as perfect as when it was built. Swallows flit in and out of the windows and make it their snug home. Here is one place where their nesting sites are unlikely to be threatened, and for centuries generations of Lismore swallows have returned annually from Africa with every chance of breeding success.

In the cemetery beneath, Catholic and Protestant names are mixed, as is often the case in Irish churchyards. In the sun trap of the roofless old cathedral, two *ogham* stones, carved with ancient runic characters, stand propped against the wall.

From Ardmore, a road may be found to take one north to the River Blackwater on the verdant banks of which, at Lismore, vast King John's Castle stands. This venerable heap is not actually so ancient. There was a castle there, built in 1185, but later destroyed by Cromwell. However, the present edifice is nothing if not imposing with its castellated battlements and towers rising over the river, surrounded by the tall, exotic trees of the lovely Lismore estate. The view from the bridge below is one of classical tranquillity, the big river approaching on a straight course and then meandering off between lush water meadows.

Above Lismore are the Knockmealdown mountains, heavily forested with great stands of mature deciduous trees and later tall lodgepole pines. After passing a corrie lake near the top one comes to the Vee, and here the traveller is rewarded with one of the most breathtaking views in Ireland. The blanket bog below gives way to a great, green plain, the Galtee mountains to the left; Slievenamon "mountain of the women" straight ahead; the Comeraghs close by and, in the distance, the Silvermines. The view stretches for a good 40 miles (64 km).

ABOVE: Workers making Waterford crystal.
OPPOSITE: The town of Waterford.

The Province of Ulster

by Ian Hill

A scattered necklace of thousands of drumlins – small hills of boulder clay, dumped as the last great ice age melted 13,000 years ago – separate the nine counties of the old province of Ulster – Armagh, Antrim, Cavan, Derry, Donegal, Down, Fermanagh, Monaghan, and Tyrone – from the rest of the island of Ireland. A natural barrier, it runs in a swathe some 30 miles (48 km) wide from the placid Irish Sea in the east to the Atlantic rollers of the west. Great earthworks, thrown up in the first century B.C., span the gaps between drumlins. A third barrier, an international border, splits off six of the counties to make Northern Ireland which comprises one sixth of the island and is home to 1.5 million people.

There have been people in Ulster since the Middle Stone Age, over 8000 years ago. They speared salmon, trapped boar, and made camp in Ireland's first recorded human settlement – a collection of round huts of woven sapling and deer hide – at Mount Sandel on the banks of the River Bann in County Antrim. The history of this culture, gathered together as the Ulster Cycle – the oldest vernacular epic in western European literature – is a heady mix of men, women, and gods; battles and lusts; spells and sorrows. It is a history open to interpretation.

The land bridge which once joined Ireland to Britain disappeared around 6000 B.C., and it was not until the fourth millennium B.C. that the next wave of settlers came in the form of Neolithic, New Stone Age farmers who risked the Irish Sea in frail boats of lathe and hide, packed with pigs, cows and sheep, and made

OPPOSITE: Most of the Antrim coast faces the North Channel, the narrow stretch of water between Scotland and Ireland. The nearness of nothern Ireland to southwestern Scotland has meant that settlers have gone in both directions.

landfall among stands of elm – always a sign of good soil – in Strangford Lough.

These new immigrants felled the forests, grew cereals, fired pots, built a distinctively northern style of stone cairn to their gods and buried their dead under the dolmens which stand eternal in many an Ulster field.

By 2000 B.C., in the Bronze Age, contemporary with the pyramids of Egypt's Middle Kingdom and the great Minoan palaces at Knossos on Crete, Ulster's tribes toiled to create the great stone circles of Down and Tyrone, while merchant adventurers taught them to make bronze axe-heads and golden ornaments.

By the coming of the Iron Age, the first Celts had arrived, conquering say some, assimilating say others, those more ancient peoples, the dark-skinned Fir Bolg, the red-haired Tuatha de Dannan, and the Cruithin of Ulster with their warrior-clan structure and their Red Branch Knights. These Gaels welcomed Patrick's Christian mission in the 5th century A.D. and resisted the subsequent Viking raids on their monasteries in the eighth century. However, in the twelfth century the Anglo-Normans took much of Ulster for the English Crown, acting at the behest of Pope Adrian IV.

The Reformation, and Henry VIII's and Elizabeth I's espousal of the Protestant cause, added another dimension. The new colonists were Protestants; the colonized remained Catholic. Eventually England's savage campaigns of attrition paid off and Ulster's Gaelic leaders were exiled to continental Europe, sailing from Donegal in 1607.

England's promotion of the Plantation of Ulster in the 17th century further marginalized the Catholic population by settling the best lands with Protestant Lowland Scots. Begun under James I and VI in 1609, the Plantation suffered severe set-backs in the rebellion of 1641 when many Protestants were massacred; massacres for which the Lord Protector, Oliver Cromwell, took sour revenge in 1649.

In 1690 William of Orange, having accepted the British Crown and representing the forces of Protestantism, defeated James II, a Catholic, at the Battle of the Boyne. This battle and its date are indelibly burned into Ulster's divided psyche, and such complexities as the mid-18th-century wave of Presbyterian republican emigration to America and the United Irishmen's Rebellion of 1798, which too had their origins among the north's Protestant non-conformist republicans, are not often weighed in this history's balance in an even-handed manner.

The year of 1916 brought the Easter Rising and 1919 the Declaration of Independence in Dublin and the Irish Republican Army's (IRA) war against British rule. These were violent times perpetrated by men who had come home from the grim battlefields of the "Great War" (the First World War, 1914–18) and were accustomed to slaughter. The ranks of the IRA, and of the opposing Ulster Volunteer Force, swelled.

As fears of a civil war in Ulster grew, the British Cabinet devised the 1920 Government of Ireland Act which aimed at imposing a solution without ignoring the demographics of the situation. In 1922 dominion status under the title of Irish Free State (later called Eire) was eventually offered to 26 southern counties. The six northeastern counties of Ulster (those reckoned to have Protestant majorities, whose political allegiance was therefore to a British rather than an Irish state) were retained inside the United Kingdom in an entity thenceforth called Northern Ireland.

In this poem Seamus Heaney describes the uneasy Anglo-Irish relationship in terms of a husband's feelings for his pregnant wife.

Your back is a firm line of eastern coast
And arms and legs are thrown
Beyond your gradual hills. I caress
The heaving province where our past has grown.
I am the tall kingdom over your shoulder
That you would neither cajole nor ignore.
Conquest is a lie. I grow older
Conceding your half-independent shore

Within whose borders now my legacy
Culminates inexorably.
FROM: "ACT OF UNION" BY SEAMUS HEANEY

Like many constitutional solutions devised as empires shrink, the 1922 act was far from perfect. There was one house of representatives in Dublin, and another in Belfast. The great majority of Protestants in Northern Ireland saw their allegiance as being to the British Crown and the government in Westminster; the great majority of Catholics were nationalists with their allegiances in Dublin to a government which would later claim the whole of Ireland as "the national territory." Elections to Stormont became a sectarian head count.

Without its "Troubles" Northern Ireland might well be seen as embodying the essence of a rural neatness the size of Connecticut. Trim hedges and wan limestone walls border its small-holdings. White sheep and dun cows graze the green fields and sturdy farmhouses nestle in clumps of sycamore. Tidy towns are linked by well-metalled roads, their grass verges clipped in orderly precision. Signs point up each historic mound of ancient stone.

In contrast, the roads of Cavan, Monaghan, and Donegal wander and camber among the hills. However, while Stormont's Protestant Unionist government undoubtedly built better roads than those in Eire, it saw little wrong in its discriminatory attitude to Catholics. But, the times they were a-changing. In 1968 students protested, not only on the streets of Washington and Paris, but also on those of Belfast and Derry. By 1969 Civil Rights marches were prevalent in the "six counties." That year also brought their suppression. The "Troubles" had begun.

Today, as Ulster's tragic melodrama continues to unfold, the great majority of the population – though still segregated by the sour dance of religion and history – looks on aghast from opposing wings, wishing that peace could bring down the curtain, permanently, on a show which has long outrun any purpose it once had.

OPPOSITE: Glenariff Forest Park is set in a u-shaped valley, one of the nine Glens of Antrim, leading to the sea at Waterfoot. It is an area of spectaular beauty and, as a nature reserve, contain several species of protected flora.

Antrim

Antrim's Spanish gold

There was a time, in the late 16th century, when there were upwards of 3000 Spaniards in the old province of Ulster, the majority of them making for the castle of Dunluce on Antrim's north coast. They were the survivors of many thousands more shipwrecked when the pride of the invincible Armada of Philip II of Spain foundered off Ireland's western shores.

Philip, who had been married to Mary Tudor when she was queen of England, and having endured enough harrying from the ships of Mary's half-sister Elizabeth I, made it his mission to destroy England's fleet once and for all, thus bringing victory to the cause of Catholic Counter-Reformation. So, on 30th May 1588, his fleet of 141 ships weighed anchor off the port of Lisbon and turned north into the Atlantic.

The English will tell you that it was the commando tactics of the English privateers, operating at long range among and behind the enemy lines under the daring command of naval captains like Francis Drake, which defeated the Armada, while the Spanish maintain that it was the unusually strong equinotial gales off the Shetland Isles, north of Scotland, which brought the Armada to its sea-sodden knees.

In truth it was a combination of the two. By the

BELOW: The Giants Causeway, near Portrush, is one of Ireland's most famous landmarks.
OPPOSITE: A view of north Antrim farmland.

time the great ships took shelter off Ireland's windswept western shores they were under-supplied and overloaded – crammed with the soldiery from other ships already sunk.

One of the last ships to go down was the three-masted galleon, Girona, which struck a reef off Lacada Point east of Dunluce Castle, near to midnight in late October 1588. She was carrying a complement of 1300 men, just nine of whom survived. It is said that in the darkness their panic-stricken captain mistook the Chimneys in the Giant's Causeway for the real chimneys of Dunluce, whose ruthless commander, Sorley Boye MacDonnell, was known to be fiercely anti-English.

The wreck left a trail of stone arquebus balls across the ocean floor as well as chestfuls of golden trinkets, much of which MacDonnell would later use to finance the repair of his favoured stronghold.

Other Spanish galleons foundered off the west coast, and many thousands – including the flower of Spain's richest families – perished, broken-limbed on golden beaches. Others fell to the sword, pikes and gallows of the Irish, greedy for plunder. Hundreds, naked, starving, fevered and sick from a diet of wet biscuit and putrified meat, were ridden down by English cavalry.

MacDonnell took his forenames, Sorley Boye, from the Gaelic Somhaile Buidhe, the "summer-soldier, yellow-haired" for the Viking who traditionally raided from the north each summer. He had both Viking and Scots blood in his veins, was Lord of the Western Isles and was among the most astute of the Celtic politicians opposed to Elizabeth I's territorial claims. His family having been driven out of Scotland by the Campbells, Sorley Boye established power in Antrim and made treaties with the O'Neills, the then kings of "the Great Irishry," so called by the English more out of fear than respect.

In July 1575, Sorley Boye had watched helpless from the mainland as the English put 500 of his clanswomen and their children to the sword on Rathlin Island off the coast of Antrim. Maddened with sorrow, he took his revenge ten years later on New Year's Day 1583, at Bonamargy east of Ballycastle, by burning the Abbey at night and

OPPOSITE: Harbour at Carrickfergus, County Antrim.

slaughtering until the grass ran red with blood.

The English offered parley, but Sorley Boye and his Redshanks – named thus after their custom of fighting bare-legged even in the winter's frosts – then set out to snatch Dunluce, craftily and bloodily from the English hands. The castle's weakness lay in its constable's taste for his young Scots mistress who was in fact playing Mata Hari for Sorley Boye. On the night of All Hallows she let down a rope and man-sized basket to enable the waiting Redshanks to scale the cliffs and hang the constable from the walls in the basket's place. So Sorley had the castle, but the English had his son's head. They had found him hiding in a freshly dug grave and cut his throat. At the subsequent peace and conciliation talks he was shown his son's head on a pike. "My son," he observed chillingly, "hath many heads." Not surprisingly, for a man who understood the heart of darkness in other men's souls, he and his descendants, in the end, owned most of the county of Antrim.

Off the coast, west in the setting sun, lies the Donegal peninsula of Inishowen and Ireland's most northerly point, the island of Inishtrahull. East is Rathlin Island which has as yet escaped the manicured tyranny of the golf course. Instead it is rich in the spring and summer with the scent of wild flowers, its lakes speckled with the rings made by tiny brown trout, its blustery shores filled with the cries of the thousands of cliff-breeding sea-birds. However, when the clouds darken the sky, it is too easy to imagine Sorley Boye's anguish as he stood on the mainland, watching his people slaughtered at the place they now call Crook Ascreidlin, "the hill of the screaming."

South of Ballycastle, one road runs south over the moors, where the buzzards wheel searching for red Irish grouse, and through the market towns of Ballymoney, Ballymena and Antrim, their citizens resigned to being the butt of many jokes concerning their Scots heritage and accent and, allegedly, taut purse strings.

Glenaan, "the glen of the rushes," ends in Cushendall where Layde Old Church graveyard is calcium-rich with the bones of MacDonnells. Sorley himself is locked, inviolate, as he requested, in a tomb at Bonamargy. At last, had he known the Spanish, he could have said to his people: *No tengo más que darte.*

Armagh

Ulster's flowery vale

History, legend and myth combine to provide the epic of the golden-haired princess Macha, who dominated the times in which she lived, becoming, for the Celts, their goddess of lusts and wars for 1000 years from 700 B.C. onwards. In one of her many guises she married Nemhedh, a darkly handsome mercenary come lately from Scythia, northeast of the Black Sea, and later died at the top of the forest hill he cleared for her giving the hill its name: Ard Macha, "Macha's Height," Armagh.

To the west, Navan Fort is all that remains of the ancient capital of Ulster where, at An Eamain or "Macha's twins," in another guise, another of Macha's husbands, Cruinnuig, forced his wife – who could allegedly run like the wind – to race against the horse of Connor, King of Ulster. Pregnant, Macha begged him to postpone the race, but he refused at the cost of her life. Having won, Macha died giving birth to twins, cursing as she did so the men of Ulster to suffer the pains of childbirth.

Macha's city, Armagh itself, sits on two hills, with the Catholic and Protestant cathedrals facing each other across a valley. Protestant St Patrick's stands where the pragmatic saint, conscious of the area's political and religious significance, built his second church in 444 ad. It must have looked its best at the end of the 18th century when it was restored by Armagh's own Francis Johnston, the man who gave the city, and so much of Dublin, its Georgian charms. Now, Johnston's delicate touches stand defaced by lesser talents, its orangey sandstone exterior forbidding, the carved heads grim in their frieze.

The cathedral tower affords a fine perspective over the medieval town, with its narrow streets coiling up the cathedral hill. Across the valley the 39-peal carillon and the exuberant Byzantine interior of twin-spired St Patrick's Catholic Church attest to the success of the 19th century primate cardinals in charge of the original financing. In the wave of compassion which swept Europe in the wake of Ireland's Great Famine even the emperors of France and Austria found it in their hearts to support the cathedral's fund-raising bazaar in 1865 – from which a long-case clock still awaits collection by its purchaser. The red hats of all its cardinals hang, with some pomp, inside.

For an understanding of the key role that the Church has played in Armagh's history, you only have to walk through the wonderful, tree-lined, Georgian Mall. Many of its encompassing limestone buildings are a testament to the architect, Johnston, and his sponsor Archbishop Robinson, harking back to a time when clerics were rich and sure patrons of the arts. There were few advisory committees then; few bureaucrats; few rapacious consultants.

At the south end of the Mall stands the old jail, now minus gallows; at the north end Johnston's 1809 Court House. On the east stands the one-time schoolhouse, which is now the delightfully arcane Armagh County Museum. How improving it must have been for the school's pupils to be pulled by the ears and lined up in ranks to watch malfeasants, hobbling in irons from north to south to be held for deportation or worse. How reassuring for townhouse residents looking down from their elegant balconies.

The acerbic Jonathan Swift, who seems to have enjoyed escaping his duties as a Dublin dean, often came north, staying on occasion with the Achesons at their manor house in south Armagh – "bandit country" to the English tabloids during the "Troubles." While old Sir Archibald Acheson, the county sheriff, was a dull stick, strong on public colonial virtues, his young wife, Anne, it seems, was quite the reverse. To his satisfaction, prosperous obscurity was how the sheriff deemed his own life, mindless it seems of the poor, starving on the village edge. It was a situation meat for Swift's satirical pen, and indeed he chased off a dozen or so poems mostly mocking M'Lady's concerns for her ageing coquettish

OPPOSITE: Slieve Gullion Forest Park is in the southern part of County Armagh.

house guest, who dallied with her over cards into the small hours, and made so free with her house and garden, if not, as far as is discreetly recorded, her physical affections.

Further verses for Lady Anne were quite scatological in the details of the functioning of the outdoor privies Swift ordered built for her comfort. However, Swift's concerns stretched well beyond the confines of Lady Anne's hospitality. He criticized the emigration to America forced upon so many of his Ulster Scots Presbyterian neighbours. Not that he tolerated their religion, but more he recognized the contribution to the relative stability of the early 18th century Ulster economy made by their Calvinist work ethic. He contrasted the relative wealth of the north with the appalling poverty in southern counties, though he wrote of himself "as a stranger in a strange land," and he spoke of "three terrible years dearth of corn, and every place strowed with beggars." For even in prosperous Armagh, the poor were always with him.

By all accounts he was happy in Armagh, that is until Sir Archibald finally woke up to his "frolick" with Lady Anne. It was in the wake of this scandal, rebuffed by society and exasperated by what he perceived as the government's economic follies, that Swift wrote A Modest Proposal, his most famous and savage of satires, in which he recommends the eating of Ireland's starving children, thus turning them into an economic asset. Soon after Swift's final visit to Markethill, Lady Anne left her husband for ever, and went to live with her mother.

County Armagh was also the birthplace of the Protestant Orange Order which was founded in 1795. Today, members of the Order, wearing their distinctive orange sashes, march across Northern Ireland on 12th July each year, and often, in contentious rehearsal, several weekends beforehand. "Flashpoint Feared" run the anticipatory headlines. Many republican Catholics see such marches as provocatively supremacist, and while some marchers delight in this shrewd observance, others would prefer that these parades be regarded simply as colourful celebrations of folk history, as

LEFT: *An aerial view of Armagh, the town that serves as the seat of both the Catholic and Church of Ireland primates.*

unthreatening as New Orleans' Mardi Gras, and surely to be welcomed in a province not given much to dancing in the streets.

In mid-August, in rituals not dissimilar – banners billowing in the Armagh breezes – the members of the Catholic Nationalist Ancient Order of Hibernians also march to the accordion, fife and drum. In truth, only the slogans and narrative paintings on the huge

ABOVE: Armagh's northern border is Lough Neagh.
OPPOSITE: Gosford Castle, Market Hill, County Armagh

banners and the icons on the green, rather than orange, sashes distinguish matters for a stranger.

Away from politics, Armagh is best savoured listening to the music in its uillean pipers' clubs; following its road-bowls champions along high-hedged lanes; walking through its Bramley apple orchards in May; or by just sitting on a wall in Armagh's Mall, gentle evening breeze tugging at the chestnut blossom, while white flannelled sportsmen, out there between the ranks of historic cannon, play leisurely cricket on its green, green grass.

Belfast

City of pubs and churches

Belfast now, sitting in a saucer of green hills astride the currently-being-gentrified River Lagan, is a medium-sized, post-industrial, Victorian city with a surfeit of engaging pubs, architecturally extravagant churches, and an improbable number of street-level car parks.

Making the world's headlines with harrowing regularity, Belfast is remarkable and compelling principally because it is the war zone for a few hundred violent activists from two opposing religions, from a fistful of blue collar enclaves, who for the last 25-plus years have resolutely defied the massed powers of the British Crown. Since 1968 more than 3000 people have died: shot; blown to bloody fragments; garrotted; bludgeoned; burned; and countless more exhausted by grief. Since then electronic images of their deaths have spun outwards, endlessly, into the expanding universe.

During the badland times of the early 1970s the few strangers here were journalists and soldiers. Good citizens rushed home from work, if they had any, and the only people on the night-time streets were the police, the hacks, the army and the revolutionaries and counter-revolutionaries. The place had a bizarre romance. Bars closed soon after dark, disgorging television crews, assassins, racketeers, touts, informers and spies from a dozen nations back onto the cracked and drizzled pavements. Barristers and solicitors, who were then the new rich, dined well in a shifting geography of small and sometimes eccentric restaurants.

Over the years, a certain number, bombed or burned out from their ghettos, or in general fear of such assaults, moved as refugees to quiet country towns. However, since the first days of the brokered peace in the summer of 1994, the mood has been cautiously robust. The city, where the streetwise greeting has always been "'bout ye?,"an abbreviation of "How's about you?,"has never lost its ironic confrontational sense of humour, nor its mendicant economy so heavily dependent on American, British and EU subsidy. It burgeons with cafés, theme pubs, ethnic eateries and the cool fashionable restaurants of media-chefs, all packed with visiting social anthropologists, incognito Hollywood stars researching superficial scripts and the even newer rich, the cohorts of the new local industries of peace and reconciliation.

Post-stress monitoring, conflict consultancy, social engineering, and empowerment of the socially disenfranchised are among the specialities. These optimistic agencies are staffed in the main by the well-funded, the self-promoting, and the often self-appointed, taking their cheques from the United States of America and the EU, from Canada, the perpetually concerned Scandinavians and from Britain itself. Their members have lives more fulfilling than those whom they would comfort.

Unemployment, outside these new and fashionable conceits is still unacceptably high. The much lauded and welcomed visits of presidents and rock stars bring the city's citizens the well-deserved glow of media attention, but whether these public delights create long-term benefit is still to be assessed and segregation by religion in voting-ward and in education persists.

The politics of peace aside, for the enquiring visitor there isn't an engaging taxi driver in the city who hasn't an explanation for each withering kerbside wreath; each gable-end political mural with its Balaclava'd heroes, dove of peace in one hand and Kalashnikov in the other; each bombed out gap in a street's architecture.

The city's affluent middle-classes, and its not-so-affluent youth, seek their urban pleasures in a narrow southern-facing triangle of streets – styled over-optimistically as The Golden Mile – taking as its base a line from the solid Victorian confidence of the City Hall to the foxed charm of the Old Museum Arts Centre. The triangle's apex is located just past the curvilinear delights of the Botanic Gardens' Palm House in the prosperous University suburbs.

ABOVE: City Hall and Donegall Square, Belfast.

Within these confines are found the art galleries, arts festivals, bars, bistros, cafés, charity shops, launderettes, museums, opera houses, pizza parlours, restaurants, sandwich bars and theaters thought necessary for middle class life.

But curiously, for a city with such a confrontational sense of its own presence, the people of Belfast have no generic title, as have Bostonians, Dubliners, Glaswegians, Londoners and Parisians. Belfastonians? Belfasters? Belfastians? None have the confident ring of acceptance. However, the citizens do have numerous rituals. For instance, they will show every one of their visitors the tiles and stained glass of the Victorian Crown Liquor Saloon, an interior which has made it, in effect, a national monument. If that is too crowded they will lead the way to nearby Robinson's, Morrison's, The Spinner's and Dempsey's, all pubs which attempt – with varying degrees of success – to recreate the Irish rural past of village spirit grocers and small-town gentleman's book-lined clubs.

Graduate migrants, who left years ago because of

the "Troubles" return to Lavery's Gin Palace comforted to find its customers caught in the same 1960s time warp. The more emboldened may find themselves in the Empire, a deconsecrated church, where "in your face" stand-up comedy offers a rare insight into the city's mood. For it is a truism that adversity and fear produce the best jokes.

Reading the city's current frame of mind from its media is a harder job. During the bad times, journalists and management on the three daily newspapers, one overtly nationalist, one primarily unionist, one trying to be somewhere in between, covered the complexities of the stubborn brutalities and conspiracies with admirable impartiality.

But just as the new peace, when it came, caught the traffic planners severely off guard (they had not had to worry about traffic jams for a quarter of a century), it also placed new burdens on the media.

When news was brought to the journalists' keyboards by the very sound of the bomb itself, by the

235

flame lighting up the nightscape outside the newsroom, by the bombers' coded telephone call, by a paramilitary group's faxed claim and politician's faxed counter-claim, peace can leave holes in the news menu.

Some lacunae have been filled by new terrors. Female and male rape; drug-associated killings; attacks on the elderly; ex-terrorist guns for hire; punishment maimings, and, newly revealed after having been bravely and doggedly researched, the appalling history of child sexual abuse inside the Catholic church.

With regard to "good news" the feeling prevails that it is churlish – for the moment anyway – to question anything which might herald peace and prosperity. So while the arrival of a massive chainstore creates 300 jobs and is hailed as a sign of acceptance into the canon of western affluence, little thought is given to the family-owned stores which will fold in consequence.

The real city begins just north of The Golden Mile. Here, where the feel-good factor reigns supreme, customers sipping pints in the Kitchen Bar, Bittle's Bar, The Morning Star, and White's Tavern, will speak with the voice of an older Belfast. The same voice would be heard in the city-village suburbs where hairdressers' establishments don't yet have weakly punning names, and spades and garden forks are still stacked each morning outside family-owned general stores, whose stock-in-trade still speaks of rural–urban links, not yet broken, of small gardens, of allotments, and of summer barbecues.

ABOVE: Queens University, Belfast, bears a more than passing resemblance to Magdalen College, Oxford.

Among the middle classes, many of whom have seen bombs only through the filter of television, the new mood is confident. The new and circular Waterfront Hall speaks for restored civic pride. Plans for riparian stadia, science parks, a national gallery, pile up in planners' offices.

Service industries prosper. Pavements are refurbished, the street furniture is new and international, the trading names in the shopping malls of Donegal Place and Royal Avenue, the city's major commercial boulevards, are those of any British high street.

A few hundred years ago there was little here except a rough castle by an estuary sandbank. Choir boys fished for salmon in the Lagan, apprentices complained of too many oysters in their diet. In time the linen and shipbuilding trades would make the city rich and polluted, supplying its merchants with the money to create its solid but decorative Victorian architecture for their businesses, the cramped rows of redbrick houses and mean streets for their workers, and the city parks for the orderly and educational enjoyment of their tradespeople.

Since those industries atrophied, this city, like many others in this European archipelago, has had to struggle for its new wealth. Further back in history its aetiology can be read in the legacies of two men, one an hereditary toff, the other an architect, opportunist and politician. One sold Belfast, the other built it. Such were the financial irresponsibilities of the 2d Marquis of Donegall that he had seen the inside of a debtor's prison before he inherited the whole city in 1799. Thereafter, so profligate was his lifestyle that, after his death in 1844, his son's advisors had to sell what was left of his inheritance to pay off the family's debts, thus opening up Lagan's banks to bankers and industrialists.

Stability was assured by Charles Lanyon, the most prosperous industrialist of them all who among other things gave the city an architectural language that all of its citizens could understand. His banks borrowed their vernacular from the houses of the medieval merchant princes of Italy. His church spires soared towards God. His prison's bulk put fear into so many hearts, his towering Courts of Justice intimidated the miscreant, his viaducts carried the railways, his tree plantations made solid the shifting bogland.

By his Queen's Bridge, named for Queen Victoria, he gave the city the Custom House and what is now the First Trust Bank, plus the Northern Bank in Waring Street nearby. Meanwhile, the New House of Correction (now Crumlin Road Prison) and the equally imposing Court House provided intimidating symbols of law and order.

So the student newly arrived in Belfast would do well to take a walk on this unofficial "Lanyon Trail," before sitting down among the bookcased and leathered delights of the Linenhall Library to begin, yet another, doctorate on yet one more aspect of the heritage of the "Troubles."

Cavan

County of lakes and waterways

Just as the old men, pipe smoking dark tobacco in public houses in County Down, oblige with the fiction that there is one island in Strangford Lough for every day of the year, those in County Cavan will proffer you the obverse. Cavan, a lakeland labyrinth, has, they boast, a lake in the county for each and every day of the 365. A "disappearing" one, over a limestone sump, takes its curtain call each leap year.

Fanciful or not, it is a description which will suffice for the county's fortunes, precarious enough at times, and its principal legends have water at their fount. At its center is a scatter of lakes linked by waterways natural and unnatural.

The 250 mile-long (402 km) Shannon, Ireland's greatest river, and major provider both of the country's indigenous hydro-electric power, and its water-based tourism, has its source in the moistness of the western slopes of Cuilcagh Mountain. Here, water sparkles down in the deep pool under the lichen-covered trees and the river, which takes its name from Sionna, grand-daughter of Lir, the god of the seas, begins its journey to the Atlantic. Meanwhile it neighbour, the River Erne, rises near Crosskeys and flows first south, then, in Lough Gowna, turns north towards Fermanagh's two broad lakes, Upper and Lower Lough Erne.

In the mid-19th century the proximity of these two rivers, the Shannon and the Erne, inspired the construction of the ill-planned Ballinamore–Ballyconnell Canal which it was hoped would complete the circuit of commercial canals that was to link Dublin to Belfast. However, this was never to be. As the budget overran, as canal budgets always seemed to, several economies of scale were made: depth was reduced to just over 3 feet (1 m), while canal towpaths, which were expensive to construct, were maintained despite the patent impossibility of operating a horse-tow across the wider lakes. By the time the canal was completed in 1860, having taken 14 years to build, a sad catalogue of penny-pinching, mismanagement and general ineptitude had rendered it vir-

tually unusable and certainly no match for the increasingly commercial railway companies.

From the minute it was officially opened, water leaked from locks, banks caved and when what would be the last boat to do so passed through its locks in 1936, it took three weeks. Official records show that only eight boats had paid tolls on the 36 mile (58 km) journey, in either direction, in the 76 years since construction had been completed.

Today, in a period of post-industrial nostalgia and increasing leisure time, there is a burgeoning desire to observe – gin and tonic in hand – the manicured outdoors and the remnants of that once labour-intensive environment. The European Commission has funded much of the re-opening of the Ballinamore–Ballyconnell Canal, now promoted – logically, but with little eye for the nuances of nostalgia with which its attractions are imbued – as the Shannon–Erne Waterway.

The massive, hand-chiselled locks tower over the boats as always, but a credit card-like device allows captains-for-the-week, piloting their shallow, plastic-skinned hire-cruisers, to operate the huge wooden lock gates by sweatless and silent electric power. Bankside alder, willow, hazel, flag iris, watchful heron and dipping grebe accustom themselves to the habits of these new invaders of their once-silent water world.

If Cavan had a county song, there would be none better than "An Bonnán Bui," "The Song of the Yellow Bittern," written by the 18th-century poet Cathal Mac Giolla Ghunna and remembered in stone in Blacklion. Now bittern, cuckoo, and corncrake are gone, driven out by pesticides, soil enrichment, the draining of callows and watermeadows, and the early cutting of grass for silage. On both sides of the border, bird protection agencies offer – to little avail – subsidies to farmers who will cut hay late to enable the secretive

OPPOSITE: Lough Ramar in County Cavan is a popular destination for the fishing fraternity.

corncrake to rear its young in peace.

Now every lakeshore is dotted with the discreet green of the umbrellas of Dutch, English, French, and German fishermen, and farm houses, turned "Bed and Breakfast" (B&B), install "picture windows," crazy-paved patios and barbecue pits and scatter their beds with duvets.

The multitudes of tiny pubs are still held in family names, the shop fronts are mostly still clear of the 1970s garishness so beloved of men of small commerce in most other Irish counties. On garage forecourts and on the factory floor premises of the local light industries, "Country and Irish" – a more lachrymose version of Country and Western – music, echoes tinnily across the wavelengths.

On the wooden pub counter, the local paper offers pictures of weddings and priests; of roughly-suited, factory-sponsored brass bands in the local festival and of shop re-fittings. There are court reports to pore over: of farmers caught without road tax; of the results of planning appeals. Old men speak slowly, courteous enough but secretive; the younger debase their badinage with an excess of expletives. Everybody smokes and on the bumpy bog roads between the towns, turf smoke filters into everyone's cars.

Turn on the car radio and there is a dedication from nearby Ballyjamesduff.

Oh, the grass it is green around Ballyjamesduff,
And the blue sky is over it all;
And tones that are tender, and tones that are gruff,
Are whispering over the sea.
'Come back, Paddy Reilly, to Ballyjamesduff,
Come home, Paddy Reilly, to me.'
FROM: "COME BACK PADDY REILLY"
BY PERCY FRENCH (1854–1920)

I'm not sure the fastidious Percy would have liked it sung Country and Western style.

Derry
History's fulcrum

Derry, the most complete of Ireland's walled cities, and the administrative and emotional heartland of the county of Derry, has more than once played a pivotal role in European history. While the city's strategic position on a hill overlooking one of Ireland's largest rivers has long made it a sought-after prize for ambitious warriors, prelates, carpetbaggers and politicians, its sobriquet, "the Maiden City," attests to the three centuries its walls have stood inviolate.

In the early centuries of Christendom, a monastery – with its many trades and center of administration –

was the nearest thing Ulster had to a town. So Columba, also known as Columcille, a prolific founder of monasteries who built his first here in A.D. 546 , is regarded as Derry's founder. He built high on an island hill just off the left bank of the estuary of the plenteous River Foyle, pragmatically choosing an oak

BELOW: Mussenden Temple, Downhill, County Londonderry, was modeled on the Temple of Vista, in Rome. It was built in the eighteenth century, during an age that found inspiration in the Classical heritage of ancient Greece and Rome. OPPOSITE: Sheep fattening in rural Binevenagh.

grove for his setting. The grove had previously been a place of pagan worship and the saint's men were canny enough not to chop down too many trees when they built, for oak has always had a particular resonance in Irish mythology.

Doire, pronounced near enough "Derry," is Irish for "oak grove" and the sessile oak, *Quercus petraea*, is one of the great mythical trees of the island, lending to the early Irish runic *Ogham* script its sign for "D," from dair for "oak."

Having survived as an important Christian stronghold, Derry featured heavily in Henry II's plan to annex Ireland in the 12th century. He had a powerful ally in the form of Rome which had had enough of the independent Irish church, so, with Pope Adrian IV's approval, Henry himself led an invasion in October 1171. In 1177 he dispatched the much-feared Somerset knight, John de Courcy, and a force of Anglo-Normans north to take Ulster, that most recalcitrant of provinces. The Irish proved to be little match for his mailed knights, Flemish crossbowmen, Welsh longbowmen, and de Courcy ringed the coast with stout castles; two are still standing at Dundrum and Carrickfergus. However, in the end the wilds of the county defeated him and so Derry survived as the Irish power base and focus of the Columban monasteries.

Over the next few centuries, siege and repulse came and went until 1566 when the English forces at last took the city, installing men and munitions in the ancient Christian temple, Teampull Mhor. However, the arsenal exploded the following year and the garrison fled.

In 1613, to stabilize the situation, James I took the advice of Sir Thomas Phillips, a plausible Welsh adventurer with lands at Coleraine, to bring the city and surrounding lands under the control of the livery companies of the City of London. Uneasy though the alliance was – the land was still the domain of resentful Irish chiefs and unruly woodkern – all parties agreed and set up what amounted to a joint

LEFT: Glenelly Valley, County Londonderry. The valley has been designated an area of outstanding natural beauty by the U.K. government. The Glenelly river has been a source of gold, for centuries, and visitors to the area can pan for nuggets of the precious metal.

stock company, not unlike the one that was currently settling the Virginias.

While it was a decision they lived to regret, thus it was that Derry gained the prefix "London," a form of address used infrequently now by any but the most ardent loyalist.

Somewhat reluctantly, the livery companies – officially referred to as "undertakers" – established several settlements: the Roe Valley to the Haberdashers, the Fishmongers and Skinners; the Bann to the Clothmakers, Merchant Tailors, Ironmongers, Mercers, Vintners and Salters; and the Foyle to the Goldsmiths, Cordwainers, Paint-stainers and Armorers as well as the Grocers. Meanwhile, Phillips had Limavady all for himself.

The conditions laid out in the Printed Book of Agreement were tough. However, few shared the king's grand design for an Ireland pacified by investment, viewing it instead as simply another scheme by the Crown to raise their taxes and they made little effort to honor promises to build stone forts, schoolhouses and churches or to deport all Celts of fighting age to Connacht. England, by this time, had been deforested so there was a ready market for barrel staves and ships' timbers. While the colonizers skimped, cutting down the great oaks for profit rather than for building, Irishmen, who should have been deported, were kept as tenants on poor uplands, a cheaper solution than importing settlers from England.

In 1619 the Crown reacted strongly to this defiance, decreeing that unless the "undertakers" agreed to pay double the taxes their lands would be forfeited. Sullenly they paid. However, in 1635, the new king, Charles I, who shared little of his father's enthusiasm for an Irish colony, summoned the companies, conjoined as the still extant The Honorable The Irish Society, before the Court of Star Chamber and ordered them to give up their lands once and for all.

Luckily for the companies, this blatant show of royal autocracy added to the disquiet about royal judgment felt by England's increasingly pro-republican parliamentarians, thus setting the power of two cities, London and Derry, against the Crown and ultimately sparking the English Civil War (1642–49). It would not be the first, nor last, time that Derry would play a key role in European history.

Twice during the 1640s the city walls held out against Irish attacks, and twice the city was held by Protestant parliamentarians against Royalist besiegers. However, the most famous siege of all came almost 40 years later while Catholic James II fought Protestant William III, formerly Prince of Orange, for the British throne.

The citizens of Derry were mainly Scots and English Protestant planters and although William was Dutch, and his army financed mainly by Rome's Pope Innocent XI, the majority of Derry's settlers supported him. On 18th December 1688 a handful of Protestant apprentices, the student class of their day, shut Ferryquay Gate and did not open it until 28th July 1689. Inside the walls, 7000 of the 30,000 townsfolk died from hunger and pestilence. Rats were a shilling a head, but the city's resolve did not falter. Under pressure the defenders hoisted a crimson banner signifying "No Surrender" which is still the cry of the Protestant Orangemen parading the province every year on 12th July. The siege tied up Jacobite forces, and so helped crown the man who became William III, turning, yet again, the tide of European history.

Today, elegant Georgian doorways decorate the hilly streets; The Honorable The Irish Society is still a major landowner. The elegant spire of Protestant St. Columb's Cathedral, built by The Society between 1628 and 1633 in what is known as the "Planters' Gothic" style, dominates the old city. Outside the walls are the sectarian enclaves: the tiny Protestant Fountain area and sprawling Catholic Bogside, the latter a no-go area for British troops during much of the recent "Troubles." On the Bogside's edge, a gable wall reads, 'You are now entering Free Derry." Of course, this is a sentiment with far reaching implications which would find a large number of opponents both in the city and much further afield. But then Derry must be used to that by now.

OPPOSITE: Downhill Strand, County Londonderry, is part of a complex of beaches that is claimed to be the longest beach in Ireland. It is a popular place with surfers, in spite of its windy nature – which no doubt contributes to the excitement when on the board. However, these winds also bring plenty of glider enthusiasts to the area as well, and it has been used by the Ulster Gliding Club since the 1930s.

Donegal
Edge of the known world

On a good day the Donegal air is bright and salty and as fresh as if it had been scrubbed by the very Atlantic. A roar of breakers funnels up the valleys from crescents of untrodden golden sands. A buzzard quarters high in the blue; a dipper darts under the bubbling stream, here, on what was once the edge of the known world. But on a bad day, when winter rain lashes its pot-holed village streets, Donegal sees itself as a lost county, cut off from and ignored by Dublin. When, in 1920, an elaborate constitutional "solution' to the "Irish Problem' was enacted by offering dominion status to a 26-county Irish Free State and Home Rule to the six northeastern counties (Antrim, Armagh, Down, Fermanagh, Derry and Tyrone), the three other counties of the old province of Ulster (Cavan, Donegal and Monaghan) were separated off and joined in the new dominion.

The economy they joined was subsequently drained by civil war, and they were the far counties on the new state's periphery. Neutrality during the Second World War, plus high trade tariffs and state censorship, led to economic and social lethargy and further isolation, even after Eire become a Republic in 1948. The whole of the country, and particularly the western counties, remained trapped in some 1930s time warp well into the 1950s, and even today there is a certain amount of catching up still to do.

But many in the Northern Ireland part of Ulster prefer it that way. Belfast's chattering classes scour the lonely valleys and the steep-streeted villages with their tiny ocean harbors, seeking out near derelict cottages to preserve in aspic. Soon turf is once again stacked by the wall, green wellies by the door, Chardonnay in the gas-powered icebox, Irish music among the Mozart CDs. The bungalow rash, scattered high on far hilltops too windy for comfort, their condensation-shrouded picture windows leaking blue television-given light, is much deplored.

In a circle of jagged rocks which makes up the tiny bay, the Atlantic boils, rolling white stones as big and as round as cannonballs. A waist-high iron winch, used long ago to haul the lobster boats, rusts amongst the sea-pinks. For the holiday-home hunting family from Northern Ireland, negotiating through the parish priest has secured the agreement of all the descendants – now spread from Boston to Sydney – to sell an abandoned property. A four-wheel drive vehicle stands high over the sheep-cropped grass.

Some – mostly tweed-suited painters and poets – bought cottages decades ago; others might also have established their second home earlier but, over the years of the "Troubles," there were stories of IRA terrorists in safe havens in Donegal's border villages; of "northern' registered cars vandalized. Many cut back on their Donegal holidays; others, the more staunchly Unionist, rejected altogether a state they saw as soft on terrorism. But now they are back, crowding the bars with north Down accents; tapping their feet with the fiddlers and playing golf over the sheep-studded links.

The secret of sexing breakfast in Donegal's unsophisticated eating houses – where lunch is dinner, and high tea is the best of the evening meals – is soon revealed: a "gentleman's" has two eggs, a "lady's" only one. Outside, the sun sparkles and the heather purples on the valley's slopes. Lamb graze up as far as the start of the talus; their cutlets, were they on offer, would taste of wild sage and bog mint. The soda and potato breads, if they had not been store-bought, would have been delicious. But, ironically, it is only in the "big houses," now turned into expensive guesthouses, where the mistress of the house bakes the peasant breads once reserved for servants and stirs the home-made jams fresh from summer hedgerows. Indeed, but for these oases of newly commercialized "auld dacency," and for a handful of bistros catering – in Derry's Donegal hinterland – for the Maiden City's nouveau riche, few restaurants offer the chance to savor the riches of Donegal's coastline:

OPPOSITE: An aerial view of Letterkenny, County Donegal.
FOLLOWING PAGE: Trawbreaga Bay, Inishowel Peninsular.

oysters snuggling in coves, carpets of mussels in inshore beds, crab, crayfish, squat-lobster and shrimp taken in pots whose floats dot the choppy indigo seas. For the majority of diners the choice remains undistinguished – sirloin steak, fried chicken, bland farmed salmon – while in the county's little ports and in the massive overcrowded harbor of Killybegs, where Victorian architecture stands uneasily in the Klondyke atmosphere of a frontier town, thousands of tons of fresh brill, dab, haddock, hake, herring, mackerel, monkfish, plaice, ray, scad, skate, sprat, squid, and turbot are landed almost every week.

Yet more is transferred, creaking and rocking, onto "mother ships" bound for other lands. Over 90 percent is destined for export: to glisten in boxes in Rungis market in Paris, on the marble slabs of the Maravillas

market-house in Madrid, or to be salted, frozen and dried for the canneries of Lagos. Apologists explain the native neglect of fish as a folk memory of the Great Famine, or as a response to the church's insistence on a meatless Friday. For the Church's writ is still large here, and each summer 15,000 barefooted souls spend three days and nights in the 1500-year-old ritual penance of St. Patrick's Purgatory on Station Island in Lough Derg, subsisting on a diet of water, black tea and dry bread.

Up the slopes, faint patterns point to transhumance where the sod-roofed "booleys" stood. Once, many in the county had three homes: a hut by the shore for when diving tern told of inshore herring; a stream-side winter cottage; and a "booley" used at autumn grazing. Not entirely unlike the county's Northern Ireland visitors: roughing in Donegal at weekends, renting in Mediterranean hills during the summer.

BELOW: The fishing port of Killybegs, County Donegal.
OPPOSITE: A view of Lough Swilly, County Donegal.

Down

St. Patrick's county

Though the man himself is all of Ireland's apostle saint, St. Patrick's Day is not much celebrated in the northern counties. A few tired bunches of what may be shamrock, normally imported from the Netherlands, are sold over florists' counters. Some take a holiday in solidarity with the Republic's national saint; others stay steadfastly at their desks, shunning such "Roman" fripperies. Well before the multi-national supermarkets started spreading the word according to Mammon and greedily eroding the concept of the universal holiday, uncertainty about allegiances cast a doubt over the whole proceedings.

Even in Downpatrick, the saint's supposed burial place, his day's commemorations – a motley parade of school bands and "floats," prominently sponsored by local business men – have neither the penitential nor

BELOW: Scutch Mill, once used for linen making, now preserved in the Ulster Folk and Transport Museum.
OPPOSITE: Silent Valley, the Mountains of Mourne.

the colorful vigor which are applied to local saints' days in southern European countries. The parade's defenders will offer up that perennial Irish excuse, 'Sure wouldn't it be grand? If only we had the weather.'

Aside from the rain the suspicion exists in Ireland that St. Patrick's Day is really a matter for Americans whose celebrations – beer dyed grass green in South Boston; a bilious river in Chicago; a jolly, if anachronistic, parade in New York – stretch over almost a week. Thus Irish passport holders, north and south of the border, who are affluent enough – or whose employers connive at business meetings located in America in mid-March – fly west on Aer Lingus, celebrating all the way there and back in a sentimental miasma of Irish Americana. Accountants, one presumes, look the other way.

For many it comes as a surprise, perhaps, that our Irish saint was the son of a Roman official, Calpurnius, based in Wales, and that his efforts to proselytize among the then native inhabitants of this island were focused mainly, not in the south, but in Ulster. "I, Patrick," he wrote, in dog Latin, in his Confession, "a sinner, the simplest of men…was taken away into Ireland in captivity."

Incarcerated for six years "near the western sea," tradition has it that he tended sheep as a slave on the lonely slopes of Slemish Mountain in County Antrim, having been sold to the unsympathetic Irish chieftain, Milchu. But Patrick, it seems, had little gift for geographical description and so topographical clues in his writings reproduced, faithfully or otherwise, in the 9th century Book of Armagh, are few. After a period away – some authorities would have it that he took holy orders in England; others that he studied in Auxerre in France – he was ordered to return to Ireland, presumably on the suspect grounds that he knew the territory, although according to the Confession he was simply acting in response to a voice which had called to him in a vision: "We beg you, holy boy, to come and walk amongst us once again."

He died at Saul 60 years later having converted most of the north, adopted the druidic chant as St.

OPPOSITE: Spelga Reservoir, in the Mourne Mountains, teems with brown trout for the dedicated angler. All you need is a fishing license to take advantage of it.

Patrick's breastplate, accommodated pagan ritual dates within his church's calendar and having – in true saintly fashion – resisted demons disguised as blackbirds, banned snakes and adopted the shamrock as the symbol for the Holy Trinity.

Abbeys and friaries followed in his wake, his successors building where the landfall was good and where clean water flowed. St. Comgall raised a monastery school at Bangor, baptized a mermaid and sent St. Columbanus and St. Gall to mainland Europe to preserve Christianity's flickering light during the continent's Dark Ages. St. Finnian built an abbey at Newtownards, St. Mochaoi another at Nendrum.

But despite the multitude of legends surrounding Patrick, the warriors he faced down, the demons he expelled, we know nothing of his views on chastity, fornication, and masturbation, matters so worrying for the churches in Ireland.

There are those historians who will claim the few stones at Saul are all that are left of his church, destroyed, as in all such legends, by the invading Danes. Now the saint stands, remembered in a vast statue high on Slieve Patrick, "Patrick's Hill." A cluster of stone structures in a pretty little valley to the south are deemed St. Patrick's Wells and curative properties are claimed for their waters which still spill, like some primitive shower device, in one of the enclosures now referred to as "the women's baths."

When Patrick came to the area he would have seen what are still Downpatrick's two dominant hills, each topped with a fort, referred to in common parlance as a "dun." On one he built a church thus giving to later generations the name, Dun Patrick.

Of course a dead saint is as useful as a live one, and somewhat less troublesome. So when the Anglo-Norman colonizing forces came north under the command of the self-styled "Prince of Ulster," John de Courcy, they were just as pragmatic as the good saint had been before them. Alfreca, de Courcy's wife, wishing to create an administrative focus to which dissidents must attend – and so be kept under supervision – decreed that Patrick's remains had been discovered buried at Downpatrick, thus securing the town's status. Such appealing myths have acquired great potency over the centuries as the massive boulder-like gravestone, inscribed "Patric'(sic), but dating from only 1900, attests.

Fermanagh

A diet of stones and fishes

Mossy headstones in the graveyard on the island of Galloon in the western part of the county of Fermanagh strike notes which resonate across time. On many, a skilled mason of the 18th century has carved, with great craft, those symbols of death which said so much to the people of his time. Here, among the coarse, wet and fresh cut grass, are the cold icons of man's mortality: crossed bones, sand-timer hourglass, bell, coffin and skull.

Yet, it is not the bell tolling the inexorable passing of the hours – recorded by the falling grains of sand – nor the sombre closed-for-ever coffin lids, nor the piratical crossed bones, but rather it is the carved skulls which evoke times before the dawn of Ireland's written history. For they echo the carvings of a cult from the core of Celtic mysticism which can trace its lineage down the centuries in the enigmatic stone heads found scattered across the multitude of islands in this quiet county of reedy lakes, and of fish, and of time standing still.

Major-General, the Honorable Sir Galbraith Lowry Cole, scion of the Cole family who came to the county

of Fermanagh in the 1600s, also looks down in stone effigy, cavalry sabre in hand, over the four hills of Enniskillen, the island county town. Were the sabre a telescope, he could scan the 50 watery miles (80 km) of the two Loughs Erne which dominate Fermanagh, fed by the River Erne which winds its way north and west from its bubbling County Cavan source to where it enters the sea among Donegal's surf beaches.

At the general's stone feet, as it were, is Enniskillen. Its one long main street curls east to west, traversing four hills, two bridges and changing its name a handful of times as it does. The hills offer an encapsulation of its strengths. On the farthest, Portora Royal School traces its origins back to 1608 and the Plantation – the playwrights Oscar Wilde and Samuel Beckett, are among its alumni. On the next are the Anglican Cathedral of St. MacCartin's, Catholic St. Michael's and the Wesleyan Chapel. The next is the Townhall's hill. The fourth hill, Fort Hill, is the

BELOW: Lough Navar Forest, County Fermanagh.
OPPOSITE: Lough Erne, County Fermanagh.

general's.

At its foot, by the East Bridge, stands the Cenotaph, where, at 11.00 a.m. each Remembrance Sunday in early November, old men with burnished medals, Boy Scouts with shining shoes and nurses in uniform, gather in silence to remember friends, fathers, grandfathers and great-grandfathers (of all religions and of no religion) who gave their lives during the two world wars. At the 1987 Remembrance Day service the IRA detonated a bomb among those so gathered, killing 11 and shattering the bodies of many more.

No other killing so moved Ireland. War-hardened reporters, who had seen it all, could not fight back tears. President Reagan and Charles Haughey, the Republic of Ireland's Taoiseach (Prime Minister), spoke of their revulsion, the Pope of his shock. On stage, in concert in America, Bono, of the Dublin group U2, cursed Irish-Americans who fund the terrorists.

There is a new Cenotaph now, and dotted along the rows of solid Georgian merchants' houses which flank this main street, are the Convent School, the Orangemen's Hall, the Court House, the Presbyterian Church, the two local newspaper offices, a scattering of bistros, gift shops and a dozen atmospheric pubs made cosmopolitan with the accents of Dutch, French, German and Swiss who have cruised and fished the great lakes as holidaymakers, undeterred, even through the worst of the "Troubles," letting the county know its future is tourism.

"Cole's Pole," as the Enniskillen people term the pillar on which the general's statue stands, is fluted and Doric. Over the centuries the Coles, who became the earls of Enniskillen, came, both directly, and by intermarriage with Planter and Gaelic families, to control every rolling arable acre, every lakeside castle – Archdale, Caldwell, Coole, Crevenish, Crom, Hume, Magrath, Maguire, Monea, Portora, Saunderson and Tully – and even policed the lakes through the 17th and 18th centuries. The family ran the county as a private fiefdom. Thirteen of them were members of the British Parliament in the period 1661–1885.

Socially they were as other Anglo-Irish families. They employed professionals to sail their yachts, engaged governesses to teach their daughters French,

OPPOSITE: An aerial view of Enniskillen.

had their sons tutored to serve as high sheriffs at home, and as generals abroad. They vied with their neighbors as to who could build the finest house and sculpt nature to its most ordered. Thus Fermanagh's inheritance from the Coles includes: Castle Coole, Ireland's finest Palladian mansion; Florence Court, a more modest Georgian concoction; battle honors for Enniskillen's Cathedral and misty photographs of aged yachts, so beloved of coffee-table book editors.

There, an interest in the family might have ceased had they not dabbled in scientific pursuits natural to the area. The name of Lady Dorothy Galbraith Cole is still associated with her work in recording the county's cult. For the Celts of the 3d century B.C., the carved human head was the house of the spirit, and just as the cross is the icon of the Christian, so decapitation, not crucifixion, figures in Celtic myth.

Carved heads are found on the ruined churches and crosses scattered liberally by the lakes, none more fascinating than the six half-pagan, half-Christian images cemented into the tiny 12th-century, ruined church on White Island. The first figure on the left is a squatting female – grotesque – cheeks bulging; mouth grinning; legs wide apart. She is aroused, bestriding the bridge from pagan exultation and Christian disapproval. Such figures are termed Sheela na Gigs and their presence in holy Ireland has given many a god-fearing archaeologist hours of soul-searching.

The Coles' other scientific diversion was fish. Quite rightly so, for the Erne and its catchment has much to reveal. There are big trout to troll for on the Lower Lough Erne and plenty of smaller ones to take the mayfly. Salmon, almost destroyed by the hydro-electric barrier at Ballyshannon, are effecting a return.

There is also the delightful charr – olive black, pink-spotted – a distant relative of the salmon, left behind in a scattering of Irish loughs when the ice age retreated. The many sub-species of charr swimming in Ireland's isolated lakes are mostly named after those who first recorded them for scientific journals. In Lough Eske is found Cole's charr, named for the 3d earl of Enniskillen, whose donation of the first specimen in the 1860s was but one of his many contributions, for which the British Museum is no doubt eternally grateful.

Monaghan

Lost for words

Whereas the county of Cavan – its surface dimpled with little hollows filled with water – had its name Anglicized from the descriptive Irish for "the hollow place," An Cabhan, County Monaghan takes its anglicized title from the equally appropriate Irish, Muineachan, "the place of little thicketed hills." However, despite the wild beauty of its scenery and the neat geometry of its Planters' and English garrison towns with their slim-spired Gothic churches and stout Georgian houses, this county has tended to receive a bad press from its many native authors.

While rough woodland and vanilla-scented gorse spreads over the poor soil of humpy hills, the water –

and there is water everywhere – drains down over the boggy ground into little reed-fringed lakes whose shores are often too sodden to approach with any degree of safety.

Once this was a good place to hide, if you were desperate enough. First, Stone Age peoples, and later the early Christians, retreated here from their invaders, who contented themselves, in the main, with the richer lands east and west which offered easier pickings with less likelihood of ambush. The Vikings and the Normans kept to the plains of Louth, leaving only small bands of marauders supporting the Irish chiefs who operated hit-and-run forays from the damp chill of Monaghan's mist-shrouded hollows. Even when Oliver Cromwell invaded in 1649, his massacres of the Catholic Irish were kept mainly to the coast, though his subsequent mass deportations were not.

Throughout the 17th century, the Planters, mostly from Scotland, took only the best land, clearing it to grow flax and raise sheep, and, if they prospered, gentrifying it with meadows and copses of beech, lime, sycamore and chestnut imported to decorate a valley's sweep or a hill's profile. In Monaghan's villages, as in those of eastern Antrim, the Scots Ulster tongue, with its Scottish pronunciations, its economy of put-down and its directness of humor, survives in the language of the fair day, the corner shop counter and the harvest.

But the land around Inniskeen, Inis Caoin, 'the pleasant island" on the little River Fane, is now comprehensively signposted as "Kavanagh Country," as rural tourism searches for its niche to market.

LEFT: Dartry Forest, County Monaghan, was formerly the estate of the earls of Dartry, the descendants of Protestant settlers who gave Monaghan much of its character. Today it is a forest park open to the public. It offers a panorama of the rugged terrain of Monaghan, all woods and gorse scattered across a rolling terrain covered in what the poet Patrick Kavanagh called "a stony, grey soil."

Here, the harsh lives of its poor farmers working the "black hills" were immortalized by that irascible, embittered, cruelly critical, but wonderful poet, Patrick Kavanagh (1904–67):

My black hills have never seen the sun rising,
Eternally they look north towards Armagh.
Lot's wife would not be salt if she had been
Incurious as my black hills that are happy
When dawn whitens Glassdrummond chapel.
FROM: 'SHANCODUFF" BY PATRICK KAVANAGH

Kavanagh was born the son of a subsistence farmer who supplemented his income by cobbling. The poems he wrote were linked closely to the landmarks around his home. "Inniskeen" and "Shancoduff" are among his most affectionate. While such works as his autobiography, *The Green Fool*, and his roman à clef, *Tarry Flynn*, celebrate the charms and delights of his bucolic upbringing, they also rigorously condemn the crass absurdities of rural poverty. His major work, *The Great Hunger*, is decidedly anti-pastoral and never won favor with any establishment; his grimmer visions of the poor farmer's life running contrary to the idyllic conventions of the Irish literary revival. In short, Kavanagh opposed art as nationalism, heritage as future and the rosy-tinted view of a mystical, mythical landscape, and in Dublin his cantankerous nature and his unflinchingly savage criticism of fellow writers left him with few friends.

John McGahern is another writer to come from the poor farmlands of south Ulster. The son of a police sergeant, he grew up in Cootehill on the Monaghan-Cavan border in the late 1930s and his grim tales tell of harsh, uncommunicative and introspective local family life, wrought hard under an incessant rain.

His first novel, *The Barracks*, was published to critical acclaim in 1963. Two years later his second, *The Dark*, was banned under the Republic's Church-inspired 1929 Censorship of Publications Act and also cost him his job as a teacher. The unspoken emotions he dissects expose a repressive world of ordinary people from both sides in the civil war of 1922: of policemen, nurses and teachers; of ancient hatreds passed down from generation to generation, submerged in the Irish omertàs which make taboo so many aspects of tenderness and sexual expression; of the fear and secrecy surrounding the country's age-old political vendettas.

Following the banning of The Dark, McGahern was forced to leave Ireland for a time. Now returned, his acute and painful presentation of the dark, closed side of rural Ireland have brought him respect, but no popular affection.

Monaghan's metropolises: Ballybay, Bailieborough, Castleblaney, Carickmacross and Clones all run to the pattern of south Ulster Plantation towns, with the wide main street, the crisp spire of the Planters' Gothic Church, the stern court house, the solid market house, the charming almshouse, the castle, the tumbled abbey, the Norman ruin, the drumlin hill and the little lake.

Some towns are bright as new pins, prosperous from new light industries; others reek of neglect. Here, wind blows chip papers across main squares – "diamonds" in the local parlance – past pollution-blackened high crosses whose carved depictions of Adam and Eve are almost indistinguishable amid the grime and street detritus. Old paint bubbles, and cracks cover the once-fine Georgian window-sills, protected here and there by cast-iron spikes, originally designed to deter fair day cattle, or their roistering herders keen on a sit-down after a pint or two. Street names are often the last memorials to the town's long-departed founding fathers.

Visiting the county town of Monaghan itself must have made a lasting impression on the enquiring minds of boys and girls growing up on farms and in tiny villages. Its history would, no doubt, have been drummed into them at their school desks. They would have been told that it traces its past back to the Crannog – a man-made island – in the lake in the grounds of St. Louis Convent which was used by the local chieftains as their 14th-century base.

Today, the town's pride rests on other things, such as its new theater, The Garage. Here, many of Ireland's more adventurous touring theatrical companies, from north and south of the border, carry on the island's long tradition of "fit ups" – whereby actor-managers brought the classics, farce and melodrama to the stages of even the smallest towns – as well as celebrating, to good effect, the sometimes uncomfortable truths contained in the works of the wetland writers.

Tyrone

From here to the White House

This is a wild county where buzzards swoop over empty moors and the genetic skeins of so many US presidents and frontiersmen were knitted together. Woodrow Wilson's family still farm land at Dergalt on the Plumbridge Road outside Strabane. Whitewashed and thatched over its oak roof timbers, the old house is furnished as it should be: a dresser stands on the clay floor; a kettle sings in the hearth; a portrait of Judge James, Woodrow's grandfather, hangs above it. Wilson's grandmother, Annie Adams, came from Sion Mills, a few miles further south. She met James in 1807 on an emigrant ship sailing west from Ulster for the Americas. They had ten children of whom the

BELOW: Gortin Glen Forest Park, County Tyrone.
OPPOSITE: An aerial view of Omagh, County Tyrone.

tenth was Woodrow Wilson's father, Joseph.

Five Ulstermen had signed the Declaration of American Independence in 1776 and, indeed, much of what was written in the declaration can be traced back to the writings of another Ulster-Scot, one who never made the tortuous voyage west. The philosopher, Francis Hutcheson, who died 40 years before, had written extensively on rights which were unalienable, on liberty, and the pursuit of happiness.

ABOVE: Cranagh, Glenelly Valley and Sperrin Mountains, County Tyrone.

No surprise then that, in all, over a dozen Ulstermen – descendants of those who made up this second wave – made it to the White House: Susanna Boylston Adams, mother of John Adams, the second president (1797–1801), came from Ulster-Scots farmers; the fifth president (1817–25), James

Monroe, took his family name from Mount Roe, just across the Tyrone border, in Derry; while the sixth president (1825–29) was John Quincy Adams, son of John Adams.

Andrew Jackson, the seventh president (1829–37), claimed to have been born in 1767 on an emigrant ship on the high seas. He led the fight against the English at the Battle of New Orleans. The grandfather of Andrew Johnson, the seventeenth president (1865–69), emigrated from the tiny village of Ballyclare – which also claims Mark Twain's family roots – in 1750. Chester Alan Arthur, the twenty-first president (1881–85), was, like Jackson and Buchanan, a first generation American. His father William left Dreen, Cullybackey, in 1816. Grover Cleveland, the twenty-second and twenty-fourth president (1885–89 and 1893–97), owes his Scots-Irish ancestry to his maternal grandfather, Abner Neal, a bookseller who left Ulster late in the 18th century.

Benjamin Harrison, the twenty-third president (1889–93), had two great, great, grandparents of Ulster descent. The family of William McKinley, the twenty-fifth president (1897–1901), left Conagher near Ballymena in 1743 and Richard Milhous Nixon, the thirty-seventh president (1969–74), had ancestors who left Ulster in 1853.

Details of all the presidents past and present – President Clinton's people came from Ballycassidy – and of all the presidents' men and women can be found among the displays at the Ulster-American Folk Park at Camphill, near the county town of Omagh, with its unevenly matched double-spired Sacred Heart Church.

Over chauvinistic to some, uncomfortably parochial or too exclusively Protestant in its origins to others, the park nevertheless certainly offers much to the understanding of today's Ulster. Some of the information is amusing; some arcane; some instructive. John Paul Getty's family, we learn, came from Ulster-Scots stock. So did those of Henry "Billy the Kid" McCarty, James Butler "Wild Bill" Hickok, William Frederick "Buffalo Bill" Cody and Robert Leroy Parker, more famous under his alias, 'Butch Cassidy.'

So, too, did the families of three of the earliest astronauts, John Glenn, Neil Armstrong and James B. Irwin, as well as those of Gene Kelly and Marion Mitchell Morrison, the latter better known as John Wayne. The film, The Searchers, embodied much of what the Ulster-Scots stood for.

In truth, however, the Sperrin Mountains north and west of Omagh may better serve to place man's efforts in nature's perspective. They emit an eerie air of ominous other-worldliness scarce in the north. But there are good trout in the bubbling streams which rush under the pretty arched, stone bridges. There is even a little gold panning and the rare (and protected) freshwater mussel which may secrete the even rarer freshwater pearl. What if the clouds scudding behind you over the lonely moor do cast an ominous shadow, hurrying you to the village pub before dusk?

Once densely forested – now speckled with grid-planted forest parks – the county was the last stronghold of the O'Neills and the O'Donnells, earls of Tyrone and Tryconnell, holding out against the English until the Flight of the Earls in 1607.

Those who stayed behind rebelled in 1641, massacring Scots and English settlers in a killing to be rued in 1649 when Cromwell took revenge at Drogheda, putting the town to the sword. No trace of the true O'Neills is to be found, bar their crowning place on top of a tree-ringed hill at Tullaghoge outside Cookstown.

An even grimmer history surrounds Harry Aimbreidh O'Neill's 500 year-old, twin-towered ruin near Newtownstewart. His sister was grossly disadvantaged – those that spoke of her said she had a head like a pig. But Aimbreidh (pronounced "Avery') wanted her wed and offered a dowry large enough to attract a flutter of suitors. He also added a sub-clause of Shakespearean subtlety, namely that any suitor to gain the dowry must commit himself to marriage without seeing the girl. A later change of intent would mean not only loss of the dowry, but also of the suitor's life by the hangman's noose.

It is said that such was his sister's affliction and fortune that 19 men were put to the scaffold. Was it for her pleasure? Or his madness? Who can judge him now, not knowing the needs of the 15th century? However, such was his unshakable resolve and determination that a few of his genes must surely have become intertwined with those of the men and women who conquered the American wilderness.

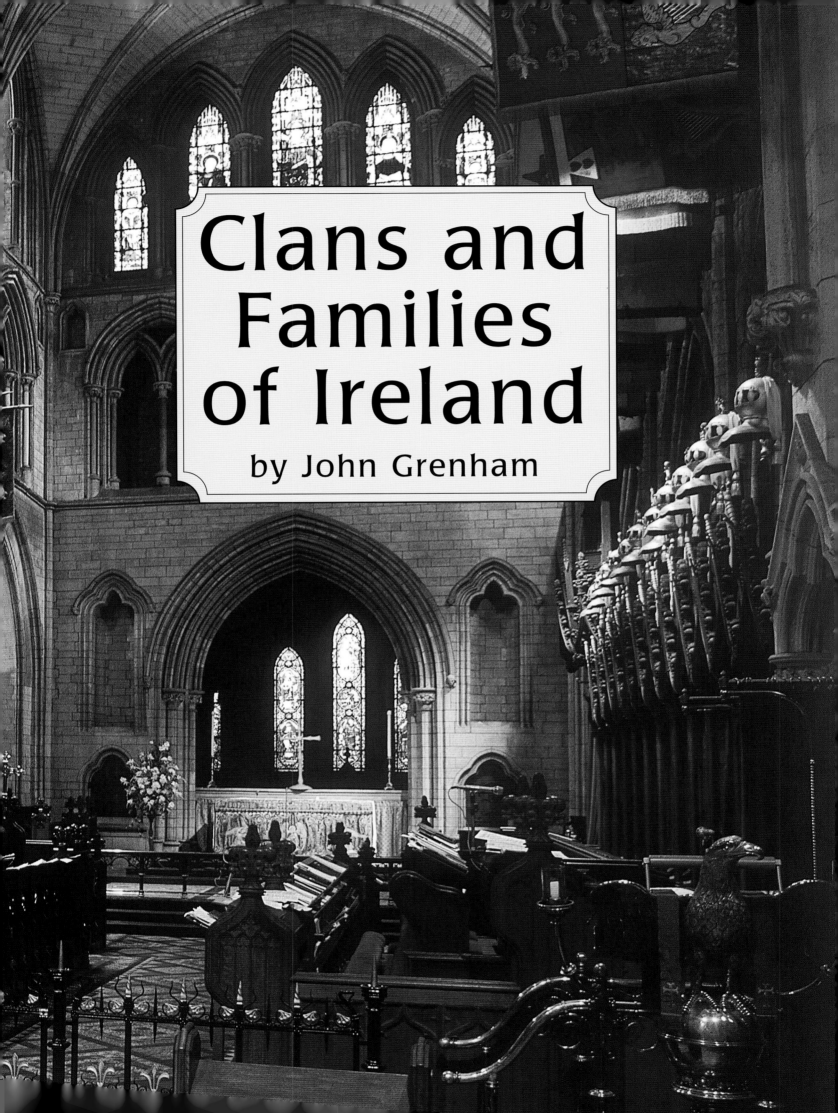

Clans and
Families
of Ireland

by John Grenham

Heraldry and Ireland

Heraldry is the study and description ("blazoning") of coats of arms, and of the rights of individuals and families to bear arms. It has its origins in the first half of the twelfth century, when knights in continental Europe first began to use markings on their shields to identify themselves in battles and in tournaments. Developments in medieval weaponry and armor made this necessary. Helmets encased the head, and armor covered the whole body. As a result, the individual was completely anonymous; the urgency of knowing whether the large, armor-clad individual galloping at you was a friend or an enemy is self-evident.

At first, military necessity was paramount. Large, clearly identifiable patterns, involving two or three colors divided into a number of compartments related to the physical construction of the shield make up the earliest arms. Later, when animals and other symbols were added, the need for quick recognition again meant that a large degree of stylized convention was used, so that the heraldic lion, for instance, bears only a passing resemblance to the real thing.

The military origin of arms is also the most likely explanation for their emergence at almost exactly the same time in England, France, Germany, and Italy. The eight Christian crusades against Islam between 1096 and 1271 involved knights from all of these countries, and provided a context in which a system of military recognition was essential. The endurance of heraldry is no doubt partly due to the fact that it spread over the whole of Europe virtually simultaneously. Crosses and fleurs-de-lys, Christian symbols *par excellence*, also take their origins in heraldry from the Crusades.

But heraldry would long ago have died out completely if the only need it met was military. Individual recognition and family identity are powerful and universal human needs and, towards the end of the thirteenth century, a further change came about as the social and non-military aspects of heraldry evolved and it became established that coats of arms were personal and hereditary. The symbols used could now relate to the name, the office, or the territory of the bearer, and were dictated less by the imperative of immediate recognition. One of the results from this period on was the creation of so-called "canting" arms, based on a pun on the name in Ireland, the arms of the Aherne family, displaying three herons, are an example. The main non-military use of arms was on seals, as a means of proving the authenticity of documents, and the practice of using birds or animals to fill empty space around the arms on these seals gave rise to "supporters," now regarded as part of the arms of peers. Eventually, arms were also used on tombs, and then on works of art and possessions.

The symbols used in heraldry have a variety of origins: In the Christian nature of the crusades, in the (supposed) character of the individual or family itself, in some event which is identified with the family. There is no strict attachment of significance to

ABOVE: The Book of the Boyles, *a hand-made masterpiece of the heraldic art, showing the descent of the Earls of Cork and Orrery.*
OPPOSITE: The insignia of the Order of St. Patrick, instituted by the English in Ireland during the eighteenth century

269

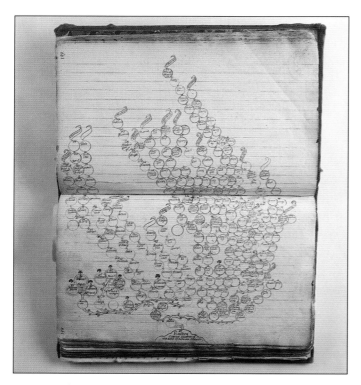

ABOVE: The line of descent of the Ui Fiachrach, from Roger O'Ferrall's Linea Antiqua. *The semi-historical Fiachra is at the bottom, and the various families and offshoots, including the Madigans, the O'Hanlons, and the Moonys, grow upwards and outwards.*

OPPOSITE: The herald's tabard, worn by the Ulster King of Arms on ceremonial occasions.

particular symbols, although the reasons for some symbols are self-evident; the lion is conventionally regal, the unicorn is a symbol of purity, the boar is a Celtic symbol of endurance and courage, and so on.

As arms proliferated, a natural need arose for rules to prevent different individuals and families using the same or similar symbols and arrangements of symbols. The first result was the evolution of the peculiar technical vocabulary used in describing arms, a highly stylized and extremely precise mixture of early French, Latin and English, still used in heraldry today. Then came the creation of the offices of King of Arms or King of Heralds throughout most of Europe in the fourteenth century. The principal functions of these were the recognition of arms, the recording of the possession of arms, the granting of arms and adjudication in disputes between bearers of arms. By the end of the fifteenth century, since the right to bear arms depended on family and ancestry, they had also become genealogists.

Irish Heraldic Traditions

Arms first arrived in Ireland with the Normans, who brought with them all the social structures on which European heraldry depended; up to then, although some evidence of the use of military symbolism among the Gaels survives, heraldry in the true sense did not exist. Norman heraldry shows clearly its military origins, with a preponderance of clear, simple devices, (known as "ordinaries") designed for easy recognition. Examples of these are found in the arms of the de Burgos, de Clares, Fitzgeralds, and other families of Norman extraction.

A separate heraldic tradition is found in the arms of the Anglo-Irish. This can be dated to the mid-sixteenth century, when the Tudor monarchs of England began to address themselves seriously to taking possession of Ireland, and establishing the full panoply of English law. Accordingly, the office of Ulster King of Arms, with authority over all arms in Ireland, was set up in 1552 as part of the household of the vice-regal court, the administration of the English king's deputy in Ireland. Inevitably, the early records of the office contain many examples of Anglo-Irish heraldic practice, characterized by great elaboration, with individual shields often containing as many as a dozen charges, reflecting the preoccupations of the Anglo-Irish with family relationships. Whereas Norman arms are clearly military, the arms of the Anglo-Irish are part of a much more settled society, concerned above all about status.

The third tradition of heraldry in Ireland relates to the original inhabitants, the Gaelic Irish, and is more problematic, since heraldry was a natural aspect of the social life of both Normans and Anglo-Irish, but originally had no part in Gaelic society. The characteristics of the arms in use among the important Gaelic families do have a number of common features, however. In part this is due to the role of genealogy in early Irish society, the myth of a common origin was a potent means of unifying the different Celtic and pre-Celtic peoples of Ireland, and the enormously elaborate Gaelic pseudogenealogies, tracing every family in the country back to the same individual, were designed to reinforce that myth. In addition, on a more mundane level the nature of Gaelic law meant that, in effect, what you could own

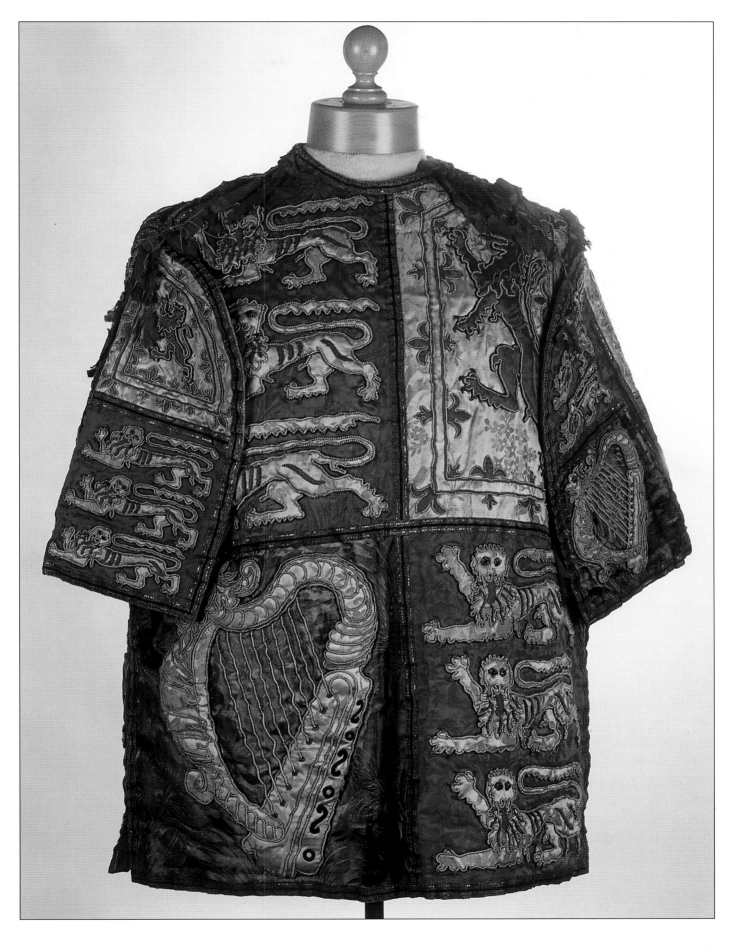

depended on who you were related to. These two factors, the importance of the origin myth and the property rights of the extended family, are reflected in the heraldic tradition which grew up in Ireland from about the fifteenth century.

Unlike the military simplicity of the Normans or the conventional elaborations of the Anglo-Irish, the symbols used in the arms of Gaelic Irish families tend to relate to pre-Christian myths, often in quite obscure ways. Thus, for example, the Red Hand of the O'Neills, now also associated with the province of Ulster, in heraldic terms *a dexter hand appaum gules*, also occurs in various forms in the arms of other Gaelic families. The reason would appear to lie in the name of the son of Bolg or Nuadu, the Celtic sun-god, in some accounts the divine ancestor of all the Celts. This son was known as Labraid Lámhdhearg, or "Labraid of the Red Hand." The association with the ancestral power of the sun-god is clearly a very good reason for the choice of symbol.

In a similar way, the stag that appears in the arms of the MacCarthy, the O'Sullivan, the Healy, and many other Munster families relates very clearly to the kingship myth of the rainn peoples. In this myth, the legitimacy of the ruling house is confirmed when a stag enters; the animal is hunted, and the border of the territory is defined by the chase; the future ruler is the individual who eventually slays the stag. What the many families displaying the stag in their arms have in common is that they were originally part of the great Eoghanacht tribal grouping which dominated Munster until the time of Brian Boru. The stag was self-evidently an appropriate choice of symbol.

As in Ulster and Munster, so in Connacht the arms of the ruling family, the O'Conors, and of a whole host of others connected with them – Flanagan, O'Beirne and many more – all display a common symbol, in this case the oak tree. Again, the reason lies in pre-Christian belief, in the old Celtic reverence for the oak, and its resulting association with kingship; the medieval sources record ruling families having at least one sacred tree outside the family's ring-fort.

As well as the association of heraldic symbolism with pre-Christian myth, the nature of the property relations within the extended family meant that arms were used in ways quite different from those practiced among the Normans and Anglo-Irish. In particular, most of the arms were regarded as the property of the sept (defined by Dr Edward MacLysaght as "a group of persons inhabiting the same locality and bearing the same surname"), rather than being strictly hereditary within a single family, as was and is the case under English and Scottish heraldic law.

In summary, two of the three heraldic traditions in Ireland, the Norman and the Anglo-Irish, form part of the mainstream of European heraldry, while the arms found among the Gaelic Irish have particular characteristics which set them apart.

The Genealogical Office

The Genealogical Office is the successor to the Office of Ulster King of Arms which, as noted above, was created in 1552 with full jurisdiction over arms in Ireland. Ulster retained this power for almost four centuries, until 1943, when the title was transferred to the College of Arms in London and the office of Chief Herald of Ireland was created to continue to fulfil the functions of Ulster in independent Ireland. The new name given to the office of the Chief Herald, "The Genealogical Office," was somewhat inaccurate,

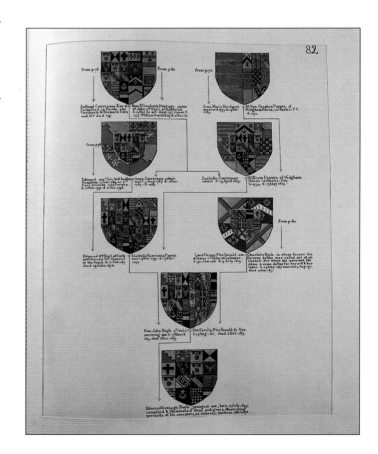

since its primary concern continues to be heraldic rather than genealogical.

Over the first 150 years of its existence, the office was almost exclusively concerned with Anglo-Irish heraldry, recording, registering, and legitimising the practice of arms that had grown up. From the start of the eighteenth century Ulster began to acquire other duties, as an officer of the crown intimately linked to the government. These duties were largely ceremonial, deciding, and arranging precedence on state occasions, as well as introducing new peers to the Irish House of Lords and recording peerage successions. When the chivalric Order of St Patrick was introduced in 1783 as an Irish equivalent of such long-established English institutions as the Order of the Garter, Ulster became its registrar, responsible for administering its affairs. He also continued to have responsibility for the ceremonial aspects of state occasions at the court of the English viceroy. The heraldic and ceremonial duties of Ulster continued down to the twentieth century.

Today the office of the Chief Herald remains principally concerned with the granting of arms to individuals and corporate bodies, the ceremonial aspect having lapsed with the establishment of the Republic of Ireland. One aspect of the office's work today is perhaps connected to this, however. This is the practice of recognising chiefs of the name, instituted in the 1940s by Dr Edward MacLysaght, the first Chief Herald. The aim was simply to acknowledge the descendants of the leading Gaelic Irish families, and this was done by uncovering the senior descendants in the male line of the last chief of the name who had been duly inaugurated under the old Gaelic laws. The practice is a courtesy only; Irish law does not recognize hereditary titles.

One final aspect of the contemporary Genealogical Office is worthy of mention. This is the State Heraldic Museum, established in 1909 by Sir Neville Wilkinson, then Ulster, and continued by his successors, including the present chief herald. Now housed in what was the old Kildare St Club, the Museum shows the diversity of arms in use in Ireland, as well as demonstrating the variety of uses to which heraldic designs have been put, including livery buttons, postage stamps, heraldic banners, signet rings, coins and notes, corporate and county arms, book-

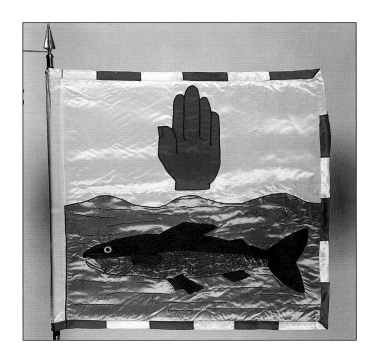

ABOVE: The Heraldic banner of the O'Neills.
OPPOSITE: A line of descent for some nineteenth century members of the Boyle family.

binding, heraldic china and porcelain, and much more. It is a permanent reminder that heraldry retains an important and familiar place even today.

Clans and Families of Ireland

The history of Ireland is a drama of war, invasion, plantation, immigration, emigration, conflict, and solidarity. Like all history, however, it is composed of countless individual family histories, each unique. Surnames are the point where history and family history intersect, marking individuality and kinship.

The intermingling of cultures in Ireland – Gaelic, Viking, Norman, British – has created a huge number of surnames and left ambiguity surrounding the origins of many of them, an ambiguity that is itself an feature of Irishness. No description of Irish surnames can afford to ignore this by selecting only those that match the history of one part of the island or the population. What follows is an account of the two hundred or so most common surnames in Ireland today, chosen purely because they are the most common, and therefore including many usually regarded as English or Scottish. Any surname borne by an Irish person, whatever its origin, is an Irish surname.

Aherne

Aherne is an anglicization of Ó hEachthianna, from Eachthiarna, meaning "lord of horses," and is also found in the variants "Hearn" and "Hearne." Eachthiarna was a relatively common personal name in Gaelic society, borne by, for instance a brother of Brian Boru. The surname originated, in fact, in the sept or tribe of Brian, the Dál gCais, and has always been strongly associated with their homeland in County Clare. The family territory was in the southeast of the county, around Sixmilebridge, up to the end of the Middle Ages, when they migrated south and east, to counties Cork, Limerick and Waterford. To this day, Ahernes are most numerous in counties Cork and Waterford.

The arms of the family include three herons, in an obvious pun on the name.

Allen

The name has two quite distinct origins, one Scots Gaelic, the other French. Ailín, meaning "little rock," is the root of the Scottish name, originally MacAllan. The first recorded arrivals bearing the Scottish name came in the fifteenth century, as hired soldiers ("gallowglasses") imported to Donegal by the O'Donnells, and the migrations of the following two centuries brought many more.

In other cases, the surname derives from the old Breton personal name Alan, which in turn came from the Germanic tribal name Alemannus, meaning "all men." The same root provided the modern French name for Germany, Allemagne. Followers of the invading Normans were the first to carry the Breton version of the name to Ireland.

Irish families bearing the name may be of either origin, though the fact that two-thirds of the Allens are to be found in Ulster – they are especially numerous in counties Antrim and Armagh – suggests that the majority are of Scottish extraction.

Armstrong

This surname originates in the area along the western Scottish borders; the first recorded bearer was Adam Armstrong, pardoned in Carlisle in 1235 for causing another man's death. They were among the most notorious of the riding Border clans, who also included the Elliots, the Grahams and the Johnstons, famous for their lawlessness and plunder. When the power of these clans was savagely broken after 1603 by James I, the Armstrongs scattered, and many migrated to Ulster, where a large number, settled in County Fermanagh. Even today, Fermanagh is home to the largest concentration of Armstrong families in Ireland, although the name is quite common throughout Ulster, particularly in counties Antrim and Tyrone.

As well as those of Scottish origin, however, a good number of Irish Armstrongs are of Gaelic Irish extraction. Many of the Trin-Laverys of County Antrim and the Trainors of counties Tyrone and Monaghan had their surnames mis-translated as Armstrong, from the presence of the Irish for "strong," tréan, in their original names.

Barrett

The name Barrett is now concentrated in two widely separated parts of Ireland, in County Cork and in the Mayo-Galway region. The Irish version of the name is Baróid in the south and Bairéid in the west, and this may reflect two separate origins. At any rate, families of the surname first appeared in these areas in the thirteenth century, after the Anglo-Norman invasion. Its Norman origin derives it from the old Germanic personal name, Bernard or Beraud. A separate derivation gives its origin as the Middle English "Barat," a nickname for a quarrelsome or deceitful person.

The western family, originally based around Killala in Mayo, were thoroughly absorbed into Gaelic society very quickly, and in the Middle Ages began to split into various sub-clans, among them McAndrew, Timmons, and Roberts. The Cork settlers were not so Gaelicized, giving their name to the large barony of Barretts in the middle of the county.

The arms of the family are based on word play, a pictorial version of barrettes, French for "short bars."

Barry

The first bearer of the surname to arrive in Ireland was Robert de Barri, one of the original band of Norman knights who landed at Bannow in County Wexford in May 1169, and a brother of Giraldus Cambrensis, historian of the invasion. The name comes from the earlier association of the family with the island of Barry, seven miles southwest of Cardiff in Wales. From the start the family were prominent in the settlement of east Cork, and were soon absorbed into the native culture, forming subsepts on Gaelic lines, the most important being Barry Mór, Barry Óg and Barry Roe. The names of two of these are perpetuated in the names of the Cork baronies of Barrymore and Barryroe, and many other

Cork place names are linked to the family: Kilbarry, Rathbarry and Buttevant (from the family motto Boutez en avant), to mention only three. The surname is now very numerous in Ireland, but still inextricably associated with County Cork.

As well as the Norman origin, two relatively uncommon Gaelic surnames, Ó Beargha and Ó Báire, have also been anglicized as Barry.

Beatty

In Ulster, where it is found most frequently by far, this surname is generally of Scottish origin. In Scotland it originated as "Baty," a pet form of Bartholomew. The family were well known in Galloway and along the Borders, where they were one of the infamous "riding clans." After the destruction by James I of these clans, many Beatties migrated to Ulster during the Plantation. Their settlements were concentrated especially in County Fermanagh, where they remain numerous.

Some Beatties, outside Ulster, also have a separate Gaelic origin, from Mac Biataigh, meaning "provider of food." The same original was also sometimes transliterated as Betagh.

Bell

The surname is one of the 100 most common in Ireland, and is found most frequently by far in the northern part of the country, particularly in Ulster, where it is especially numerous in counties Antrim and Down.

In Ulster, Bell is almost always of Scottish origin, the family being one of the infamous "riding clans" along the Borders, descended from Gilbert le fitz Bel, bel meaning "beautiful" or "handsome." After the destruction of the power of these clans in the early seventeenth century, many Bells migrated to Ulster during the Plantation.

The name may also, more rarely, be a phonetic anglicization of the Scots Gaelic Mac Gille Mhaoil, which was also turned into MacIlveil and MacGilveil.

Boyd

This surname originated in Scotland, and is now most common in Ulster, particularly in counties Antrim and Down. Two separate derivations are claimed for the name. The most commonly accepted links it with the Scottish island of Bute in the Firth of Clyde, in Gaelic Bód; the Gaelic for "of Bute" is Bóid. Another derivation connects the family with the Stewarts, claiming that the descent is from Robert, son of Simon, one of the Norman founders of the Scottish Stewarts. Robert was known as Buidhe, meaning "yellow," from the color of his hair, and this is taken as the origin of the surname. Whatever the truth, the earliest recorded bearers of the name certainly used the Norman prefix de. These were Robertus de Boyde of Irvine and Alan de Bodha of Dumfries, both living in the early thirteenth century.

Boyle

Boyle, or O'Boyle, is now one of the fifty most common surnames in Ireland. In Irish the name is Ó Baoghill, the derivation of which is uncertain, but thought to be connected to the Irish geall, meaning "pledge." In the Middle Ages the family were powerful and respected, sharing control of the entire northwest of the island with the O'Donnells and the O'Dohertys, and the strongest association of the family is still with County Donegal, where (O)Boyle is the third most numerous name in the county.

The majority of those bearing the name are of Gaelic origin, but many Irish Boyles have separate, Norman origins. In Ulster, a significant number are descended from the Scottish Norman family of de Boyville, whose name comes from the town now known as Beauville in Normandy. The most famous Irish family of the surname were the Boyles, earls of Cork and Shannon, descended from Richard Boyle, who arrived in Ireland from Kent in 1588 and quickly amassed enormous wealth. His earliest known ancestor was Humphrey de Binville, a Norman lord in Herefordshire in the eleventh century.

Bradley

Although Bradley is a common English surname, derived from the many places in England so called, in Ireland the vast majority of Bradleys are in fact descended from the Ó Brolchóin sept. How English ears could have heard this as the equivalent of "Bradley remains one of the many little mysteries of Anglo-Irish relations. Brollach, the root of the name, means "breast."

The name originated in County Tyrone, and the territory inhabited by Ó Brolcháin families covered the area where the present-day counties of Tyrone, Derry, and Donegal meet. From early times they appear to have migrated widely; one branch established itself in the Western Highlands of Scotland, while another settled in County Cork. The many Bradleys in that county to this day descend from this branch. Despite their travels, however, most Bradley families in Ireland today still live in their northern ancestral homeland.

Brady

The surname derives from the Irish Mac Brádaigh, coming, possibly, from brádach, meaning "thieving" or "dishonest." The name is among the sixty most frequently found in Ireland, and remains very numerous in County Cavan, their original homeland, with large numbers also to be found in the adjoining county of Monaghan. Their power was centered on an area a few miles east of Cavan town, from where they held jurisdiction over a large territory within the old Gaelic kingdom of Breifne. There have been many notable poets, clergymen and soldiers of the name, including Thomas Brady (1752-1827), a field marshal in the Austrian army, the satirical Gaelic poet Rev. Philip MacBrady, as well as three MacBrady Bishops of Kilmore, and one MacBrady Bishop of Ardagh. The pre-Reformation Cavan Crozier, originally belonging to one of these MacBradys, is now to be found in the National Museum in Dublin.

Breen

There are several distinct Gaelic origins of the surname, both Mac Braoin and Ó Braoin, from braon, meaning "moisture," or "drop." The Mac Braoin were originally located near the town of Knocktopher in County Kilkenny, but migrated to Wexford after the Anglo-Norman invasions in the twelfth and thirteenth centuries. County Wexford is still the area of the country in which the surname is most common, though a separate Wexford sept, the Ó Briain, also had their surname anglicized as Breen. These were descended from Bran Finn, son of Lachta, King of Munster, and uncle of Brian Boru. However, the O'Breens, rulers of Brawney, a territory near Athlone in counties Offaly and Westmeath, were the most powerful of the name in the Middle Ages; as they lost power the name mutated, and many in the area are now to be found as O'Briens. The surname is now also quite common in north Connacht, County Fermanagh, and in County Kerry.

Brennan

This is one of the most frequent surnames in Ireland and is to be found throughout the country, though noticeably less common in Ulster. It derives from the two Irish originals Ó Braonáin and Mac Branáin. The Mac Branáin were chiefs of a large territory in the east of the present County Roscommon, and a large majority of the Brennans of north Connacht, counties Mayo, Sligo, and Roscommon, descend from them. Ó Braonáin originated in at least four distinct areas: Kilkenny, east Galway, Westmeath and Kerry. Of these the most powerful were the Ó Braonáin of Kilkenny, chiefs of Idough in the north of the county. After they lost their land and status to the English, many of them became notorious as leaders of bands of outlaws.

A separate family, the Ó Branáin, are the ancestors of many of the Brennans of counties Fermanagh and Monaghan, where the name was also anglicized as Brannan and Branny.

Browne

This is one of the most common surnames in the British Isles, and is among the forty commonest in Ireland. It can derive, as a nickname, from the Old English Brun, referring to hair, complexion or clothes, or from the Norman name Le Brun, similarly meaning "the Brown." In the three southern provinces of Munster, Leinster and Connacht, where the name is usually spelt with the final "e," it is almost invariably of Norman or English origin, and was borne by some of the most important of Norman-Irish and Anglo-Irish families, notably the earls of Kenmare in Kerry and Lord Oranmore and Browne and the earls of Altamont in Connacht. The assimilation of the Connacht family into Gaelic life is seen in their inclusion as one of the "Tribes" of Galway.

In Ulster, where it is more often plain "Brown," the surname can be an anglicization of the Scots Gaelic Mac a' Bhruithin ("son of the judge") or Mac Gille Dhuinn ("son of the brown boy"). The largest concentrations of the name in this province are in counties Derry, Down and Antrim.

Buckley

The common English surname Buckley derives from a number of places of the name, and was used as the anglicization for the Irish Ó Buachalla, derived from buachaill, meaning "boy" or "herdsman." In seventeenth-century records, the surname is principally found in County Tipperary, but today counties Cork and Kerry have the largest concentrations. Numerically, it is one of the most frequent Irish surnames; almost three-quarters of the Buckleys in the country live in Munster, however. Other, rarer, anglicized versions of the name are Bohilly, Boughla, and Boughil.

One well-known Corkman of the name was Dermot Buckley, one of the last of the eighteenth-century Rapparees, or highwaymen, whose exploits around the Blackwater valley were legendary.

Burke

Burke, along with its variants Bourke and de Burgh, is now by far the most common Irish name of Norman origin; there are over 20,000 Burkes in Ireland, a fraction of the world-wide total. The first person of the name to arrive in Ireland was William Fitzadelm de Burgo, a Norman knight from Burgh in Suffolk, in the invasion of 1171. He succeeded Strongbow as chief governor. He received the earldom of Ulster, and was granted vast tracts of Connacht. His descendants adopted Gaelic customs almost wholesale, and very quickly became one of the most important families. In Connacht, which remained the center of the family's power, new septs were formed on native Irish lines. William Liath de Burgh, a great-grandson of the original William, was the ancestor of the two most influential clans, the MacWilliam Uachtar of County Galway, and the MacWilliam Íochtar of County Mayo. Other descendants founded families with distinct surnames; "Philbin" derives from Mac Philbín, son of Philip (de Burgh); Jennings is an anglicization of Mac Sheoinín, son of John (de Burgh); Gibbons, found in Mayo, was originally Mac Giobúin, son of Gilbert (de Burgh).

Burns

The surname Burns is Scottish and northern English in origin, and in Ireland is found most frequently in counties Antrim, Down, and Armagh, and in Ulster generally, which is home to more than two-thirds of the Irish who bear the name. It comes from the Middle English burn, meaning "a stream," and would have referred to someone who lived close to a river or stream.

The most important source of the name is the Scottish Clan Campbell. The ancestors of the poet Robert Burns moved from Burnhouse near Loch Etive to Forfar, where they became known as the Campbells of Burness. In 1786, Robert and his brother adopted the spelling "Burns" as a surname, and his subsequent celebrity inspired others to follow his example.

In Ulster, Burns was also used as an anglicization of the Irish O'Byrne and MacBrim.

Butler

The surname Butler, found in both England and Ireland, is Norman in origin, and originally meant "wine steward," from the same root as modern French bouteille, "bottle." The name was then extended to denote the chief servant of a household and, in the households of royalty and the most powerful nobility, a high-ranking officer concerned only nominally with the supply of wine.

In Ireland the most prominent Butler family is descended from Theobald Fitzwalter, who was created "Chief Butler" of Ireland by Henry II in 1177. His descendants became the earls of Ormond in 1328 and dukes of Ormond after the restoration of Charles II in 1660. Up to the end of the seventeenth century, the Butlers were one of the most powerful Anglo-Norman dynasties, sharing effective control of Ireland with their great rivals the Fitzgeralds, earls of Desmond and earls of Kildare. From the Middle Ages right up to the twentieth century their seat was Kilkenny Castle.

Byrne

Byrne or O'Byrne, together with its variants Be(i)rne and Byrnes, is one of the ten most frequent surnames in Ireland today. In the original Irish the name is Ó Broin, from the personal name Bran, meaning "raven." It is traced back to King Bran of Leinster, who ruled in the eleventh century.

As a result of the Norman invasion, the O'Byrnes were driven from their original homeland in County Kildare into south County Wicklow in the early thirteenth century. There they grew in importance over the years, retaining control of the territory until the early seventeenth century, despite repeated attempts by the English authorities to dislodge them.

Even today, the vast majority of the Irish who bear the name originate in Wicklow or the surrounding counties.

Cahill

The original Irish from which the name derives is Ó Cathail, from the common personal name Cathal, sometimes anglicized "Charles," which may in turn derive from the Old Irish catu-ualos, meaning "strong in battle."

Families of the name arose separately in different parts of Ireland, in Kerry, Galway, Tipperary and Clare. Originally the Galway family, located in the old diocese of Kilmacduagh near the Clare border, were most prominent, but their position was usurped by the O'Shaughnessys, and they declined. The southern families flourished, and the name is now most common in counties Cork, Kerry and Tipperary, while it is relatively infrequent in its other original homes. The arms illustrated are those of the Munster Cahills.

Campbell

Campbell is a Scottish surname, one of the ten most numerous in that country, and one of the thirty most numerous in Ireland, with over two-thirds of those who bear the name living in Ulster. It is particularly common in counties Armagh, Down and Antrim. Originally a nickname, it comes from the Scots Gaelic cam beul, meaning "crooked mouth."

Clan Campbell was founded by Gillespie Ó Duibhne, who lived in the thirteenth century, and was the first to assume the surname. His descendants included the most famous branch, the Campbells of Argyll, one of whose members was responsible for the massacre of MacDonalds of Glencoe, which led to the famous feud between the two clans.

The vast majority of Irish Campbells are descended from the Scottish family, although in County Tyrone the surname may be an anglicization of the Irish Mac Cathmhaoil, from Cathmhaol, meaning "battle champion."

Carroll

One of the twenty-five most common Irish surnames, Carroll comes, in the vast majority of cases, from the Irish Ó Cearbhaill, from Cearbhall, a very popular personal name thought to mean "fierce in battle." It is widespread today throughout the three southern provinces of Connacht, Leinster and Munster, reflecting the fact that it arose almost simultaneously as a separate surname in at least six different parts of Ireland.

The most famous of these were the Ely O'Carrolls of Uíbh Fhailí, including modern County Offaly as well as parts of Tipperary, who derived their name from Cearball, King of Ely, one of the leaders of the victorious native Irish army at the battle of Clontarf in 1014. Although their power was much reduced over the centuries in the continuing conflict with the Norman Butlers, they held on to their distinctive Gaelic customs and way of life until the start of the seventeenth century.

Casey

Casey, O'Casey and MacCasey come from the Irish cathasach, meaning "vigilant in war," a personal name which was quite common in early Ireland. This, no doubt, accounts for the fact that Ó Cathasaigh arose as a separate surname in at least five distinct areas, in counties Cork, Dublin, Fermanagh, Limerick and Mayo, with Mac Cathasaigh confined to the Louth/Monaghan area. In medieval times, the Dublin and Fermanagh Caseys were the most prominent, though their power had been broken by the seventeenth century; the name is still common in north County Dublin to this day, as it is in Mayo and north Connacht generally. However, most present-day bearers of the surname are to be found in Munster, not only in Cork and Limerick, but also in Kerry and Tipperary.

The arms shown are those of the County Limerick sept, part of the great tribe of the Dál gCais, who claimed descent from Cas, a semi-mythical prehistoric figure. The depiction of the eagle, with its legendary ability to look into the sun without blinking, may be connected to one of the old tribal gods of the Dál gCais, Derctheine, the fiery-eyed one

Cassidy

In Irish Ó Caiside, "descendant of Caiside," from Cas, meaning "curly-headed," the surname is inextricably associated with County Fermanagh, where the family were famous for centuries as poets, churchmen, scholars and hereditary physicians to the great Maguire chieftains. In Fermanagh, their original seat was at Ballycassidy, north of Enniskillen. As their healing skills became widely known, many Cassidys were employed by other chiefs, particularly in the north of the country, and the name is now particularly common in counties Donegal, Monaghan and Antrim, as well as in the original homeland of Fermanagh. Although less numerous elsewhere, the name is now also familiar throughout Ireland, with the smallest numbers to be found in Connacht.

Clancy

The Irish version of the surname is Mac Fhlannchaidh, from the personal name Flannchadh, which, it is thought, meant "red warrior." It originated separately in two different areas, in counties Clare and Leitrim. In the former, where they were a branch of the McNamaras, their eponymous ancestor being Flannchadh Mac Conmara, the Clancys formed part of the great Dál gCais tribal group, and acted as hereditary lawyers, or "brehons," to the O'Brien chieftains. Their homeland was in the barony of Corcomroe in north Clare, and they remained prominent among the Gaelic aristocracy until the final collapse of that institution in the seventeenth century. The Leitrim family of the name were based in the Rosclogher area of the county, around Lough Melvin. Today, the surname is still most common in Leitrim and Clare, with significant numbers also found in the adjacent counties. The best-known bearer of the name in modern times was probably Willie Clancy, a world-famous uilleann piper and folklorist from County Clare, who died in 1973.

Clarke

Clarke is one of the commonest surnames throughout England, Ireland and Scotland, and has the same remote origin in all cases, the Latin clericus, originally meaning "clergyman" and later "clerk" or "scholar." In Irish this became cléireach, the root of the surname Ó Cléireigh, which was anglicized in two ways, phonetically as "Cleary," and by translation as "Clerk" or "Clarke." Up to the beginning of this century, the two surnames were still regarded as interchangeable in some areas of the country. By far the largest number of Clarkes (with or without the final "e") are to be found today in Ulster, a reflection of the great influx of Scottish settlers in the seventeenth century. Even in Ulster, however, without a clear pedigree it is not possible in individual cases to be sure if the origin of the name is English or Irish. Austin Clarke (1896-1974), poet, dramatist and novelist, was one of the most important Irish literary figures of the twentieth century.

Cleary

Ó Cléirigh, meaning "grandson of the scribe" is the Irish for both (O) Cle(a)ry and, in many cases in Ireland, Clarke, as outlined above. The surname is of great antiquity, deriving from Cléireach of Connacht, born c. 820. The first of his descendants to use his name as part of a fixed hereditary surname was Tigherneach Ua Cléirigh, lord of Aidhne in south County Galway, whose death is recorded in the year 916. It seems likely that this is the oldest true surname recorded anywhere in Europe. The power of the family in their original County Galway homeland was broken by the thirteenth century, and they scattered throughout the island, with the most prominent branches settling in Derry and Donegal, where they became famous as poets; in Cavan, where many appear to have anglicized the name as "Clarke," and in the Kilkenny/Waterford/Tipperary region.

Coleman

Although Coleman is a common surname in England, where it is occupational, denoting a burner of charcoal, in Ireland the name is almost always of native Irish origin and generally comes from the personal name Colmán, a version of the Latin Columba, meaning "dove." Its popularity as a personal name was due to the two sixth-century Irish missionary saints of the name, in particular St Columban, who founded monasteries in many places throughout central Europe and whose name is the source of many similar European surnames: Kolman (Czech), Kalman, (Hungarian), Columbano (Italian). The original homeland of the Irish Ó Colmáin was in the barony of Tireragh in County Sligo, and the surname is still quite common in this area. In the other region where the surname is now plentiful, County Cork, it has a different origin, as an anglicization of the Irish Ó Clúmháin, which has also been commonly rendered as "Clifford."

Collins

Collins is a very common English surname, derived from a diminutive of Nicholas. As with so many such names, in Ireland it may be either of genuinely English origin, or an anglicized version of an original Irish name. Two such Irish names were transformed into Collins: Ó Coileáin, originating in County Limerick, and Ó Cuileáin of West Cork. The Ó Coileáin were forced to migrate from Limerick to the home territory of the Ó Cúilleáin in the thirteenth century, so that it is now virtually impossible to distinguish between the two originals. The name is extremely numerous in Cork and Limerick, and indeed throughout the southern half of the country.

Conlon

Conlon and its associated variants (O') Conlan and Connellan, are anglicized versions of a number of Irish names. Ó Connalláin, from a diminutive of the personal name Conall, "strong as a wolf," originated in counties Galway and Roscommon. Ó Coinghiolláin, whose derivation is unclear, arose in County Sligo. The third of the Irish originals, Ó Caoindealbháin, comes from caoin, "fair" or "comely" and dealbh, meaning "form," and is principally associated with the midlands and County Meath. This last name was also anglicized "Quinlan" or, in Munster "Quinlivan." The most common anglicization, "Conlon," is now distributed throughout Ireland, with particular concentrations in the original homelands of north Connacht and the midlands.

Connolly

Again, a number of original Irish names have been anglicized as "Connolly." The Ó Conghalaigh, from conghal, "as fierce as a wolf," were based in Connacht, where the English version is now often spelt "Connelly." The name arose as Ó Coingheallaigh in West Cork, while Ulster Connollys derive from both the Ó Conghalaigh of Fermanagh, who gave their name to Derrygonnelly, "Connolly's oakwood," and the Monaghan Connollys, for whom a number of separate origins are suggested, as a branch of the southern Uí Neill, or as a branch of the MacMahons. Whatever their origin, the Monaghan family have been the most prominent of the Connollys, recorded as having "Chiefs of the Name" up to the seventeenth century, and producing, among others, Speaker William Conolly [sic], reputedly the richest man in eighteenth-century Ireland, and James Connolly, labor leader, socialist writer, and signatory of the 1916 Proclamation of Independence. The arms illustrated are those of the family of William Conolly [sic].

Conway

In Ireland Conway may be of Welsh or Irish origin. In the former case it derives from the fortified town of Conwy, from the river of the same name, which term is thought to mean "reedy." Descendants of settlers of the name are to be found in counties Kerry and Antrim, and elsewhere. The Irish origins of the name are manifold: it is the anglicized version of at least four separate names, including, in County Sligo, Ó Conbhuidhe, ("yellow hound"), also anglicized "Conboy"; in Mayo Ó Connmhacháin, sometimes also given as "Convey"; in Munster Mac Connmháigh, from condmhach, meaning "head-smashing," also anglicized "Conoo," and in Derry/Tyrone Mac Conmidhe ("Hound of Meath"), which has also been rendered as "MacConomy," "Conomy" etc. The surname is now numerous throughout Ireland, with perhaps the largest single concentration in County Mayo.

Corcoran

The English version may derive from a number of Irish originals: Ó Corcrdáin, Mac Corcráin, Ó Corcáin, and Ó Corcra, all stemming originally from corcair, meaning "purple." The name has also been anglicized "Corkery" and "Corkin." It arose separately in different locations, in the O'Carroll territory encompassing parts of Offaly and Tipperary, and in County Fermanagh. The name is now rare in Fermanagh, and it seems likely that the many Corcorans found in Mayo and Sligo are part of this group. Further south the name is also common now in Cork and Kerry as well as in Tipperary.

Costello

The origin of the surname Costello provides a perfect illustration of the way the native Irish absorbed the invading Normans. Soon after the invasion, the de Angulo family, also known as "Nangle," settled in Connacht, where they rapidly became powerful. After only three generations, they had begun to give themselves a surname formed in the Irish manner, with the clan taking Jocelyn de Angulo as their eponymous forebear. Jocelyn was rendered Goisdealbh in Irish, and the surname adopted was Mac Goisdealbhaigh, later given the phonetic English equivalent "Costello." Their power continued up to the seventeenth century, centered in east Mayo, where they gave their name to the barony of Costello. Today the surname is widely spread throughout Ireland, with the largest concentrations still in the historic homeland of Connacht.

Coughlan

Two original Irish versions of Coughlan (and its variants (O') Coghlan, Coglin, and Cohalan) exist, Ó Cochláin and Mac Cochláin, both derived from cochall, meaning "cloak" or "hood." The Mac Cochláin were part of the great tribal grouping of the Dál gCais, claiming descent from the semi-mythical Cas, which also produced O'Briens and the McNamaras. Their territory was in the present County Offaly, where they remained prominent up to the eighteenth century. County Cork was the homeland of the Ó Cochláin, where the name has long been associated with the baronies of East and West Carbury, and Barrymore. Interestingly, the surname tends to be pronounced differently in different areas of County Cork, as "Cocklin" in the west and "Cawlin" in the east.

Craig

Craig is Scottish in origin, describing a person who lived near a steep or sheer rock, from the Scots Gaelic creag. It was very common near Edinburgh and the Lowlands in the fifteenth and sixteenth centuries, and was brought to Ulster by seventeenth-century Scottish settlers. In Ireland, it is still almost exclusive to Ulster, where it is now one of the most numerous surnames, being particularly frequent in County Antrim, with large numbers also to be found in counties Derry and Tyrone. The most famous Irish bearer of the name, who organized the Ulster Volunteer Force against Home Rule after 1912, was prime minister of Northern Ireland from its creation in 1921 until his death in 1940. He was created Viscount Craigavon in 1927, and the new town of Craigavon in County Armagh is named after him.

Cronin

The surname in Irish is Ó Cróinín, from a diminutive of crón, meaning "yellow" or "swarthy." A more accurate rendition of the original pronunciation would be "Croneen," and this survives in place names embodying the name Cooscronin ("Cronin's hollow") and Liscroneen ("Cronin's fort") in west Cork, and Ballycroneen in Imokilly barony in east Cork. As the place names imply, the origin of the family lies in Cork, in particular in the west of the county, where they were originally part of the Cora Laoighdhe. In the Gaelic genealogies of this tribal grouping, the Cronins are recorded as hereditary owners of territory to the west of present-day Clonakilty.

Crowley

In form Crowley is English, a habitation name from an Old English term meaning "wood of the crows," and no doubt some of those in Ireland bearing the name derive from English stock. However, the vast majority are of Gaelic Irish extraction, with Crowley an anglicization of Ó Cruadhlaoich, from cruadh and laoch, meaning "hardy" and "warrior." The Cruadhlaoch from whom the family take their name was in fact one of the MacDermots of Moylurgin Connacht, who lived in the mid-11th century. Some time later, probably in the thirteenth century, some members of the family migrated from Connacht to County Cork, and their descendants prospered and multiplied while the original western branch of the family declined. The vast majority of Irish Crowleys today are connected to the Cork branch, and that county is still home to most of them. Up to the seventeenth century they remained powerful, particularly in the Carbery region of the county, and acquired a reputation as formidable soldiers, literally living up to their name.

Cullen

The surname Cullen may be of Norman or Gaelic origin. The Norman name has been derived both from the city of Cologne in Germany, and from Colwyn in Wales. In Ireland this Norman family was prominent principally in County Wexford, where their seat was at Cullenstown castle in Bannow parish. Much more numerous in modern times, however, are descendants of the Ó Cuilinn, a name taken from cuileann, meaning "hollytree." The name originated in southeast Leinster, and this area has remained their stronghold, with the majority to be found even today in counties Wicklow and Wexford. The most famous individual of the name was Paul Cullen (1803-78), Cardinal and Archbishop of Dublin, who presided over, and guided, the revival of the power of the Catholic Church in nineteenth-century Ireland.

Cunningham

In form, Cunningham is originally Scottish, taken from the place of the same name near Kilmarnock in Ayrshire. This name was originally Cuinneagán, from the Scots Gaelic cuinneag, meaning "milk-pail," and was given its present form through the mistake of a twelfth-century English scribe, who transcribed the ending as "ham," a purely English suffix meaning "village." Many Scottish Cunninghams came to Ireland in the seventeenth-century Plantation of Ulster, and their descendants now form the bulk of those with the name in that province, where it is most numerous. As well as these, however, many of native Gaelic stock also adopted Cunningham as the anglicized version of their names. Among these were the Mac Cuinneagáin (MacCunnigan) of County Donegal, the Ó Cuineagáin or Ó Cuineacháin (Kennigan/Kinahan) of County Antrim, the Ó Connacháin (Conaghan) of counties Tyrone and Derry, the Mac Donnegdin (Donegan) of County Down and the Ó Connagdin (Conagan) of County Armagh. The most numerous, however, were the Ó Connagáin and Mac Cuinneagáin of Connacht, where the surname remains most common outside Ulster.

Curran

Curran, together with its many variants (O')Curren, Corhen, Currane, Curreen, etc. may come from the Irish Ó Corraidhín, or Ó Corráin, both deriving from corradh, meaning "spear." The former version arose in County Donegal, where it still remains very numerous, while the latter was the name of several independent septs living in south Leinster/Waterford, Kerry, Galway and Leitrim. Today, the heaviest concentration of the name is found in Ulster, with the smallest number in Connacht, but the name is numerous and widespread throughout Ireland. Its most famous bearers were John Philpot Curran (1750-1817), the barrister and nationalist, and his daughter Sarah, who was secretly engaged to Robert Emmett. Thomas Moore's song She is Far From the Land was inspired by her story.

Daly

The surname (O) Daly (and its variants Daily, Daley etc.) is Ó Dálaigh in Irish, deriving from Dálach meaning "one who is present at assemblies." The meaning of the name may be conncected the tradition of scholarship and poetic achievement associated with those who bear it, since the ollamh of Gaelic Ireland had a place of honor at the tribal dáil as a man of learning and a poet. The medieval genealogists located their home in the present County Westmeath, and they spread throughout the country by acting as ollamhs to prominent families. From an early date Dalys were also prominent in County Cork, especially around the peninsula of Muintervarra, or Sheep's Head, in west Cork. The likeliest explanation is that the name had a separate origin in the south. Even so, the O'Dalys of Desmond had an equally strong association with poetry and learning: So potent were the poems of Aonghas Ó Dálaigh of Ballyroon that he was murdered by a victim of one of his satires. The name is now common across Ireland, with the greatest concentrations in the south and west, and in County Westmeath.

Delaney

In its form, Delaney is a Norman name, from De l'aunaie, meaning "from the alder grove," and doubtless some of those bearing the name in Ireland are of Norman stock. However, in the vast majority of cases it was adopted as the anglicized form of the original Irish Ó Dübhshláine, from dubh, meaning "black," and slán, meaning "defiance." The original territory of the Ó Diúbhshláine was at the foot of the Slieve Bloom mountains in County Laois. From there they spread also in neighboring County Kilkenny, and the surname is still strongly associated with these two counties. The most famous historical bearer of the surname was Patrick Delaney (1685/6-1768), Church of Ireland clergyman, renowned preacher and close friend of Jonathan Swift, of whom he wrote a celebrated "Defence."

Dempsey

In the original Irish Dempsey is Ó Díomasaigh, from diomasach, meaning "proud." The name was also occasionally anglicized "Proudman." The Ó Díomasaigh originated in the territory of Clanmalier, on the borders of what are now counties Laois and Offaly, and remained powerful in the area until the seventeenth century. James I recognized the strength of the family by granting the title "Viscount Clanmalier" to Terence Dempsey. The loyalty of the family to the crown was short-lived, however, and the Williamite wars later in the century destroyed their power and scattered them. The surname is now found throughout the country. In Ulster, Dempsey is common in County Antrim, where it may be a version of "Dempster," a Scottish name meaning "judge," or possibly an anglicization of Mac Díomasaigh, also sometimes rendered as "McGimpsey."

Dillon

In Ireland Dillon may be of Gaelic or Norman origin, the former from Ó Duilleáin, possibly from dall, meaning "blind," the latter from de Leon, from the place of the same name in Brittany. This, of course, accounts for the lion in the family arms. The Norman family have been prominent in Ireland since the arrival of their ancestor Sir Henry de Leon in 1185. He was granted vast estates in counties Longford and Westmeath, and his descendants retained their power up to modern times; with County Westmeath becoming known simply as "Dillon's Countiy." Another branch of the family settled in County Mayo, where they are still well known today. After the Williamite wars of the seventeenth century, a number of members of the family served in Continental armies. The best-known Irish regiment in the French army was "Dillon's Regiment," many members of which made their way to America to fight against the British in the War of Independence.

Doherty

Doherty and its many variants (O')Dogherty, Docherty, Dougharty, etc., comes from the Irish Ó Dochartaigh, from dochartach, meaning "unlucky" or "hurtful." The original Dochartach, from whom the clan descend, lived in the tenth century and has traditionally been claimed as twelfth in lineal descent from Conall Gulbain, son of Niall of the Nine Hostages, the fifth-century monarch supposedly responsible for kidnapping St Patrick to Ireland, and progenitor of the great tribal grouping of the Uí Néill. Conall gave his name to the territory he conquered, Tír Chónaill, the Irish for Donegal, and to the subgroup of the Uí Néill, the Cineal Chonaill, the race of Conall, the collective name for the many families which claim descent from him, such as the Gallaghers and the O'Donnells as well as the Dohertys. The original homeland of the O'Dohertys was in the barony of Raphoe in County Donegal, with the chief seat at Ardmire in the parish of Kilteevoge. They remained powerful chiefs in the area for five hundred years, until Sir Cahir O'Doherty's rising of 1608 against English seizures of Irish land, which ended in defeat and his execution.

Dolan

In Irish the surname is Ó Dúbhshláin, from dubh, meaning "black" and slán, meaning "challenge" or "defiance." Other anglicized versions include "Doolan" and "Dowling." It first arose as part of the Uí Máine tribal grouping in south Roscommon and east Galway, and from there spread to the northeast into counties Leitrim, Cavan and Fermanagh. It remains numerous in all five counties today, and is particularly common in County Cavan. In places it is also given as an anglicization of Ó Doibhilin, probably derived from dobhail, meaning "unlucky," and more usually rendered into English as "Devlin." Many of the Dolans of County Sligo are of this stock.

Donnelly

Donnelly is Ó Donnáile in Irish, from Donnáil, a personal name made up of donn, meaning "brown" and gal, meaning "bravery." The original ancestor was Donnáil O Neill, who died in 876, and was himself a descendant of Eoghan, son of Niall of the Nine Hostages, the fifth-century king who supposedly kidnapped St. Patrick to Ireland. Their territory was first in County Donegal, but they later moved eastwards into County Tyrone, where the center of their power was at Ballydonnelly. Many of the family were hereditary bards, but their chief historical fame is as soldiers, especially in the wars of the seventeenth century. One modern bearer of the name who combined both traditional roles was Charles Donnelly (1910-37), poet and republican, who was killed fighting with the International Brigade in the Spanish Civil War.

Doran

Doran is in Irish Ó Deoráin, a contracted form of Ó Deoradháin, from deoradh, meaning "exile" or "pilgrim." The surname has also been anglicized as "Dorrian," principally in the northern counties of Armagh and Down, where a branch was established in early times. The major fame of the family, however, was in Leinster, where for centuries they were hereditary judges and lawyers ("brehons") to the rulers of the ancient territory of Uí Cinnsealaigh, the MacMurroughs. This territory took in all of the present County Wexford as well as adjoining parts of south Wicklow and Carlow, and the Dorans are still most numerous in this area today, with the place name "Doransland" in Wexford providing evidence of their long association with the area. In modern times, Dorans have been famous as Wexford sportsmen, with families from Enniscorthy, Monamolin, and Gorey prominent in football, hurling, and cycling.

Dowd

At the end of the nineteenth century, the vast majority of bearers of this surname, by a proportion of four to one, were "Dowd" rather than "O'Dowd." Since then, a large-scale resumption of the "O" has reversed the proportions, with "O'Dowd" now by far the most popular. The original Irish name was Ó Dubhda, from dubh, meaning "black." In the traditional genealogies, the family is one of the Uí Fiachrach, a large tribal grouping tracing its origin back to Fiachra, brother of Niall of the Nine Hostages, the fifth-century monarch supposedly responsible for kidnapping St Patrick to Ireland. The O'Dowds were the most powerful in this group, and for centuries their territory included large parts of northwest Mayo and west Sligo; the name is still numerous in the area today. The surname also appears to have arisen separately in two other areas of the country: in Munster, where the anglicizations "Doody" and "Duddy" are quite frequent in the Kerry area, and in Derry, where the anglicization is almost invariably "Duddy."

Dowling

Although it may sometimes appear as a variant of "Dolan," in most cases Dowling has a separate origin. In form the name is English, derived from the Old English dol, meaning "dull" or "stupid," but in Ireland it is generally an anglicization of the Irish Ó Dúnlaing. The original territory of the Ó Dúnlaing was in the west of the present County Laois, along the banks of the river Barrow, which was known as Fearrann ua nDinlaing, "O'Dowling's country." The leaders of the family were transplanted to Tarbert in County Kerry in 1609, along with other leaders of the "Seven Septs of Laois" – the seven Gaelic families who dominated County Laois – but the surname remained numerous in its original homeland, and spread south and west into Carlow, Kilkenny, Wicklow, and Dublin, where it is now very common. As a first name Dúnlang was popular in early medieval times in Leinster, where it was also anglicized as "Dudley."

Doyle

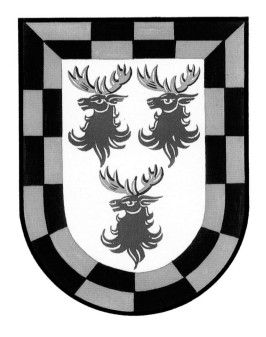

This name, one of the most common in Ireland, derives from the Irish Ó Dubhghaill, from dubh, "dark," and gall, "foreigner," a descriptive formula first used to describe the invading Vikings, and in particular to distinguish the darker-haired Danes from fair-haired Norwegians. The common Scottish names "Dougall" and "MacDougall" come from the same source, and reflect the original pronunciation more accurately. In Ulster and Roscommon, these names now exist as "McDowell" and "Dowell," carried by the descendants of immigrant Scottish gallowglasses, or mercenaries. The strongest association of Doyle, however, is with southeast Leinster, counties Wexford, Wicklow, and Carlow in particular, though the name is now found everywhere in Ireland. The stag portrayed in the arms is regarded as a symbol of permanence and endurance, a theme reflected also in one of the family mottoes Bhí mé beich mé, "I was and will be."

Driscoll

In 1890, over 90 percent of those bearing the name recorded themselves as "Driscoll;" today, in a remarkable reversal of the nineteenth-century trend, virtually all are called "O'Driscoll." The surname comes from the Irish O hEidirsceoil, from eidirsceol, meaning "go between" or "bearer of news." The original Eidirsceol from whom the family descend was born in the early tenth century, and since then they have been strongly associated with west Cork, in particular the area around Baltimore and Skibbereen, where they remained powerful up to the seventeenth century. They were part of the Corca Laoighde tribal grouping, descended from the Érainn or Fir Bolg, Celts who were settled in Ireland well before the arrival of the Gaels, and retained a distinct identity despite the dominance of the victorious newcomers. Their arms reflect the family's traditional prowess as seafarers, developed during their long lordship of the seacoast around Baltimore.

Duffy

In Irish the surname is Ó Dubhthaigh, from dubhthach, meaning "the dark one." Several different families of the name arose separately in different places, the most important being in Donegal, Roscommon and Monaghan. In Donegal the family were centered on the parish of Templecrone, where they remained powerful churchmen for almost eight hundred years. The Roscommon family, too, had along association with the church, producing a succession of distinguished abbots and bishops. The area around Lissonuffy in the northeast of the county, which is named after them, was the center of their influence. From this source the name is now common in north Connacht. The Monaghan O'Duffys were rulers of the area around Clontibret. They also contributed a great deal to the church, with a huge number of parish clergy of the name. They flourished through the centuries, and Duffy is now the single most common name in County Monaghan.

Duggan

The Irish Ó Dubhagáin is anglicized principally as "Duggan," but may also be found as "Dugan" or "Doogan," the latter representing a more accurate rendition of the Irish pronunciation. The principal family of the name had their territory near the modern town of Fermoy in north Cork, and were part of the Fir Máighe tribal grouping which gave its name to the town. Along with the other Fir Máighe families they lost their power when the Normans conquered the territory in the twelfth and thirteenth centuries. The family name is found in the parish and townland of Caherduggan in that area. Another sept of the same name is famous in the Uí Miáine area of east Galway/south Roscommon principally because it produced John O'Dugan (died 1372), chief poet of the O'Kellys, and co-author some verses now known as *Topographical Poems*, a long, detailed description of Ireland in the twelfth century. The arms of the family appear to derive from a pun on some of the elements of the name dubh, meaning "dark" and in, meaning "light'.

Dunne

Although "Dunn" is also an English surname, from the Old English dunn, "dark-colored," the vast majority of those bearing the name in Ireland descend from the Ó Doinn, from donn, used to describe someone who was swarthy or brown-haired. The Ó Doinn first came to prominence as lords of the area around Tinnehinch in the north of the modern County Laois, and were known as lords of Iregan up to the seventeenth century. At that time the surname was generally anglicized as "O'Doyne." Today the name is still extremely common in that part of Ireland, though it is now also widespread elsewhere. Perhaps because of the stronger English influence, in Ulster the name is generally spelt "Dunn," while it is almost invariably "Dunne" in other parts.

Dwyer

In Irish the surname is Ó Duibhir or Ó Dubhuidhir, made up of dubh, meaning "dark" and odhar, meaning "tawny" or "sallow." The resumption of the "O" prefix has now made "O'Dwyer" much the most common version. Their original homeland was in the mountains of west Tipperary, where they held power and resisted the encroachments of the English down to modern times. The surname is still extremely common in this area, but Dwyers and O'Dwyers have now also spread into the neighboring counties of Limerick, Cork, and Kilkenny. The most famous bearer of the name in modern times was Michael Dwyer, who took part in the 1798 Rising against the English, and continued his resistance up to 1803. He was transported to New South Wales in Australia, and became High Constable of Sydney, where he died in 1826.

Egan

Egan in Irish is Mac Aodhagáin, from a diminutive of the personal name Aodh, meaning "fire," which was anglicized "Hugh" for some strange reason. As well as Egan, Aodh is also the root of many other common Irish surnames, including O'Higgins, O'Hea, Hayes, McHugh, McCoy, etc. The MacAodhagáin originated in the Uí Máine territory of south Roscommon/east Galway, where they were hereditary lawyers and judges to the ruling families. Over the centuries, however, they became dispersed southwards, settling mainly in north Munster and east Leinster. As well as Connacht, their original homeland, they are now most numerous in Leinster, though the surname is now also relatively widespread throughout Ireland. In both Connacht and Leinster the surname has also sometimes been anglicized as "Keegan'.

Fahy

Fahy in Irish is Ó Fathaigh, probably from fothadh meaning "base" or "foundation." Another, rarer, English version of the name is "Vahey." Strangely, it has also been anglicized as "Green" because of a mistaken association with faithce, meaning "lawn." The name still has a very strong association with County Galway, where the historic homeland was situated. The area of the family"s power was around the modern town of Loughrea in the south of the county, and the surname is still most plentiful in this area, despite the upheavals and migrations which have spread the name quite wide-ly throughout Ireland. The best-known bearer of the name was Francis Arthur Fahy (1854-1935), songwriter and literary man, who paved the way for the Irish Literary Revival through his life-long involvement with the Gaelic League and the London Irish Literary Society.

Farrell

As both (O')Farrell and (O')Ferrall, this name in Irish is Fearghaíl, from the personal name Fearghal, made up of fear, "man," and gal, "valor." The original Fearghal or Fergal from whom the family claim descent was killed at Clontarf in 1014. His great grandfather Angall gave his name to the territory they possessed, Annally in County Longford. The present name of both the county and the town derives from the family, the full name in Irish being Longphuirt Uí Fhearghaíll, O'Farrell"s Fortress. They ruled this area for almost seven centuries, down to the final catastrophes of the seventeenth century, after which many members of the family fought with distinction in the armies of continental Europe. Today the surname is one of the most common in Ireland, with a wide distribution throughout the country, though the largest concentra-tion remains in the historical homeland of Longford and the sur-rounding areas. The most famous modern Irish bearer of the name was Michael Farrell (1899-1962), whose novel Thy Tears Might Cease achieved international recognition in the 1960s.

Ferguson

The surname is common in Scotland, and in Ireland is almost entirely confined to Ulster because of the Scottish connection. It is particularly numerous in counties Antrim, Derry, Fermanagh, and Down. Most Irish Fergusons claim descent from Fergus, prince of Galloway, who died in 1161, whose descendants included the Fergusons of Craigdarrach in Dumfriesshire, and of Atholl and Dunfallandy in Perthshire. The connection remains somewhat speculative, since the root of the name, the personal name Fergus, was common and widespread in medieval Scotland, and almost certainly gave rise to a large number of different families bearing the surname. Sir Samuel Ferguson (1810-86) was a precursor of the Irish Literary Revival, publishing many translations from Irish and versions of Irish myths, as well as contributing greatly to the scientific study of early Irish antiquities.

Finnegan

In Irish the surname is Ó Fionnagáin, from Fionnagán, a diminutive of the popular personal name Fionn, meaning "fairhaired." It arose separately in two areas, on the borders of the present north Roscommon and north-east Galway, between the modern towns of Dunmore and Castlerea, and in the territory taking in parts of the present counties of Monaghan, Cavan, and Louth. Descendants of the Connacht family are still to be found in the ancestral homeland, but the majority of modern Finnegans are descended from the Ulster family, and the name remains particularly numerous in counties Cavan and Monaghan. It is now also common throughout Ireland, with the exception of the southern province of Munster.

Fitzgerald

Fitzgerald is a Norman name, made up of Fi(t)z, Norman French for "son of," and Gerald, a personal name of Germanic origin from geri, "spear" and wald, "rule." The family trace their origin to Walter FitzOther, keeper of Windsor forest in the late eleventh century, whose son Gerald was constable of Pembroke Castle in Wales. Gerald"s son Walter accompanied Strongbow in the invasion of Ireland, and adopted the surname Fitzgerald. Over the following eight centuries the family became one of the most powerful and numerous in Ireland. The head of the main branch, the duke of Leinster, known historically as the earl of Kildare, is the foremost peer of Ireland. The power of the Munster branch, the earls of Desmond, was severely disrupted in the wars of the sixteenth century, but gave rise to three hereditary titles, in existence since at least 1333, which still survive: The Knight of Kerry, the Knight of Glin, and the White Knight, now a Fitzgibbon. The surname is now common, but remains concentrated in the ancient homeland of the earls of Desmond, counties Cork, Limerick, and Kerry.

Fitzpatrick

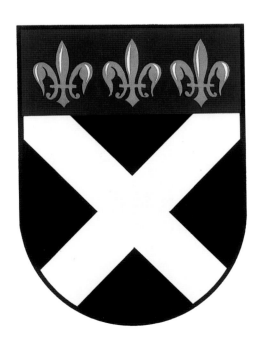

Despite its Norman appearance, "Fitz-" being Norman French for "son of," in the vast majority of cases Fitzpatrick is an anglicization of the Irish Mac Giolla Phádraig, meaning "son of the servant of (St) Patrick." Similarly to other surnames containing Giolla, it has also been anglicized as "Kilpatrick" and, more rarely, "Gilpatrick," principally in Ulster, where it is most common in counties Fermanagh and Monaghan. The original GiollaPhidraig from whom the surname is taken was the tenth-century ruler of the ancient kingdom of Upper Ossory, including parts of the present counties of Laois and Kilkenny. The surname was anglicized to Fitzpatrick in the early sixteenth century, when the chief of the family accepted the title of lord baron of Upper Ossory from Henry VIII. Partly due to this, they managed to retain possession of a large portion of their original lands right up to the nineteenth century. Although the surname is now common and widespread throughout Ireland, the largest concentration is still to be found in County Laois, part of their original homeland.

Flaherty

In Irish Flaherty and O'Flaherty are Ó Flaithbheartach, from flaitheamh, meaning "prince" or "ruler," and beartach, meaning "acting" or "behaving." Although the literal translation is "one who behaves like a prince," a more accurate rendition would be "hospitable" or "generous." The family"s original territory included the whole of the west of the modern County Galway, including Connemara and the Aran Islands, whence the title of their chief, lord of Iar-Chonnacht and of Moycullen. They occupied and controlled this area from the thirteenth century on, and survived as a power in the area down to the eighteenth century. Although the name is now common and widespread, the largest numbers are still to be found in County Galway.

Flanagan

In Irish the surname is Ó Flannagáin, a diminutive of flann, a personal name which was very popular in early Ireland, and means "red" or "ruddy." Perhaps because of this popularity, the surname arose separately in a number of distinct locations, including counties Roscommon, Fermanagh, Monaghan, and Offaly. Of these, the most important families historically were those of Roscommon and Fermanagh. In the former location they were long associated with the royal O'Connors, traditionally deriving from the same stock, and supplying stewards to the royal household. In Fermanagh they ruled a large territory covering the west of Lower Lough Erne, and based at Ballyflanagan, now the townland of Aghamore in Magheraboy parish. Today the surname is widely distributed around Ireland, though the largest concentration remains in their original homelands, southwest Ulster and north Connacht.

The family arms display the royal oak, symbol of the O'Connors, proclaiming their long association with this family, though the tree does not cover the whole shield, a significant difference.

Fleming

"Fleming" is an ethnic name simply meaning "an inhabitant of Flanders." It is a common surname in Britain, reflecting the importance of the wool trade between England and the Netherlands in the Middle Ages, when many Flemish weavers and dyers settled in England, Wales, and southern Scotland. It arrived in Ireland in two ways: Following the Norman invasion, when families of the name became prominent in the areas around Dublin; and through the Plantation of Ulster in the seventeenth century, when many Scottish bearers of the name arrived. Today, although widespread elsewhere, the surname is most numerous in Ulster, particularly in counties Antrim and Derry, but the most historically important Fleming family was one of the earlier southern arrivals, a family that held large tracts of land in counties Meath and Louth down to the seventeenth century, and acquired the title "lords of Slane'.

Flynn

In Irish the name is Ó Floinn, from the adjective flann, meaning "reddish" or "ruddy," which was extremely popular as a personal name in early Ireland. As might be expected, this popularity led to the surname coming into being independently in several different parts of the country, including Clare, Cork, Kerry, Mayo, Roscommon, Cavan, Antrim, and Monaghan. The most historically important of these were the families originating in Cork and Roscommon, with the former ruling over a territory in Muskerry between Bailyvourney and Blamey, and the latter centered on the area of north Roscommon around the modern town of Castlerea. In County Antrim the Irish version of the name was Ó Fhloinn, with the initial "F" silent, so that the anglicized version became "O'Lynn," or simply "Lynn." The O'Lynns ruled over the lands between Lough Neagh and the Irish Sea in south Antrim. (O')Flynn is now numerous throughout Ireland, though significant concentrations are still to be found in north Connacht and the Cork! Waterford areas, roughly corresponding to the original homelands.

Foley

The original Irish for the surname is Ó Foghladha, from foghlaidh, meaning "pirate" or "marauder." It originated in County Waterford, and from there spread to the nearby counties of Cork and Kerry. These are the three locations in which it is still most numerous, though it is now common throughout the southern half of the country. The best known modern Irish bearer of the name, Donal Foley (1922-81), journalist and humorist, came from the original homeland of County Waterford. Another Foley, Congressman Tom, was Speaker of the U.S. House of Representatives from 1989 to 1995. In places in Ulster the surname MacSharry (Mac Searraigh) was sometimes mistranslated as "Foley" or "Foaley," because of a mistaken belief that it was derived from searrach, meaning "foal'.

Ford

In form, this is a common English name for someone who lived near a ford. In Ireland, where it is more often "Forde," it may indicate English ancestry, since many English of the name settled in Ireland. However, in the majority of cases it is a native Irish name, an anglicization of at least three Irish distinct originals: Mac Giolla na Naomh, meaning "son of the devotee of the saints," also anglicized as "Gildernew;" Mac Conshnámha, from conshnámh, meaning "swimming dog," also anglicized "Kinneavy;" and Ó Fuaráin, from fuar, meaning "cold," and also anglicized as "Foran." Clearly, the English clerks transcribing Irish names had scant knowledge of the language they were hearing. Mac Conshnámha originated in north Connacht, where the sept were chiefs in the area now part of County Leitrim from the thirteenth century. Mac Giolla na Naomh was principally a south Connacht name, while Ó Fuaráin originated in County Cork. The name is still most common in Cork, though large numbers are also to be found in the Connacht counties of Galway and Mayo, as well as in Dublin.

Fox

Fox is a common English surname, based on a nickname, and a significant number of Irish Foxes will be of English descent. In the majority of cases, however, Fox is a simple translation of Ó or Mac an tSionnaigh, "descendant" or "son of the fox" respectively. From early times the Mac an tSionnaigh were widely scattered, allowing their name to be anglicized phonetically in an extraordinary number of ways depending on local accents and dialects – MacAshinna, MacShanaghy, Shinny, Shannon, Shinnock, Tinney and MacAtinna are some of the variations.

Ó Sionnaigh has a more particular history. Tadhg Ó Catharnaigh ("Kearney") was Chief of Teffia in County Meath in the eleventh century and, for his wily ways, become known as An Sionnach the fox. As his descendants prospered, becoming proprietors of the barony of Kilcoursey in County Offaly and acquiring the title "Barons Kilcoursey," they adopted his nickname as their surname, and the chief of the family took "The Fox" as a title. They lost their property after the rebellion of 1641-2, but the descent from the last chief remains unbroken. John William Fox, The Fox, chief of his name, recognized as such by the chief herald of Ireland, lives in Australia.

Gallagher

(O')Gallagher in Irish is Ó Gallcobhar, from gall, meaning "foreign" and cabhair, meaning "help" or "support." The original Gallcobhar from whom the family claim descent was himself descended from Conall Gulban, son of Niall of the Nine Hostages, the fifth-century monarch who was reputedly responsible for the kidnapping of St Patrick to Ireland, and who was the founder of the Uí Neill dynasty. The O'Gallaghers claim to be the most senior branch of the Cinéal Conaill, the group of families who all descend from Conall Gulban. Their territory was in Tír Chonaill (literally "Conall's Land"), in what is now County Donegal. From the fourteenth to the sixteenth centuries they were hereditary commanders of the cavalry of the forces of the O'Donnell princes of Tír Chonaill. Today Gallagher is the single most numerous surname in County Donegal, and is also very common in the adjoining counties of Derry, Fermanagh and Tyrone. Though less common elsewhere in Ireland, it has spread throughout the country over the centuries.

Gorman

Gorman is a relatively common name in England, where it is derived from the Middle English personal name Gormund, from gar, meaning "spear," and mund, meaning "protection." A few Irish Gormans may be of this connection, but in the vast majority of cases in Ireland the surname comes from the original Irish Mac Gormáin, from a diminutive of gorm, meaning "blue." The original homeland was in County Laois, in Slievmargy, but they were dispossessed by the Prestons, a Norman family, and removed to counties Clare and Monaghan. The Clare branch became well known in later years for the extent of their wealth and hospitality, and for their patronage of poetry. From Clare they spread also into the adjoining county of Tipperary. When the native Irish began to resume the old O and Mac prefixes to their names in the nineteenth century, the Clare family mistakenly became "O'Gorman," probably following the error of the then best known bearer of the surname, Chevalier Thomas O'Gorman (1725-1808), an Irish exile in France. In Tipperary, the name has generally remained "Gorman," while in Monaghan the original MacGorman still exists, along with the other two versions.

Graham

Graham is a Scottish surname, deriving from the place name Grantham, also known as Graham, in modern Lincolnshire in England. It was taken to Scotland in the twelfth century by William de Graham, a Norman baron who held the manor of Grantham, and from whom virtually all modern bearers of the name are descended. In Ireland it is overwhelmingly concentrated in Ulster, in particular counties Down and Fermanagh, as well as Armagh, Monaghan and Tyrone. The Irish Grahams are mostly descended from a branch of the family which migrated from Midlothian to the Scottish borders in the Middle Ages and became, with the Armstrongs, the most powerful of the outlaw "riding clans." When the power of these clans was savagely broken by James I, many migrated to the north of Ireland, settling especially in County Fermanagh. Unlike the other clans, from that base the Grahams spread widely through the surrounding counties.

Greene

Green(e) is an extremely common English surname, generally referring to someone who lived near a village green. Many Irish bearers of the name, particularly in Ulster, are probably of this connection. However, Green(e) was also used as the anglicized version of a wide variety of Irish names containing uaithne, "green," or glas, "grey-green." Ó hUaithnigh, anglicized as both "Green" and the phonetic "Hooney," arose in County Cork. In County Clare the original, from the same Irish stem, was Ó hUaithnigh, more rarely anglicized as "Hooneen" and "Huneen." In Ulster, Mac Glaisín, "McGlashan," and Mac Giolla Ghlais, "McAlesher," relatively common in counties Antrim and Derry, also became Green. Further, Ó Griana, Mac Griana, found in northwest Ulster, and Ó Grianáin, from counties Cavan and Sligo, were also phonetically rendered as Green, although the root of the names is the Irish grian, meaning "sun."

Griffin

While the name is English in appearance, in the great majority of cases Irish Griffins are descended from the Ó Gríobhtha. Both the English and Irish versions ultimately have the same source, the name of the legendary monster, the gryphon, used as a nickname for someone fierce or dangerous. The name arose separately in at least two areas: In County Kerry, centered on Ballygriffin in Glanarought barony, and in County Clare, where the seat was at Ballygriffy, near Ennis. From these two starting points the families spread and intermingled, and today Griffin is among the 100 most common Irish surnames, found principally in the original homelands of Clare and Kerry, as well as in the adjoining counties of Cork and Limerick.

Hall

Hall is an extremely common English surname, found widely in Scotland also, denoting someone who lived near a large house, or who was employed in a manor or hall. In Ireland, it is most common in Ulster, where its source is predominantly Scottish; the Halls were one of the outlaw "riding clans" who migrated to Ulster when their dominance over the Scottish Borders was broken by James I. The name is particularly associated with County Antrim. Elsewhere, it is also found in Munster, brought during the sixteenth and seventeenth century plantations, and in Leinster, due to the long association of parts of that province with English rule. It is rare in the western province of Connacht.

Hamilton

The surname is one of the most common and famous in Scotland, coming from the Norman baron Walter Fitzgilbert de Hameldone, a supporter of Robert the Bruce in the fourteenth century. His name came from the now deserted village of Hameldone (Old English hamel, "crooked," and dun, "hill') in the parish of Barkby in Leicestershire. The arrival of Hamiltons in Ireland is inextricably linked to the Plantation of Ulster in the seventeenth century, when a large number of the powerful Scottish landowners granted territory in the province were members of that family. They gained possession of vast tracts of land in counties Armagh, Cavan, Fermanagh and Tyrone, and settled many of their kinsmen on these estates. Sir Frederick Hamilton fought in the army of the Swedish King Gustavus I Adolphus before settling in Ulster, and his grandson Gustavus Hamilton was created Viscount Boyne in 1717.

Hayes

Hayes is a common surname in England, where it derives from various places of the same name and from the Norman De la Haye, but in Ireland it is almost always the most common anglicization of the Irish Ó hAodha, from the personal name Aodh, "fire," which was very popular in early Ireland. No doubt this popularity accounts for the fact that the surname originated separately in at least twelve different locations, including southwest Cork, Limerick/Tipperary, south Donegal, Sligo, Monaghan, Meath, Mayo, north Tyrone, south Down, Armagh, and Wexford. As well as Hayes, the surname was also anglicized as "O'Hea," particularly in southwest Cork, and as "Hughes," since Aodh was invariably translated as "Hugh." This last anglicization is most common among the five septs originating in the Ulster counties.

Healy

There is an English surname Healy, derived from the Old English heah, "high," and leah, "clearing," "wood," but almost all of those bearing the name in Ireland are descendants of one of two Irish families, the Ó hEilídhe, from Éilídhe, "claimant," and the Ó hEaladaighthe, from ealadhach, "ingenious." The Ó hEilídhe had territory in southeast County Sligo, on the shores of Lough Arrow, one of the most beautiful parts of the country, where their seat was at Ballyhely. The Ó hEaladaighthe, whose name was originally given the more phonetically accurate equivalent "Healihy," were based in the parish of Donoghmore in Muskerry in County Cork, where they retained considerable power and wealth up to the seventeenth century. The surname is very common and widespread today, though significant concentrations are to be found around the original homelands in Connacht and Cork. The best-known modern bearer of the flame was the journalist, John Healy, of the Connacht family, renowned for his passionate defence of the rural way of life.

Hegarty

In Irish the surname is Ó hÉigceartaigh, from éigceartach, meaning "unjust." The name appears to have arisen first in the area now divided between counties Derry and Donegal, where the Ó hÉigceartaigh were a branch of the Cinel Eoghain, that large group of families claiming descent from Eoghan, one of the sons of Niall of the Nine Hostages, the fifth-century monarch who supposedly kidnapped St Patrick to Ireland. However, today the surname is much more common in County Cork, at the other end of the country. Traditionally, the Cork (O')Hegartys were claimed as a branch of the more historically prominent northern family, but ecertach was a common personal name in Munster, and it seems more likely that the surname arose separately there. At any rate, O'Hegartys are recorded in west Cork as early as the thirteenth century, and remain strongly associated with the area.

Hennessy

The original Irish form of the name is Ó hAonghasa, from the personal name Aonghas, anglicized "Angus," one of the pre-Christian Celtic gods. This was quite popular, and it gave rise to the surname in several distinct localities: in the north of the present County Offaly, from where the family later spread into the adjoining counties of Clare and Tipperary; in southwest County Cork, where they formed part of the Corca Laoidhe tribal grouping, descended from pre-Gaelic origins, and in east Cork, in the territory between the present towns of Fermoy and Mitchelstown. The east Cork family produced the most famous bearer of the name, Richard Hennessy (1720-1800), who fought with Dillon's Brigade in the French army, and founded the famous brandy distillery in 1765. Today the surname is still strongly associated with County Cork, though significant numbers also appear in counties Limerick, Tipperary, and Clare. In the latter area, the name has also been anglicized as "Henchy" and "Hensey."

Henry

There are several Irish, Scottish and Norman originals for this surname. In Munster it is often the anglicization of Mac Innéirghe, from innéireighe, meaning "abandonment," and has also been rendered into English as MacHenry and MacEnery. This family were prominent in County Limerick. In County Tyrone, it is found as an anglicization of Ó hInneirghe, from the same root. At least two other Gaelic Irish sources for the name exist in Ulster, the Mac Éinrí, descended from Henry, son of Dermot O'Cahan (died 1428), situated in the north Antrim/Derry area, and the Ó hAiniarriadh, originally from southeast Ulster. In addition, the surname appears in Connacht, where it seems to derive from a branch of the Norman FitzHenrys, who settled in west Galway in the Middle Ages. To complicate matters further, Ulster contains many Scottish surnames based on Henry as a personal name – Henderson, Hendry, McKendry, Hendron etc. – which have long been confused with similar-sounding Gaelic Irish surnames in the same areas.

Hickey

The original Irish for Hickey is Ó hIcidhe, from iceadh, meaning "healer." The Hickeys were part of the tribal grouping, the Dál gCais, which produced Brian Boru, the high king of Ireland who defeated the Vikings in 1014. This grouping had its territory in the area now part of County Clare and north Tipperary, and it is this area with which the Hickeys remain closely identified. Their surname arose because of their position as hereditary physicians to the royal O'Brien family. From their original homeland, the name spread first into the neighboring County Limerick, and from there even wider, so that Hickey is today one of the most common and widespread of Irish surnames.

Higgins

In form, Higgins is an English name, from the medieval given name "Higgin," a diminutive of "Hicke," which was in turn a pet form of Richard. In Ireland, however, the vast majority of those bearing the name are of Gaelic Irish stock, Higgins being used as an anglicization of the Irish Ó hUigín, from uiginn, meaning "Viking." The original Uigin from whom they claim descent was grandson to Niall of the Nine Hostages, the fifth-century king who founded the powerful tribal grouping the Uí Néill, and they are therefore regarded as part of that grouping. Originally based in the midlands, part of the southern Uí Néill, they moved west over the centuries to Sligo and Mayo, and more than half of those bearing the surname today still live in the western province of Connacht. Don Ambrosio O'Higgins rose to become viceroy of Peru for Spain, and his son, Bernardo, is widely remembered in South America as the Liberator of Chile. Ambrosio was born in Ballinvary, County Sligo, and took the Spanish title baron de Valenar, Baron Ballinvary.

Hogan

The Irish version of the surname is Ó hÓgáin, from a diminutive of og, meaning "young." The original Ógán from whom the family claim descent lived in the tenth century and was an uncle of Brian Born, the High King who defeated the Vikings at Clontarf in 1014. Like Brian Boru, they were part of the Dál gCais tribal grouping, whose original territory took in Clare and parts of Tipperary. The (O')Hogans were centered on Ardcrony, near the modern town of Nenagh in north Tipperary, where their chief had his seat. From there the surname spread far and wide, and is today one of the most common in Ireland, with particular concentrations close to the first homeland, in counties Clare, Tipperary, and Limerick. In addition, significant numbers are to be found in Cork, where it is thought that the name may have had a separate origin, in the southwest of that county.

Hughes

Hughes is common in England and Wales, where it is a patronymic, deriving from the father's name, and quite a few Irish bearing the name, particularly in Ulster, will be of English and Welsh stock. Elsewhere, it is almost always one of the anglicizations of the Irish Ó hAodha, from the personal name Aodh, "fire," the second most popular such anglicization after "Hayes," since Aodh was invariably translated as "Hugh." Perhaps because of the example of the settlers, Hughes was the most frequent anglicization amongst the Gaelic Irish in Ulster, where there were Ó hAodha at Ballyshannon (County Donegal), Ardstraw (County Tyrone), Tynan (County Armagh), Famey (County Monaghan), and south County Down. In places, too, Hughes became the English version of Mac Aoidh or Mac Aodha, more usually given as Magee or McHugh.

Hurley

Hurley has become the English version of at least three distinct original Irish names: The Ó hUirthile, part of the Dál gCais tribal group, based in Clare and north Tipperary; the Ó Muirthile, based around Kilbritain in west Cork; and the Ó hIarlatha from the district of Ballyvourney, also in Cork, whose name is more usually anglicized "(O')Herlihy." The principal concentrations of Hurleys are today found in counties Tipperary and Limerick, where they spread from the original Dalcassian homeland, and in Cork. An interesting example of the pseudo-translation of surnames is found in Clare, where some whose name was originally Hurley have now become "Commane," since the Irish for the hurley-stick used in the sport of hurling is camán.

Johnston

In form at least the surname is Scottish, deriving from the place of the same name in Annandale, which was originally "John's town." The original John was a Norman landowner in the twelfth century, and instead of taking on the patronymic "Johnson," his descendants adopted the place name as their surname, becoming Johnston(e)s. This family, the source of virtually all Scottish bearers of the name, became one of the strongest and most unruly of the Border clans. Their long feud with another clan, the Maxwells, was notorious for its ferocity. When the clans were eventually scattered by James II, many Johnstons fled to Ulster. Many settled in County Fermanagh, where the surname is the second most numerous in the county. As well as these Johnstons, however, many others whose name was originally Johnson adopted the Scottish name. Such adoptions occurred predominantly in Ulster, and affected those of Scottish and of native Irish origin, with the MacIans of Caithness translating their surname as Johnson, and then altering it to Johnston in many cases, and the MacShanes of the Armagh/Tyrone district, a branch of the O'Neills, doing likewise.

Jones

Jones is an extremely common surname in England and Wales, one of the wide range of names derived from the personal name "John." It is a patronymic, coming from the genitive form "John's." Its widespread popularity in Wales is due to the form adopted in the Welsh translation of the Authorized Version of the Bible, Ioan, phonetically close to the modern surname. In Ireland it is quite widespread, coming among the two hundred most frequent names, and is understandably most closely associated with areas where English influence was strongest.

Joyce

Joyce derives from the Breton personal name Iodoc, a diminutive of iudh, meaning "lord," which was adopted by the Normans as Josse. A number of English surnames arose from this Norman original, including Joce, Joass, and Joyce, this last being far more frequent in Ireland than anywhere else. The first bearer of the name in Ireland was a Thomas de Joise, of Norman Welsh extraction, who married a daughter of the O'Brien princes of Thomond in 1283, and settled in the far west of Connacht, on the borders of the modern counties of Mayo and Galway. Their descendants became completely gaelicized, ruling that territory, today still known as "Joyce's Country," down to the seventeenth century. The surname remains strongly associated with the area, with a large majority of Joyces originating in counties Galway and Mayo. The most famous modern bearer of the name was James Joyce (1882-1941), author of *Dubliners*, *A Portrait of the Artist as a Young Man*, *Ulysses*, and *Finnegans Wake*, said to have been the only twentieth-century novelist to publish nothing but masterpieces.

Kane

Kane and O'Kane are the most common anglicized versions of the Irish Ó Catháin, from a diminutive of cath, meaning "battle." Kane and O'Kane are most frequent in Ulster, where Ó Catháin arose as a surname in the Laggan district of east Donegal, as part of the Cinéal Eoghain, the large group of families descended from Eoghan, son of Niall of the Nine Hostages, the fifth-century monarch who founded the Uí Néill dynasty and was supposedly responsible for the kidnapping of St Patrick to Ireland. In the twelfth century these Ulster Ó Catháin conquered a large territory to the east of their original homeland around Coleraine and Keenaght in what is now County Derry, and remained powerful and important in that area down to the wars of the seventeenth century. Their last chief died in the Tower of London in 1628. Two other common surnames, McClosky and McAvinney, are offshoots of Ó Catháin, stemming respectively from the twelfth-century Bloskey Ó Catháin, and Aibhne Ó Catháin. Kane remains particularly common in the Coleraine district of County Derry, and in the adjoining county of Antrim.

Kavanagh

Kavanagh, along with its variants Cavanagh, Cavanaugh, etc., is the English version of Caomhánach, one of a very few Gaelic Irish surnames not to include "O'" or "Mac." It means "follower of (St) Caomhan," a name which is itself a diminutive of caomh, meaning "gentle" or "tender." It was first borne as a surname in the twelfth century by Dónal, illegitimate son of Dermot MacMurrough, king of Leinster. He became known as "Dónal Caomhánach" after he was fostered by a successor of the saint based probably at Kilcavan in Bannow parish in south County Wexford.

Although this Dónal first bore the name, the majority of the Kavanagh septs descend from Art MacMurrough Kavanagh, king of Leinster, who died in 1418. The territory of the Kavanaghs at this period comprised nearly all modern County Carlow, and most of north and northwest County Wexford. The power of the Kavanagh chiefs was broken by the start of the seventeenth century.

Despite their loss of power and property, the line of descent remains unbroken; the title is now held by Andrew MacMorrogh Kavanagh of Borris, County Carlow.

Keane

Like Kane, Keane is an anglicization of Ó Catháin, from a diminutive of cath, meaning "battle." As an anglicization, however, it is more common in Connacht than in Ulster, the homeland of the Kanes, because Ó Catháin arose separately as a surname in County Galway, where the family were a branch of the historic Uí Fiachra tribal grouping. Traditionally it has been believed that the prominent Clare Keanes were an offshoot of the Ulster Ó Catháin, but the closeness of Clare and Galway must make this doubtful. A distinct family, the Ó Céin from County Waterford have anglicized their name as "Kean," but without the final "e." The famous actors Edmund Kean (1787-1833) and his son Charles (1811-1880) were of this family.

Kearney

Keamey is common and widespread in Ireland, and has a number of different origins. In the west it originated in County Mayo, near Moynulla and Balla, the territory of the Ó Cearnaigh (from cear- nach, meaning "victorious"), where it has sometimes also been anglicized as Carney. A separate family of the same name, but anglicized as (O)Kearney, arose in Clare, and migrated in early times to the area around Cashel in County Tipperary. In Ulster the name derives from Mac Cearnaigh, also from cearnach; they were part of the Cinéal Eoghain, the large group of families descended from Eoghan, son of Niall of the Nine Hostages, the fifth-century monarch who founded the Uí Néill dynasty and was supposedly responsible for the kidnapping of St Patrick to Ireland. The most historically important family, however, were the Ó Catharnaigh, from catharnach, meaning "warlike." These were chiefs of a large territory in the midlands, in the modern counties of Meath and Offaly; one of their number became Baron Kilcoursey, from the place name in Offaly. The composer of the Irish national anthem was Peadar Kearney (1883-1942).

Keating

Although Keating is found as a surname in England, where it derives from the Old English Cyting, from cyt, meaning "kite," in Ireland it is almost always of Norman origin. The family arrived with the Cambro-Norman invaders in the twelfth century and soon became thoroughly Irish, settling in south Leinster, and particular- ly in County Wexford, where the name is still very common. The most famous historical bearer of the name was Geoffrey Keating (or Seathrún Céitinn) the poet and historian who lived in the first half of the seventeenth century and wrote *Foras Feasa ar Éirinn*, a narrative history of the country defending it against the accounts given by foreign writers. In modern times the painter Sean Keating (1889-1977) specialized in traditional scenes, and was president of the Royal Hibernian Academy for fourteen years.

Kelleher

Kelleher, and its variants Keliher, Kellaher, etc., are the English versions of the Irish name Ó Céileachair, from Cúileachar, meaning "uxorious," "overly fond of one's wife." The original Cileachar from whom the family claim descent was a nephew of Brian Boru, and part of the famous Dál gCais tribal grouping. Although the family originated in Clare, homeland. of the Dál gCais, they migrated southeast to County Cork in the fourteenth century and it is now in that county and the adjoining County Kerry that the surname is most frequently found. It is sometimes abbreviated to "Keller," a name more usually associated with Germany, and in this form is recorded in County Cork.

Kelly

Kelly comes from the Irish Ó Ceallaigh, based on the popular personal name Ceallach, which may mean either "bright-haired" or "troublesome." The most prominent families are the O'Kellys of Uí Máine, or Hy Many, an ancient territory taking in east Galway and south Roscommon, also known simply as "O'Kelly's Country." Their pedigree takes them back to Máine Mór, first chief of the area bearing his name, who lived in the fifth century. His descendant Ceallach I (died c.874) was the twelfth chief, and the surname derives from him.

Despite the loss of most of their possessions in the catastrophic wars of the seventeenth century, the succession to the position of head of the sept has continued unbroken down to the present incumbent, Walter Lionel O'Kelly of Gallagh and Tycooly, count of the Holy Roman Empire, known as "the O'Kelly," and recognized as such by the chief herald of Ireland.

Today, Kelly and O'Kelly are almost as numerous in Ireland as Murphy, and are to be found throughout Ireland.

Kennedy

Kennedy in Irish is Ó Cinnéide, from a compound word meaning "ugly-headed" or "rough-headed." The original bearer of the name, from whom the family claim descent, was a nephew of Brian Boru. His descendants were one of the most powerful families in the famous Dál gCais tribal grouping, and migrated from their homeland near Killaloe in Clare into adjoining north Tipperary, to become lords of Ormond for over four hundred years up to the sixteenth century. From there the surname spread farther afield; becoming one of the most numerous and widespread in Ireland. In Ulster, many Kennedys are originally of Scottish stock, the MacKennedys being a branch of the Clan Cameron. The surname is now also very common in Galloway and Ayrshire. The most famous modern bearer of the name was, of course, John F. Kennedy, thirty-fifth president of the U.S., descended from a Wexford branch of the Dalcassian family.

Kenny

In Irish Kenny is generally Ó Cionaodha, from the personal name Cionaodh, of uncertain origin. It was borne by a high-king of Ireland Cionaodh mac Irgalaig in the eighth century, and seems to have become popular after this. At any rate Ó Cionaodha arose as a separate surname in a number of places, including County Tyrone, and the Galway/Roscommon region. This latter family was the most important historically, lords of Munter Kenny, and it is from them that the majority of Irish Kennys spring. In Ulster, Kenny was also the anglicization of the separate Ó Coinne, based in County Down, and became a synonym for a number of other names, including McKenna, Canning, and Keaney. The stage designer and director Sean Kenny (1933-1973) had achieved international fame when he died suddenly.

Keogh

Keogh, and its variant Kehoe, are the anglicizations of the Irish Mac Eochaidh, from eoch, meaning "horse." It arose as a surname in three distinct areas. The first was in south Roscommon, around Moyfinn in the barony of Athlone, which used to be known as "Keogh's country." This family was part of the Uí Máine tribal grouping. The second was in west Tipperary, near Limerick city; the place name Ballymackeogh marks the center of their territory. The third and most important, both numerically and historically, was in Leinster, where the original homeland was in north Kildare, whence they migrated first to Wicklow and then south to Wexford. It is in Wexford that the name has been most commonly anglicized Kehoe. The surname is now most frequent in Leinster, though it has become widespread throughout Ireland.

Kerr

Kerr is Scottish and northern English in origin, describing a person who lived near overgrown marshland, kerr in northern Middle English. As might be expected, it is principally found in Ulster, where the majority of those bearing the name are descended from one of the Scottish Border riding clans, whose enforced migration in the seventeenth century also brought large numbers of Armstrongs, Johnstones, and others to the province, where they settled, initially at least in County Fermanagh. A separate Scottish family of the name is part of the Clan Campbell in Argyllshire. As well as these Scottish origins, however, Kerr (along with Carr) was used as the anglicization of a number of native Ulster names, including Mac Giolla Chathair and Mac Ciaráin (Kern) in Donegal, Ó Cairre and Mac Cairre in County Armagh, and Mac Giolla Cheara in County Monaghan.

Kiely

Kiely is the anglicized version of the Irish Ó Cadhla, from cadhla, meaning "beautiful." It was popular as a personal name among the tribal grouping the Dál gCais, who acquired the high-kingship of Ireland under Brian Boru in the eleventh century. Their base was in the Clare/Limerick area, and this is the part of the country in which the surname is still most numerous, although it has now spread widely throughout Munster. The best known contemporary bearer of the surname in Ireland is the journalist and novelist Benedict Kiely, whose stories and essays are well-loved for their relaxed, anecdotal style.

King

King is one of the most common surnames in Ireland, and is distributed throughout the country. In Ulster, many, though not all of those of the name, will be of English stock, bearing the English surname which originated simply as a description of someone of kingly bearing. The majority, however, are of native Irish origin, since King was used as a (mis)translation of a number of Irish names which contained sounds similar to rí, "king." Among the many such names are Mac Fhearadhaigh ("McAree/McGarry") in County Monaghan, Ó Maolconaire and Ó Conraoi ("Conroy/Conry") in County Roscommon, Mac Conraoi, ("Conroy") in County Galway (where the change to King was almost total), Ó Conaire ("Connery") in Munster. In Ulster, in counties Antrim, Tyrone, and Down, Mac Fhinn ("Maginn") was also changed, by phonetic misrepresentation rather than mistranslation, to King.

Leary

Leary and O'Leary derive from the original Irish (Ó Laoghaire, from Laoghaire, meaning "a keeper of calves". Although there was a fifth-century king who gave his name to Dún Laoghaire, the port south of Dublin, no connection exists with the surname, which originated in County Cork and is even today to be found predominantly in that area. The family originally inhabited the rocky sea-coast of southwest Cork, between Roscarbery and Glandore, but the coming of the Normans displaced them, and they migrated to the mountains of Iveleary, which now incorporates their name, where they were and are particularly associated with the district of Inchigeelagh.

Lee

In appearance Lee is a common English name, used either for a person who lived near a pasture or meadow, from the Old English lea, or for a person from one of the many places so called, such as Lea in Shropshire, and many bearing the name in Ireland today will be descended from English settlers. In the majority of cases, however, Lee is the anglicized version of a number of original Irish names: (Ó Laoidhigh, from laoidheach, meaning "poet" or "poetic," which arose separately in Connacht in west Galway, and in the south in the Cork! Limerick area, and Mac Laoidhigh, ("McLee") from the same stem, which is found in County Laois. In Ulster Mac an Leágha ("McAlee"), was also sometimes anglicized as Lee, as was, in County Monaghan, Mac Giolla Eachaidh ("McCloy"). The most historically notable of the families were the O'Lees of Galway, powerful subchieftains under the O'Flahertys.

Lenehan

Lenehan is the anglicized version of the Irish (Ó Leannacháin, possibly from leannach, meaning "sorrowful." It appears to have arisen separately in two localities, in County Roscommon in the west, and in the south in the Limerick/Tipperary region. Bearers of the surname are found in both areas today, but it is most common in the south. The most prominent contemporaries of the name are Brian Lenihan (b. 1924) and his younger sister Mrs Mary O'Rourke, of the Roscommon family, who both served in a variety of ministerial positions in the Irish government from the 1970s to the 1990s.

Lennon

Lennon is primarily the anglicized form of the Irish Ó Leannáin, from leannán, meaning "lover." However, Ó Leannáin has also sometimes been anglicized as "Linnane" or even "Leonard." Additional uncertainty is caused by the fact that Lennon has occasionally been used as the English version of completely different Irish surnames, in particular Ó Lonáin or Ó Lonagáin ("Lenane" or "Lannigan") based in west Cork, and Ó Luinigh ("Lunney") originally from Donegal and now strongly associated with the adjoining County Fermanagh. The primary Irish source of Lennon, Ó Leannáin, arose separately in east County Galway, in County Mayo, and in County Fermanagh. Historically, the most important were the Fermanagh family, who held land and ecclesiastical office in the parish of Inishmacsaint. Today, Lennon remains common in Ulster, but elsewhere has spread from its traditional homelands to become most frequent in the eastern province of Leinster.

Long

In appearance, Long is a typical English or Scottish name, derived from a nickname for a tall person. In addition, the Norman names de Lung and de Long have become "Long." Many in Ireland bearing the surname today are of English, Scottish or Norman descent. However, there were also two native Gaelic families, the Ó Longáin and the Ó Longaigh, whose name have been anglicized Long.

Ó Longáin, also anglicized as "Langan," arose in County Armagh, but spread throughout the north, and is now most common in County Donegal. It probably shares its linguistic origin with Ó Longaigh, deriving from long, "ship," meaning "seafarer".

Ó Longaigh arose in County Cork. The earliest records, dating from the fourteenth century, show them as hereditary occupiers of church lands in the parish of Cannovee in mid-Cork. This, together with the neighbouring parish of Moviddy, are the areas most strongly associated with the family. Like virtually all of the native aristocracy, they lost their possessions in the wars of the seventeenth century. The descent from the last duly inaugurated chief of the name, Dermod O'Longy, remains unbroken. The official title is "O'Long of Garrenelongy."

Lynch

Lynch, which is today one of the most common surnames throughout Ireland, is unusual in that it has two completely distinct origins. The first is Norman, from de Lench, possibly derived from a place name now forgotten. The family settled initially in County Meath, and a branch then established itself in Galway, where they rapidly became one of the strongest of the "Tribes of Galway"; one of their number, James Lynch, mayor in 1493, is reputed to have hanged his own son for murder when no one else could be found to carry out the sentence. The arms illustrated are for this family. The second origin for the name is Gaelic, from the Irish Ó Loingsigh, from loingseach, meaning "seaman." This arose quite separately in a number of areas, including Clare/Limerick, Sligo, west Cork, Cavan, Donegal and the north Antrim/Derry region, where they were chiefs of the old kingdom of Dál Riada in medieval times. As the variety of geographical sources implies, the Gaelic origin is responsible for the wide frequency of the surname today.

Lyons

Lyons is one of the commonest surnames in Ireland, particularly in the three southern provinces. In Ulster especially it may be a variant of the English and Scottish surname "Lyon," which can derive, as a nickname, from "lion," from the first name Leo or Leon, or from the place name Lyon-la-Forêt in Normandy. Elsewhere, however, Lyons is virtually always the anglicized version of one of two Irish names, *Ó Laighin,* from *laighean,* meaning "spear," or *Ó Liatháin,* possibly from *liath,* meaning "grey." *Ó Laighin* originated in two areas, in County Kerry and in east County Galway, where the family's territory was centered on Kilconnell. In Kerry, however, the name was almost invariably anglicized as "Lyne." The *Ó Liatháin* family are reputed to have originated in County Limerick, but are now to be found much more frequently in County Cork, particularly in the north of the county, where the village of Castlelyons records their presence. *Ó Liatháin* has also been anglicized as "Lehane".

Macauley

MacAuley and its many variants – Cawley, Gawley, Macauley, Magawley etc. – may be either Scottish or Irish in origin. They are anglicizations of two distinct Irish surnames, Mac Amhalgaidh ("son of Auley") and Mac Amhlaoibh ("son of Auliff"). The former derives from a native personal name now obsolete, and the family bearing the surname were rulers of a territory in what is now Offaly/Westmeath. The latter derives from a Gaelic version of the common Norse name "Olaf," and the family claim descent from Amhlaoibh, son of the first Maguire king of Fermanagh, who ruled at the end of the thirteenth century. They gave their name to the barony of Clanawley in that county. An entirely distinct family, the MacAuliffs of Munster, are descended from Amhlaoibh MacCarthy. In Scotland also the surname and its variants have the same two distinct origins, from the Gaelic and Norse personal names. The Scottish origin is most common in the northeast of Ulster, where a branch of the Dumbartonshire MacAuleys settled in the sixteenth century.

MacBride

MacBride comes from the Irish Mac Giolla Bhríghde, "son of the follower of (St) Bridget'; St Bridget was a famous abbess of Kildare, who died in 525. Also derived from the same Irish original are the surnames Kilbride, Gilbride, MacIlvreed, MacGilbride and others. The principal Irish family of the name were based in the north of County Donegal in Raymunterdoney, where they were very prominent in the church, a number of the family becoming bishops. A branch migrated to County Down in early times, where the surname remains quite numerous. In Ulster also, the name may have a Scottish origin, from the descendants of one Gillebride, progenitor of one branch of the Clan Donald. The best known contemporary bearer of the surname was Sean MacBride (1904-1988), active on the Republican side in the War of Independence and after, Minister for External Affairs from 1948 to 1951, founder-member of Amnesty International, winner of the Nobel Peace Prize in 1974, the Lenin Peace Prize in 1977 and the American Medal for Justice in 1978.

MacCabe

MacCabe derives from the Irish Mac Cába, from cába meaning "cape" or "cloak." The family are thought originally to have been a branch of the MacLeods of Harris in the Hebrides. They came to Ireland from there in the mid-fourteenth century to act as gallowglasses (mercenaries) to the O'Reillys and the O'Rourkes, the ruling families in the kingdom of Breifne, the territory now part of counties Longford and Cavan. They became completely hibernicized and adopted the customs and practices of the Irish, including internecine war; having established themselves in neighboring Fermanagh by the fifteenth century, they continued the struggle for control with the Maguires up to the final catastrophe of the seventeenth century. The surname also became prominent in other adjoining counties, in particular County Monaghan.

McCann

There is dispute as to whether McCann comes from the Irish MacAnna, "son of Annadh," or Mac Cana, from cana, meaning "wolf cub." At any rate, the major family of the name were known as lords of Clanbrassil, an area on the southern shores of Lough Neagh in the modern County Armagh, which they conquered from the O'Garveys. They appear to have been a branch of the Cinéal Eoghain, the large group of families claiming descent from Eoghan, one of the sons of Niall of the Nine Hostages, the fifth century founder of the Uí Néill dynasty. The death in 1155 of one of their chiefs, Amhlaoibh Mac Cana, is recorded in the Annals of the Four Masters with praise for his chivalry, his vigor, and the fine strong drink he made from the apples in his orchard. Today, the surname is found principally in counties Armagh, Tyrone, and Antrim, though it has also spread southwards into the provinces of Leinster and Connacht.

MacCarthy

MacCarthy comes from the Irish Mac Cárthaigh, from cárthach, meaning "loving." The original Carthach from whom the surname is taken was king of Cashel c.1040, at a time when Donncha, son of Brian Boru, was king of Munster. The MacCarthys and the O'Briens, with their respective allies, waged bitter, intermittent war on each other for almost a century and a half. In the middle of the twelfth century, the struggle was resolved with the expulsion of the MacCarthys from their home in the Golden Vale in County Tipperary. They moved south, into the historic territory of Desmond, which includes the modern counties of Cork and Kerry, with which they have strongly associated ever since.

Despite their displacement, the MacCarthys dominated much of Munster for almost five centuries, with four distinct branches: those led by the MacCarthy Mór ("Great MacCarthy"), nominal head of all the MacCarthys, who ruled over much of south Kerry, the Duhallow MacCarthys, who controlled northwest Cork; MacCarthy Riabhach ("grey") based in Carbery in southwest Cork; and MacCarthy Muskerry, on the Cork/Kerry border.

MacCormack

MacCormack and MacCormick are both derived from Mac Cormaic from the extremely popular Irish and Scottish personal name Cormac. This popularity meant that the surname arose independently in a large number of places throughout Ireland (and Scotland), and is today widely scattered. It seems likely also that the creation of these surnames took place at a later date than many of the other native Irish names. The only family of any early consequence were based in County Fermanagh, around Kilmacormick, "MacCormack's church," and were a branch of the Maguires. The most famous bearer of the surname is undoubtedly John MacCormack (1885-1945), the operatic and concert tenor, who achieved extraordinary international fame in the first half of this century.

MacCullagh

MacCullagh and MacCullough are very numerous in Ulster, and almost entirely confined to that province. They may have a native Irish, or a Scottish origin. The Irish original is Mac Con Uladh or Mac Cú Uladh, both meaning "son of the hound of Ulster," and generally anglicized as MacCullagh, though they also sometimes appear as Coloo, MacAnaul and MacNully. The family were based in east County Antrim and north Down. The Scottish origins are various, coming from Mac Cullaich, from cullach, meaning "boar," common in Galloway, and from Mac Lulich, (lúlaogh meaning "little calf), which originated in Argyllshire. A member of this latter family was briefly King of Scots. In Scotland, the surname is generally given today as MacCulloch. In Ulster MacCullagh is more common in the west of the province, in particular in County Tyrone, while MacCullough appears more frequently in the east, in counties Antrim and Down.

MacDermot

MacDermot comes from the Irish Mac Diarmada, from the personal name Diarmuid, the meaning of which may derive from dia, "god" and armaid "of arms." The individual from whom the surname is taken lived in the twelfth century, and was a direct descendant of Maolruanaidh Mór, brother of Conor, king of Connacht, the ancestor of the O'Connors, who ruled in the tenth century. Diarmuid's descendants are associated with an area in the north of the modern County Roscommon roughly corresponding to the baronies of Boyle and Frenchpark. For many centuries their seat was a large castle on MacDermot's Island, in Lough Key near the modern town of Boyle.

The Moylurg branch remained powerful until the final post-Cromwellian confiscations. In the seventeenth century, the MacDermots of Moylurg moved to Coolavin, beside Lough Gara in the neighboring County Sligo, where the line of descent from the original MacDermot chiefs remains unbroken.

The surname is now one of the most common in Ireland, found throughout the island, but still most frequent in Roscommon.

MacDonagh

MacDonagh, and its many variants, MacDonough, Donogh, Donaghy etc., all derive from the Irish Mac Donnchadha, from donnchadh (often anglicized "Donagh"), a popular first name meaning "brown one. The early popularity of the name meant that the surname based on it arose separately in two places: in County Cork, where the MacDonaghs were known as "Lords of Duhallow," and in County Sligo, where the family were rulers in the barony of Tirreril. The Sligo MacDonaghs were in fact a branch of the MacDermotts, claiming Donagh MacDermott as their ancestor. Today the name is rare in Cork, but has become very widespread in the western province of Connacht. The best-known modern bearer of the name is Donagh MacDonagh (1912-1968), the poet, dramatist and lawyer, whose most successful play, Happy as Larry, has been translated into a dozen languages.

MacDonald

MacDonald is extremely numerous and widespread throughout Ireland. It is commonly a confusion for MacDonnell (q.v.), and shares the same origin, coming from the Gaelic personal name Domhnall, meaning "world mighty." However, true MacDonalds are descendants of the Scottish clan of the name. They are one of the group of Scottish clans who claim descent from Conn of the Hundred Battles, the legendary Irish king, through Colla Uais, who colonized the Hebrides. Their name comes from Donald of Islay, one of the sons of Somhairle, lord of Argyle. By the fifteenth century they were the most powerful clan in Scotland, controlling the entire western coast of the country. Their involvement in Ireland was continuous from the thirteenth century, when they first arrived as gallowglasses, or mercenaries; such was their fame that they were employed in virtually every local war, spreading and settling throughout the country over the following centuries. Inevitably, their main connection remained with Ulster. A secondary influx into that province of settlers bearing the name occurred in the eighteenth century, when the Highland clearances caused great forced migration from Scotland.

MacDonnell

MacDonnell, often confused with MacDonald, comes from the Irish Mac Domhnaill, from the personal name Domhnall, a compound made up of "world" and "strong." It is common and widely distributed throughout Ireland. The principal source of the name outside Ulster is in the old kingdom of Thomond, in the Clare/Limerick area, where the MacDonnells were hereditary poets to the O'Briens. Many other southern MacDonnells will in fact be descendants of MacDonald gallowglasses (see MacDonald). In Ulster, the most prominent native family were the MacDonnells of Clankelly, rulers of Fermanagh before the rise of the Maguires. Displaced by their loss of power, they settled in the north of the adjoining County Monaghan, and remain numerous in the area. The MacDonnells of Antrim are in fact descendants of the Clan Donald. In the sixteenth century Somhairle Buidhe ("Sorley Boy") MacDonnell conquered a large part of that county and defended it tenaciously against Gaelic Irish and English intrusions. In 1620 his son, Randal MacSorley MacDonald, was created earl of Antrim.

MacEvoy

MacEvoy (or MacAvoy) is the phonetic anglicization of Mac Fhfodhbhuidhe, possibly from the Irish fiodhbhadhach, "man of the woods." The most prominent family of the name originally held power in the barony of Moygoish in modern County Westmeath, but migrated southwest, where they became one of the well-known "Seven Septs of Leix," ruling over an area in the parishes of Mountrath and Raheen in County Laois. In the early seventeenth century the most important leaders of the family were forcibly transported to County Kerry, together with other members of the "Seven Septs," but the surname remains numerous in the Laois/Westmeath region. In the north of the country, MacEvoy was used as an erroneous equivalent of Mac Giolla Bhuidhe, "son of the fair-haired youth," a Donegal name usually anglicized as "McIlwee" or "MacKelvey," and of Mac an Bheatha, "son of life" (MacVeigh), a surname common in the Armagh/Louth region.

MacGillycuddy

The surname comes from the Irish MacGiolla Mochuda, meaning "son of the devotee of (St) Mochuda." Its adoption was unusual. St Mochuda was a native of Kerry who founded a monastic settlement at Lismore in County Waterford. When his fellow Kerryman Ailinn O'Sullivan became bishop of Lismore in the mid-thirteenth century, he started the practice of O'Sullivans paying special devotion to this saint. As a result, some used Giolla Mochuda as a kind of title. The first to use Mac Giolla Mochuda was Conor, recorded as having slain Donal O'Sullivan Beare in 1563. His family, descendants of Donal Mor O'Sullivan (see O'Sullivan), continued to be known as "MacGillycuddy O'Sullivan" or "MacGillycuddy alias O'Sullivan" into the seventeenth century, when MacGillycuddy became established as a surname in its own right. Even then, less-well-off members of the family continued to be known as "O'Sullivan" for some time.

The family controlled a large territory in the Kerry baronies of Magunihy and Dunkerron; the name of the mountains in Dunkerron, MacGillycuddys Reeks, records their ownership.

MacGovern

MacGovern is the phonetic anglicization of Mag Shamhradháin, from a diminutive of samradh, "summer." The name is closely linked with the original homeland where it first arose; in the traditional genealogies, Shamhradhán, the eleventh-century individual from whom the surname comes, was himself descended from Eochaidh, one of the O'Rourkes, who lived in the eighth century. His name was given to the area of County Cavan where the MacGoverns held sway, the barony of Tullyhaw (Teallach Eochaidh), in the northwest of the county. The particular centers of their power were Bawnaboy, Lissanover, and Ballymagauran. This last includes an earlier anglicization of Mag Shamhradháin, "Magauran" or "MacGowran," now much less common than MacGovern. From Cavan, the name has now spread throughout Connacht and Ulster, and is particularly numerous in the adjoining counties of Fermanagh and Leitrim.

MacGowan

MacGowan (or Magowan) is the phonetic anglicization of the Irish Mac Gabhann and the Scottish Mac Gobhann, both meaning "son of the smith." In Ireland the surname originated in central County Cavan, in what was once the ancient kingdom of Breifne, where the MacGowans were among the most powerful families. However, in Cavan itself a large majority translated their surname and became Smiths (see also the entry for that name). Outside Cavan, in the adjoining counties of Leitrim, Donegal, Sligo and Monaghan, MacGowan was the most popular English form, and the surname is most numerous in those counties today, with the largest number in County Donegal. There, a family of MacGowans held Church lands in the parish of Inishmacsaint. Because of their prominence, a separate Donegal family based near Raphoe, the Mac Dhubháin (from a diminutive of dubh, "black") also anglicized their name as MacGowan, adding to the numbers bearing the name in that county.

MacGrath

MacGrath, and its many variants: Magrath, MacGraw, Magra, comes from the Irish MacRaith, from the personal name Rath, meaning "grace" or "prosperity." Two native Irish families adopted the name, one based on the borders of the modern counties of Donegal and Fermanagh, around Termon MacGrath, the other in County Clare, where they were famous as hereditary poets to the ruling O'Brien family of Thomond. Today neither area can be claimed to have large numbers of the surname. The southern family spread eastwards, into counties Tipperary and Waterford, while the northern family's descendants are now mainly to be found in County Tyrone, where they settled around Ardstraw after being driven from their homeland by the O'Donnells. The most remarkable bearer of the name was of this family, Meiler Magrath (1523-1622), who managed to be, simultaneously, Catholic Bishop of Down and Connor and Protestant Archbishop of Cashel. His rapacity was notorious, and he held six Anglican bishoprics, four of them at the one time, as well as the income of seventy parishes. For his pains he lived to be a hundred years old.

MacGuinness

MacGuinness, together with its variants Guinness, Magennis, MacNeice, MacCreesh, and others, comes from the Irish Mac Aonghasa, from the personal name Aonghas ("Angus"), made up of aon "one" and gus "choice." The surname originated in Iveagh, in what is now County Down, where the family displaced the O'Haugheys in the twelfth century, ruling over the region down to the seventeenth century. The center of their power was at Rathfriland. In the sixteenth century they accepted the Reformation, but joined in the later wars against the English and were dispossessed of all their lands. The name is now common in Connacht and Leinster, as well as in its original homeland of Ulster.

A southern offshoot of the family adopted the variant MacCreesh, and in Monaghan, Fermanagh, and south Down that name was used as an equivalent of MacGuinness. North of the original homeland, in County Antrim, a similar process occurred, with MacNiece or MacNeice the variant adopted there. The Guinness family who founded the famous brewery were originally from County Down.

MacHugh

Along with its principal variant MacCue, MacHugh comes from the Irish Mac Aodha or Aoidhe, from the very popular personal name Aodh, meaning "fire." In various forms, Aodh is the root of a large number of common surnames (see Hayes, Hughes, and Magee). At least three distinct families in west Ulster and Connacht adopted Mac Aodha: a branch of the O'Flahertys of Connemara in west Galway, another family based near the modern town of Tuam in north Galway and, in Fermanagh, a family who claim descent from Aodh, a grandson of Donn Carrach Maguire, the first Maguire ruler of the county. Today the surname is most numerous in County Donegal and in north Connacht, though it is also common in Leinster. In parts of Ulster Fermanagh in particular it was considered interchangeable with Magee until quite recently.

MacKenna

MacKenna is the English form of the Irish surname Mac Cionath. The Mac Cionath were originally based in Meath, but in early times were brought north into Clogher as hired fighters by the rulers of that territory, and quickly became lords in their own right of Truagh, a territory on the borders of the modern counties of Tyrone, and Monaghan. Their power endured down to the seventeenth century, their last chief being Patrick McKenna, who died near Emyvale, County Monaghan, in 1616. The surname is still very numerous in the area of the original homeland, but over the centuries has spread throughout the country. Juan MacKenna (1771-1814) was born at Clogher in County Tyrone, and was a general under Bernardo O'Higgins in the fight for Chilean liberation.

MacKeon

MacKeon has a wide range of synonyms and variants, including Keon, MacKeown, MacGeown, MacOwen and, in Ulster, MacEwan, MacCune, MacKone, Magowen and, occasionally, Johnson or Johnstone. The reason lies in the Irish and Scottish original of the name, Mac Eoin, "son of Eoin (John)', which arose independently in a number of areas. In Ireland the principal areas of origin were in the Kiltartan region of County Galway, at Creggan and Derrynoone in County Armagh and in Sligo/Leitrim in north Connacht. This last family were the most prominent historically, and it is thought that the Galway family were an offshoot. In County Antrim, the surname is almost entirely of Scottish origin, and derives from Eoin Bissett, who came to the Glens of Antrim from Scotland in the thirteenth century. The form MacKeown is largely confined to northeast Ulster, while MacKeon is most common in Connacht and west Ulster. As so often with variations in spelling, however, no absolute rules are possible.

MacLoughlin

MacLoughlin is the form of the name most frequent in Connacht and Leinster, while McLaughlin is most common in Ulster, particularly in counties Antrim, Donegal and Derry. Both forms derive from the Irish and Scottish Mac Lochlainn, from the personal name Lochlann, from loch, "lake" or "fjord," and lann, meaning "land." It was a Gaelic name used for Scandinavia, and was applied to the Viking settlers of the early Middle Ages, and became a popular name in its own right. The surname containing it has at least three origins in Ireland: in County Clare, where the MacLoughlins claimed descent from Lochlann, a tenth-century lord in the barony of Corcomroe; in the Inishowen peninsula of County Donegal, where the family were among the most powerful in Ulster down to the late middle ages, and in County Meath, where the descendants of the tenth-century high king, Maolseachlann (or Malachy II), were first known as O'Melaghlin, later corrupted to MacLoughlin.

MacMahon

MacMahon (or MacMahon) comes from the Irish Mac Mathghamha or, in the modern version, Mac Mathdúa, from mathghamhqain, meaning "bear." The surname arose separately in two areas, in west Clare and in County Monaghan. In the former, the MacMahons were part of the great tribal grouping, the Dál gCais, and claim decent from Mahon O'Brien, grandson of Brian Boru. The last Chief of the Name was killed at the battle of Kinsale in 1602. The Ulster MacMahons were based in the barony of Truagh in the north of County Monaghan, and ruled the kingdom of Oriel between the thirteenth and sixteenth centuries. Their last chief, Hugh MacMahon, was beheaded by the English in 1641. Today, although widespread throughout Ireland, MacMahon remains most common in the two ancestral homelands of Clare and Monaghan.

After the defeats of the native Irish in the seventeenth century, many of the Clare MacMahons emigrated to serve in the Irish Brigade of the French army. One of their descendants, Patrick MacMahon (1808-93), became President and Marshal of France.

MacManus

MacManus is the anglicization of the Irish Mac Mághnais, from the popular Norse personal name Magnus, derived ultimately from the Latin magnus, "great." Although the Viking settlers are responsible for the introduction of Magnus as a personal name the surname it gave rise to is entirely Irish. It came into being in two distinct areas: in County Roscommon, where the family claim descent from Mághnais, son of the twelfth-century High King, Turlough O'Connor; and in County Fermanagh, where the original ancestor was Maghnuis Maguire, son of the chieftain Donn Mór Maguire. In Fermanagh they were second in power only to the Maguires themselves, and from their base on the island of Ballymaguire (now Belleisle) on Lough Erne controlled the shipping and fishing on the lake. Cathal Óg MacManus (1439-1498), chief of the name, dean of Lough Erne and vicar-general of the diocese of Clogher, was responsible for the compilation of the Annals of Ulster. Today the surname is most common by far in its original homelands, and especially in County Fermanagh.

MacNally

MacNally, MacAnally and Nally all share the same Irish origins, in the two Irish names Mac an Fhailghigh, "son of the poor man," and Mac Con Uladh, "son of the hound of Ulster." As might be expected, the latter name is almost entirely confined to Ulster, in particular to that part of the modern province originally called Ulaidh, the southeast, in particular counties Armagh and Monaghan. Today, the anglicized versions of the name remain very common in these counties, with the "Mac-' forms in the majority. Outside Ulster, the principal origin of the name is in northwest Connacht, in counties Roscommon and Mayo, where it is said that the name was adopted by the descendants of Norman settlers. The most common form in these counties is the simple "Nally." One extremely prominent bearer of the name was the Reverend David Rice MacAnally (1810-1895), a sheriff and Methodist preacher who is said to have weighed more than 360lbs (160kg).

MacNamara

MacNamara comes from the Irish Mac Conmara, "son of the hound of the sea." The surname arose in County Clare where the family were part of the famous Dál gCais tribal grouping. They were second only to the O'Briens, to whom they were hereditary marshals. From relatively minor beginnings they grew in power to become rulers of the territory of Clancullen, a territory including a large part of what is now east Clare, where they held sway for almost six centuries, down to the final defeat of Gaelic culture in the seventeenth century. Today, the surname is widespread throughout Ireland, but the largest concentration remains in the area of the original homeland, in counties Clare and Limerick. Brinsley MacNamara (1890-1963), the novelist and playwright, and the most famous modern bearer of the surname, was in fact John Weldon. He adopted the pseudonym as protection; his most famous work, The Valley of the Squinting Windows, was highly critical of Irish rural life.

Madden

Madden is is the anglicized version of the Irish Ó Madaidhín, from a diminutive of madadh, meaning "hound." In early times, the family were part of the Uí Máine tribal grouping based in east County Galway, and ruled the area up to the late Middle Ages. Even today, the surname is most numerous by far in east Galway. A branch of the family moved south to the Clare/Limerick region in early times, and anglicized their name as "Madigan," and this separate surname is also still most strongly associated with its original homeland. The most famous bearer of the name was Richard Robert Madden (1798-1886), doctor, traveller, historian and fervent opponent of the slave trade.

Magee

Magee, and its variants McGee, MacGee, etc., come from the Gaelic Mac or Mag Aodha, from Aodh (anglicized "Hugh"), a very popular personal name meaning "fire," which also gave rise to a large number of other surnames, including Hays, Hughes, McHugh, and McCoy. The form "Magee" reflects the pronunciation of Ulster and Scottish Gaelic, with "Mag-' most common in the east of the province, and "Mac-' in the west; Ulster is the area where the name is most common by far. It can be of either Scottish or Irish origin. Three Irish families of the name are recorded: in the area now on the borders of counties Donegal and Tyrone, in the territory around Islandmagee on the coast of Antrim, and in Fermanagh, where they descend from Aodh, great-grandson of Donn Carrach Maguire, the first Maguire ruler of that region. The remainder of the Ulster Magees are descended from seventeenth-century settlers from Scotland, where the surname is most common in Dumfries, in Ayrshire, and in Galloway. In County Cavan, Mag Aodha has also sometimes, strangely, been anglicized as "Wynne," from a mistaken resemblance to gaoth, "wind".

Maguire

Maguire, with its variants MacGuire, McGwire etc., comes from the Irish Mag Uidhir, meaning "son of the brown(-haired) one." The surname is common throughout Ireland, with particular concentrations in Cavan, Monaghan, and Fermanagh; in Fermanagh it is the most numerous name in the county. From the time of their first firm establishment, in Lisnaskea around the start of the thirteenth century, all the associations of the family have been with Fermanagh. By the start of the fourteenth century, the chief of the family, Donn Carrach Maguire, ruled the county, and for three hundred years after there were no fewer than fifteen Maguire chieftains of the county. By 1600, County Fermanagh virtually belonged to them.

As for so many other Gaelic families, however, the seventeenth century was catastrophic for the Maguires. First, a junior branch, based around the area of the modern town of Enniskillen, were dispossessed and their lands parcelled out in the Plantation of Ulster. Then, as a result of their participation in the rebellions of the Cromwellian and Williamite periods, virtually all the remainder of their possessions in Fermanagh were taken.

Maher

Maher, and its principal variant Meagher, are the anglicized versions of the Irish Ó Meachair, from meachar, meaning "hospitable." The surname originated in Ikerrin near the modern town of Roscrea in north Tipperary, where the family retained their traditional lands right up to the modern period. The name remains very strongly linked to the traditional homeland, with the bulk of present-day Mahers living or originating in County Tipperary. Thomas Francis Meagher (1823-1867) was one of the founders of the revolutionary "Young Ireland" movement. Transported to Australia, he managed to escape to the U.S., where he became Brigadier-General of the Irish Brigade of the Union Army during the Civil War, and was later Governor of Montana.

Malone

Malone is the anglicized form of the Irish Ó Maoil Eoin, meaning "descendant of a devotee of (St) John," maol being the Irish for "bald" and referring to the distinctive tonsure sported by Irish monks. The family was an offshoot of the O'Connors of Connacht, and lived up to the ecclesiastical origin of their surname in their long connection with the famous Abbey of Clonmacnoise, with a long line of Malone bishops and abbots. Today they are largely dispersed from this area, and the largest concentrations are to be found in counties Clare and Wexford. The most famous bearer of the name was Edmund Malone (1741-1812), a friend of Samuel Johnson, James Boswell, and Edmund Burke amongst others, whose complete edition of the works of Shakespeare remained standard for almost a century.

Martin

Martin is an extremely common name throughout the English-speaking world and, in its many variant forms, throughout Europe; its popularity is largely due to the widespread fame of the fourth-century saint, Martin of Tours. In Ireland, the surname may be of English, Scottish or native Irish origin. The best-known Martins, powerful in west Galway and Galway city for centuries, were of English extraction, having arrived with the Normans. The largest number of Irish origin stem from the Mac Giolla Mhártain, "son of the follower of (St) Martin," also anglicized as "Gilmartin," who were a branch of the O'Neills. They originally held territory in the barony of Clogher in County Tyrone, but were displaced westwards into the adjoining counties of Sligo and Leitrim, where they are most numerous today. The Scottish origin of the name is similar, from an anglicization of Scots Gaelic Mac Gille Mhártainn. Richard ("Humanity Dick") Martin (1754-1834), of the Galway family, was one of the founders of the Royal Society for the Prevention of Cruelty to Animals.

Meehan

Meehan, along with its variant Meighan, comes from the Irish Ó Miadhacháin, from miadhach, meaning "honorable." Historically, the most notable family of the name were an offshoot of the MacCarthys of the kingdom of Desmond in south Munster. However, as early as the eleventh century they migrated north to County Leitrim. From there they spread slowly into the adjoining counties, and are now numerous throughout east Connacht, Donegal and Fermanagh. This family preserved a sixth-century manuscript of St Molaise of Devenish from generation to generation for more than a thousand years; it is now held in the National Museum in Dublin. A separate family appears to have adopted the surname in the Clare/Galway region, where the name is also numerous. In Monaghan, and there alone, it has been anglicized as "Meegan".

Molloy

Molloy, along with Mulloy and O'Molloy, is the anglicized version of a number of distinct Irish names. The Ó Maolmhuaidh, from maolmhuadh meaning "proud chieftain," were part of the southern Uí Néill, the southern branch of the large tribal grouping claiming descent from Niall of the Nine Hostages, the fifth-century king who supposedly kidnapped St Patrick to Ireland. They held power over a large part of what is now County Offaly, where the surname is still very common. A second family were the Ó Maoil Aodha, "descendant of the devotee of (St) Aodh," from maol, literally "bald," a reference to the distinctive tonsure sported by early Irish monks. As well as Molloy, this surname has also been anglicized as "Miley" and "Millea." The name arose in east Connacht, in the Roscommon/east Galway region, and remains numerous there today.

Moloney

Moloney, along with its variants Mullowney and Maloney, is the English version of Ó Maol Dhomhnaigh, meaning "descendant of the servant of the church," Maol means "bald," and refers to the distinctive tonsure common in the early Irish Church, while domhnach means "Sunday," and was used by extension to refer to the place of worship on that day. The surname arose in County Clare, near the modern town of Tulla, and remains extremely common there, as well as in the adjoining counties of Limerick and Tipperary. Mullowney has also sometimes been used as the anglicization of the Ulster surname Mac Giolla Dhomhnaigh, meaning "son of the servant of the church," usually anglicized as "Downey" or "MacEldowney," which is found principally in counties Antrim and Derry. Both of these name were sometimes used for the illegitimate offspring of clergymen.

Monaghan

Monaghan is the English version of the Irish Ó Manacháin, from a diminutive of manach, meaning "monk," and some of the family adopted the semi-translation "Monks." Most of the surname in Ireland descend from one Manachain, a chieftain who lived in Connacht in the ninth century, and it is with that province, specifically with east Roscommon close to the river Shannon, that the family are most closely linked. Up to the end of the thirteenth century they were rulers of this area, known as "the Three Tuathas." The name has spread from the original homeland, and is now common also in Mayo and Galway. In County Fermanagh, where the name is also numerous, the family are thought to be part of the original inhabitants of the area, the Fir Manach, from whom the county gets its name. Their base was in the district of Lurg. From here the name has now also scattered in the adjoining counties of Monaghan and Derry.

Mooney

Mooney comes from the Irish Ó Maonaigh, which may derive from the Old Irish maonach, meaning "dumb," or from maoineach, meaning "wealthy." It arose as a surname independently in each of the four provinces. In Ulster, it was the name of a family based in the parish of Ardara, in County Donegal. The Connacht family were located in the parish of Easky in the barony of Tireragh in County Sligo, where "Meeny" is often the English version used. In Munster, reflecting the different pronunciation, the English is often "Mainey." But the most notable family arose in Leinster, in the modern County Offaly, where they were concentrated around the parish of Lemanaghan. Their descendants are by far the most numerous today, although the name has now spread throughout Ireland.

Moore

Moore is today one of the most common surnames in Ireland, among the top twenty. It may be of English, Irish, Welsh or Scottish origin. In England the name may derive either from someone who lived near a moor or from a nickname for someone of dark complexion, from "moor," meaning Negro. This is frequently also the ultimate origin of the name in Scotland and Wales, where it is often rendered "Muir," although in places it is thought to come from mór, "big." The Irish origin of Moore is Ó Mórdha, also anglicized O'More, from mórdha, meaning "stately" or "noble." The principal family of definite native Irish origin were of County Laois, where they were the leading sept of the famous "Seven Septs of Laois," whose resistance to the English led to the forced resettlement of the most prominent individuals in County Kerry. At this point, it is virtually impossible to say in any single case which of the various origins of the surname is the most accurate.

Moran

Moran is the anglicization of two distinct Irish names, Ó Mórain, from mór, meaning "big," and Ó Mughráin, whose origins remain unclear. The former arose in County Mayo, near the modern town of Ballina, where the eponymous ancestor Móran held power. The latter family were part of the Uí Máine tribal grouping. Their two branches were based around Criffon in County Galway, and the modern village of Ballintober in north Roscommon. Today, as might be expected, the vast majority of Morans are of Connacht origin. One of the most famous bearers of the name was Michael Moran (1794-1856), better known by his nickname of "Zozimus," who was blinded in infancy and made his living on the streets of Dublin with his recitations and ballads. A monument to him stands in Glasnevin cemetery.

Morgan

In origin Morgan is Welsh, deriving from the Old Welsh morcant, meaning "sea-bright." The majority of Irish Morgans are almost certainly of Welsh or Welsh Norman stock. The surname is common in Connacht and Leinster, but most numerous in Ulster. Here, it is possible that some are descended from the Clann Morgunn of Sutherland in Scotland, or from a separate family based in Aberdeenshire. There is also a Gaelic Irish family in Ulster, the Ó Murcháin, who were based in County Monaghan, whose surname was anglicized Morgan. The writer Lady Sydney Morgan (1783-1859) had immense success with her books on the politics and society of France and Italy, and her salon in Kildare Street was the center of Dublin literary life.

Moriarty

Moriarty is the English version of the Irish Ó Muircheartaigh, made up of muir, "sea," and ceardach, "skilled," thus "one skilled in the ways of the sea." The name is undoubtedly linked to their original homeland, on both sides of Castlemaine harbor in south County Kerry. The continuity of their association with the area is remarkable, even by Irish standards. They have lived in the area since the surname came into being in the eleventh century, and ninety percent of present births of the surname are still in County Kerry. This continuity is all the more tenacious for the fact that they had lost virtually all their power in the area by the fourteenth century. David Moriarty (1814-1877) was a Catholic bishop of Kerry notorious for his vehement denunciations of all opposition to the British government, saying of the Fenian leaders "eternity is not long enough nor Hell hot enough for such miscreants.' Ó Muircheartaigh was also a surname found in Meath and the midlands, but in these areas it has been anglicized as "Murtagh".

Morris

Morris is a common surname throughout the British Isles, and in virtually all cases is derived, directly or indirectly, from the personal name Maurice, which comes from the Latin Maurus, meaning "moorish" (see Moore). A large number of those bearing the name in Ireland, where the name is most frequent in Leinster, with significant numbers also in Ulster and Connacht, will be of English, Scottish or Welsh origin. There was also an Irish family, the Ó Muirgheasa, (from muir, "sea" and geasa, "taboo") part of the Uí Fiachrach tribal grouping in County Sligo, whose surname was originally anglicized Morrissey and later shortened to Morris. Ó Muirgheasa was also the surname of a family in County Fermanagh who anglicized their name to Morris. The most prominent family of the name, one of the famous "Tribes of Galway," were of Norman extraction and originally known as de Marreis.

Mullan

Mullan, together with its variants Mullin, Mullen, Mullane and Mullins, can have a variety of distinct origins. First, it may be the anglicization of the Irish name Ó Maoláin, from a diminutive of maol, "bald" or "tonsured", which arose separately in a number of areas. The County Galway family of the name claim descent from Maolan, himself descended from a king of Connacht. A different family of the same name were based in the Keenaght district of County Derry, and were followers of the O'Cahans (see Kane). In County Monaghan a family of the name arose around the modern town of Clones; their name has also been anglicized as Mollins. Yet another family hails from south County Cork, where the name is frequently given as Mullins. As well as all of these, many MacMillans, Scottish settlers in Ulster in the seventeenth century, adopted MacMullan, often shortened to Mullan. There is also an English name Mullins, from the Middle English miln, "mill", and a good number of Irish bearers of the name are undoubtedly of this origin.

Mulligan

Mulligan comes from the Irish Ó Maolagáin, from a diminutive of maol, literally meaning "bald" and referring to the distinctive tonsure of the early Irish monks. In the early Middle Ages they were rulers of the territory of Tír MacCartháin, in the baronies of Boylagh and Raphoe in County Donegal, and held power down to the plantation of the seventeenth century. After this they were dispersed, and migrated south to Mayo and east to counties Fermanagh and Monaghan. Some members of the family anglicized their surname, by quasi-translation, to Baldwin. Milligan is another common variant, found most frequently in counties Antrim, Down and Derry. Hercules Mulligan (1740-1825), born in Coleraine, acted as a secret agent for George Washington during the War of Independence.

Murphy

Murphy is the anglicized version of two Irish surnames, Ó Murchadha and Mac Murchadha, both derived from the popular early Irish personal name Murchadh, meaning "sea-warrior." Mac Murchadha ("son of Murchadh") is exclusive to Ulster, where the family were part of the Cinéal Eoghain, the tribal grouping claiming descent from Eoghan, himself a son of the fifth century founder of the Uí Néill dynasty, Niall of the Nine Hostages. In Ulster today, Murphy remains most numerous in County Armagh.

Elsewhere in Ireland, O Murchadha (descendant of Murchadh) is the original Irish. This arose separately in Cork, Roscommon, and Wexford. The most prominent were the Wexford Uí Murchadha, who took their surname from Murchadh or Murrough, grandfather of Dermot MacMurrough. Their chief seats were at Morriscastle ("O Murchu's Castle"), Toberlamina, Oulart ,and Oularteigh. In the late sixteenth century, Dónal Mór O'Morchoe (as the name was then anglicized) was overthrown, and virtually all his territory confiscated. The branch based at Oularteigh, managed to retain their lands. The arms illustrated are for this family.

Murray

Murray is a common surname throughout Ireland, among the twenty most numerous. It can be of Scottish or Irish origin. The Scottish surname, Murray or MacMurray, derives from Moray in the northeast, a name that originally meant "settlement by the sea." The earliest recorded ancestor of this family was one Hugh Freskin, a Flemish settler who obtained large grants of land in Morayshire in 1130; his descendants took their name from his property. Many in Ireland, in Ulster particularly, are of this connection.

In Ireland the surname came from Ó Muireachaidh, "descendant of the seaman." The most prominent family were based in the south Roscommon/east Galway region, and were part of the Uí Máine tribal grouping. As well as these, however, a separate family are recorded in Cork, in the barony of Carbery, and Mac Muireachaidh, anglicized as Murray and MacMorrow, is found in County Leitrim and north County Down. In addition Mac Giolla Mhuire, "son of the servant of Mary", another County Down name, has sometimes been anglicized as Murray, as well as the more obvious MacIlmurray and Gilmore.

Nolan

Nolan is now among the most common surnames in Ireland. It is the anglicized form of Ó Nualláin, from a diminutive of nuall, meaning "famous" or "noble." The family are strongly linked with the area of the modern County Carlow, wherein pre-Norman times they held power in the barony of Forth, whence their ancient title of "Princes of Foharta." Their power was greatly diminished after the arrival of the Normans, but the surname is still strongly linked with the area The prevalence of the surname in the modern counties of Mayo and Galway is explained by the migration of a branch of the family to that area in the sixteenth century; they obtained large tracts of land, and their descendants are many. The most famous modern bearer of the surname was Brian O'Nolan (1911-1966), better known under his two pen-names of FIann O'Brien and Myles na Gopaleen, whose genius for comic invention has only been fully appreciated since his death.

O'Brien

O'Brien is in Irish Ó Briain, from the personal name Brian. Its meaning is problematic. It may come from bran, meaning "raven", or, more likely, from Brion, borrowed from the Celtic ancestor of Welsh which contains the element bre-, meaning "hill" or "high place." The name would then mean "lofty or eminent."

The historic origin of O'Brien containing it is clear. It simply denotes a descendant of Brian Boru, ('Brian of the Tributes"), high king of Ireland in 1002, and victor at the battle of Clontarf in 1014. The first individual clearly to use O'Brien as a genuinely hereditary surname was Donogh Cairbre O'Brien, son of the king of Munster, Dónal Mór. His descendants spilt into a number of branches, including the O'Briens of Aherlow, the O'Briens of Waterford, the O'Briens of Arra in north Tipperary, and the O'Briens of Limerick, where the surname is perpetuated in the name of the barony of Pubblebrien. Today the name is numerous and widespread throughout Ireland, with particular concentrations in these areas, as well as in the original homeland of Clare.

O'Callaghan

O'Callaghan, along with its variants (O')Callagan, Callahan etc., comes from the Irish Ó Ceallacháin, from the personal name Ceallachán, a diminutive of ceallach. This was traditionally taken to mean "frequenter of churches," but is now thought to have an older meaning "bright-headed." The personal name was favored by the Eoghanacht, the tribal grouping who controlled the kingship of Munster before the 11th century, and the family trace their descent from one of the Eoghanacht kings, CeallachAn (d.954).

Cárthach, the ancestor of the MacCarthys, traced his ancestry from the same king; and a bloody succession feud between the MacCarthys and the O'Callaghans continued well into the twelfth century, ending with the MacCarthys in the ascendant.

By the end of the thirteenth century the O'Callaghans had taken control of that part of County Cork which came to be known as Pobal Uí Cheallacháin, O'Callaghan's Country. Here their principal bases were the castles at Clonmeen and Dromaneen, and from them they retained virtually uninterrupted control until the family lost virtually everything in the great confiscations following the wars of the seventeenth century.

O'Connell

O'Connell, along with Connell, comes from the Irish Ó Conaill, "descendant of Conall," a personal name probably derived from con, "hound," and gal, "valor." Because of the popularity of the personal name at its root, O'Connell arose separately as a surname in Connacht, Ulster, and Munster. The most prominent and numerous of these were the O'Connells of Munster, where the family were lords of the barony of Magunihy in east Kerry.

Driven from this area by the O'Donoghues, they moved south and the center of their power shifted to Ballycarbery, also in County Kerry. Today a majority of the O'Connells in Ireland are still found in County Kerry, and adjoining County Cork. This family produced the most famous bearer of the name, Daniel O'Connell (1775-1847), whose political campaigning won for Irish Catholics the right to hold office.

In Ulster, especially in counties Antrim, Tyrone, and Down, many Connells and MacConnells are of Scottish stock, their names derived from a phonetic transliteration of Mac Dhomhnaill (the 'Dh-' is not pronounced). This family were a branch of Clan Donald.

O'Connor

O'Connor, with its variants Connor, Conner, Connors, etc., comes from the Irish Conchobhair, from the personal name Conchobhar, perhaps meaning "lover of hounds" or "wolf-lover." The surname rose in five distinct areas, in Connacht (O'Conor Don), in Offaly (O'Conor Faly), in north Clare (O'Conor of Corcomroe), in Keenaght in County Derry, and in Kerry (O'Connor Kerry).

The Offaly family take their name from Conchobhar (d.979), who claimed descent from Cathaoir Mór, a second-century king of Ireland. The O'Connor Kerry were chiefs of a large territory in north Kerry, displaced northwards by the Norman invasion to the Limerick borders. Today, the descendants of these O'Connors are the most numerous, concentrated in the Kerry/Limerick/Cork area.

The O'Connor Don family is the most famous of all. They take their surname from Conchobhar, king of Connacht (d.971), the direct ancestor of the last two high kings of Ireland, Turlough O'Connor and Roderick O'Connor. Unlike the vast majority of the Gaelic aristocracy after the seventeenth century, the O'Connors of Connacht retained property and influence. The family seat remains in the ancestral homeland, in Castlerea, County Roscommon.

O'Donnell

O'Donnell comes from the Irish O Domhnaill "descendant of Domhnall", a name meaning "world-mighty." The surname arose simultaneously in a number of areas, among them west Clare and east Galway. The most famous O'Donnells, however, are undoubtedly those based in Donegal.

The O'Donnells of Tír Chonaill were part of the great Uí Néill tribal grouping, claiming common descent from Niall of the Nine Hostages. In early times, they inhabited a relatively small territory around Kilmacrenan. From the late Middle Ages their power and influence grew until, by the fourteenth century, they were lords of Tír Chonaill, roughly identical to modern County Donegal.

Their dynasty continued for over three centuries, until its defeat, together with the remaining pre-eminent Gaelic families, in the Nine Years' War. In this conflict, Red Hugh O'Donnell (1571-1602) and his brother Rory, first earl of Tyrconnell (1575-1608) almost inflicted a decisive reverse on the English. Rory O'Donnell took part in the "Flight of the Earls," the departure from Lough Swilly in Donegal in 1607 of the most powerful Irish leaders.

O'Donoghue

(O')Donoghue, with its variants Donohue, Donahoe, Donohoe, etc., comes from the Irish Ó Donnchadha, derived from the popular personal name Donncha, from donn, meaning "brown." The surname means "descendant of the brown-haired (or brown-complexioned) man." The popularity of the personal name meant that the surname arose in a number of places, including Galway/Roscommon, Cork, Tipperary and Cavan. The anglicized versions vary, with "Donohoe" more common in Galway and Cavan.

The O'Donoghue of Desmond, or south Munster, were the most historically important. They shared their ancestry with the O'Mahonys. Like the O'Mahonys, the Desmond O'Donoghues saw their power greatly diminished by the rise of the MacCarthys. Ultimately they were displaced from their original homeland in west Cork, and settled in southwest Kerry. Here they split into two: The O'Donoghue Mór, based around Lough Leane near Killarney, and O'Donoghue of the Glen, based in Glenflesk. O'Donoghue Mór shared the fate of the most of the Gaelic aristocracy, dispossession and poverty, but the O'Donoghue of the Glen retained both the family property and an unbroken succession to the title.

O'Donovan

O'Donovan comes from the Irish Ó Donndubháin, from donn, "brown" and dubh, "black" or "dark", the surname thus meaning "descendant of the dark brown (-haired/complexioned) man." The original Donnduban from whom the surname derives was king of Uí Chairpre in what is now east Limerick, and died in 980. In the late twelfth century, as a result of the vicious struggle between the MacCarthys and the O'Briens for dominance in Munster, the O'Donovans were forced to migrate into the neighboring county of Cork. There they gave the name of their kingdom to the modern barony of Carbery. Their territory reached from the southeast coast almost as far as the modern town of Bantry. Their principal seat was at Castledonovan, in the center of Drimoleague parish.

The family remained prominent in the area down to the seventeenth century, when, the chiefs of the family were dispossessed in the punitive confiscations, but Colonel Daniel O'Donovan, the head of the family at that time, regained some property in the area after the treaty of Limerick in 1691, and re-established the family seat at Bawnlahan in the parishes of Myross and Castlehaven.

O'Grady

O'Grady, along with Grady, comes from the Irish Ó Grádaigh, from grádach, meaning "noble." The surname originated in County Clare, where the Ó Grádaigh were part of the Dál gCais tribal grouping who claimed descent from Cas, a son of Oiloll Ollum, the semi-legendary third-century king of Munster. They thus shared common ancestry with the pre-eminent family of the Dál gCais, the O'Briens, and took a prominent part in the O'Briens' struggle against the rival Eoghanacht MacCarthys, descended from Eoghan, another son of Oiloll Ollum.

Although Clare was their homeland, from a very early date the family had strong associations with County Limerick, in particular the area around Kilballyowen. This was acquired by the then head of the family, Hugh O'Grady, in 1309, and has remained the principal seat of the family down to the present day. Unlike so many others of the native aristocracy, the O'Gradys sided with the English in the sixteenth century, and intermarried with a number of powerful English families, thus retaining their influence and possessions through all the vicissitudes of the seventeenth and eighteenth centuries.

O'Hara

O'Hara is a phonetic anglicization of Ó hEaghra. The family claim descent from Eaghra, lord of Luighne (the modern Leyney) in County Sligo, who died in 976 and who was himself, in the traditional genealogies, of the family of Oiloll Ollum, king of Munster. The O'Haras remain strongly associated with County Sligo, where they were chiefs in two areas, Ó hEaghra Buidhe ("fair") around Collooney, and Ó hEaghra Riabhach ("grey") at Ballyharry, more properly 'Ballyhara.' In the fourteenth century a branch of the family migrated north to the Glens of Antrim and established themselves in the area around the modern town of Ballymena. There they intermarried with powerful local families and acquired great prominence themselves. Apart from Dublin, Sligo and Antrim are still the two regions where the surname is most concentrated.

O'Keeffe

O'Keeffe, and Keeffe, are the anglicized versions of the Irish Ó Caoimh, from caomh, meaning "kind" or "gentle." The original Caomh from whom the family descend lived in the early eleventh century, and was a descendant of Art, King of Munster from 742 to 762. Originally the territory of the family lay along the banks of the Blackwater river in Cork, but the arrival of the Normans displaced them, like so many others, and they moved west into the barony of Duhallow, where their territory became known, and is still known, as Pobal O'Keeffe. The chiefs of the family retained power down to the eighteenth century, despite their involvement in the various rebellions, but were eventually dispossessed. Even today, Pobal O'Keeffe is still the area in which the name is most common, with surrounding areas of County Cork also including many of the name. It remains relatively rare outside that county.

O'Mahony

O'Mahony, the most common contemporary form of the name, comes from the Irish Ó Mathghamhna, stemming, like MacMahon, from mathghamhan, meaning "bear." The surname was adopted in the eleventh century by one of the dominant families of the Munster Eoghanacht peoples, the Cinéal Aodha; the individual from whom the name derives was the child of a marriage between Cian, chief of the Cinéal Aodha, and Sadhbh, daughter of Brian Boru. With the rise of the MacCarthys in the twelfth century the influence of the O'Mahonys declined, and was largely confined to the two areas of west Cork with which they are still most strongly associated, the Iveagh peninsula and the barony of Kinalmeaky, around the modern town of Bandon. In these areas they retained a large measure of power and wealth until the final collapse of Gaelic power in the wars of the seventeenth century. The most famous modern bearer of the name was Eoin ("the Pope") O'Mahony (1904-1970), barrister and genealogist, who founded and organized the annual clan gathering of the O'Mahonys.

O'Neill

O'Neill is in Irish Ó Néill, from the personal name Niall, possibly meaning "passionate" or "vehement." A clear distinction needs to be kept in mind between the family bearing this surname and the Uí Néill, the powerful tribal grouping claiming descent from Niall of the Nine Hostages. Out of the Uí Néill came many other well-known surnames, including O'Doherty, O'Donnell, O'Hagan, and others, Within the Uí Néill the two principal sub-groups were the Cinéal Eoghain and the Cinéal Cónaill, claiming descent from two sons of Niall, Eoghan and Conall respectively. The O'Neills were the leading family of the Cinéal Eoghain, ruling the ancient territory of Tír Eoghain, comprising not only the modern County Tyrone, but also large parts of Derry and Donegal. The first to use the name in recognizable hereditary fashion was Donal, born c.943.

In the fourteenth century a branch of the Tír Eoghain O'Neills migrated eastwards and, under the leadership of Aodh Buidhe ("Yellow Hugh"), wrested large areas of Antrim and Down from Norman control. The territory at the center of their power, Clandeboy, took its name from them (Clann Aodha Buidhe), and they in turn became known as the Clandeboy O'Neills.

O'Rourke

O'Rourke comes from the Irish Ó Ruairc, from Ruarc, a personal name derived from the Old Norse Hrothekr (whence also "Roderick"), meaning "famous king." Further Viking influence is seen in the frequency in the family of such names as Lochlann, Amhlaoibh (Olaf) and Sitric.

The O'Rourkes were of the same stock as the O'Connors of Connacht, part of the large tribal grouping of the Uí Briain, claiming common descent from Brion, a fifth-century king of Connacht. In the early Middle Ages, the O'Connors and the O'Rourkes were engaged in a long and bloody struggle for supremacy in Connacht, a struggle which ended in the victory of the O'Connors.

The Ruarc from whom the surname derives was a ninth-century king of Breifne, an area covering most of the modern counties of Leitrim and Cavan, along with part of County Longford. The first to use his name as part of an hereditary surname was his grandson, Seán Fearghal Ó Ruairc, who died in 964.

O'Shea

O'Shea, Shea and (O')Shee are anglicizations of the Irish Ó Séaghdha, from the personal name Séaghdha, meaning either "hawk-like" or "fortunate." The surname arose in south Kerry, on the Iveragh peninsula, where the family held power in the early Middle Ages. Despite the later decline in their influence, they were not displaced, remaining extremely numerous in their original homeland down to the present day. The surname is also found in some numbers in counties Tipperary and Kilkenny. These are the descendants of family members who migrated north as early as the fourteenth century. They became prominent in Kilkenny especially, where the name was more often anglicized (O')Shee. The most famous bearer of the name in Irish history was Katharine O'Shea, mistress and later wife of Charles Stewart Parnell; their love affair brought about Parnell's downfall and changed the course of Irish history.

O'Sullivan

The original Irish is Ó Súileabháin, deriving from súil (eye). The dispute over the meaning of the remainder of the name is understandable, since the two principal alternatives are "one-eyed" or "hawk-eyed." In Irish mythology, they are part of the Eoghanacht tribal grouping, descended, along with such prominent families as the MacCarthys and O'Callaghans, from the mythical Eoghan, supposedly one of the original Gaelic invaders. In historical times the O'Sullivans split into two major branches, the O'Sullivan Mór, based on the shores of Kenmare Bay in County Kerry, and the O'Sullivan Beare, around Bantry and the Beara peninsula in County Cork. Cork and Kerry are the areas in which popular tradition places the earliest Gaelic settlements, and even today, four out of five families of the name still live in the two counties, where it is the single most common surname.

O'Toole

O'Toole, along with Toole, comes from the Irish Ó Tuathail. This derives from the personal name Tuathal, meaning "ruler of the people", used by many Irish kings and heroes and accordingly incorporated into a surname in a number of distinct areas, among them south Ulster, Mayo and Kildare. Today the vast majority of those bearing the name are descended from the Kildare O'Tooles. The individual from whom the surname is taken was Tuathal, king of Leinster, who died c.958; the first to use the surname in true hereditary fashion appears to have been his grandson Doncaon, slain at Leighlin in 1014.

Although the original territory of the O'Tooles lay in County Kildare, in the twelfth century they were displaced by the invading Normans and migrated into Wicklow, where they controlled an area roughly identical to the old diocese of Glendalough, with the center of their power in the region around the Glen of Imaal. Despite the proximity of Dublin, the center of English rule in Ireland, the O'Tooles maintained a fierce independence. It was only in the seventeenth century, with the final and general collapse of Gaelic power, that the O'Tooles were "pacified," as the English put it.

Patterson

Patterson is now found throughout Ireland, though it is common only in Ulster, being particularly frequent in County Down. Originally it is a Lowland Scottish name, meaning, simply, "Patrick's son", and was also used as an anglicization of the Highland Gaelic surname, Mac (Gille) Phádraig, meaning "son of the follower of Patrick." In addition, there is a surname, Mac Pháidín, from Páidín, a diminutive of Patrick, which arose separately in both Ulster and Scotland, and which has been anglicized as Patterson, as well as the more usual (Mc)Fadden and (Mc)Padden. The founder of the Belfast Natural History Society was Robert Patterson (1802-1872).

Power

Power is originally a Norman name, which may derive from the Old French poure, meaning "poor", or from pohier, meaning a native of the town of Pois in Picardy in France, so called from the Old French pois, meaning "fish", a name given it because of its rivers. The surname is also found in Ireland as "Le Poer", and in the Irish version "de Paor." The first Norman settlers of the name were in County Waterford, where members of the family retained large estates up to the nineteenth century, and the surname is still most numerous by far in that county, although it has also spread into the adjoining counties of Kilkenny, Cork, Tipperary and Wexford. The family which founded Power's distillery, famous for its whiskey, were from Wexford, with their seat at Edermine near Enniscorthy.

Quigley

Quigley is the principal English version of the Irish Ó Coigligh, from coigleach, meaning "unkempt." The main origin of the family was in County Mayo, where they were part of the powerful Uí Fiachrach tribal grouping. From there they were dispersed at an early date, principally to the adjacent territories now part of counties Sligo, Donegal and, Derry, where the name is principally found today. There appears also to have been a separate Ó Coigligh family which arose in County Wexford, where the name has been anglicized for the most part as "Cogley", although Quigley is also frequent.

Quinn

Quinn is now one of the most numerous of Irish surnames, among the twenty most common, and is to be found throughout the country. The name arose separately in four distinct areas. In three of these near the modern town of Corofin in County Clare, in the glens of north Antrim, and in County Longford the Irish original from which the surname derives is Ó Coinn, from Conn, a popular personal name meaning "chief" or "leader." The most notable of these families is that based in Clare, where the barony of Inchiquin bears their name; in early times they were chiefs of the Clan Heffernan, and their descendants are today Earls of Dunraven and Mountearl.

The fourth area is Tyrone, where the surname is today the most common in the county. Here the individual from whom descent is claimed was Coinne, a great-great-grandson of Niall of the Nine Hostages, the fifth-century monarch who founded the dynasty of the Uí Néill. In the fighting forces of the O'Neills, the Ó Coinne were traditionally quartermasters.

Redmond

Redmond is a Norman surname, derived from the personal name Raymond or Raimund, which is made up of the Germanic roots ragin "counsel", and mund, "protection." The first of the name in Ireland was Alexander Redmond (or "FitzRedmond"), who was granted the Hook area of County Wexford in the first wave of the Norman settlement. The descent of the senior lines of this family is very well documented down to the twentieth century, while the junior lines have flourished and multiplied, to the point where Redmond is now an extremely common name in the county. Other branches have now also established themselves throughout Ireland. There is also a native Irish family of County Wexford, the MacDavymores, who adopted the surname of Redmond in the early seventeenth century, taking it from Redmond MacDavymore. This family were a branch of the powerful MacMurroughs, and were based in the north of the county, while the Norman Redmonds are most strongly associated with south Wexford, where they first settled.

Regan

Regan, along with its variants Reagan and O'Re(a)gan, comes from the Irish Ó Ríagáin, perhaps from ríodhgach, meaning "impulsive" or "angry." It originated independently in at least three different areas. In the Meath/Dublin region it was borne by one of the Four Tribes of Tara, who migrated to County Laois, where their descendants are still to be found. A second family claims descent from Riagán, a nephew of the eleventh-century High King Brian Boru; their homeland was the historic kingdom of Thomond, in what is now County Limerick. East Cork, around the modern town of Fermoy, was the original territory of the third family of Ó Riagáin. Their influence in the wider area of east Cork is recorded in the townland names of Coolyregan in Brigown parish, and two Ballyregans, in the parishes of Cloyne and Carrigtohill. By the sixteenth century most members of this family had migrated to the southwest, however, and it is with west Cork that the name is most strongly linked today.

Reid

Reid, with its variants Reed and Read(e), is now one of the 100 most common surnames in Ireland. In form it is English, and can derive from a nickname for someone who is red-haired or ruddy (from the Old English read), from a name for someone who lived in a clearing in a wood (Old English ried), or from the various places in England called Read or similar. No doubt many bearing the name in Ireland are of English stock. In addition, a number of Scots Gaelic surnames – MacRory, Ruaidh ("red"), and MacInroy – were frequently anglicized Reid, and many Reids in Ulster especially are descended from Scottish settlers. However, there were also two Gaelic families, the Ó Maoildeirg ("Mulderrig" – "red chieftain") of Mayo and Antrim, and the Ó Maoilbhríghde ("Mulreedy" – "devotee of St Brigid") of County Roscommon, whose surnames have often been anglicised Reid, by semi-translation and abbreviation respectively. Nano Reid (1905-1981) was one of the best known Irish painters of her generation, celebrated for her skillful evocation of the landscape of her native County Louth.

Reilly

Reilly, with its variants Riley and (O')R(e)ily, comes from the Irish Ó Raghallaigh, and is extremely common and widespread throughout Ireland. It originated in the old kingdom of Breifne, which included areas now in counties Cavan and Longford, where the O'Reillys were long the dominant family. Their prosperity may be gauged by the fact the "reilly" was at one point a colloquial term for money in Ireland. After the collapse of Gaelic power in the seventeenth century large numbers emigrated to serve in the armies of France, many in Colonel Edmund O'Reilly's regiment of foot. The connection with the original homeland is still strong, however; even today (O')Reilly is the single most numerous surname in both Cavan and Longford.

Riordan

Riordan, with its variants O'Riordan and Reardan, comes from the Irish original Ó Rioghbhárdáin (Ó Ríordáin in modern Irish), riogh-meaning "royal", and bárdán a diminutive of bard, "poet." The surname originated in the area between the modern towns of Thurles in County Tipperary and Birr in County Offaly. Very early, perhaps even in the twelfth century, the Ó Rioghbhdrdáin migrated south to County Cork, where they settled in the west of the county, in Muskerry particularly, and the strength of their association with this part of the country remains remarkable; a large majority of those bearing the name originate in County Cork. Seán Ó Riordáin (1916-1971), born in Ballyvourney, County Cork, is considered by many to have been the finest Irish-language poet of the twentieth century.

Robinson

Robinson is one of the 100 most common surnames in Ireland. In form it is English, from Robin, a diminutive of Robert, though it is also common in Scotland, where in many cases it has been used as a synonym of Robertson, a surname used by the Clan Donnachie. Many Robinsons in Ulster, where the name is among the twenty most common, will be of this connection. The majority elsewhere are almost certainly of English stock. The best-known contemporary bearer of the name is undoubtedly Mary Robinson (née Bourke), who was elected President of Ireland in 1990. Before her election she was already widely respected as a constitutional lawyer and human rights campaigner.

Roche

Roche, together with its variants Roach, Roch, etc, is a name of Norman origin. Although the obvious derivation is from the French roche, "rock", the earliest bearer of the surname in Ireland, Richard FitzGodebert de la Roche, in fact adopted the surname after his place of origin in Wales, Rhos in Pembrokeshire. He was one of the first Norman arrivals, coming in 1167, and acquiring with others of his family large tracts of south County Wexford. Over the centuries the family became thoroughly hibernicized, to the point where they were prominent in the many rebellions against English rule, the best-known being Father Philip Roche, who led the Irish in the Battle of Horetown in 1798. The name is still strongly linked with County Wexford, where a townland of Rochestown exists today, but over the centuries many of the family migrated south, particularly to the area around the modern town of Fermoy in County Cork, where they prospered greatly. They also spread further afield and multiplied throughout the southern province of Munster; Roche is today one of the commonest surnames in that area.

Rogers

Rogers is one of the most common surnames in Britain and Ireland. Its English origin is simple: it means "son of Roger", a very common personal name made up of two Germanic elements: hrod, "renown" and geri "spear." It is also common in Scotland, where it is frequently spelt Rodgers. Many bearing the name in Ireland are of English and Scottish descent. However, the Gaelic Irish surname MacRuaidhrí, from the personal name Ruaidhri, meaning "red king," was also anglicized as Rogers. Two Mac Ruaidhrí families are notable in early times, one based in County Tyrone, a branch of whom migrated north to County Derry, the other in County Fermanagh, possibly an offshoot of the Maguires. In these areas the surname was also anglicized MacRory and MacCrory.

In addition, many individuals in the sixteenth and seventeenth centuries were identified by the fathers' names. A son of Ruaidhrí Ó Briain might, for example, be known as Mac Ruaidhrí Ó Briain. In a significant number of cases the Mac Ruaidhri became an hereditary surname in its own right, instead of Ó Briain, and was then anglicized "Rogers".

Rooney

Rooney is the anglicized version of Ó Ruanaidh, from Ruanadh, a personal name meaning "champion." The principal family of the name originated in County Down, where their territory was centered on the parish of Ballyroney, which includes their name. They have produced many poets, the most recent of whom is Pádraig Rooney, winner of the Kavanagh Prize for Poetry in 1986. Two other families, both from County Fermanagh, have also anglicized their surnames as Rooney, the Ó Maolruanaidh ("Mulrooney"), and the Mac Maolruanaidh ("Macarooney"), both prominent in the early history of the county.

Ryan

Ryan is today one of the commonest surnames in Ireland. Unlike many other common surnames, however, it has one major origin, in the family of Ó Maoilriaghain, meaning "descendant of a devotee of St Riaghan." The anglicization "Mulryan" began to fade as early as the seventeenth century, and is today virtually unknown apart from a few pockets in counties Galway and Leitrim, possibly derived from a different family. The surname first appears in the fourteenth century in the barony of Owney, on the borders of counties Limerick and Tipperary, where the Ó Maoilriaghain displaced the O'Heffernans. Even today the surname is highly concentrated in this area. In Carlow and adjoining areas Ryan may also derive from Ó Riaghain, sometimes confused with Regan. Patrick J. Ryan (1883-1964) emigrated to the U.S., won a gold medal for hammer-throwing for that country in the 1920 Olympics, and then returned to farming in Pallasgreen in Limerick.

Scott

Scott is a very common surname in Ireland, and is particularly numerous in Ulster. It derives ultimately from the Latin Scottus which, confusingly, means "Irishman." After the Irish colonization of that country in the sixth century, "Scotland" eventually became the English name for the territory controlled by the Gaelic-speaking descendants of the settlers, more or less the Highlands. In the course of time, by extension, the name was applied to all of what we now know as Scotland. "Scott" as a descriptive name was initially used for the Highlanders but, like the name of the country, in the end came to refer to all Scots. A Lowland Scottish family, based along the Borders, are in fact the forbears of many Ulster bearers of the name. They were one of the notorious "riding clans," many of whose members settled in Fermanagh in the seventeenth century after their power was broken by James II.

Sheehan

Sheehan is the anglicization of the Irish Ó Stodhacháin, from a diminutive of sìodhach, meaning "peaceful." The principal family of the name were part of the Dál gCais, the tribal grouping occupying an area now in counties Limerick and Clare which produced Brian Boru, High King of Ireland in the eleventh century. Some of the traditional genealogies have the descent of the Sheehans from one Sidhechan, a contemporary of Brian Boru and distantly related to him. Initially they appear to have lived in the south of County Limerick, in the barony of Connello. In very early times, however, they migrated south, into the northeast of the present County Cork, where they are still most numerous. Over the course of the centuries, large numbers have also migrated into County Kerry, while a significant number also remained in their homeland of Limerick. In these areas, the surname is very common indeed.

Sheridan

Sheridan is the English version of Ó Sirideáin, from the personal name Sirideán, which is possibly related to sirigh, "to seek." The surname arose in the modern County Longford, where the Ó Sirideáin held hereditary church offices and land in the parish of Granard. They later moved to the adjoining county of Cavan, where they became followers of the rulers of Breifne, the O'Reillys. Cavan is still the area in which the surname is most common, though it has now spread throughout the northern half of the country. The most famous bearer of the name was the playwright Richard Brinsley Sheridan (1751-1817), born in Dublin, whose three masterpieces, The Rivals, The School for Scandal and The Critic display brilliant comic invention.

Smith

Smith is a surname famous for being ordinary, it is the most common name in England, Scotland, Wales and Ulster, while it is the fifth most common in Ireland as a whole. Antrim and Cavan are the areas in which it is most numerous. Its English origin, designating an armorer, smith or farmer, and many bearing the name, in Ulster especially, will be of English stock. The Scottish originals anglicized as Smith are Mac Gobha and Mac Gobhann, both meaning "son of the smith." These were also anglicized phonetically as (Mac)Gow and (Mac)Gowan. At least two major families of the name are recorded, branches of the Clan Donald and the Clan MacPherson. The principal Irish name is Mac Gabhainn, also "son of the smith", and is strongly rooted in County Cavan, where the Mac Gabhainn were one of the most powerful families. The vast majority of the family in Cavan anglicized their name to Smith. Among less prominent families adopting Smith were the Ó Gabhainn ("O'Gowan") of Drummully in Fermanagh and of County Down, and the Mac an Gabhan of Ballymagowan in County Tyrone.

Stewart

Although coming among the top sixty in the list of the most common names in Ireland as a whole, Stewart or Stuart is to be found almost exclusively in Ulster, where it is of Scottish origin. The surname is occupational, referring to an administrative official (modern English "steward"), and this word derives from a compound of the two Old English terms stig, "house", and weard, "guardian." The surname arose in various locations in Scotland, no doubt due to the fact that every local lord and bishop would have his own steward. Its popularity as a surname was also influenced by the royal family, the Stuarts, who ruled Scotland from 1371 to 1603, and Scotland and England from then until 1688. They were hereditary High Stewards of Scotland for six generations before they acquired the throne, and this is the source of their surname. The spelling "Stuart" is the French version of the name, popularized in the sixteenth century by Mary, Queen of Scots, who was educated in France.

Sweeney

Sweeney, along with its variants MacSweeny and MacSwiney, comes from the Irish Mac Suibhne, from suibhne, meaning "pleasant." The original Suibhne from whom the surname derives was a Scottish chief based in Argyle around the year 1200. His people were of mixed Viking and Irish descent, and their fame as fighters meant that they were much in demand in Ireland as gallowglasses, or mercenaries. Suibhne's great-great-grandson Muchadh Maer Mac Suibhne settled in the Fanad district of the modern County Donegal in the fourteenth century, and his offspring soon split into distinct groups, the principal ones being Mac Suibhne Fanad and Mac Suibhne na dTuath. For over three centuries, up to the final defeat of the seventeenth century, they fought as gallowglasses in the struggles of Ulster, mainly on behalf of the O'Donnells. Members of both groups also made their way south to Cork in the late fifteenth century and served the MacCarthys, acquiring territory of their own in Muskerry. The Cork family prospered and multiplied, and today the surname is more numerous in the Cork/Kerry area than in its original Irish homeland of Ulster.

Tobin

Tobin is in Irish Tóibín, which is a Gaelicized version of the Norman "St Aubin", after the place of the same name in Brittany, so called from the dedication of its church to St Albin. The family came to Ireland in the immediate aftermath of the Norman invasion, and by the early thirteenth century were well established in counties Kilkenny and Tipperary; their power in the latter county is attested by the (unofficial) title "baron of Coursey", by which the head of the family was known in the Middle Ages. In the course of time the surname also spread into the adjoining counties of Cork and Waterford, and this is the area in which it remains most common by far today. The two best-known contemporary bearers of the name in Ireland are the comic actor Niall Tóibín and the novelist and poet Colm Tóibín.

Wallace

Wallace comes from the Anglo-Norman French le waleis, meaning simply "the foreigner" or "the stranger", which was used in different parts of Britain to denote Scots, Welsh or Breton origin, strangeness obviously being in the eye of the beholder. In medieval Ireland the name was generally used to mean "the Welshman", and arrived in the wake of the Norman invasion; the first Norman invaders came from Wales. The surname became, and remains, numerous in the major urban centers of population: Dublin, Cork, Limerick and Galway. It is most numerous, however, in Ulster, where bearers will generally be of Scottish descent. In Scotland the name was more usually applied to descendants of the small pocket of Strathclyde Britons who survived into the Middle Ages. This was the origin of Scotland's national hero, Sir William Wallace. The best-known Irish bearer of the name was the composer William Vincent Wallace (1812-1865), who became world famous after the success of his operas Maritana, and Lurline.

Walsh

Walsh is among the five most numerous surnames in Ireland, found across the country, with particular concentrations in Connacht in counties Mayo and Galway, in Munster in counties Cork and Waterford, and in Leinster in counties Kilkenny and Wexford. It is a semi-translation of the Irish surname Breathnach, meaning "British" or "Welsh," also sometimes anglicized as "Brannagh." The surname thus has the same origin as Wallace, but arrived at its present form by a more circuitous route. Unlike most Hiberno-Norman families, such as the Burkes and the Fitzgeralds, who can trace their ancestry to a small number of known individuals, the Walshes have many different origins, since the name arose independently in many different places, for obvious reasons. Two exceptions should perhaps be mentioned: the descendants of Haylen Brenach, one of those who arrived in 1172, became very well known and prosperous in the south and east of the country, while "Walynus," who arrived in 1169, is said to have been the progenitor of the Walshes of Tirawley in County Mayo, and the brother of Barrett, the ancestor of the Barretts of the same county.

Ward

Ward is common and widespread throughout Ireland, England and Wales. In Britain it is generally an occupational surname, derived from the Old English weard, meaning "guard." Some in Ireland may be of English stock, as, for example, in the case of the family who now hold the title of Viscounts Bangor in County Down. In the vast majority of cases, however, Ward in Ireland is the anglicization of Mac an Bháird meaning 'son of the poet (bard)'; the equivalent Scottish surname almost always became "Baird." Two families are historically prominent, one based near the modern town of Ballinasloe in County Galway, and the other near Glenties in County Donegal. Both families were professional hereditary poets, as their surname implies, to the O'Kellys and the O'Donnells respectively. A branch of the northern family also became poets to the O'Neills in County Tyrone. Today the largest single concentrations of the surname are to be found in the original homelands, counties Galway and Donegal.

Whelan

Whelan, along with its common variant Phelan, comes from the Irish Ó Faoláin, from a diminutive of faol, "wolf. Taken together, the two names come among the fifty most numerous in Ireland. The family originated in the ancient kingdom of Decies, part of the modern county of Waterford, where they were rulers up to the Norman invasion. From this center the surname has now spread to the adjoining counties of Kilkenny, Cork, Wexford and, further north, Carlow. It is also to be found throughout the country, however. The best known modern bearer of the name was Seán Ó Faoláin, the novelist and short story writer, whose writing career spanned six decades. His family name was originally Whelan. His daughter Julia is also a distinguished novelist.

White

White is of the most common surnames in England, Wales, Scotland and Ireland. In England its most common origin is as a descriptive nickname for someone who was fair-haired or pale, and a sizable proportion of those bearing the name in Ireland will be of English extraction; such families were prominent in Clare, Waterford and Kilkenny. In some cases, as families were absorbed by Gaelic culture, White was phonetically hibernicized Mac Faoite. After the final collapse of the Gaelic order in the seventeenth century this was re-anglicized as MacWhitty and MacQuitty, as well as the original White. In the north of Ireland, many Whites are of Scottish extraction. The surname was a semi-translation of the Highland Gaelic Mac Gille Bháin, "son of the fair-haired servant or youth", and was also adopted by many of the MacGregors and Lamonts when they were outlawed and their own names proscribed. Elsewhere in Ireland White was sometimes used locally for many Irish originals containing, or thought to contain the elements bán ("white") or fionn ("fair").

Woods

In appearance at least, Woods, together with Wood, is of course an English name, denoting a person who lived near a wood or, in some cases, a woodcutter. In Ireland, however, the majority of those bearing the surname are of native Irish extraction. The Irish for a wood is coill, plural coillte , and many Irish names containing elements which sounded similar in untutored English ears were mistranslated as "Woods." Among such names are: Mac Giolla Comhghaill ("MacIlhoyle"/"Coyle"), "son of the follower of St Comall", found in Donegal and Monaghan; Mac an Choiligh ("MacQuilly"/"Magilly"), "son of the cock", from County Roscommon; Mac Giolla Chomghain ("MacElhone"), "son of the follower of St Comgan" in County Tyrone, and Mac Caoilte ("Quilty") in Munster. The only family whose surname actually did contain coill were the Mac Conchoille, "son of the hound of the woods," who were also anglicized phonetically as MacEnhill. They were based near Omagh in County Tyrone. The form Woods is more than ten times commoner in Ireland than in England and Wales.

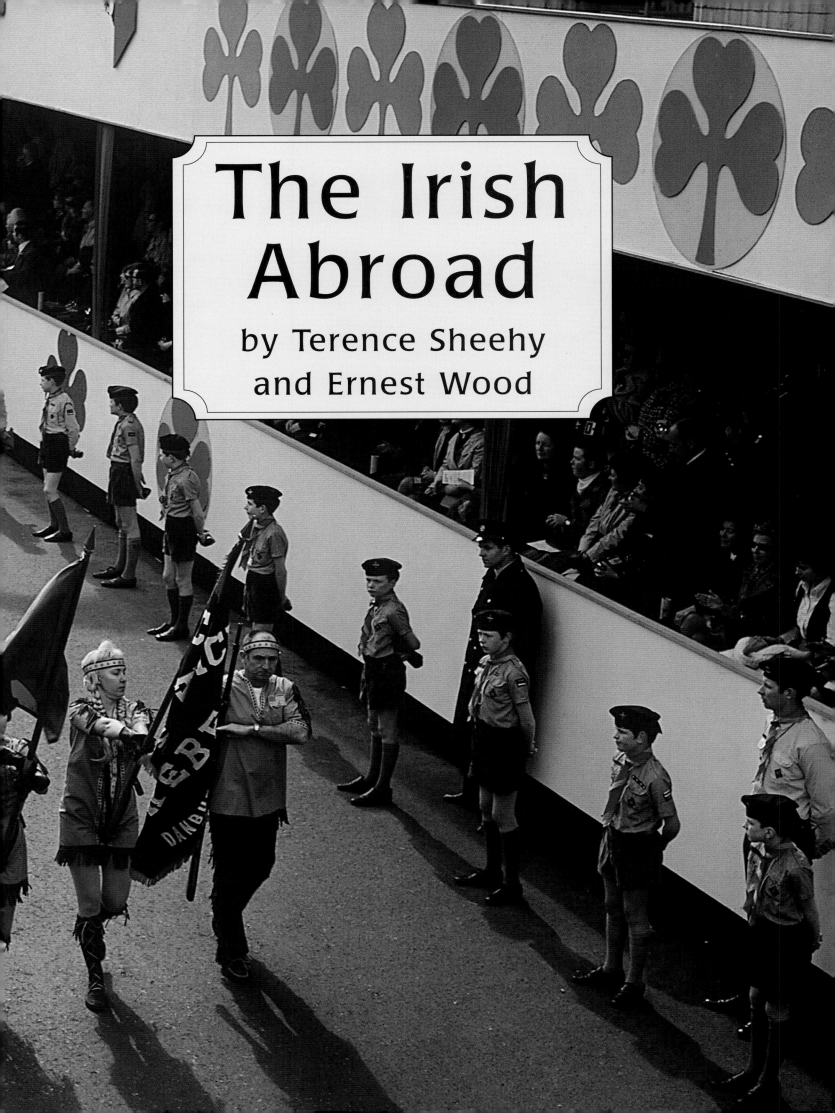

The Irish Abroad

by Terence Sheehy
and Ernest Wood

The Irish Abroad

The great paradox of Irish history is that because of it there are many more millions of Irishmen and Irishwomen – Irish born, and of Irish descent – living in Canada, in Australia, in New Zealand, in South America, and in Great Britain, as well as in the United States of America, than there are living in the Emerald Isle today.

Of the success of his fellow countrymen abroad, even Jonathan Swift, author of *Gulliver's Travels* and that most cynical of political observers, was moved to write: "I cannot too highly esteem those gentlemen of Ireland, who, with all the disadvantages of being exiles and strangers, have been able to distinguish themselves in so many parts of Europe, by their valor and conduct, above all other nations."

The Irish in the United States of America

The Irish Catholic millions who fled the potato famine of the mid-nineteenth century certainly changed the story of immigrant America. They were the first group to come in a large, sudden wave that was very different in social makeup from the establishment already here. They were not, however, the first Irish to come to America.

In the early years, the Irish in America were but a scattered few. As early as 1586, Edward Nugent served in North Carolina with Captain Ralph Lane. The first immigrant group – 140 Northern Irish Presbyterians – set sail from Ulster to New England on the Eagle Wing in 1636 – more than 200 years before the famine Irish came over. More than halfway across the

Previous pages: St. Patrick's Day celebrations in Ireland include a commemoration of the vast community overseas. Opposite: A monument to John F. Kennedy. Following pages: The British surrender at Yorktown in 1781. Irish soldiers filled the ranks on both sides during the American Revolution.

Atlantic, the ship met a fierce storm. Convinced the tempest was a sign that their trip was against God's will, the emigrants returned home.

The Irish, however, had looked to the west, and to the future.

It was not long before Irishmen joined the colonization of the New World. An attempt in the 1650s to found a colony in Maryland called "New Ireland" failed, but by the end of the century the Irish were established in Pennsylvania, Maryland, Delaware and New York. Some Irish did very well for themselves. Thomas Lewis of Belfast, who landed in America in 1656 and became a merchant in Albany, N.Y., was one of the wealthiest men in the colony when he died in 1684. The Colonial Governor of New York at the time was Thomas Dongan, an Irish Catholic from County Kildare.

The early colonies were not always so welcoming, however. When Thomas Dongan tried to settle Irish folk on his lands in Massachusetts in about 1710, the local government refused him permission. New England Puritans did not only dislike Catholic Dongan, however, they disliked the Presbyterian Irish too – along with everyone else who did not follow their Puritan creed. In 1692 the people of Salem executed an Irishwoman named Granny Glover as a witch because they thought her native Gaelic was the language of the Devil.

But America was a big country, and there was plenty of room for the Irish. Thousands of miles away another colonial governor played an entirely different role in the Irish colonization of America. Hugh O'Connor, born in Dublin in 1734, fled to Spain to escape troubles with the English and wound up – with his name translated into Spanish as Hugo Oconór – first as a Spanish soldier in New Spain and, from 1767 to 1770, as Governor of Texas.

The rate of emigration to America was at first just a trickle. From North Carolina to upstate New York

there had been a few organized Irish settlements before the American Revolution. But most were relatively small. William Johnson, an Indian agent born in Ireland, settled sixty Irish families in Warrenbush, N.Y., in 1740, for example. But the first U.S. Census in 1790 counted only 44,000 people who had been born in Ireland and 150,000 more of Irish ancestry in a total American population of three million. Catholics constituted only a small fraction of the Irish immigrants – the Church estimated it had about 35,000 faithful in the United States.

No one can say the Irish were not a visible and vital part of the Colonies and the young Republic, however. St. Patrick's Day was celebrated in Boston as early as 1737, and General George Washington recognized it as an official holiday for his Colonial troops. An Irishman named Patrick Carr was one of the five persons killed in the Boston Massacre. Three Irishmen pulled down the statue of King George III in New York's Bowling Green and had it melted down for bullets. And Daniel Junior, born in Maryland of Irish ancestry, is credited with coining the phrase: "No Taxation Without Representation." The Irish even accounted for eight signatories of the Declaration of Independence – four of them born in Ireland. However, Irishman Charles Carroll III of Maryland was the only Catholic to sign. On July 8, 1776, John Nixon, whose parents had emigrated from County Wexford in the 1680s, was the first to read the document aloud in public. Later Irishman Thomas Fitzsimons was the only Catholic to sign the U.S. Constitution.

During the revolution some thirty-eight percent of the American forces were Irish. The British Army was heavily Irish as well. But as much as each side relied on their own, they hated the other's Irish. Wrote a British officer of the Americans:

"The rebels are chiefly composed of Irish redemptioners and convicts, the most audacious rascals existing." And an American said: "The British regiments [are] composed of the most debauched weavers prentices, the scum of the Irish Roman Catholics who desert upon every occasion."

No matter what America thought of them, however, the Irish were enthusiastic about America – and willing to do most anything to get here. Many who could not afford the passage came to be sold upon arrival as indentured servants along with the merchandise that the ship brought. In 1734, the Charleston Gazette advertised "Irish servants, men and women, of good trades, from the north of Ireland, Irish linen, household furniture, butter, cheese, chinaware and all sorts of dry goods." By the 1770s there were not enough ships to carry all the people who wished to leave Ireland.

Depending on the weather, the trip from Ireland to America on a sailing ship usually took between four and eight weeks, with an extra two weeks for Southern ports such as Charleston or Savannah. Later, steamships made the voyage quicker – about two weeks – and easier. Prophetically, the first steamer to cross the Atlantic from east to west, in 1837, was Irish – the Sirius out of Cork. Steam travel did not take over immediately, however. As late as 1856, only five percent of immigrants were traveling by steamer. The same slow, crowded conditions that the Irish had endured in sailing ships for more than a hundred years prevailed. But when steam travel developed in earnest, the switch from sail was quick. By 1863, forty-five percent of emigrants were traveling by steamships. In 1866, the number had grown to eighty-one percent, and by 1870 hardly any traveled by sail any more.

Emigration from Ireland to America topped 20,000 for the first time in 1830. A year before the potato blight began in 1845, 75,000 Irish emigrated, two thirds of whom went to the United States. However, by 1847, when the effects of the blight had become undeniable, these numbers had doubled. The following year, most Irish emigrants turned en masse towards America. The numbers continued rising steadily until 1851, when 219,000 Irish left for the United States. In all, the famine years accounted for as many as 1.5 million deaths and sent more than a million Irish to America.

The Irish who fled the famine and those who followed were different from the Irish who migrated to America during the seventeenth, eighteenth and early nineteenth centuries. While the "Famine Irish," as they came to be known, were both Protestant and Catholic, by far the greater number were Catholic. And while the earlier immigrants and those who came during the famine years often traveled as families those who followed more often than not were sin-

ABOVE: *President Andrew Jackson was Scots-Irish.*
LEFT: *Twelve Irishmen were among the defenders of the Alamo in 1836.*
BELOW: *America's railroads were built by Irish workers.*

gle people. They were young – overwhelmingly between fifteen and thirty-five years old. They came in about equal numbers of women and men. And they came to stay. Only about ten percent of the Irish returned home, compared to eighty percent of some immigrant groups.

In the earliest years, more Irish settled in Pennsylvania than in any other colony, followed by New York and Maryland. From there, they moved west and traveled down the Shenandoah Valley into Virginia and North Carolina. In South Carolina and Georgia the Irish landed at Charleston or Savannah and spread west from there. Augusta, Georgia, was settled by Irishman William O'Bryan in 1735. Old maps of Georgia show places named Limerick, Clare, Killarney, Tyrone, Blarney, Cork, Belfast, Newry and Donegal. From western Carolina, Virginia and Pennsylvania the Irish pushed west into Tennessee

FRANK LESLIE'S ILLUSTRATED NEWSPAPER.

[July 30, 1870.]

313

NEW YORK CITY.—SCENE OF THE RIOT AT ELM PARK, EIGHTH AVENUE AND NINETIETH STREET, BETWEEN PROTESTANT

and Kentucky. There, as in the eastern colonies, the Irish were frontier farmers, settling the virgin territory of the new world.

There always had been organized Irish settlements and individuals who brought groups of Irish to America. In the mid-1700s, Boice Cooper settled first in Portsmouth, then in Pemaquid, Maine. He returned to Ireland, where he gathered a group of settlers and brought them back to Maine. In the 1820s and 1830s,

impresarios who received grants of land from the Mexican government settled colonies of Irish Catholics in south Texas. One town settled this way was named San Patricio de Hibernia (St.. Patrick of Ireland). By 1850, San Patricio and neighboring Refugio counties were more than half Irish – while people of Mexican descent numbered only one sixth of the population.

Settlement patterns changed when the "Famine Irish" arrived in the mid-nineteenth century. Instead of moving to farms, most settled in cities or followed work on canals and railroads through rural areas until they reached the cities at the other end. When they did live on the frontier, most Irish settled in frontier towns such as Butte, Montana, where there was a thriving copper-mining industry. The gold

LEFT: *Rioting between Catholic Irish and Protestants was widespread in nineteenth-century America.*
ABOVE: *Civil War General Phil Sheridan was the child of Irish immigrant parents who settled in Ohio.*

fields of California also attracted a healthy share of Irish.

However, Irish settlements were spread thinly outside the cities. Between 1899 and 1910, the decade in which Oklahoma gained statehood, for example, only 122 of the 440,000 Irish – one in 3,600 – who entered the United States declared the new state to be his destination. Which is not to say that the ones who did go there had lost their Irishness. Shamrock, Oklahoma, an oil boom town developed between 1912 and 1915 by Edwin L. Dunn, a Tulsa Realtor of Irish ancestry, had a main street named Tipperary Road and others named Dublin, Ireland, Cork and Killarney. Its newspapers were named the Blarney and the Brogue, and many of its buildings were painted green.

It is ironic that the Irish, who had been a rural people in their own country and who in earlier generations had been farmers in America, should now become city dwellers. Perhaps they avoided frontier life because their culture was essentially a sociable one. In 1821 a homesick farmer in Missouri compared rural life in Ireland to America: "I could then go to a fair, or a wake, or a dance .... I could spend the winter's nights at a neighbor's house cracking jokes by the turf fire ... but here everyone can get so much land ... that they calls them neighbors that live two or three miles off."

San Francisco probably exemplifies better than any other city how willing the Irish were to relocate in order to find jobs. In 1852, only 5.1 percent had come directly from Ireland, while 44.6 percent had come from New York, Philadelphia, Boston, New Orleans and other cities in the Eastern United States. James Phelan was one. When but a boy he had emigrated to New York, where he worked as a grocery clerk. Then, with the first word of gold in California, he left for San Francisco, where he ran a saloon, invested in real estate and founded a bank. By 1870 he had become one of the city's ten richest men. The American Irish, however, were prepared to relocate from farther afield than New York. In 1852, for example, some 44.5 percent of San Francisco's Irish had first settled in Australia, Hawaii or other Pacific Rim lands. They uprooted themselves once more to seek their fortunes in the California gold fields.

Coming from their small farms to American cities, the Irish who arrived after the famine mostly took unskilled jobs. The women became domestic servants or worked in mills. The men performed the most difficult, backbreaking and dangerous tasks, such as mining, digging canals or laying railroads. In the pre-Civil War South, they often were given jobs that were too dangerous for valuable slaves. Irish from Boston, for example, to replaced slaves digging the Brunswick Canal in Georgia, where one writer noted, "... if the Paddies are knocked overboard or get their backs

OPPOSITE: *Many Irish served in the U.S. army, including with Custer at the battle of the Little Big Horn in 1876.* ABOVE *New York is perhaps the capital of overseas Ireland.* RIGHT: *St Patrick's Cathedral, New York.*

broke, nobody loses anything." Crews laying railroad tracks in the mountains around Port Jervis, New York, lowered Irish drillers in wicker baskets from ledges down to the blasting areas. There, the man would drill his hole, plant the charge, light the fuse and – if all went well – be pulled to safety before the charge went off. Railroad building was so hazardous that there was said to be "an Irishman buried under every tie" of the American railroad system.

Irish women succeeded as domestics because they arrived single, already spoke English and were willing to work eighty-hour weeks and put up with little privacy and constant demands on their time. With room and board and sometimes uniforms provided, the typical Irish maid could send home her share of cash to finance the emigration of others. If they did not take work as domestics, most immigrant Irish women found work in mills. In 1870, 57.7 percent of the women working in the textile mills in Lowell, Massachusetts, had been born in Ireland.

Some of their success in finding and keeping such employment was due to the efforts of labor unions. But even when they were not organized, the Irish had a tradition of helping each other find and keep work. When organized, the Irish became able leaders in many trades, ranging in diversity from millinery and carpet weaving to team driving. They also appeared as members of organizations as diverse as Knights of Labor, the American Federation of Labor and the Actors Equity Association. Though not actually a labor union, the famous Molly Maguires were a secret society of Irish Pennsylvanian miners who used violence to strike back at unscrupulous and oppressive mine owners. They operated from the 1850s until their capture in the 1870s. Twenty of the Mollies, including leader John Kehoe, were hanged in what is believed to be the largest civilian, non-slave execution up to that time.

Of all the professions associated with the Irish, however, the police take the top position. New York had a police marshal named John McManus in 1815. But it was not until the 1840s that most cities established large, modern police forces. The timing could not have been better for the famine Irish, who joined in large numbers, seeking the security of a public-service job and the excitement that police work

385

involved. By the time of the Civil War, New York's police force was twenty-eight percent Irish, despite accounting for only sixteen percent of the city's population. Elsewhere, the Irish filled police forces from Boston to New Orleans to San Francisco. They also had a tradition of serving in volunteer fire departments – whose colorful history included racing other units to fires and brawling with rival fire companies for the privilege of putting out the blaze. Though tamed by city regulations, the Irish continued to serve as firefighters when fire departments, too, became public after the Civil War.

It is more than a little ironic that the Irish cared so much for public service in America – because the American public cared so little for the Irish. The animosity was long standing. In 1692 a government official in Maryland wrote that his region was "pestered" by Scotch and Irish immigrants, and in 1729 a Pennsylvanian Quaker named James Logan, himself having immigrated from Ireland thirty years earlier, expressed the fear that "if they continue to come, they will make themselves proprietors of the province." When large numbers of Irish really did arrive after the famine, an eminent Bostonian showed little interest in welcoming them. "Our Celtic fellow citizens," he wrote, "are almost as remote from us in temperament and constitution as the Chinese." In the popular stereotype, Irish women, especially those employed as domestics, were foolish and careless, and Irish men were drunken, dirty, violent and lazy. By the 1850s, many early Presbyterian Irish immigrants began calling themselves "Scotch-Irish" to set themselves apart from the new arrivals.

More serious was anti-Irish violence. In Massachusetts alone, houses were stoned (Boston, 1829), Yankee laborers rioted against Catholics employed on construction jobs (Lowell, 1831), and a convent was burned (Charlestown, 1834) - all this before the famine immigrants arrived. Philadelphia had to declare martial law to stop anti-Catholic and anti-Irish riots in 1844. By the 1850s, the Know-Nothing Party – the leading edge of the Nativist movement that advocated "America for Americans" - was marshaling both public opinion and physical vio-

RIGHT: Boston was the birthplace of Louis Sullivan, father of the skyscraper and the child of Irish immigrants.

lence against the Irish. Riots broke out in Philadelphia, Newark, Baltimore, Brooklyn, St.. Louis and several Massachusetts cities.

By the 1870s, a generation had passed since the Great Famine across the sea. And the Irish were moving up from the backbreaking laboring positions they had been forced to take on their arrival. They were established. They now could capture the great prize of the American democracy: political power.

Most notably, in the decade following the Civil War the Irish captured control of Tammany Hall, the New York City political machine. Founded in 1789, the Society of Tammany had, since the early 1800s, relied on and, indeed, manipulated the votes of immigrants to keep its machine in power. William Marcy Tweed - "Boss Tweed" as he later came to be known – the son

PUCK.

OFFICE OF "PUCK" 23 WARREN ST NEW YORK.

FIRED FROM THE FEAST.
THE HARPER OF DYNAMITE AND DISCORD NOT WANTED AT THE IRISH BANQUET.

of Irish immigrants, gained control of Tammany during the Civil War and, by 1870, had used its system of political spoils to enrich himself and build a huge base of power and patronage. In 1871 he was replaced by "Honest John" Kelly, another son of Irish immigrants, who, after his death in 1885, was succeeded by Richard Croker, who had emigrated from County Cork as a boy during the potato famine. Croker was succeeded by yet another Irish political boss, Charles Murphy, a former saloon keeper who ruled Tammany until his death in 1924.

The irony was that while the Irish generally practiced politics of passion when it came to Ireland, they practiced politics of pragmatism in their new American home, because, to the Irish, politics was a profession like any other. If their political activities provided public services, it was largely to keep voters happy and politicians in office. The result was "machine politics."

For an immigrant group that arrived in America destitute, the machine offered an invaluable transition to American life, providing the social services not available elsewhere. The neighborhood precinct captain brought coal in winter, beer in summer,

MAYER MERKEL & OTTMANN LITH. 23-25 WARREN ST. N.Y.

LEFT: A cartoon shows Irish nationalist leader O'Donovan Rossa expelled from an Irish immigrants' association dinner in New York.

food when the cupboard was bare and legal aid to those in trouble. The same captain, or party operatives further up the political ladder might even be able to provide the most valuable service: a government-patronage job. In Chicago, for example, forty-three percent of the policemen, firemen and watchmen in the city were first- or second-generation Irish by 1900 – though only fourteen percent of the male workforce was Irish.

Such a system was naturally ripe for abuse. In Chicago, politicians became famous for "boodling" - the practice of selling city franchises to businesses. Vote fraud and coercion by street gangs were rampant. The system lent itself to the rise of flamboyant characters able to woo ethnic voters. New York's mayor Oakley Hall, a prime example of this, decked himself out for Saint Patrick's day 1870 with a shamrock in his lapel, green tie, green kid gloves and green coat. Moreover, the system cultivated strong ethnic power bases. For example, in 1879 twenty-seven percent of San Francisco's 38,000 voters had been born in Ireland, and the Irish ran city politics there from the time of the Civil War to the early twentieth century. As for the East Coast, during the late 1880s the Irish controlled sixty-eight cities and towns in Massachusetts.

Then there were the bosses. Philadelphia's Irish boss, William McMullen, was a man whose background was solidly working class. He got his start in politics with the rowdy firefighters of the Moyamensing Hose Company, and he ran a saloon for a living. He held political office of one sort or another from 1856 until 1901. By contrast, the Fitzgeralds and the Kennedys of Boston, beginning with Mayor John F. "Honey Fitz" Fitzgerald and culminating with his grandson, President John Fitzgerald Kennedy, became as near in public perception to a royal family as America has known.

Some of the bosses, such as Daniel Peter O'Connell – boss of Albany, New York, from 1921 until his death in 1977 – ran their dynasties from behind the scenes. A few, like Boston's flamboyant James Curley, whose political career ran from 1899 until 1949 and included four terms as mayor and four in Congress, were independent of the machine. But others made no apologies. "Of course workers get the jobs," said Jersey City boss Frank Hague about the patronage

CLOCKWISE, FROM TOP: Joseph McCarthy, the anti-communist Senator from Wisconsin; President John F. Kennedy with members of his cabinet; and Ronald Reagan: Three Irish-Americans who had a profound effect on the politics of the postwar United States.

system, "What would you think of an executive who hired fellows that knocked the company or didn't take any interest in it?" Said Kansas City boss Tom Pendergast: "I'm not bragging when I say I run the show in Kansas City. I am boss. If I was a Republican they would call me 'leader'"

Whether first arriving in America or migrating to a new city within their new country, most Irish settled into ethnic neighborhoods. In Milwaukee in 1850, for example, forty-seven percent of the Irish lived in a single ward. Most were poor, and though they could sometimes approximate the rural housing they had known at home, most had to settle for a very different kind of urban existence. Mayor Daley's neighborhood, Bridgeport, was first called the Cabbage Patch because residents grew cabbages on vacant land. In New York, however, the density of Irish tenement neighborhoods nearly doubled when

the Famine Irish arrived. The Irish urban experience is generally thought to be the first American instance of a pattern of immigrant settlement – the ghetto – that other ethnic groups would follow.

More important than neighborhood, and as important as Irishness itself to the settlers, however, was the family. Nearly all of the remittances that early immigrants sent home went, in fact, to pay for family members – most often siblings – to come to America. The family, however, did more than pay for passages. They provided a valuable transition to the New World. Without someone to meet them, arriving immigrants could be in for a rude shock. In 1829 a band of Irish immigrants landed on the Texas coast with no one to meet them, and at the same time an icy "norther" blew through. The immigrants huddled around fires made from driftwood until Mexican ranchers gave them food and clothing and found

them temporary shelter in an abandoned mission. In cities, debarking immigrants often were met by "agents" who swindled them as they pretended to find them lodging or jobs. As a result, the Hibernian Society of New Orleans in the 1850s asked the city to place police on the docks to protect new arrivals, particularly the women. By 1897 a survey taken of Irish women arriving in Boston found that only seventy-six of the 22,945 who arrived that year were not met by family members or friends.

Because so many arrived single, poor and wanting to earn money to send home finding work was usually the first priority for Irish immigrants in America. And the nature of their work often kept apart the men, who labored in transient trades, and the women, who stayed put as domestics or millworkers. The result was fewer and later marriages than most other ethnic groups. In New York in the 1870s, for example, the marriage rate of the Irish was only one quarter the rate of the Germans.

After marriage, however, these same factors conspired to create a distinct Irish homelife. Like most immigrants, the Irish married within their own ethnic group whenever possible. But unlike many immigrant groups who welcomed newly arrived siblings, cousins and other relatives to live with them, the Irish usually lived as nuclear families. Even when together, men and women were relatively independent of each other, having lived on their own for so long before marriage. What's more, the mobile and hazardous nature of the men's work left large numbers of deserted or widowed Irish women. In Boston in the 1870s, twenty-two percent of Irish families had women as their heads.

Wherever there is difficulty, people also often look to religion for support. The Irish were no exception in their need for spiritual comfort, but the Catholic Church also provided many of the social services that were not forthcoming from government or secular charities: hospitals, orphanages, asylums and almshouses. Prime examples of church affiliated

helpers were the Society of St. Vincent de Paul, which provided food and shelter for the poor; the Sisters of the Good Shepherd, who worked to save women from prostitution; and the Sisters of Mercy, who provided shelter and employment assistance for young women. These are just a few of the Catholic agencies that assisted the new immigrants.

The Catholic Church, however, was probably more important for its role in creating an Irish-American ethnic identity. For while Irish people had been emigrating to America for two centuries, only in the mid-nineteenth century did the words "Irish" and "Catholic" became synonymous. There are two reasons for this. First, Catholicism was one of the objects of English repression in Ireland. Such repression is certain to bind any people together. Second, and consequently, the Irish were the first large Catholic group to emigrate to America. From numbering one percent of the population in the 1790 census, the number of Catholics grew to over seven percent in 1850 and to ten percent – constituting the nation's largest single faith – in 1860. Immigration following the potato famine caused a tremendous growth in the Catholic

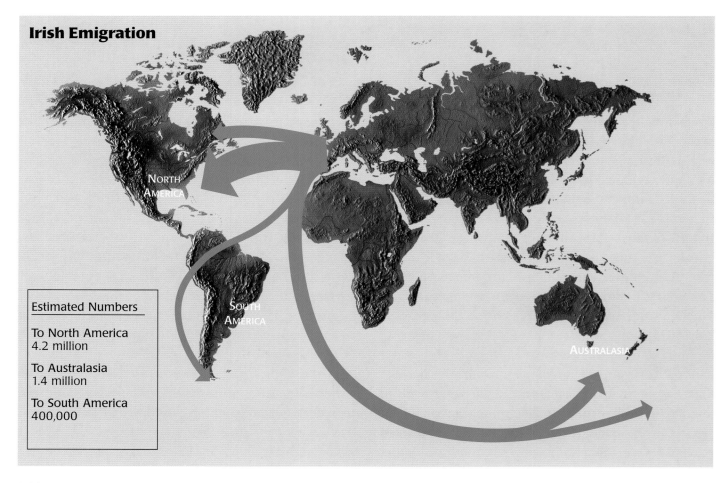

Irish Emigration

NORTH
AMERICA

SOUTH
AMERICA

AUSTRALASIA

Estimated Numbers

To North America
4.2 million

To Australasia
1.4 million

To South America
400,000

population – from less than one million in 1840 to about three million in 1860.

Until the second decade of the twentieth century, the Irish in America had suffered from their history. Poverty and political oppression at home had been a real handicap, and involvement in Irish nationalist causes had been a distraction from improving their lives in America. By the twentieth century, however, the Famine was ancient history. And with the creation of the Irish Free State, nationalism all but disappeared. At the same time, Irish-American accomplishments opened the way for the success and assimilation that formed part of the American Dream.

As early as World War I, Irish families were already sending more of their children to college than the average American family. Their chances of achieving a managerial or white collar position were accordingly greater than the American average, too. By the 1970s, according to national statistics, Irish Catholics had overtaken Irish Protestants and British Protestants as well in terms of total years spent in education, occupational prestige, and income. Only Jews were more successful as an ethnic group. Had not so many young men become priests and so many women become nuns, the Irish level of achievement in secular and material terms would have been even greater.

Historically, the Irish found success easier in the West, where everybody was a newcomer, than in the East, where they had to battle entrenched establishments.

Wherever they settled, however, the Irish were firm believers in the bootstrap theory: With enough hard work anyone could escape poverty. One theory claims that poverty and lack of business skills actually aided the Irish in their business success and cultural assimilation. Forced to work for American bosses for a generation or two, the Irish learned the American way of doing business, so that when they did open their own businesses they were not hampered by Old-World ways.

Today, some fourteen to sixteen million Americans, six to seven percent of the total population, are entirely or mostly of Irish extraction – and about three times that number have a smaller proportion of Irish blood. Most live where they always have: about seventy percent live in cities in the north and west – with sixty percent of those resident in the New-England and Middle-Atlantic States. Among Irish Protestants, nearly seventy percent live in the south. True to their roots, and in contrast to the northern Catholics, many live rural lives.

On March 17, however, Americans of all types all over the country wear green in celebration of St. Patrick's Day. In Chicago, the stripes down the middle of Dearborn Street are painted green for the St. Patrick's Day Parade – and the Chicago River is dyed green. There are green derby hats and green balloons and green windbreakers everywhere you look. Labor unions and Democratic organizations and a pipe band from the Chicago Police Department participate in the parade. There are also marching bands from public and parochial schools, playing songs like "When Irish Eyes are Smiling." Many of the musicians have shamrocks painted on their cheeks. But many of the musicians are black. Or Hispanic. Or from any of dozens of ethnic groups that are not Irish, perhaps because St. Patrick's Day is the one ethnic holiday that has been wholeheartedly embraced by the American public. In New York, Italian Governor Mario Cuomo, black Mayor David Dinkins, and Jewish former mayor Edward Koch marched down Fifth Avenue with the St. Patrick's Day parade. Said Koch: "Only in New York do you have a St. Patrick's Day Parade with a governor, Mario Cuomo, marching with the invalids in wheelchairs, the Mayor marching with gays and lesbians, and me, a Jewish boy ... marching with the police department's Holy Name Society."

The Irish and Canada

It is not generally known that Irish fishermen were putting down their nets off Newfoundland as early as 1595! Many Irish fishermen settled in Newfoundland in the 1700s, and one third of the population of Nova Scotia is of Irish descent. The Irish fishermen came mainly from Waterford, Tipperary, and Wexford. The failure of the 1798 Rising, and the subsequent excesses of the Yeomanry in Ireland, sent thousands to Canada, and the famine of 1822 brought more settlers in ever increasing numbers. Today there are millions of Canadians who can reckon to be of Irish descent.

To escape the famines in Ireland great numbers

came in 1846. They landed in Quebec – in Montreal – over 32,000 of them, and the following year over 70,000 came. The tragedy was that the majority of them, already suffering from the effects of starvation, came from the crowded hulks of the "coffin" ships, bearing with them the last stages of cholera, and burial in mass graves on the shore became the fate of many. Some 10,000 Irish bodies have made a corner of a Canadian field far greener than any green field abandoned in Ireland.

Canada was often a "back door" for those Irish emigrants who survived, to move on to the United States. Because so many of these poor people were very sick, Grosse Isle, on the St. Lawrence river at the entrance to the city of Quebec, became the quarantine island in 1834. Many a valiant priest and doctor fell mortally ill after tending to the needs of the dying

ABOVE: Montreal has one of the most spectacular St.Patrick's Day parades in the world.
LEFT: Point Pelee, Ontario, still has the pretty yet daunting landscape that greeted Irish settlers to the province.
OPPOSITE: The first Irish settled in Newfoundland in the 1700s.

famine victims.

It is a deeply moving experience to stand before a large, simple, unhewn stone, erected in 1859 by Irish railroad navvies constructing the railway bridge in Montreal, where they discovered the bones of their fellow countrymen, women and children, who were buried in mass graves on the site of the old emigration sheds at Point St. Charles. The inscription on the rough boulder reads:

"To
Preserve from Desecration
The remains of 600 emigrants
who died of ship's fever
AD 1847-8
This stone
is erected by the workmen
of
Messrs Peto, Brassey and Betts
Employed in the construction
of the
Victoria Bridge
AD 1859"

And yet many Irish Canadians survived, and every year, on March 17th, the Irish Society of Montreal has one of the most spectacular St. Patrick's Day parades in the world, with the reviewing stand packed with civic dignitaries, including the Irish Ambassador, and with Royal Canadian Air Force jets flying over the parade in salute.

Those who survived made good in many places. From 1823 to 1825 emigrants, mostly from Munster, made their homes in Upper Canada in settlements such as Peterborough, Lanark, Renfrew, Carleton and Northumberland. In 1826 some 20,000 settled in the Lake Erie district alone. The Orangemen from Ulster headed mainly for Toronto.

The Irish and Australia

It is worth remembering that the voyages of Captain James Cook to the South Seas were contemporary with the American Revolution, and the loss of the American Colonies deprived the British government of a dumping ground for convicts. In 1783 the transportation of convicts was switched from America to

New South Wales. The first convict expedition, 750 in number, set sail for Australia in 1787. In 1791, Irish prisoners started to arrive, thus forging the first Irish-Australian links. Ireland was then a nation in desperate political turmoil, and the first prison ships contained many simple country folk, driven in desperation to political "crimes." For many it became, under a fearfully oppressive military goading, a choice of transportation for life, or hanging by the neck, or even suicide. The convict ships themselves were not much better than the slave ships traveling the Middle Passage between Africa and the Americas during the same period. Frequently the convicts were kept in irons throughout a horrendous six-month voyage during which they suffered hunger, thirst, the lash and harassment from their captains and crews.

Not all the Irish convicts were poor folk or agricultural laborers, for, after the rebellion of 1798, Presbyterian ministers and professional men, such as doctors, were among the more educated revolutionaries to be transported. Many of the early political prisoners were Presbyterian ministers from County Derry, County Down and County Antrim. Very soon, Irish convicts formed a large percentage of the prisoner population in Australia, and the authorities were greatly concerned at their numbers, their escape attempts, their standard of intelligence, and the fact that Catholic priests as well as Presbyterian ministers were among the arrivals.

The beautiful harbor of Cork was the normal point of departure for convict ships from Ireland to Australia, and the public records of correspondence between Dublin Castle and the Governor in Australia give details of regular ship loads of convicts, usually several hundred at a time, of both men and women as well as many teenagers. Many of those transported were Catholics who found, on arrival in their penal settlements, that the Church of Rome was not recognized, and they were obliged to attend the state religious services of the Protestant faith. Although there were priests among the early convicts, they were not allowed to perform their religious duties and it was not until 1803 that the first Catholic priest was permitted to celebrate mass on Sundays, in a peculiar

OPPOSITE: Fremantle was where the last Irish convicts transported to Australia arrived, in 1867.

official climate where "No Popery" was the order of the day. Appropriately enough, on the site of the house in Sydney where the first Catholic service was held, there now stands the Catholic Church of Saint Patrick.

The rebellions of 1798 and 1803 in Ireland, land of insurrection, were followed by the rising of the Young Ireland movement in 1848. The most remarkable leader of the rising was John Mitchel, born in 1815 in Dungiven, County Derry. The son of a Presbyterian minister, and a law graduate of the College of the Holy and Undivided Trinity, in Dublin, he became editor of "The Nation," the journal of the Young Ireland movement, and eventually founded his own newspaper, "The United Irishman." Because of his revolutionary writings, Mitchel was arrested in Dublin and, under a hastily arranged Treason Felony Act, he was sentenced to 14 years transportation to Van Diemen's Land.

He wrote an account of his days as a political prisoner in Australia in his now famous "Jail Journal", or "Five Years in British Prisons." He escaped to America in 1853, and his journal was first published as a series of newspaper articles in New York a year later.

Mitchel gives a fascinating description of his days in exile, where his fellow conspirators were segregated in police areas. The English and Scottish settlers were fair minded men who refused to regard him or his associates as felons. The convict class were taboo among the free settlers, but political prisoners were accepted into normal society, and rode horses, hunted kangaroo and farmed.

Mitchel was joined by his wife and family in Van Diemen's Land, and describes in "Jail Journal" the first election of representatives under the new Constitution – one-third Crown nominees and two-thirds elected by the people. This was the beginning of the end for corrupt governors and their gangs of highly-paid officials.

In his "Journal" on October 14th, 1850, Mitchel gives this description of a non-convict Irish settler family: "This morning we took a conveyance, a sort of spring cart, and drove 16 miles through the valley of the Macquairie river, the Sugar-loaf, where dwells a worthy Irish family, emigrants of thirty two years ago from the County of Cork. Their name is Connell. We had promised to visit them on our way back from

Avoca; and Mr Connell had kindly sent for our horses to Oatlands, and has them ready for our ride tomorrow up to the lakes. Mr Connell and his wife have had severe hardships in their early days of settlement – a wild forest to tame and convert into green fields – wilder black natives to watch and keep guard against and wildest convict bushrangers to fight, sometimes in their own house. Mrs Connell is a thorough Celtic Irish woman – has the Munster accent as fresh as if she had left Cork last year, and is, in short, as genuine an Irish Vanithee or 'Woman of the House' as you will find in Ireland at this day – perhaps more so – for Carthaginian 'civilization' has been closer and more deadly in its embrace among the valleys of Munster, than it could be among the wilds of the Sugar-loaf forests. Most of their laborious toil and struggle is over: their farm smiles with green corn fields, and their sheep whiten their pastures; their banks are well furnished with bees, and Mrs Connell's mead is seductive; the black Tasmanians have all disappeared before convict civilization; and even the bushrangers are not 'out' so often these late years. Still it is needful that every lonely house should be well supplied with arms."

In 1853, Mitchel made his escape from Van Dieman's land disguised as a priest, made his way to Sydney, then a beautiful seaport town of 80,000 inhabitants, and thence, via Tahiti, to San Francisco, and on to New York where he worked as a journalist, and then to the state of Tennessee where he farmed. He finally returned to Ireland in 1874, and was elected MP for Tipperary, but was not allowed to take his seat in the House of Commons because he was a convicted felon and an escaped convict. He died in Newry in 1875.

Not all the early Irish settlers in Australia were there for political reasons and one of the most famous exceptions was the explorer Robert O'Hara Burke. He was born in St. Cleran, in County Galway, in 1820, the son of a British Army officer. He was educated in Belgium, joined the Austrian army, and attained the rank of Captain. He later returned to Ireland and joined the Royal Irish Constabulary. Restless, like many an Irishman, he emigrated to Australia, and became an Inspector of Police in the state of Victoria. When the state decided to explore the continent he was chosen to lead one of the first

expeditions because of his military and commanding background.

Many intrepid explorers worked at opening up the interior of the great continent, and all suffered from the immense drought and tropical heat. The Robert O'Hara Burke expedition was no exception. Financed by the state and by popular appeal, the expedition purchased camels, horses, and supplies, and picked the men who were to attempt the crossing of the unknown continent from Victoria in the South to the Gulf of Carpentaria in the North – some fifteen degrees south of the equator. Leaving Melbourne, Burke and his team set out to be the first white men to cross the vast continent from south to north. The expedition left in August 1860, and a month later reached Menindee on the River Darling. Already the camel expert had left the party, in high dudgeon at the impetuous Irish leader of the expedition, who had rashly decided to push on into the unknown, uncharted outback. Not waiting for the main support of his expedition, Burke and two companions with their horses and camels and several months supplies, headed north for Eyre Creek in Queensland. Crossing the Tropic of Capricorn they reached the Cloncurry and the Flinders rivers, and they viewed the northern seas before starting on their return journey. Four months into the new year they missed the back-up party at Cooper's Creek. Again the impatient Burke decided to press on and complete the remainder of the return journey by a different route. By May their last camel was dead and they were near starvation in the wilderness. By the end of June the deputy leader of the expedition was dead; Burke died later of starvation, and only John King survived.

Although this remarkable journey was technically a failure, the citizens of Melbourne were deeply moved by the gallantry of the captain from Galway, and erected a monument to his heroic memory. The monument features statues of Burke and his companion, William Wills. His foray into the unknown inspired many to follow his exploratory zeal, and to open up the interior of Australia.

Fremantle in Western Australia, over 11,000 miles

OPPOSITE: The great Australian bowler, Bill "Tiger" O'Reilly, took 144 wickets in 27 Test matches between 1932 and 1946, a career interrupted by World War II.

from home, was to be the last port in Australia to receive Irish political prisoners in January 1868, 63 of them, after the ill fated Fenian Rising of 1867. The exciting stories of the adventures of the Irish convict political prisoners in Australia would make a dozen epic action-packed movies! The average Australian of today, with Irish roots, is generally aware that about half of the population has some link with Ireland.

The Irish and New Zealand

To the average Irishman today, New Zealand is best known as the nation which produces the legendary "All Blacks" Rugby Football Union team, and as a very distant country which has always had the friendliest and most understanding relationship with Ireland. The great difference between the New Zealand and the Australian connection with the Emerald Isle is that basically Australia, through a quirk of history, was populated originally by convicts sent from Britain. New Zealand, however, was never a convict settlement and thus was totally different. It was, indeed, a haven of refuge for escaped convicts from Australia, many of them Irish. Aptly named originally, the "Friendly Islands", and first discovered by the Dutch explorer, Tasman, it fell to Captain Cook, in 1770, to proclaim the region of which he had made a detailed coast-line survey, a British Dominion.

Most of the emigrants from Ireland to New Zealand were of Presbyterian stock from the province of Ulster. For example, from 1875 onwards, the emigration agent for the Northern port of Ireland sent some 4,000 Irish settlers to New Zealand. Many of these settled in Tauranga. Most of the early settlers set up their homes all around the coastline of the north and south islands. Among the very first settlers in the north island, in Wellington, were hundreds of Irish origin, and the first Catholic priest there as parish priest was a Father O'Reilly. Similarly, many hundreds of Irish who had come from Australia were among the first citizens of Auckland, in the north island in the 1840s. With the discovery of gold in the

LEFT: The bulk of the Irish who settled in New Zealand were from the Protestant community in Ulster, although Irish Catholics were among the founders of the cities of Auckland and Wellington.

1860s, Irish miners worked their claims, and then settled in Lake Wakatipu, Kingston and Queenstown.

From the time of the Famine of the 1840s until the time of Gladstone and Parnell in the 1870s, Irish immigrants were few and far between, the majority going to the United States of America, to Canada and to Britain. Under various settlement schemes, about 20,000 Irish immigrants, mainly from the north of Ireland, and mostly laborers, settled in places such as Katikati which was a highly organized and successful settlement of Orangemen.

The Irish and South America

Long before the first arrivistes came to join in the South American wars of freedom from centuries of Spanish oppression, there were famous leaders of Irish stock who had helped put the countries of their adoption on the map.

The most famous of these was Bernardo O'Higgins, a founding father of modern Chile. His father was Don Ambrosio, a Spanish government representative who became Viceroy of Peru. Don Ambrosio was born near Daingean in County Offaly, in 1720, from where he went to Cadiz, and then to Buenos Aires. This remarkable man began his merchant life with a stall in the market place, and eventually became a cavalry captain. He founded the city of San Ambrosio, initiated the highway from Santiago to Valparaiso, and also built the city of Osorno. The Spaniards rewarded him for his services by creating him the Marquis of Osorno and, in 1795, Viceroy of Peru. He died in Lima, Peru in 1801. His son, Bernardo O'Higgins, later to become the liberator of Chile, and president of its congress, lived from 1780 to 1846. He was educated initially in Peru, and then in England and Spain, and returned to join the revolutionary movement against the Spanish oppressors. He trained as a soldier, and in a matter of a few years became commander of the army of Chile. Various battles were fought and lost, in the mountains of the Andes, against superior Spanish forces who were better trained and equipped. Bernardo eventually joined forces with the Argentinian General San Martin, and together with their Army of the Andes, equipped with 10,000 pack mules, they forced the Spaniards out of Chile, and captured its capital Santiago. In 1817

Bernardo was chosen president of the new republic.

After various battles, during one of which the new President was wounded, the Spanish Royalist forces were finally beaten, and O'Higgins had the unenviable task of putting the nation's affairs in order upon its return to normal civilian life.

To help rid the country and its neighboring coastal nation of Peru of Spanish power, O'Higgins set about founding a navy for Chile. His flagship was called the

"O'Higgins" and a Chilean naval force under the command of its first Admiral, Admiral Cochrane, chosen by O'Higgins, went to war to assist Peru against the Spaniards. Simon Bolivar was to become the liberator of Peru, and for a time O'Higgins lived in exile in that country while the affairs of Chile were in chaos. He died on October 23rd, 1842, and lies buried in Santiago. In honor of this Irish liberator, the main street in Santiago is called after O'Higgins, a permanent reminder of Irish-South American links.

ABOVE: King Louis XIV of France gave a refuge to Irish soldiers who left their homeland after the Treaty of Limerick in 1691 ended the fighting in Ireland between the armies of James II and William III.

Another great contributor to the freedom from Spain of the South American Republics was Admiral William Brown, founder of the Argentinian navy. He was born in Foxford, County Mayo, on June 23rd 1777. He emigrated to America, with his family, when

403

A View & Representation of the Battle of Mon...
1. Prince Eugene of Savoy. 2. The Wood of Sart. 3. The Attack of the Emperialists & the Engli... ...ttack of the Dutch by the Prince of Orange. 7. The Village of Malplaquet. 8. The Village of Bla...

he was nine years old, and at the age of nineteen, after some years at sea, he was press-ganged into the British navy. He finished up as a captain in command of a British merchant ship.

Captain William Brown arrived with his family in Buenos Aires in 1812. At this time the revolutionary leaders of Buenos Aires were at war with Spain and recognising the abilities of Brown, they offered him the command of the navy. Together with another captain from Ireland, he put together quite a formidable little fleet of merchant ships converted to warships, and a third Irishman, John Santiago King, assisted in the command. After some famous victories. he retired from the sea to live in his beloved city. He died at his modest property there on May 3rd 1857.

The links between Ireland and South America have frequently been forged through soldiers or sailors of fortune offering their services to the emergent South American Republics, and yet there have been many links in peace-time. In our time there are many individual Irish missionaries who have volunteered to devote their lives to work among the poor and oppressed in the slums of South American capital cities, and in remote rural areas, where the peasantry are under constant threat of starvation or, worse, oppressive military regimes.

One of the strangest battles ever fought by Irishmen was in the service of Mexico, against the "Imperial" might of the United States of America. Today, because of an educational system which owes much to the Irish Christian Brothers, many Mexicans are aware of Ireland and her history and every year, on the feast of Saint Patrick, they pay tribute, in Mexico City, to the "memory of the Irish soldiers of the heroic Saint Patrick's Battalion, martyrs who gave their lives for the cause of Mexico during the unjust North American invasion of 1847." It is a curious story, and a plaque on the wall in the Plaza San Jacinto, in a suburb of Mexico City, names 71 Irishmen of the Mexican Saint Patrick's Battalion who were either hanged or imprisoned by the invading United States Army. It was an unjust war, the war by which the state of Mexico was forced to give up its

LEFT: *An Irish brigade fought in the French army against a British and Dutch force at the battle of Malplaquet in September 1709.*

405

territories to satisfy the greed of Americans for Texas, Nevada, New Mexico, Arizona and California.

At its start, the United States Army sat on the Rio Grande facing the Army of Mexico. Of the thousands of troops encamped, half were immigrants, and almost 500 were Irish, and Catholic at that. The Mexican priests assiduously worked on this fact during the months of waiting, and their propaganda war was highly successful, as several hundred American soldiers, mostly raw Catholic country boys from Ireland, were persuaded to cross the Rio Grande and form the "San Patricio" battalion with their own green flag, in the Mexican Army! Captain John O'Reilly was their leader, and the battalion, like the Lincoln Brigade almost a century later in the service of the Spanish Republic, fought for "Democracy", this time alongside the Mexicans against the United States forces in 1846 and 1847. It was a case of homesick, illiterate country boys deserting an "Imperial" army for a romantic and lost cause, the Mexican people and Irish peasants versus the generals.

Ireland and the Continent

Following the conversion to Christianity in the fifth century, Irish monks burst forth from Ireland in vast numbers as the "peregrini" - wanderers for the sake of Christ - who spread throughout Europe, and as far as Kiev, in Russia. Staff in hand, wearing a rough-spun habit and cowl with a rope cord tied at the waist, and shod with sandals, they favored the "half-corona" hairstyle, the hair tonsured right across the front of the head, and they must have looked somewhat eccentric to pagan Europe. They carried no material possessions with them and brought civilization - Latin, Greek and Christianity. They set up their stalls at the court of the Emperor Charlemagne and shouted "knowledge for sale".

Irish monks and pilgrims, in the course of history, were duly replaced by young men who trained for the priesthood in France, when persecution forbade such schools of learning in their native Ireland. For centuries, half of the priests of Ireland were trained in the Irish College in Paris - founded in 1578, in Nantes, and in seminaries in other cities. Small wonder that today the people of France feel so much at home as tourists in Ireland, and similarly, the Irish in France feel not only close to the French people, but can conjure up ghosts and visions of many an Irish saint and scholar who has trodden the same roads before them through the glorious French countryside, and through the majestic Gothic cathedral cities.

France has been a friend to insurgent Ireland since the days of Henry III of France, who tried to assist the Rebellion of the province of Munster in the fight against the forces of the English Virgin Queen, in 1572. The France of 1688 provided military advisers, troops and officers to James II in his fight against William of Orange. The French Revolution had a profound effect on the movement known as the United Irishmen, founded by Theobald Wolfe Tone, which endeavored to unite Irish Presbyterian and Catholic in a form of republicanism.

The Irish struggle for freedom continued, largely with the aid of the French. It was the French who helped inspire the insurrection of 1848, and it was in France that the Fenians - the Irish Republican Brotherhood - first learned their trade, and became heavily influenced by the French revolutionary philosophy of violence and dynamite, anti-clericism, and the destruction of religious education in schools - aspects of the less acceptable face of modern anarchical revolution.

Austria has had a special fascination for the wandering Irish since the monks of the 9th century. Ever chivalrous, when the mad militant Prussian, Frederick the Great, declared war on Maria Theresa of Austria, Irishmen flocked to her aid and joined her regular army. So much so, that at one time there were no less than 30 Irish generals in the Imperial Army. The best known descendants of these generals were Brownes, Fitzgeralds, Nugents, O'Donnells, O'Connells, Lacys, O'Briens and Taaffes and in 1915, Viscount Taaffe was Field Marshal, Minister of State, and Chamberlain to the Emperor Franz Joseph. Many other Irishmen achieved eminence and it is probable that many Austrian citizens today, particularly in Vienna, who bear Irish names, are unaware of their ancestral connections with the Emerald Isle.

Another big Irish invasion of Europe came as the forces of the Virgin Queen, Elizabeth I, smashed up the old Gaelic order in Ireland and forced its aristocratic leaders to flee abroad in defeat and exile. This became known as the "Flight of the Earls" when the

ABOVE: The Arc de Triomphe in Paris contains a memorial to Irish soldiers who fought for France.

princely O'Donnells and the O'Neills sailed for Spain. Later, as the Williamite forces defeated the Irish at the Battle of the Boyne in 1690, and at Limerick in 1691, 10,000 officers and men sailed into exile and formed Irish brigades in the armies of the Continent. These were known as the "Wild Geese". As Thomas Davis, the poet of "The Nation" tells us:

"The recruiting for the Brigade was carried on in the French Ships which smuggled brandies, wines and silks, etc., to the western and south-western coasts. Their return cargoes were recruits for the Brigade, and were entered in their books as "Wild Geese". Hence this became the common name in Ireland for the Irish serving in the Brigade. The recruiting was chiefly from Clare, Limerick, Kerry and Galway".

The Green Flags of the Irish Brigades on the Continent soon carried the battle honors of Cremona, Spire, Luzzara, Blenheim, Cassano, Ramillies, Almanza, Alcira, Malplaquet and Denain. The names of Irish Officers appear today in honor on the Arc de Triomphe in Paris and, in the opening words of his essay on "The Irish Brigade", Thomas Davis observed: "When valor becomes a reproach, when patriotism is thought a prejudice, and when a soldier's sword is a sign of shame, the Irish Brigade will be forgotten or despised".

It is probable that, between the 1600s and the 1800s, up to three quarters of a million Irishmen fought and died in European wars, starting with the first 30,000 members of the Irish brigades who served under Louis XIV. The names of the Irish generals are like a roll call of the most famous clans in Irish history and include Dillon, O'Mahony, Butler, O'Farrell, Dunsany, O'Gara, O'Donnell, McCarthy, O'Neill, Burke, Barry and Murphy. Some reached the greatest heights as, for example, Marshal Patrick McMahon who became President of the Republic of France in the 1870s.

Index

Acknowledgements

The Editor and Publishers would like to thank Professor Bill McCormack of Goldsmiths College for his considerable help as a consultant on the History of Ireland section.

Thanks must also be expressed to Ashley Brent, Stella Caldwell, Terry Forshaw, Cara Hamilton, Jonathan Hilton, and Stephen Mitchell for their contributions to the production of this book.

All pictures Chrysalis Images except page 117 Galen Rowell/Corbis, 118(T) Hulton-Deutsch/Corbis, 118(B) All Star Picture Library, 119(L) Temp Sport/Corbis, 119(R) Eye Ubiquitous/Corbis, 120 David and Peter Turnley/Corbis, 121 Neal Preston/ Corbis